PATRICIA STORACE

Dinner with Persephone

A native of Mobile, Alabama, Patricia Storace was educated
at Columbia University and the University of Cambridge.
She is the author of a book of poems, *Heredity*, and the win-
ner of a prize for poetry from the American Academy of
Arts and Letters. Her essays have appeared frequently in
The New York Review of Books and in *Condé Nast Traveler*. This is
her first book of prose.

DINNER WITH PERSEPHONE

DINNER WITH PERSEPHONE

PATRICIA STORACE

VINTAGE DEPARTURES

Vintage Books

A Division of Random House, Inc.

New York

FIRST VINTAGE DEPARTURES EDITION, SEPTEMBER 1997

Grateful acknowledgment is made to the following for permission to reprint previously published material: *Cambridge University Press*: Excerpt from *Folk Poetry of Modern Greece* by Roderick Beaton. Copyright © 1980 by Cambridge University Press. Reprinted by permission of Cambridge University Press. • *Hestia Publishers and Booksellers*: Excerpts from "Demotiko Tragoubi Tis Xenitias," translated in this work by Patricia Storace. Copyright © 1990 by Hestia Publishers and Booksellers. Reprinted by permission of Hestia Publishers and Booksellers. • *Ludlow Music, Inc.*: Excerpt from "This Land Is Your Land" by Woody Guthrie. TRO Copyright © 1956, renewed 1958, 1970 by Ludlow Music, Inc. Reprinted by permission of Ludlow Music, Inc. • *Original Books, Inc.*: Excerpts from *Oneirocritica* by Artemidorus, translated by Robert J. White, 1990. Reprinted by permission of Original Books, Inc. • *Princeton University Press*: Excerpts from "Denial," "Syngrou Avenue, 1930," and "The Mood of a Day" from *Collected Poems of George Seferis*, translated by Keeley Sherrard. Copyright © 1967, 1981 by Princeton University Press. Reprinted by permission of Princeton University Press.

Library of Congress Cataloging-in-Publication Data

Storace, Patricia.
Dinner with Persephone / Patricia Storace.
p.   cm.
ISBN 0-679-42134-3
1. Storace, Patricia—Journeys—Greece. 2. Greece—Description
and travel. I. Title.
DF728.S76   1996
949.5—dc20   96-7650

Vintage ISBN: 0-679-74478-9

Author photograph © Jeffrey Weiner

Book design by Chris Welch

Random House Web address: http://www.randomhouse.com/

Printed in the United States of America
10 9 8 7 6

For Mrs. Emily M. Flint
and in loving memory of
Mrs. Louise S. Lovett

Ποῦ 'ναι ἡ ἀγάπη ποὺ κόβει τὸν καιρὸ μονοκόμματα στὰ δυὸ καὶ
τὸν ἀποσβολώνει

Where is love that with one stroke cuts time in two and stuns it?

—From "The Mood of a Day"
by George Seferis

In the different cities of Greece and at the great religious gatherings in that country . . . in the largest and most populous of the islands, I have patiently listened to old dreams and their consequences.

—Artemidorus of Daldis

May we believe in Greece.

—Serapheim, Archbishop of Athens and All Greece

CONTENTS

Acknowledgments   xi

MARBLE GIRLS   3

THE BLUE GLASS EYE   22

IMMORTALITY   38

FLESH AND STONE   43

METAMORPHOSIS   50

THE LIFE-GIVING WELLSPRING   64

THE TRUE LIGHT   69

I SEE ELVIS   74

A DREAM OF THE VIRGIN   85

COLD SHOULDER   93

THE SISTER OF ALEXANDER THE GREAT   97

MIRRORS AS BIOGRAPHERS   107

THE GODFATHER   124

WISHES AS HISTORIANS   144

THE PAST AS THE FUTURE   164

Contents

THE *PLANETARKHIS*   171

LUST FOR A SAINT   174

A NYMPH'S TEMPLE   178

POLYTECHNIC NIGHT   184

HOW IT ALWAYS IS   191

A DREAM OF A BODILESS ONE   198

MACEDONIA DAY   206

WEDDING   211

POMEGRANATES   216

HEADS OR TAILS   224

THE RULE OF WOMEN   234

PREGNANT MEN   238

CLEAN MONDAY   253

AT COLONUS   258

SOUL SATURDAY   260

INDEPENDENCE DAY   263

THE INVINCIBLE COMMANDER   275

CANDLES   287

THE BUS TO METAMORPHOSIS   295

TWIN PEAKS   298

THE DREAM OF LOVE AFTER THE DANCE   319

THE UNWRITTEN   356

THE DREAM OF NARCISSUS   364

THE SLEEPING VIRGIN   369

THE MARBLE KING   387

THE STATUES DANCING   396

ACKNOWLEDGMENTS

I thank Lynn Nesbit, for her support of this work. I also owe thanks to the Department of Hellenic Studies of Princeton University, and in particular to Dimitri Gondicas. Affectionate thanks also to Richard Burgi, Robert Lane, Demos Kounidis, Krista Zois, and John and Athina Davis, for evenings of white wine and Cavafy, and much more. My heartfelt thanks and love to my dear friends Sofia Theonas, Zacharias Thrillos, the poet Katerina Anghelaki-Rooke, and the painter Yiannis Zikas; nothing would have been possible without them. I am grateful to Robert J. White for his eloquent translation of the *Oneirokritika*, from which all the Artemidorus quotations are drawn. Thanks to the painter Peter Devine, for joyful hours spent looking at Greek art; and love and gratitude to Ron, involved in this book in more ways than he knows. A number of people did not want acknowledgment, for reasons of privacy; you know who you are, and you know my gratitude.

It is an honor and an education to work with the editor Erroll McDonald; the guidance of such a profound literary mind is beyond thanks.

It is rightfully against the law to remove antiquities from Greek territory; and yet I brought home ancient treasures in the form of Greek words. Thanks to my teachers, Tryphon Tzifis and Dora Papaioannou, without whose patient work I could not have shared in these precious possessions.

The chapter "Dream of Love After the Dance" includes references and quotations from the books of the archives of P.S. Delta "First Memoir" and "Memoir of 1899" which were published by Hermes Publishing House under the supervision of P.A. Zannas and Alexandros P. Zannas. The quotations have been reprinted with the permission of Alexandros P. Zannas and Asimina Zannas.

DINNER WITH PERSEPHONE

MARBLE GIRLS

Arkhe tou paramythiou, kalispera sas, is a traditional beginning of a Greek fairy tale. The fairy tale begins, good evening to you.

I lived in Athens, at the intersection of a prostitute and a saint. It was a neighborhood of mixed high-rises and a scattering of neoclassical houses, some boarded up while the owners waited to be offered the right price for their inheritance. The neighborhood hardware stores carried, along with screwdrivers and lengths of wire and caulking pastes, icon frames with electric lights in the shape of candles attached, so you wouldn't have to inconvenience yourself with oil for the perpetual flame. All the neighborhood shops—the laundry, the butcher's, the vegetable market, the TV and appliances store, the cheap dress shop and the bridal gown shop, the school supplies shop with its large-sized brightly colored picture books of Greek myths and tales of Alexander the Great—were defended by charms against the evil eye suspended over their counters. If you took the evening *volta,* stroll, that provides most Athenians with their exercise during the punishingly hot times of the year, certain streets gave you glimpses of Mount Hymettus, smudged with darkening violet light, like a drawing someone had started and then decided to cross out with ink.

The tiny cottage of an apartment I moved into yesterday has already begun to teach me what a different world I have come to, physically, socially, historically. It is no easy matter to find apartments with furniture and kitchen appliances here. In Greece, the tenant is supposed to supply these things. Until 1983, when the obligatory dowry—the *prika*—a woman brought to her husband was declared illegal, refrigerators and beds were components of the marriage agreement. And for the most part, unmarried people until fairly recently lived with their parents, and had no need for their own domestic equipment. Even now, when it is common for couples to marry later, and to live together before they do, many people I know from previous visits live in a kind of compromise between independence and family surveillance. Their parents or grandparents built family-only apartment buildings in which each child of adult age is housed on a different floor, along with members of the extended family, who wander in and out of each other's living rooms, dandling each other's babies, stirring each other's pots of *stifado,* hoping to catch a glimpse of the man Kiki has gone out with three times in the last month.

The miniature living room of this flat is dominated by a ballroom-sized chandelier, a persistent element of the middle-class Greek idea of grandeur in decoration, probably translated into homes from Orthodox churches, which usually feature monumental gilt chandeliers, their branches supporting a rain of votive offerings. There is also a glass-fronted trinket cabinet, which displays a blue and white Greek flag, some seashells, a souvenir china plate from the island of Paros, and a narghile, or hookah, the Middle Eastern water pipe. In the tiny kitchen, there is the ubiquitous dull white marble sink, and a bottle of Ajax cleanser, which promotes itself here through its claims to whiten marble. Marble is more common than wood in southern Greece, and an apartment building which takes itself at all seriously will have marble floors and steps, at least in the entrance. A narrow balcony runs the length of the two rooms, overlooking the courtyard, dotted with green trees in clay pots, an attempt at a city garden from the tenants of the ground floor. There is a balcony etiquette I will have to master, I realized yesterday, even through my jet lag. I suddenly understood the cliché about airing laundry in public, as the neighbors frankly scrutinized my lingerie and the patterns on my sheets as I hung them out to dry. The balconies are proportioned to the size of the apartment, and across the way, on a substantial balcony, a neighbor is handling her line, pins, and draped laundry with the grace and expertise of Madame Vionnet fitting a mannequin. She looks at me impassively. I know I am affording her an odd spectacle—I have never lost a freezing childhood fear of heights, and to lean out over a fatal drop to dry my laundry gives me a sudden image of the characters in North by Northwest as they scramble over Mount Rushmore with a gunman in pursuit. I have to close my eyes for each garment. A badly positioned dress drips a steady purple rain onto the balcony railing below, and a black lace bra spirals down into the courtyard when a clip pulls loose. The neighbor stares at me, and I leave the field, making a show of not clinging to the walls, disguising the symptoms of hyperventilation.

Recovering with a cup of coffee inside, I hear a scratching sound from the front room; a handful of leaflets has been thrust under the door. Greek apartments, I discover, are leafleted as thickly as American college dormitory rooms. The local movie theater offers a showing of a film starring Yuppy Goldberg, as she transliterates to Greek, and a school of foreign languages offers me French, English, German, and Italian. It takes no more than a drive from the airport to realize how critical the study of foreign languages is in Greece. One of the most common neighborhood sights is the colorful signs offering the teaching of xenes glosses.

I remember a drive I took across the United States a few years ago. From one end of the continent to another, I did not see a school for foreign languages. They were there, of course, but to be sought out. Here, though, they are ubiquitous; it is hard to walk more than a city block without seeing schools or posters advertising them, as if foreign languages were some kind of vital substance you needed constantly to replenish, a milk. In Greece, where every enterprise that involves language—publishing, entertainment, journalism, tourism—is dependent on the roughly nine million people who speak Greek, knowing one or more foreign languages is a professional necessity. Businessmen, politicians who deal with European Community officials, doctors who must keep abreast of foreign research, writers who here largely make their living on translations, all need foreign languages in order to survive. There used to be an unanswerable Greek joke phrase, "What says meow-meow on the roof tiles?" the equivalent of "Is the pope Catholic?" But friends tell me that it now has an answer—"A dog who is learning foreign languages."

The status of the language affects the country externally, too, influencing how well a country is known, whether the outlines of its history become part of the stock of common knowledge. Browsing in bookstores outside Greece, I have much more easily found works on French or German or Spanish history and biography than on modern Greece. The scarcity probably begins with childhood circumstance; lessons in those other languages were readily available. I wonder how it affects people here to have to add the learning of languages to other everyday necessities, and I wonder how it affects native English speakers to be in possession of the current lingua franca, a status once held by Latin, and before that, by Greek. Being able to rely on the dominance of English may affect English speakers' ability to approach and imagine other cultures—as if they were rich children, who have inherited such an enormous trust fund that they can choose whether or not to go to work.

The third leaflet offers a six-volume set of the classics of modern Greek literature. It is promised, as if it were in doubt, that the introductions by prominent Greek scholars will "reveal to us the greatness of the deeds and spirits" of the founders of the modern nation. Pictures of the gilt-edged volumes are set against the backdrop of a nineteenth-century painting, showing romantic warriors wearing the foustanella, the pleated Greek kilt, in repose among the ancient columns of the Parthenon—the classical past defended by the creators of modern Greece. The books are the collected writings of Kolokotronis, Krystallis, Valoritis, Solomos, and Makriyiannis, all men of the nineteenth century, when the Greek nation violently entered history. It occurs to me as I look at the elaborately bound books offered by the leaflet that I have never heard them mentioned in speeches by tour guides I have overheard in museums, or listened to on bus trips. The emphasis is usually on Thucydides, Aristotle, or Sappho; paradoxically, it is the history of modern Greece that seems more distant. The past which can be remembered as well as imagined, the recent past which directly produced the manners, customs, and political situation of the nation we travel to, seems almost too complex to approach.

Kolokotronis and Makriyiannis were military leaders of the Greek War of Independence of 1821 against the Ottoman Turks—these two soldiers so despised each other that the Greek campaign against the Turks nearly became a civil war as well. The engravings show both men wearing oriental turbans and the highly prized elaborate oriental mustaches. In features, costume, and expression, they could be chieftains from any Near or Middle Eastern country. They could be Afghan. They could be Syrian. They could be Turks. All six of them display the self-consciously stern, imposing jailor's facial expression that means authority in Greece. Taki, a Greek friend of mine, shook his head once over a picture of Franklin Roosevelt that accompanied a review of a biography, and said irritatedly, "That face. I can never understand that face, that inane smile." In the Greek vocabulary of the face, smiling does not include the nuance of power that it does in the United States. Roosevelt's sunny optimistic smile had an air, for Americans, of invincibility, of mastery of both good and bad fortune, because to possess happiness is a kind of authority in America, barely comprehensible to Taki, who saw smiling as a kind of placation, a sign of submission, and in whose native tongue the verb "to laugh" also means "to deceive." This different language of the face begins at passport control in each country. The Americans smile in their booths with an easy self-assurance that enjoyment cannot threaten; the Greeks scowl theatrically, implacably, since a smile is not considered an impressive facial expression, and a male face is meant above all to impress, not to charm.

The group of men in conventional nineteenth-century European dress are men of letters. Solomos, whose poem to freedom was set as the national anthem, is considered the national poet. He and General Makriyiannis share a quality that makes them not only eminent personalities in the struggle to found the Greek nation, but symbols of it. Solomos, the bastard son of a Greek maidservant and an Italian count who lived on the Ionian island of Zakinthos, is the symbol of the Greece created out of the embrace of European and Greek cultures. Makriyiannis, who said that Greece and Europe could never learn each other's dances, and who was instrumental in bringing about the fall of the Bavarian king who had been dispatched to rule over the new nation, is the symbol of the Greece created out of the rejection of Europe. That simultaneous rejection and embrace of Europe shifts and collides still, like tectonic plates, under the surface of the country.

Makriyiannis and Solomos had another common quality which established them as symbols of modern Greece: their relation to Greek. Solomos, who was educated in Italian and had a child's imprint of the simple Greek of his mother, had virtually to teach himself Greek in order to write poetry in the language. Makriyiannis was semiliterate, and had to learn to write Greek as an adult in order to record his memoirs. In their rebirth as Greeks, they were seen as proofs of "the Greek miracle," resurrected. And in this nation, which sees itself as the true birthplace of Christianity, and whose national history is seen as a reenactment of the life of Christ, so that the Greek national holiday is deliberately celebrated on the day of the annunciation of Mary's pregnancy, resurrection is an idea with an erotic power over the national imagination, invoked, yearned for, caressed, an image as present in pop songs as it is on church walls. Yesterday, riding in a taxi, I caught a line on the radio through the chaos of Athens traffic: "And if you cut me in half, I'll love twice as much."

Most non-Greeks, in my experience, have never heard of any of these men. I hadn't myself until the first time I came here, and felt the eerie sensation of disorientation I recognized from my childhood; I had grown up without knowing my parents, although intensely aware of their existence in my own body, made out of elements of theirs. So I knew something about beings who are powerfully present without being visible to others, and I knew something about lost worlds, even though my lost world was the past, and the lost world of Greece was the present. Greece, too, was preoccupied with questions of origins, however different the configuration. Having to use my imagination to understand the impact of tragically real events had made me aware of imagination's enormous force— for good and evil—in every aspect of our lives, even in realms supposedly free of it, in law, science, and politics, in history and economics, in learning and ignoring, in describing and in lying, in crime and in love. In Greece I saw a nation both tormented and exalted by imagination.

The doorbell rings, and I answer it a little uncertainly, not knowing quite how cautious to be. Standing outside is a small, sturdy woman with carefully architected gray curls. She is holding a tray of some unrecognizable cookies, and is dressed in a flowered smock. The entire floor smells like a swimming pool, thanks to the heavily chlorinated cleansers popular in Greek households. "Welcome to Greece," she says, "I am Kyria Maro. If you have any questions, knock at my door. I am a friend of your landlady's, so if you cannot reach her for some reason you can come to me. Any questions at all. And," she adds in grandmotherly tones, as if she were imparting some domestic golden rule about doing the dishes or the frugal use of electricity, "you know, Macedonia is Greek." She hands me the china plate and tells me to return it whenever it should happen that I have the time, and clacks down the hall in her slippers.

I look down at the plate—I have never seen any confections in these shapes before, and I can't anticipate the flavor of any of them. There is one in quadrants, like a pastry kite, another like a ridged sausage, another like a piece of fried lace. I might as well be living on the moon. It seems I will need a new body in order to live here, that the demands of a new country begin as demands on the body. I feel the weight and alienness of the food, the light, this world where a day has a different geography, and a life moves through time and space differently. I feel the tug of Greek words as a change in the force of gravity, and as the plate of pastries in my hand posits a different conception of appetite than I know, and a different conception of pleasure, I begin to understand that this language will perceive the body, and the world itself, differently from my own. This is the moment when travel is felt most absolutely, when time and space and history and emotion exert a force on the body, and the distances you are traveling inside are as great as the distance you have traveled outside.

I have some basic household staples to buy and a bank account to set up before I meet some friends in central Athens for lunch. It takes deep breaths and resolution to get myself down the three flights of stairs onto the neighborhood streets. The first month in a new country is an exhausting one; every object, every face, every incident comes at you the size of faces on a giant screen. You are exhausted from paying attention, and even sleep is sleepless, because the magnified days, the fifty-foot words, the towering new conventions insist their way into your dreams, too.

It seems almost impolite, somehow tactless, to notice how unlike any other neighborhood streets in any other country these are. I pass two or three icon stores in the space of six or eight blocks, hung with rows of sullen female saints, dead-eyed male saints, looking as if they are at the last moment of control before an explosion of anger. The more expensive images have ornate frames or silvered-over clothes. Women buy them and women tend them, lighting oil flames in front of them, burning incense, and misting them with holy water as if they were sacred house plants. I never actually saw a man buy one, not during the year I spent in Greece; and I often remembered, as I walked by these stores, that during the two periods of fierce Byzantine iconoclasm, both times the revival of icon worship was sponsored by women, the empresses Theodora and Irene. There is something disturbing about all those blank pent-up-looking faces that demands propitiation, like a child's desperate attempts to please a remote, miserable parent. And there is something poignant, too, as if they are only so alike because they need to be rescued into individuality, they need the mercy of tending, one reason little girls play with dolls. I used to spend pocket money for small toys when I was little, not nearly so much because I wanted the toys for myself as because I wanted to release them. I remember buying a palm-sized monkey and the saleslady wanting me to exchange him because he didn't have the right tag. "They're all alike," she said, and threw him into the bin overflowing with the toy monkeys. "No, they're not all alike," I said, fishing him out. "Not anymore." Outside the shop, safe in my hand, he stopped being a movie tie-in.

I walk past yet another icon shop, past those bitter faces imprisoned in their silver cells. I look for a moment past the street of Phryne, beyond a small green square, to the street of Agios Fanourios, the revealer, patron saint of illumination, who finds lost objects and gives glimpses of the future. He is also famous for having had such a monstrous mother that on his name day, one formulaic prayer runs: "God pardon the mother of Agios Fanourios."

At my intersection, Phryne, the prostitute, was a courtesan in the fourth century B.C., the lover of the sculptor Praxiteles, and the model for what seems to have been the first monumental statue of a female nude. She was also the only woman in antiquity to have won a lawsuit with only her own eloquent breasts. When she was about to be condemned by the Athenian court for immoral conduct, she pulled her dress from her shoulders down to her waist in front of the judges, who, transfixed, ruled in her favor. In a world where speech and thought were neither the rights nor the privileges of women, Phryne found a way to pose philosophical questions with her body. "Are you immoral?" she asked the judges. "Is desire immoral? What is immorality?"

This story may or may not be true. And all we know of the looks of this standard of female beauty in the Greek and Roman worlds is our dream of them. We only know the lost Aphrodite of Knidos from Roman copies and images on coins, made by artists who probably never saw the original statue, and certainly never saw the woman. In any case, the statue was rejected by the islanders of Kos, who had commissioned it; they considered its nakedness immoral.

Running parallel to the street of Phryne, forming a rough cross with it, flecked with small shops, is the street of Fanourios, a saint, who was satisfied that as a Christian he had found the answer to Phryne's questions. Following the consequences of his logic, he submitted himself to the sacred suicide of virginity and martyrdom, instead of the profane suicide of sexuality. Greek polytheists were not "pagan," in the licentious interpretation of the word given by their religious rivals. The old Greek word for pagan is *ethnikos,* which is synonymous with "national," as in the national flag. I didn't know you were *ethnikos,* says a Christian to a polytheist in one of Cavafy's poems.

The Greek polytheists regarded the body with their own kind of mystical puritanism, believing that each sexual act diminished in some degree the vital force of the partners, and even shortened their lives. Their ideal was a highly stylized and controlled kind of sexual contact, in which the "passive" partner was always to some degree humiliated, and which looks from the scenes on vase paintings to have been really very dull. Perhaps it is no accident that the body of myths assembled, invented, reinvented, and anthologized from a variety of sources by the ancient Greeks is one of the least erotic of the world's mythologies, rivaled perhaps only by the mythology of the ancient Israelites. The source of sexual tension in ancient Greek myth is not so much the drive to the ecstasy of consummation, but uncertainty as to whether either or both partners will survive the sexual act. This thread runs through all the stories of the young men and women who are killed after lovemaking with each other or the gods; through all the stories of rape, a sexual act in which there is always an implicit threat of murder; and on a global scale, through the *Iliad,* in which generations and nations die because Helen and Paris lay down together.

I realize now how much being on the courtyard side of the building shields me from the noise of the streets. Athens streets are substantially noisier to my ear than New York's, because of the ubiquitous motorcycles and from the incessant gear-shifting here, where nobody drives automatic.

I am on my way to the *laiki agora,* the farmers' market, held on different days of the week in different neighborhoods throughout the city.

The traffic is anarchic, and walking here requires acute scouting attention. Cars simply drive over curbs; motorcycles wanting to pass weave through the pedestrians on the sidewalks; and often cars are parked directly on the sidewalks, further narrowing the slim margin of safety separating pedestrians from the onslaught. Traffic is worse today because there is a bus strike—the conservative Mitsotakis government and the bus drivers' union are struggling over the government's attempt to privatize the buses. There are hints that the trolleys and taxis will soon strike in sympathy. Walking everywhere doesn't trouble me, since I am used to some five miles a day, but I wonder what it will do to elderly people like Kyria Maro if they have heavy groceries or errands downtown. A red light halts me at the *periptero,* one of the kiosks for newspapers, aspirin, batteries, and the cold drinks that are crucial in the southern Greek summer, when thirst is felt more violently than hunger. I am caught in a crossfire of stares: a motorcyclist has turned his face away from the lights toward me and is staring with dedicated attention, while the *periptero* man has me covered from the other side. It is very hard to get used to, but there is no social prohibition against frank, assessing, concentrated

staring, and my first pervasive sensation in Greece is of those eyes—
the stares of the coffee-drinking shopkeepers, the gazing icons, the
tin and glass eyes dangling from key chains and rearview mirrors and
hung over doors as protection against harm from living eyes.

The *periptero* man waves me over. "You just move here?" he asks,
framed by newspapers hanging over his head like national flags from
wooden poles. There are the Everydays, the Afternoons, the
Newses, the Free Presses, the Uprootings, as some of the dizzying
range of Greek newspapers, journals usually openly affiliated with
political parties, are called. There is *Estia,* named after the goddess
of the hearth, which in the nineteenth century serialized many of
the first modern Greek novelists, and is now one of the most vitri-
olic of right-wing papers, referring to Bosnia-Herzegovina as a
"Turkish protectorate." There are the magazines named as if they
were philosophical categories: *Images, It Is, She, Woman, One,* and the
Greek satirical paper *The Mouse.*

"Yes, I'm here for a year," I answer, aware of the constantly shifting passage through Athens of diaspora Greeks, students, tourists,
international scholars, and EEC employees. I choose a carton of
strawberry juice from the kiosk refrigerator. Except for certain
wines and cold mountain water, I have never drunk anything as perfect as Greek fruit juices, each as distinct in timbre and character as
the instruments of an orchestra.

"And you're Greek?" the *peripteras* asks.

"No," I say.

"But you speak Greek?"

"Yes, but I still talk a lot of *ardzi, bourdzi,* and *loulas,*" I say, using
a Greek phrase for nonsense that amuses people when they hear it,
a phrase that plays with the idea of being fluent in nonsense.

"So how much a week do you have to live on?" he asks.

"Enough for *horta,* greens, at the *laiki,*" I say, and catch the light
to cross.

"Well, buy your newspapers here," he calls after me, "and you
can practice your Greek too. Here we speak Greek for absolutely
nothing. Even though it is an expensive language to speak."

Just beyond, a shop window offers a new line of wedding and baptism invitations, all embossed with a gold Star of Vergina, the symbol marking some of the grave treasures of Philip of Macedonia, Alexander the Great's father. The vegetable and fruit stalls of the *laiki* are hung with the most beautiful agriculture I've ever seen: olives in many colors, grapes so real they make fancy grocers' bunches seem like Victorian wax ornaments, eggplants that are the royal porphyry that was the exclusive color of the Byzantine imperial family, branches of bay leaves that are called Daphne here, after the nymph who metamorphosed into the laurel tree to escape being raped by Apollo. "Wherever I go and wherever I stay," wrote the novelist Kazantzakis, "I grasp between my teeth, like a bay laurel leaf, Greece."

The sellers shout for the shoppers' attention. "*Aromata kai khromata,*" perfumes and colors, says one, scooping up handfuls of ruby-colored cherries. He gives me one to sample and enjoys my response. The fruit has something more than flavor; it evolves—it has drama. "It's the sun," he says. "We get more sun than any other country in Europe, and it concentrates all the sugars in the fruits and vegetables. And we pick them ripe, just before we sell them." The only other place I find with fruits and vegetables to equal this brilliance, when I travel there at the end of my year here, is Turkey.

I pass a stall with barrels of grains that are collectively called here *demetriaka,* after the Greek goddess Demeter, as we call them cereals, after the Roman goddess Ceres, a subtle reminder of complicated historical fissures and parallels. The Western world is called the Western world because it descends from the western Roman Empire, while Greece belonged to the eastern Roman Empire of Byzantium. The polarity of the relations between the two and the cultural dominance of one over the other are rarely as clear in their contrasts as they are often presented. These empires seemed not so much to face each other like black and white champions across a chessboard as to be enmeshed dynamically together, more a spiral than a chessboard, in a cultural struggle that could never be fully resolved or completely clarified, because each side was so marked by the characteristics of the other it had taken on. Each side at times confronted the other in opposition, but at others adopted the more insidious method of incorporating its rival, like two actors competing for the same role. It was even a common dream in the second century for Romans and Greeks to have dreams of each other's alphabets. The interpreter who recorded these dreams remarks, "If a Roman learns the Greek alphabet or a Greek learns the Roman alphabet, the former will take to Greek pursuits, the latter to Roman. Many Romans, moreover, have married Greek wives, and many Greeks, Roman wives, after having this dream." Elite Roman children had Greek nurses, and Greek literature and decorative arts had something like the prestige and elegance of French for nineteenth-century Russians or Persian for the Ottoman Turks. I remember having dinner with a teacher who worked at one of the most prestigious Greek prep schools, who told me her high school class had flatly refused to read Virgil's *Aeneid*. Greek high school students have a reputation for being ungovernable; I heard teachers' stories of classes who, en masse, refused exams, and of idle weeks passing while students went on strike, attending school but doing no schoolwork, in the service of various causes. These particular students held it as dogma that the *Aeneid* was a cheap imitation of Homer, with a popular Platonism, present in both the ancient Greek preoccupation with sculpture and the modern Greek preoccupation with icons, that insisted there was one ideal original, and the rest of the genre increasingly false and bloodless. "It's as if they accused Chopin of being a cheap imitation of Beethoven, without of course having heard him," the teacher said frustratedly to me. They were unable to see Virgil's poem as a radical reinterpretation of the epic and the epic hero. It was an ironic thing to hear, since the borders of influence were so permeable—the Byzantine Empire, which evolved into an empire dominated by Greeks, was founded by a Latin-speaking Roman, now one of the important saints of the Greek church, and the language of this empire, later to become Greek, was originally Latin, and remained Latin for an ample num-

ber of centuries. Besides, the Greeks had called themselves, well
into the twentieth century, Romans, and their word for quintessential Greekness had been Romiosyni, Romanness. This historical vertigo had been brought home to me by the title of a modern short
story, which described a quintessential Greek Orthodox Easter. The
title of the story was "Romaic Easter." Through the strange spiral of
this history, the Greeks evolved into their conquerors.

The Byzantine emperors, though, in the eastern empire, were
the emperors of the crossroads—not only did the Byzantines have
to claim to Rome that they were the real Romans, but they had to
declare to their rivals in the Middle East—the Persians, the Jews,
the Arabs, and the Turks—that they were the Roman Empire. Par-
taking of both the cultures of the West and the East, but fully inte-
grated with neither, Byzantium was a transvestite empire, partly
both but also neither, the Empire of the Crossroads, whose preoccupation with dual natures of all kinds, from its man-gods to Diyenis Akritas, its own epic hero, the biracial knight of the border, is its
most ineradicable legacy to modern Greece. Diyenis (of two races)
Akritas, the medieval Greek hero, son of an Arab chieftain and an
aristocratic Greek lady, was to have been the subject of the second
part of Kazantzakis's *The Odyssey: A Modern Sequel.*

A boy calls for customers to riffle through his stock of used
CDs—the one in his right hand has a picture of one of the finest
current pop singers, and I go closer to read the title: *Our National
Loneliness.*

Walking away from the perfection of the produce, I wander past
stalls selling utensils of the worst possible design, waste bins with
lids that don't fit, plastic colanders that would melt on contact with
boiling water, cheap clothes in punitively ugly prints. I can't find the
simplest glass mixing bowl, only greasy plastic, so I turn back,
changing my plan for the eggplant and olives—in any case, the
genius of the flavors will overcome the limitations of the cook, like a
person thrust from private life into fame. My marketing is snatched
from my arms suddenly by a wiry, sixtyish man, whose eyes behind

his old-fashioned glasses are brown like weak coffee, and anxious. He shoves a hand under my elbow and pulls me toward the street. "You must come with me, you must come with me," he says urgently. My thoughts are of fire, riot police, terrorists. "What is happening?"

"Hurry," he says, "hurry up. I want to have coffee with you." A struggle ensues over my packages, which I win, thanks to my new height. Having stepped through the mirror to this country, I find that I am no longer small as I was in the United States, but have become magically taller than average. "Where are you going?" he calls after me. "You will be perfectly safe. I am a doctor."

"But I am perfectly healthy." I escape down a side street past a grim-looking restaurant full of men reading newspapers and eating hot food. It is a genre of restaurant you find tucked away in city neighborhoods, patronized by old bachelor and widower habitués, with no wives or mothers to cook for them. The men settle at their separate tables as if they were distinct worlds, eating in silence, in a kind of public solitary confinement.

Another person calls to me, this time a girl in blue jeans standing on the corner beside a stack of books piled on an upended crate. "Do you need a new one?" she asks.

"What are they?" I slow down, shift my packages, and climb toward her. Athens is all ascent and descent, like San Francisco, and readjusting your balance is what walking is about as much as covering distance. She holds up a volume and flips the pages. "Dream books. *Oneirokrites.*"

Actually, I did bring one. But it was written in the second century, the *Oneirokritika,* a handbook of dreams collected by a professional dream interpreter named Artemidorus, who traveled in Greek cities, and recorded and classified the dreams people told him in order to make a manual of the art of dream interpretation for his son. It is a social history of shocking intimacy, a study of the unconscious lives of people of another world, trying to divine the future through their dreams, while we, so far away, try to divine the past. The *Oneirokritika* was translated into Arabic in 873, and was an inspiration for the great dream book of Ad-Dinawari, published in 1006; in the West, it was an inspiration for Freud's *Interpretation of Dreams*.

"I do have one," I say, "but it's old."

"You are foreign?" she asks, and I nod. "How long have you lived here?"

"Two days."

"Then you will need a new one. You will have new dreams here."

That was true, so I counted out the drachmas, and slipped the book into my string bag next to a kilo of white peaches. I passed another jewelry store—there is a remarkably dense concentration, maybe five within a space of nine blocks or so, in this modest middle-class neighborhood—thinking of a story about the great Greek poet George Seferis, who on a summer's visit to an island, I think in the 1970s, encountered a woman holding a jar of honey in one hand and a tattered book in the other. "Take my honey, my boy," she said, "and when you get back to Athens, send me a new dream book, this one is worn to pieces." And I struggled to pay attention to the aggressive Greek traffic, while remembering another traveler's experience made me careless. The importance of these *oneirokrites* was mentioned by an Oxbridge classicist named Lawson, who visited here around the turn of the century and wrote a book examining the survival of pre-Christian practices in the contemporary Greece he visited, a study which is also a travel book of great charm. Lawson's book is in many ways as much an experience of traveling in an Edwardian gentleman's England as it is of traveling in Greece, as all travel books are as much retracings as they are journeys forward, explorations too of the country left behind, which may be just as unknown as the territory ahead.

I have a personal affection for Lawson, for his both sympathetic and independent imagination and his gently satirical turn of mind. I like him for confessing to seeing a nymph in an olive grove near Sparta: "Had I possessed an initial faith in the existence of nymphs and in the danger of looking upon them, so lifelike was the apparition that I might have sworn as firmly as did my guide that it was a nymph we had seen, and might have required as strong a dose as he at the next inn to restore my nerves." Later, on the island of Mitilini, I would hear an earthy Greek rhyme recorded by Lawson about a superstition of the bad effects Christian priests have on virility, warning that "if you see a priest on the road, hang on to your balls." With endearing Edwardian discretion, Lawson had rendered it into Latin: *Si per viam sacerdoti occures, testiculos tuos teneto.* And I remember just now that Lawson had often seen advertisements in Athenian newspapers for new editions of some *Megas Oneirokritis* (Great Dream Interpreter), the same title as the book I had just bought. "In isolated homesteads," he wrote, "to which the Bible has never found its way, I have several times seen a grimy tattered copy of such a book preserved among the most precious possessions of the family, and honored with a place on the shelf where stood the icon of the household's patron-saint and whence hung his holy lamp."

I just have time to put down my shopping and run for the downtown trolley on the neighborhood's main wide avenue, dodging the underworld of stray Athenian cats. A moving van is parked outside of one of the apartment buildings, stacks of cardboard containers resting on a dolly next to it, and two sweaty black-haired men approaching it carrying a dining table. The word "Metaphors" is painted on both its sides in brilliant blue. Here it means transportation. I will never be able to use the word again without the image of a meaning heaved onto the back like household furniture to be carried to its new residence.

The trolley is of Russian manufacture and populated with women on their way to the city center for errands and shopping. It runs past the small neighborhood park, a glowing oasis that smells like a herbalist's. *Drosia,* I heard someone murmur from a bench under one of the trees yesterday, the Greek word for dew, for freshness and cool, a word that like a trembling molecule is set into the Greek notion of erotic desire. It is extraordinary to realize out of what local materials and experiences large ideas are made—that the dream of a desired body, the imagination of an embrace is shaped here by the searing merciless heat and stone that irritated Cicero; here the word freighted with the greatest weight of longing is *dipsa,* thirst, and in love poems lovers drink the dew from each other's lips, and are refreshed in each other's arms as if dew fell on them. I felt my whole body undertake the translation, yesterday, the new sense of what longing and desire might be, when I stood inside the park in a dense pool of wavering emerald shadows, where the darkness was not nocturnal but fertile. Leaving the street to find this was like kissing someone you have waited to kiss for a long time.

Most of the ladies cross themselves three times as they pass a church, built in the cruciform Byzantine way, with a dome whose Pantokrator, the image of Christ the ruler of everything, can be imagined from outside without entering. It is an odd fact that except for details regarding particular saints, you know from outside the pattern of decoration in an Orthodox church; in my New York neighborhood, there are Presbyterian, Roman Catholic, and Jewish temples, but I couldn't guess at their interiors without peering in.

I have a copy of *The Adventures of Huckleberry Finn* on my lap, which I brought with me, along with Artemidorus's *Oneirokritika,* Boswell's *Life of Samuel Johnson,* a cookbook of Claudia Roden's, and a few others. But the barrage of new sights from the window makes it hard for me to concentrate on anything else. *Huckleberry Finn* is suddenly lifted out of my hands and examined by a stout middle-aged lady wearing brown support hose and an arsenal of jewelry. She puts it back into my hands with neither prelude nor farewell, and communicates her finding to her seat partner. "*Galliki glossa,*" she says firmly, "French," gesturing toward me. "A French girl."

THE BLUE GLASS EYE

My chore is to open a bank account and then join my friends
Leda and Theo for lunch in Plaka, the lovely, crowded old
quarter of Athens, at a restaurant owned by a man who calls himself simply the Mustache, or for specificity, the Mustache from
Olympia.

The bank is affiliated with my bank in the States, and I explain to
the raven-haired representative with the dramatic makeup that I
will be here for a year and a bit and would like to open an account.
I hand her letters of recommendation from the American bank officer and my employer, and she takes them off to her supervisor.
When she returns, she says, "We open accounts in dollars under the
following conditions: You must deposit at least fifty thousand dollars
in the account. Or you must be of Greek descent." I am puzzled,
since this appears to be a branch of an American bank, and ask the
reason for these unexpected conditions. She says certainly, she will
ask her supervisor, and after a conference with him, she returns.
"There is no reason," she says.

"Okay, thanks, I just wanted to be sure," I say and gather up my
letters.

"But try the National Bank of Greece," she says, "I know for a fact that they have the kind of accounts you want. Many Greeks from America and Australia use them."

I find my way to the National Bank of Greece with obedient confidence and am told there that only the bank I have just come from offers the service I want. "Many Greeks from Australia and America use them." The bank representative then offers to translate any of my magazine articles into Greek, assuring me that he has the "competence of the University of Michigan." It is a puzzle I can't work out; there seems to be no uniform law, and no common reservoir of information about it, not even a sense that information is being deliberately withheld in order to increase some unknowable advantage. I try a third bank, and after a substantial wait, sit down with the bank officer, in shirtsleeves, as most Greek businessmen are during the hot summers, and turn-of-the-century-style mutton-chop whiskers. I hand him my letters of recommendation and my passport and wait for the verdict. "Why do you want to open an account here in Greece?" I direct him to the letter from my employer, which verifies that I will not be taking a salary from any Greek source, and tell him I have business here.

"You? You have business here? What kind of business can you have here?" He bursts out laughing theatrically, shuddering with stagy hilarity.

"What makes you laugh?" I ask him, and he picks up my passport, opens it, and begins kissing my passport picture, making sure I can see that he is using his tongue. I do have business here, though, and I am engaged in it at this very moment—my business is to remember you, I think. I give up for the day on my bank account, and walk to Plaka, cooling my temper. The bankman's arrogance and the coarse insult interest me less than his presumption—the phenomenon here for me is how unmistakably he is not thinking. He is dogmatizing, sure that he knows all that is essential about me. And this very certainty conceals the powerful drive to make me conform to his sure and certain knowledge of me—he is using it like a policeman's cosh. He is certain he knows how I am arranged, as if I were an Orthodox church—he has even, in a secular style, I think with bitter amusement, kissed my icon.

When I arrive at the Mustache's restaurant in Plaka, on a street with many of the handsome neoclassical buildings that were the architecture of preference for the new Greek state in the 1830s after its Bavarian king arrived bringing his Munich classicism with him, a group of friends and strangers is sitting inside, drinking cold drinks and watching the television over the bar. The choice outdoor tables are given over to tourists, and whenever there is a flurry of activity, one of the Mustache's friends will hop up behind the bar to fix a tray or carry a plate. If a party speaking a language someone at the table knows well arrives, the Mustache will call out "German, Maria, or Italian, Ari." But English is most in demand; the largest number of foreign tourists visiting Greece are Britons, some 1.1 million of them every year. After a spate of interpreting and waiting on table, the volunteer returns to the group table with its sips, *mezedes,* and conversation—there is something touching about this arrangement, in which working never arrests friendship. The Mustache hands me the token of the honored guest, the television remote, and a program guide, and tells me to choose any show I want. I channel surf for a moment out of curiosity. There is a trailer for a Greek detective movie—in two separate scenes, different women are slapped so hard they are knocked off their feet. I click forward to the Greek MTV channel. In the pop song video, a man backhands a woman until she finally falls to her knees. Leda shuffles the pages of the program guide and points to a comedy called *The Boss,* whispering to me that our host watches it every day, and signals me to choose it. It turns out to be a sitcom starring Tony Danza, about a household in which a woman earns her living as an executive and a man works as a housekeeper. In America, the show is called *Who's the Boss?* It is a comedy about equality; in this household, the question is more stable than the answer, which shifts between both, one, the other, and neither.

"What does the American girl like to eat?" the Mustache asks on one of his runs to the kitchen. He emerges waving a leg of goat, its fluffy tail still attached. "You like goat, Patricia?" he mocks. "Shall we have a *glendi* with goat's meat?" His wife has just brought it back from her home island, and she and his fifteen-year-old son laugh. At the table, the company consists of his wife and two children, my friend Leda, a professional tour guide, and her fiancé Theo, an architect, and two other men, a businessman and a cartoonist, a *yeliographos.* Greek makes no distinction between painting, drawing, and writing, so that a painter is a *zographos,* a writer of life, *zoi,* and a cartoonist is a writer of laughter. It is hard to imagine this man making drawings to laugh at, using the implements of his sad, exhausted-looking eyes. He finishes his coffee, on his way home to lunch, and wishes me luck. "Greece is beautiful," he shrugs, "but the Greeks are not good people. I know and you will find out."

"Well, Yiorgo," the businessman diverts him by matching disillusionment to disillusionment, "maybe she will be the only good thing America has ever sent us." He wears the gold baptismal cross Greek children receive from their godparents when they are christened and a blue glass eye on the same gold chain. The fifteen-year-old boy is obviously worried that I will be shocked by such naked cynicism, and says to me, almost protectively, as if he were telling me to cover my eyes during the scary part of a movie, "You see, our lives are very hard, so it makes us cold people." His mother has been absorbed during this in the television show, and at especially antic moments, she calls out, "*Panagia mou,* oh my holy Virgin, look at this!" Theo, Leda's fiancé, puts food on my plate from his, cutting it for me as if I were a child. It begins to seem disturbingly possible to me that the model for tender behavior in Greece is parental— but the model for erotic behavior is violence.

Leda makes me do my party piece, the recitation of a Greek nonsense verse that goes "I pass in front of your door, and you are frying fish. You throw me a meatball. Long live Cyprus!" This brings down the house. I try to imagine what sends them into paroxysms, and guess that it might have something like the effect of hearing someone with a strong Japanese accent declaim, "The Owl and the Pussycat went to sea in a beautiful pea-green boat."

The Mustache passes by and hands his little girl a beribboned chocolate motorcycle, which earns him a radiant smile; an ad comes on television for the coming broadcast of the summer Olympics in Barcelona, and he shakes his head. "I am surprised the flame got so far," he says, and I look at him questioningly. "No, you never hear about it, but there are always problems with the flame. Not mechanical problems, political problems. I remember once when the flame had to be taken from the Olympic stadium by helicopter, since the people of Olympia blocked the road to the stadium—and I can tell you we will withhold the flame for the Atlanta games, since Coca-Cola stole them from Athens, where they should be held for the anniversary. But it will not be reported."

Nineteen ninety-six is the one-hundredth anniversary of the modern Olympics, which were held first in the Kalimarmara, "the beautiful marble" stadium presented to the nation by the Onassis of his day, Averoff, who also donated the country's first battleship. Those 1896 Olympics were also the site of one of the primary myths of modern Greece, which like all true myths takes some element of politics—a political ambition, perception, or action—and transforms it through story into destiny, a destiny which is seen to be nature, as inevitable as daybreak and nightfall. The plots of modern Greek myth, though, are drawn from real events that are apotheosized, rather than imaginary events that are recreated in the world of reality.

At the 1896 Olympics, in front of an international audience and before members of the royal families of Europe, including the Prince of Wales, the future King Edward VII of England, a shepherd from the Roumeli region took the gold medal in that most charged of competitions for Greeks, the marathon. There it was—Greece reborn, after four hundred years as a fraction of the Islamic Ottoman Empire, Greece outstripping the world against all odds, and racing to catch up to the phantom figure of ancient Greece, like a body racing to seize its own errant soul, and this in front of the representatives of western Europe, which Greece held both in contempt and in awe. And by a shepherd, who like the illiterate General Makriyiannis who became the author of a classic, won against expensively trained athletes through his natural excellence alone. That he came from Roumeli, a center of the 1821 insurrection against the Turks, and a kind of equivalent to our redneck country, with Barba (Uncle) Yiorgo substituting for our Bubba, added to the savor of the event. The shepherd, Spiro Louis, appeared in photographs and engravings, while his feat was woven into literature, even appearing as the final scene of a novel by Greece's first public women's rights activist and one of its first women writers, Kalliroi Parren.

Many filaments of the modern Greek myths were there: the stunned witness of western Europe, the overcoming of a run of evil luck, the race to rejoin time to a lost eternity, and the mystical belief in Greece's natural excellence. The story is told to me in a patchwork of vehement voices, with a fury not only at Coca-Cola and the United States and the Olympic Committee, but at me, for not knowing this story, for knowing stories about ancient Marathon but not about the marathon of Spiro Louis. There is not just a bitterness at the loss of economic opportunity, but a prickly sense of being snubbed, of not being allowed the chance to prove something that needs proving. "But we could never have prepared Athens for the Olympics on time," says the Mustache's wife, "we don't have the facilities, we don't have the public transport, everyone would take the opportunity to strike and we can't even breathe. How could we expect athletes to perform in this *nefos?*" She is shouted down.

"This Olympics belonged to us; and if the rulers of the planet had recognized what they owe us, we would have solved these problems, and others, too. But we are a small country, and the superpowers decide our destiny for us," the Mustache says.

"Squashes," his wife says, "*kolokythia.* Nonsense. Look at how we punish the tourists. At the height of the season, it takes them three hours to go through passport control after a transatlantic flight and two more hours for a taxi, because all the bus drivers are on strike! We punish them and we pretend it is just happenstance."

Before a full-scale argument begins, the table finds a new outlet for its aggressions by teaching me to curse in Greek. I am taught to thrust my hand forward, in something like our high-five motion, and to snarl, "Here it is!" This, Leda thinks, is probably from a Byzantine way of wishing death on someone, a gesture of smearing them with ashes, which was a mourning custom, along with tearing the clothes, the hair, and scratching the cheeks.

I am taught to call out "Masturbator," which is mild unless you add an excruciatingly explicit diagonal pulling motion to it. "And if a neighbor annoys you," the businessman gestures with relish, "you point between your legs and tell them to write it on your balls." I don't see the use of this for myself, but he says, "Then write it on what's there."

"Or borrow the baker's," Leda suggests, "as I have done on occasion." The table starts an obscenity party, teaching me these phrases with mischievous delight, as if they were teaching them to a talking parrot. And oddly, I, who blush easily in English, can reel off the worst phrases in Greek with phlegmatic indifference. The blush seems to depend on some encounter between a child self and an adult self which can't be reproduced in a language you learn as an adult.

The businessman, whose father is from Smyrna, the port in Turkey that was once so associated with its Greek population that the Turks called it "infidel Smyrna," is telling stories about how his father went to school with Onassis, who was also from Smyrna. A round of whispered teasing follows his mention of Smyrna. "He is a Turk," the Mustache winks. "Baptized not in holy water, but in yogurt." The businessman drives the teasing off with a cryptic epigram—"If Greeks are Turks, then many Turks are also Greek; Karaghiozis-Karageuz," this last being a reference to the beloved shadow puppet figure shared in Turkish and Greek versions of the popular cycles of plays in both countries.

The businessman makes a hobby of a small vineyard, and produces his household wine from the grapes, but he is saying with a worried look that he thinks someone may have "eyed" it, because his sister found her dog there a few days ago, dead of the evil eye. "You see," he explains to me, "the eyes produce electricity, as does the mouth—the whole body is charged, but especially the eyes and mouth—and the evil eye is a product of a kind of negative magnetism in a person, who may not always be aware of possessing this power. And this negative magnetism makes the victim have an accident or get sick or lose something he treasures. Animals die of it often, since they have fewer defenses."

"Horses always die of it," adds the Mustache, "because they never vomit."

"Many people say it is just *fthonos*," Leda says, uttering one of the key pieces of Greek vocabulary, a word for a poisonous omnipresent jealousy. *Fthonos* is a word as old as Homer; it used to mean the particular jealousy and malice the gods displayed toward humans that caused them to promise a hero immortality, then snatch it back, or to lead a person into a trap. This divine malice seems now to belong only to mortals in their relations to other mortals.

"*Fthonos* surely has something to do with it," says the businessman. "We are a strange people—it is a disgrace for us to be the unwilling means for any other Greek's advancement. This is why we are so patriotic. We love the *patrida* so much—because—we hate each other." He shakes with cheerful laughter. "You don't believe me?" he asks. "Look." And he takes a newspaper from an empty chair pushed away from our table, opening it to the classified ads pages, and points to one. It is an ad from a Kyria Kalliope, offering *kafemandeia*, coffee-cup readings, tarot card readings, and palm readings. "If enemies of yours who are jealous of you have made magic against you, she can tell you their names and can bring luck again to your house." He points to another, Kyria Agapi, Mrs. Love, whose ad says that she is "dowered by God with the power to protect you from your enemies and to expel the evil eye from operating on you." She offers also consultations via phone to Greeks living abroad. I hand him back the paper. "You see?" he says.

"Can you tell me who has the evil eye?" I ask, having long since accepted that I am not being teased.

He touches the blue glass eye he wears as a safeguard around his neck. "It would help if you could always tell, but you can't. Often people with frowning brows pulled together in the center of the forehead have it—and of course people with blue eyes."

The fear of the evil eye, I know, is felt throughout the Middle East—there are charms against it in Arabic, Hebrew, Turkish, Persian—and it is an ancient fear, mentioned in Paul's letter to the Galatians. But the blue glass eye, the possible suggestion that bad luck comes from Europe, intrigues me.

The world of magic so often has its roots in the concrete social world; not so much its polar opposite, but its inseparable familiar— that blue glass eye hanging on the Smyrniote's neck reminds me of the Gothic minority in fourth-century Byzantium, a half-forgotten example of the mobile nature of racial prejudice. For in fourth-century Byzantine society, the fair-skinned and the blue-eyed were objects of physical disgust and fear, they were household slaves, street sweepers, cannon fodder as mercenaries in the army, people in daily contact with contamination, with refuse and with blood, an exploited population who it was feared would revolt one day and slaughter their masters and commanders. By the sixth century the situation had changed and the Gothic population had been absorbed, but I wonder if the blue glass eye might not have been at one time a charm against having the bad fortune to be a Goth, a charm to keep the bad luck of the blue eye out of your own face.

Perhaps the blue-eyed crusaders who sacked Constantinople, the Byzantine capital, are also concentrated in this charm, but this small unseeing eye may have been first a charm not so much of protection as of projection, that stunning psychological mechanism of the powerful, which is so often the unacknowledged presence in classical Greek tragedy, the real death's-head at the feast. It is the

means through which the murder of Iphigenia by her father is presented as social necessity, while the murderous response of her
mother Clytemnestra is portrayed as a demonic outrage. It is the
means by which Oedipus's crimes against his parents are grossly
magnified while the fact that the cycle of tragedy began with his
parents' exposing their baby to die on a hillside is a matter of convention. The blue glass eye holds a reminder that it is not only the
victim who is afraid of the murderer, but the murderer who is afraid
of the victim. Leda spoke of the evil eye as a result of *fthonos,* but it
may be equally a protection against the *fthonos* within as against the
fthonos without.

"At least there are spells against it," says the Smyrniote. "My
aunt, who by the way is a very skilled reader of coffee cups, if you
should ever like to look a bit into the future, has taken it off people
sometimes."

"And priests can too," says the Mustache's wife. "There is a
prayer against it in the prayer book."

"In the Orthodox prayer book?" I ask.

"Yes," says the Mustache's wife, "I can show you, we have one in
the knife drawer of the kitchen." She brings back a black leather
book with a ribbon marker and reads, with comments by the
others, "Healer of our souls . . . we beg you, send away, banish,
and drive out every devilish operation . . . every plot, magic and
evil and injury and evil enchantment of the eyes of the evil-doing
and malicious people, from your servant." Church Greek is hard for
me—you need dictionaries of New Testament–period Greek to
read it—but it seems almost equally hard for them; they stumble
and argue over words and have to shruggingly let whole phrases
go without the right dictionary to help with the puzzles. But Greek
is a strange lawless combination of both continuity and frag-
mentation. Although it is true that a substantial amount of ancient
and modern vocabulary is the same, it is also true that there are
nineteenth-century authors whose works need glossaries, even dictionaries. There is an enormous pride in the continuity between

ancient and modern Greek, but there is also another pride, almost a secretive ideal, in the vision of a world in which each Greek author would require a private dictionary to be approached. But in this country of Greek and Turk, ancient and modern, Roman and Byzantine, East and West, Christian and polytheist, the language itself is full of hidden kinships and ambiguities. Christians were once called atheists, in the Greek of late antiquity. "Anathema on the hour that I met you" is one of the bitterest things you can say to an old love. But go far back enough in Greek, and you will find that at one time *anathema* meant simply whatever was dedicated to a god, whether cursed or blessed—it is possible to call the Parthenon itself, begun in 447 B.C., an *anathema* of victory over the Persians. There is, it seems, an unwitting blessing even in this violent dismissal.

What is unnerving about this evil-eye prayer is that the evil eye seems to be a product of both evil and good—at times to come from malice, at others to arrive simply as a response to a human gift, beauty, or virtue or good fortune.

"So remember," says the Smyrniote, who has to go back to his office, "don't compliment anyone unless you say *ftou ftou ftou* three times, because unless you show that you cancel out the compliment by spitting, you might accidentally bring the evil eye on them."

The rest of us finish a bottle of the wiry Greek white wine, and the conversation gets dense with things for me to see and do and read. "You must watch *Lampsi* (The Shining), the most famous Greek soap opera," says the Mustache's wife, "it will be wonderful for your Greek." Her husband glares at her. "Well, it will," she holds her ground. "They repeat so much to keep you up with what you missed."

"Soap operas," the Mustache says contemptuously. "Imitation American soap operas. Has she seen the Parthenon? Are you going to take her to the son et lumière?" he roars at Theo and Leda. "The Acropolis at night, now that is beautiful. You should see the illumination, have dinner together afterward, and then come back to walk around late in the neighborhood. Maybe Patricia will hear the marble girls cry." He hardly needed my questioning look as a motive to explain. "You know of course, that the English *milordi*"—a hellenization of "my lord," whose Greek ending gives it an inexplicably sarcastic air in the hearing—"stole one of the kores who stood on the Porch of the Maidens and held up the Erectheum. They say they bought it from the Turks, but it was not the Turks' to sell. And you know we are going to have it back. Melina—Mercouri—will get it back for us. But anyway, when the *milordi* stole the kore, the Parthenon was a Turkish fortress. Greeks were only allowed there with permits, so we couldn't defend all our treasures. And the *milordi* wanted the rest. So they sent a party of Turks up there at night in secret, to take the other girls away in the darkness. But when the Turks climbed up there, they heard the girls' voices calling and sobbing for their sister, and when they got closer they heard anguished screaming like women being raped, and they dropped their shovels and ropes and ran away. The *milordi* couldn't bribe them to go up there again, and some of those Turks went mad, supposedly, they could never stop hearing the screams of women they couldn't see, and the screams were terrible, violent, because it is so hard for marble to cry. So people who live in this neighborhood used to claim that on certain nights they heard the marble girls crying for their sister who was kidnapped by force, and they say Greece won't be Greece until she comes back again."

"Gentle madam, no," says my inner voice silently and oddly as I look at the crusading insistent exaltation in his face. The phrase's source floats to the surface of my mind: a moment from *Antony and Cleopatra,* that play about passion and illusion in which the pair have to destroy each other because their love is sustained by myth, not life. Cleopatra says of Antony, "His legs bestrid the ocean; his rear'd arm/ crested the world; his voice was propertied as all the tun'd spheres . . . Think you there was, or might be, such a man/ as this I dreamed of?" Her attendant answers, "Gentle madam, no."

The party begins to break up because we are nearing siesta time, still very much a part of the Greek summer, even if it is beginning to disappear in the cities in wintertime. But the Mustache is still wound up about the *milordi* and wants to tell one more story about them, so while Theo fiddles with his car keys, the Mustache tells me a story he says he had from his grandfather.

"Where do you think the *milordi* came from?" he asks me rhetorically. "England," I reply helplessly.

"Wrong, at least in my grandfather's story. They came from Greece. They are pre-Christian Greeks, a remnant of the ancient idol-worshippers. He said you could tell they had never been Christian because you never saw them crossing themselves, as all Christians do. One time when he was visiting me here and we were riding the trolley near the English church downtown, we saw English people carrying cages and cats and leading dogs into their church. A woman on the trolley asked out loud, 'Are the English Christian?' And my grandfather said not very patiently, 'Of course not, woman. You don't see that they take their animals to church?' He explained his idea to me, that when the other Greeks became Christian, the *milordi* would not give up the old gods, and so they took all their wealth and emigrated to Europe. And those people are the ancestors of the *milordi,* and that is why they fight with us in our wars, and why they came back to take the marbles of the Parthenon with them to England, it is the old sympathy in their blood. And that is why they have houses here and so many of them feel the need to visit here every summer and to pay homage, just like they used to, to the ancient stones."

Theo is now very anxious to get on the road for home, so we leave with thanks and embraces. I run into a pharmacy before it closes for siesta to buy a tube of sunscreen. The sales clerk hands it to me in a bag printed with the Star of Vergina and the slogan "Three thousand years of Greek Macedonia." We weave through the traffic, and when someone cuts in front of us, Theo leans out the window, pulls at an imaginary penis, and shouts, "Masturbate, masturbator! Play with it more! Keep masturbating!" There is a startlingly rhetorical, formal quality to Greek insults, almost as if the speaker were trained to take a theme and elaborate on it. It is a quality taken to its

height in the orations of John Chrysostom, a Byzantine church patriarch who was a master of ornamental invective, as are a number of
high-ranking contemporary Greek clerics. I wonder if I am hearing
in Theo's imperatives of contempt a trace of the Byzantine schooling
in rhetoric, in which a student had to deliver patterned speeches
both of praise and insult.

Shutters are closing at my apartment building for the quiet
hours, and I climb the stairs as quietly as I can, looking forward to a
nap myself. I am just drifting off when a fight erupts, a trio: two
women—one mezzo, one soprano—and a man, a baritone. The
mezzo's accusations rush like fountain spray, while the soprano's
defense joins her and then rises above her even more spectacularly
like a fresh jet of water from a new source in the fountain—there is
twenty minutes at least of this, with the man's voice weaving
between both. Every time it seems to subside there is a fresh outbreak, and I am amazed at the inexhaustible jets of fury. It is a terrifying opera for someone vulnerable in the language, since you are
conscious of the prospect that the fight will escalate and you will be
swept into it, without the right words to soothe or mediate. This is
how babies must feel when their parents fight—the sense of helpless endangerment, of being an inarticulate witness to something
that may destroy you, of being captive in speechlessness, like being
adrift in an ocean and seeing a rescue ship, but knowing you can't
call loudly enough for it to hear.

Sure enough, my doorbell rings, and there is a spluttering
woman standing there. "Did you hear my radio, did it disturb you?"
she shrieks at me.

"Not at all," I say, which seems to calm her.

"It is those Albanians below, they always cause trouble and blame
it on me. They are not used to life among civilized people. But you
will say you did not hear a radio if anyone asks."

Since I did not, I will. She retreats to her own apartment.

Albanians at the moment have the reputation of being the Joads
of Greece, ignorant dustbowl characters who are perceived as

threateningly, desperately, criminally poor. Albanians pour across the borders to work illegally in Greece, and Albanian gangs supposedly rob, rape, murder, and carry their internecine quarrels into Greece. The Greeks also accuse them of maltreating the Greek minority in Albania, and there is an inflammable border dispute about southern Albania, a region which the Greeks say was unjustly incorporated into Albania and which is called here "northern Epirus," to emphasize that it is part of the Greek region of Epirus. When I was looking for apartments to rent in the newspapers, I came across a number of ads with the proscription "No Albanians."

I want to try to sleep again, but the prolonged fighting was too nerve-wracking. The Mustache's bitter remarks about the Olympics are still in my mind. On an impulse, I reach for my new dream book. The entry I am looking for shows a definitive break with the world of Artemidorus. Koka-Kola—"This vulgar, banal, and unhealthy drink that has imposed Western industrialism throughout the world has passed already into the world of dreams where it is a familiar symbol; an inauspicious dream. If you see others drinking this manufactured beverage in your dream, be on guard of superficial relationships. If you yourself are drinking it, your motives toward them may be suspect without your having realized it."

I hear shutters beginning to open on the courtyard, sounds of televisions and radios. A woman emerges onto her balcony and signals to a neighbor across the way with a *"Pssst, psst,* Katerina," exactly like Leporello in *Don Giovanni.* I had never thought about how brilliantly Mozart understood the community of balconies until now. My own telephone rings. "I knew you would come here," says my friend Kostas. I had known Kostas in the United States, where he went to college, and has some family, and I had seen him struggling with the dilemma of where to settle. In the end, with no clear resolution, he returned to Thessaloniki, the northern city which is Greece's "second capital," where he practices law now. He jokes now that it should have been London, and not either Thessaloniki or Boston, because he can't get a high enough dosage of Shakespeare in either. Kostas loves Shakespeare probably more than anyone I know, with an almost sports-fan-like fanaticism, and his conversation is usually full of hidden Shakespeare, like those drawings in children's books where you are supposed to find how many clocks or cats are hidden in the picture. I had thought about Antony and Cleopatra earlier this afternoon, and now, with impeccable Shakespearian telepathy, Kostas is on the phone.

"I knew you would come," he repeats, "I knew it in the States."

"How did you know that?" I ask, familiar with his bouts of both real and imaginary omniscience.

"I knew it because you love *A Winter's Tale* most of all the Shakespeare plays," he says cryptically, and we arrange to meet on his impending trip to Athens.

"Kosta," I ask, "do you have an *oneirokritis* at home?"

"My sister does at her place."

"Would she let me borrow it for a few weeks?"

"I think so, but you know Artemidorus, don't you?"

"Yes," I say, "I have his book with me, but there are dreams in it that nobody can dream anymore. I know what you dreamed of in the second century. But I want to find out what you've dreamed of since."

"Well, I will see if I can wrest the book from Angeliki's grip. And until I get there, keep in mind what Emmanuel Roidis, our great unread nineteenth-century novelist, said about my country: 'Every nation has its cross to bear: In England, for example, it's the weather. In Greece, it's the Greeks.' "

IMMORTALITY

I tear off a slice of the flat bread I bought yesterday from a Lebanese bakery—it leaves floury traces on the cutting board. My electricity is "on vacation," as they say here, because of sympathy strikes with the bus drivers. The hours that different neighborhoods will be without power are posted in the newspapers and announced on news bulletins during the day. Hospitals, merchants, schools, commuters, all suffer from the power cuts, but they are in an odd way an expression of a national ideal, that all experience should be communal, both in family and in political life.

I use my hours without electricity this morning to wander in my neighborhood, beginning to find my way around. The hills of Athens make it a labyrinth, easy to get lost in. You can be near a familiar main avenue and be utterly unaware of it, wandering in a cul-de-sac that seems to have no relation to your landmark. That is true of the language too, which is a language of enclaves. When you learn Greek, you aren't learning one language, but two or three, and there are uncountable ranges of patois.

I discover a street that is like a miniature village, which has grapevines bearing grapes strung from house to house. In Athens what you tread on underfoot is most likely to be figs, or oranges or lemons that drop from the fruit-bearing trees onto the streets. On another corner, a man is changing a hubcap with communal advice from his building, and I hear someone practicing a Schubert song with a pretty touch. At the summit of a hill, there is a fine neoclassical mansion, stucco wreaths under the windows, handsome entrance doors unhinged but held together by a piece of wire between one handle and another, a cat lying thirstily in the overgrown garden. The neoclassical houses followed the Bavarian king assigned to Greece by the great powers after the country earned its independence from the Turks. Otto, the son of the classicizing King Ludwig of Bavaria, who had envisioned Munich as the "Athens of the North," reimagined Athens as—Athens. The city had begun to lose all but its symbolic significance when Constantine created the eastern Rome in Constantinople in the fourth century. Athens did not give him the geographical advantage in building an eastern empire that Constantinople did, and its association with the old gods that Constantine had abandoned made it even more inappropriate as the imperial capital of a newly conceived empire of religion. Under the Ottomans, whose most significant cities remained Constantinople and Thessaloniki, as they had been for the Byzantines, Athens metamorphosed into a provincial Turkish village. Otto and his Bavarian architects set out to rebuild it—few houses were left standing after the years of the War of Independence, so they had a remarkably blank canvas, in a dilapidated Turkish town with hardly an important public building. They set about to reinvent the city, and although there are those who claim they fatally misunderstood the site, and turned Athens into the Munich of the Mediterranean, the domestic scale of the neoclassicism they inspired is endearing—these villas can take so many tones and responses toward classical architecture, witty, tender, mocking, silly, affectionate. The neoclassical houses of Athens are like a flock of young girls wearing their first evening dresses and their first formal necklaces and earrings—some graceful, some giggling, some of them awkward in their mother's "classical" clothes. These houses give a youth back to a city that can seem exhausted.

Athens is a city that brims with people, but it can often seem like a city no one lives in; it has a haunted quality. All the unseen worlds of the past, classical, medieval, Ottoman (of which there are few reminders left, except in the language, because the Greeks so hate the evidence), surround you, above and beneath. The underworld is always present, the world of the dead. And the jumble of houses—the abandoned nineteenth-century mansions in odd corners, the tiny houses that were built at the turn of the century by villagers and look exactly like village houses, the whitewashed boxes built for refugees from Asia Minor in the 1920s, now overshadowed by large apartment buildings on either side like grown-ups holding the hands of a child about to cross the street—gives Athens the feeling that everyone here is both himself and his own ghost.

I walk through an unexpected piece of countryside, apartment buildings going up on land that clearly belongs to the modest empty farmhouse still standing. Emerging from this cool shady lane, I find myself caught up in a throng of people on a paved plaza. They are carrying banners and enormous wreaths of flowers on tripods. Some are throwing handfuls of bay leaves onto the pavement. They are shouting a word over and over again: "Immortal, immortal!" I think for a moment that my Greek must be failing me, but they repeat the word often and furiously: "*Athanati, athanati!*" Tears are streaming down the cheeks of some of the women. There is no way to go forward through the throng, it is so dense, and they seem to be waiting for something.

"Please, can you tell me what is happening?" I ask a couple next to me. The man holds a small Greek flag. "We are burying our Jenny Karezi," he says. "We are burying our great actress. She will pass this way." He turns a genuinely grief-stricken face away from me, and forcefully joins the cry of "Immortal! Immortal!"

I know stories about Aspasia and Hypatia. But I have never heard of this immortal dead woman.

I can't find a passageway out of this crowd, which shifts and sways but doesn't move until people at the front catch sight of the funeral procession, when the chanting of "Immortal" trebles in volume, driven and protesting, and the mass surges forward to follow the coffin. I am swept past glass-fronted shops with sample tomb carvings in the windows, many in the popular shape of open marble books with space for a photograph. The photographs used in the storefront tombstones are of famous figures—I see a picture of a much loved young mayor of Athens, who died suddenly of a heart attack not too long ago and is still talked about with regret. There is a picture of Maria Callas, so it is clear that these carvings are a kind of advertisement, since Callas, defying the Greek state, in which civil funerals are illegal, and the virulent Orthodox prohibition against cremation, supposed to interfere with the resurrection of the body, had arranged to have her body cremated and its ashes scattered over the sea. The crowd sweeps me past a cluster of these shops, and I catch a glimpse of a memorial featuring a photograph of Marilyn Monroe. In other windows, there are elaborately decorated cakes with sugar messages reading *Kalo Taxidi,* the wish for a good journey, and *Athanatos.* This is *kollyva,* the food of the dead, made of grains, seeds, and dried fruit, funeral food throughout the Balkans. The Turks, too, have a similar commemorative food, of wheat and pomegranate seeds, which they eat to mark the martyrdom of Muhammad's grandsons, and to celebrate Noah's survival of the flood—the mixture, in their version, is based on the supplies remaining on the ark after the survivors' forty days on board.

I am swept along inside the Protonekrotafio, Athens's version of Père Lachaise, but I manage to disentangle myself from the crowd. The geography of the cemetery is complicated; I am utterly lost now as I often am here, but I have learned that bewilderment is often as effective a method of finding an entrance or an exit as certainty. I pass a life-size statue of a little girl wearing a 1930s smock and a Buster Brown haircut, baptismal cross prominently carved, and a gravestone that proudly identifies the deceased as an employee of the Greek national telephone company. A man in a straw hat and shirtsleeves is weeding graves. Tending graves is obviously a difficult business here, since water is expensive and keeping greenery alive takes committed effort—I can see that many people opt for urns full of deathless plastic roses and wreaths.

Two women near a wall are trying to revive a dying kitten by giving it sips of water; the Greeks consider spaying animals cruel, and according to European animal welfare organizations, attempt to control the stray animal population through putting out poisoned food. A row over, a priest in a long gown, ponytail, and the black fez on which chef's hats were supposedly modeled is singing a remembrance ceremony for a small group of five, before a stone tomb covered with flowers, stems wrapped in foil to keep them wet long enough to live through the ceremony. Two rows further up, toward what I hope is the exit, two women are gardening the graves of their dead, one wearing a halter top and gym shorts, the other flapping her skirt up to her thighs to make a breeze. I pick my way through the meshes of the graves, struck by the modern versions of the kind of classical grave monument that pictured the dead relative on one side clasping the hands of the living on the other. The kitschy realism of the modern carvings is absurdly fascinating—mustachioed men wearing business suits, women with permanent waves wearing pearls and stiletto heels are presented in classical poses.

On a rise overlooking what seems like a reception hall, I see a gate onto the street. Descending, I see clustered boxes and a pile of shovels outside it. It is a mausoleum for reburial; grave space is at a premium in Greece, and practical necessity has made a religious ceremony of the recycling of the remains roughly three years after the burial. The remains are removed from the grave to be ritually washed and reburied in mausoleum walls. It looks as if the workmen are taking a break. Soft-drink cans and beer bottles are propped up against open chests overflowing with white, yellow, and gray bones.

FLESH AND STONE

A glowing lemon, like a star magically transformed into a fruit, falls directly onto our table from the tree overhead. Aura, an actress whom I recently met, has spent a morning with me wandering the Archaeological Museum, probably the most visited museum in Greece, with its collection of treasures from Schliemann's digs, and sculpture familiar from postcards and art history textbooks. We finished with a visit to her namesake, a headless fifth-century statue called *Aura,* a personification of a breeze in the form of a woman whose maker battled against his own material, doing all he could to transform a block of stone that would crush bones if it fell, into the illusion of a transparent current of air, the pleats of her dress eddying unevenly around her, following the topography of her body, her bodice molded in the gust to her breasts, a nipple showing through the cloth. It is a marvelous piece of work, evoking a nakedness that will never be revealed as an underlying metaphor for air that can never be carved, stone that can never feel a breeze, much less achieve the condition of air. Aura looks nothing like it. She is not an image, but a maker of images, with round malleable features which can mimic nearly any expression, from a newborn's to a secret policeman's, and a sturdy, even rather thick, hourglass figure like a nineteenth-century actress's. When the waiter brings our iced coffees, the pattern of his expression, the narrowed eyes and rather pursed mouth, momentarily clings to her face as she looks at him. A lizard startlingly falls onto her head, and before she shoos it off the table, it is unnerving to watch her absorb its gaze, matching its impervious stare with a cousinly eye.

"And?" she says. "How did it all strike you, what you saw?" I have visited this museum enough to know the rooms where my personal landmarks are, and to have ritual pilgrimages to make, even to pieces that I know would be trivial to many other people, like a sauté pan with a handle in the shape of Aphrodite, found among grave treasure, which I yearn to have a copy of, as the ideal vessel for scrambled eggs with white truffles, along with champagne, for Valentine's Day breakfast. But for the most part, as I have to confess to Aura, I always emerge from this museum with new reactions, always aware that in looking at these statues, we partly see them and partly guess at what we are seeing. The museum inevitably disguises as well as exhibits them. The last time I visited here, I came away with a pervasive sense of the connection between these sculptures and tragedy. I was looking at the famous statue called *Poseidon,* poised to cast a spear, and motionless, and I thought how absolutely failure was worked into every keenly modeled muscle, tendon, the perfect hips of this perfect body, that it had been brought to this physical pitch, but could never breathe, never cross the boundary into life. This wouldn't matter in many kinds of art, but here it does, here it seems that the failure of perfect sculpted bodies to live is a meditation on the failure of human beings not to die.

Now that I am living here, I have a new way to imagine the statues, not as rare, but as ubiquitous, like the painted icons I encounter in workshops, shops, homes that shelter them as the polytheist homes housed their patron deities, churches, restaurants, streets. The ancient dreamers who told Artemidorus their dreams literally lived with these statues, dreaming of the meanings of seeing them-

selves anointing and cleaning them, as they did in daily life, sweep-
ing in front of them, sprinkling everything in the temple with
water, defacing them in moments of distress, or angrily throwing
the statues from a house outside. Their statues had social meanings
as well as religious ones, which were reflected in their dreams: connotations of victory and public honor, because of the practice of
honoring athletes with statues, and connotations of freedom—if a
slave dreamed of his own statue in bronze, it portended freedom,
because bronze statues were erected only for free men. No woman,
then, could ever dream that she was free, since the statues representing women were nearly always of supernatural women, or of
dead women and their domestic attendants on grave monuments.
The ancient dreamers saw statues with specific associations; they
liked the gods to be seated or immovable, in stable positions, and in
their usual costumes, "in the form we have imagined him to be," as
Artemidorus says of Zeus. They might see the sun god, Helios (it
was a better omen to see a representation of him in a dream than to
see the god himself); Heracles, who was a good omen for men
engaged in lawsuits; Tyche, the goddess of chance, whom it was
always desirable to see seated or reclining, not shifting positions.
For the modern dreamers, statues seem mostly symbolic of tenden-
cies in their inner lives: if you see a statue, you can expect to meet
a person who will become your ideal; a statue of a famous person
predicts good news, or some reward for an effort; seeing yourself as
a statue may mean something has gone wrong with you as a human
being, in your emotional life. Under the headings of dreams about
icons, though, are guides for the dreamer to specific personal
patronage and protection, like the codes Artemidorus assigned to
the dream statues. But that doesn't imply a simple continuity,
because while our wishes and needs may be similar, the selves we
wish with have changed. A modern dreamer making a statue,
according to several of my dream books, wishes to perfect some
aspect of himself, and is preparing for an opportunity to do that.
The second-century interpretation of this dream—a common

dream, since Artemidorus based his interpretations on many instances of dreams and their outcomes that he compiled on his travels—is that it is good for adulterers, orators, forgers, and for all deceivers, since the art of making statues shows "what does not exist as though it actually does." My modern dream books are splendid catalogues of the imagery of modern Greek life—if you riffled through a book of photographs of Greece, like the wonderful *Yeitonia* (Neighborhood) of Andreas Skhinas, you would see many of the dream images that come to life behind closed Greek eyes. But while the modern dream books document the dreams, they leave alone the question of who the dreamers might be.

And today, as I was looking, I tell Aura, I was struck not only by the beauty of the statues, but by the limitations of the conception of beauty they represent, not just in the way it creates a convention of perfection, and then is bound to its own convention, unable to respond to physical features outside it, but an actual limitation. Aura asks what I mean, and I struggle to find out myself. I mean that the beauty they embody is only at the threshold of what beauty is, a fragment. This is beauty only as it is idealized, not as it is experienced, beauty only as it is desired, and not beauty as it is loved. It misses the beloved ugliness that is also part of our sense of beauty, part of the specific beauty of a body and face that you love. It misses the shocking joy of the attainable. And it misses something else. Think of the human genitals, with their humility and magnificence, a beauty too complex to be idealized. The statues of the women have no genitals, and the statues of the men have dainty, symbolic genitals, made symmetrical so as not to spoil the line of the body.

"You are making me think about a phenomenon that occurs in our language, because it is so old," Aura says, putting on her sunglasses. "What happens is that sometimes after moving through different eras, and grammars, and absorbing elements of other languages, a phrase or a word will pick up meanings that comment on each other. I am thinking just now of the verb 'to idealize,' which can also mean 'to sublimate,' although it is not a very common

usage. Think about how our ideal of the body changed with Christianity from the beautiful athlete's body to the ruined emaciated
saint's body you see in icons. John the Baptist is always shown nearly
naked, like the old gods and the boy athletes, but his arms and legs
are sticklike, tortured-looking, as if he is diseased. And yet this body
is a kind of ideal, the ideal Christian body, with its hollow throat,
the sacralized misery of its limbs and sacred torment on its face,
with which it bargains for the eternal life that beauty couldn't win.
In both worlds, though, it was the male body that expressed the
ideal, physical, moral, social. If you look in the *Nichomachean Ethics*
you will read how Aristotle, a thinker riddled with assumptions
about class presented as biological observation, as you would
expect a tutor dependent on the nouveau riche Macedonian royals
to be, describes a man's slow impressive gait as evidence of his great
soul. Ideas about the body are so built into social imagery that the
ancient word for beggar, *ptokhos,* very like the modern adjective for
'poor,' literally means someone who crouches. Women, of course,
were supposed to crouch, and look down submissively. The type of
woman who did not is represented by the many scenes of the Ama-
zons fighting the Greeks, who of course defeated them—the name
of one of the famous Amazon warriors, Antiope, means 'the woman
who looks straight into your face.' As for the Christian male body,
go to Nea Moni on Chios, and to Patmos—you will see the ambitions of the new bodies, the ones that belong to the emperor of
heaven, no longer bodies at all, but instruments, so their loss cannot
matter, as the loss or aging of the athlete's beautiful body does.

"To idealize and to sublimate. We honored our statues as representing excellence and divinity—but we have also at times violently
hated our own art. Statues like my namesake, for instance, and like
many others that will never be found, are not just headless because
of accidents, but because they were attacked by angry Christians, or
by the emperor's troops, who would decapitate them, and sometimes bury them, neutralizing their demonic powers by building
churches over them. Imagine lynchings of statues. Saint Augustine

himself cheered like a football fan when he saw a crowd attack a
statue of Heracles. They tore its gold beard off. But those buried
statues have, in a way, risen again. Let me tell you a story from our
revolutionary war. You know General Makriyiannis, the illiterate
who wrote the memoir and became the first master of modern
Greek prose? During the war, he acquired two statues, one a
woman, the other he thought was a prince; he was awed by their
craftsmanship, and mentions that you could see the raised outlines
of their veins. He rescued them from some soldiers, who had
abducted them during a raid on the island of Poros, and were planning to sell them for a fine profit to some Europeans at Argos.
Makriyiannis took the soldiers aside and told them that no matter
what the sum, they should never allow these statues to leave our
country. He told them, 'It was for the statues that we fought.' "

We order two more coffees, staving off the confrontation with
the shadeless sidewalk and frantic Athenian traffic. Aura wants to
know what impressions I have of Greek theater, but I haven't yet
been to a play, I have only so far had encounters with Greek television programs. I am amused by the national soap opera, with its
shipping magnates, scandal-making politicians, and the incestuous
charge of its love affairs, which seem to occur almost exclusively
within the family circle, a brother in love with his brother's wife, a
stepson courting his stepmother persistently in corners of the family mansion. It is startling too, to see the fine work of the actors lav-
ished incongruously on television material—Greek actors make
their living largely on TV, supplemented by stage work and the small
Greek movie industry, so sitcoms and soap operas are populated
with many fine, classically trained actors, and serial adaptations of
Greek fiction are finely crafted and eagerly awaited cultural events.

I have also been painfully stunned by the daily scenes of women
being beaten and slapped, in comedies, in dramas, in serials, in
movies, from the fifties to segments taped last week. I kept a log for
a week, to test whether the shock of seeing these matter-of-course
beatings was making me exaggerate their frequency, but "daily"

wasn't even an adequate description. Fistfights between men were much rarer than the episodes of men hitting women, so incessant that they seemed as much a matter of national taste as of dramatic necessity. In one week of casual viewing, I saw a sister beaten by a brother in a lyrical island drama, a daughter in a high-spirited comedy slapped sharply across the face by her father, a wife in a soap opera slapped by a husband for impertinence, a melodrama in which a wife was repeatedly beaten savagely and then raped by her husband's brother, an episode of a dramatic serial in which a woman's boyfriend seduces her by slapping her until he reveals to her her desire for him, and a comedy about a dominating mother and a village boy who cannot seem to lose his virginity, even after his marriage. The movie concludes with his mother calling for him downstairs in the night, while his young bride waits upstairs. He asserts to his mother that he is now master of the house, and that it is up to him to command. Upstairs, in his bridal chamber, he slaps his wife, and climbs on top of her, able at last to consummate the marriage. It is hard for me to imagine the effect this incessant imagery has on children—schoolgirls and boys watching movies with their parents after supper, watching twenty minutes of a movie before they start their homework after school. Only a week of this reminds me that one of the most important, if not the most important of nineteenth-century Greek novels, a classic of Greek realism, is called *The Murderess,* about a woman who concludes that the lives of Greek women are intolerable, and begins to murder little girls, to spare them.

"I had never quite grasped how shocking such violence must seem to an outsider," says Aura, "almost as if it were a pillar of our culture, even celebrated." She sips at her coffee. "To idealize and to sublimate. Now that I think of it, I am not aware of anything in our criminal code that defines beating or any kind of physical violence to women as a criminal offense. But for the mutilation or any physical damage done to statues, the penalties are very severe."

METAMORPHOSIS

Today is the Feast of the Metamorphosis, known to us as the Transfiguration, when Christ allowed his disciples to glimpse the radiant divinity he had previously withheld from his face. This shimmering alteration is a part of all miraculous tales, even present in one as familiar as Cinderella, in the changing of the pumpkin into a coach and the metamorphosis of an abused, miserable, dirty child into a glowingly beautiful and lovable woman. In Greece, it is one of the commonest subjects for icons, Christ's face like the sun surrounded with golden rays, and disciples dropping awed to their knees before him, while the word "Metamorphosis" sparkles somewhere in the painted scene, here in this country of the double nature, where even the language has a double nature, divine and mortal. "Leukos Oikos," the White House, people say in the classically flavored Greek which deifies what it names; *aspro spiti,* white house, people say giving directions, using the word for house that emerged from the crusaders' word *hospitum.* The idea of metamorphosis is here too as a fantasy shaping political life. The Ottoman province Greece had been, the fantasy went, after 1821 would be revealed as an eternal idea, and would take back, piece by piece, all that it had lost—first from Rome, which it felt had usurped its classical culture. Then it would be revealed again as a territorial empire, with Istanbul, transformed again into Constantinople, as its capital. And at last it would be recognized as the Empire of Time itself, governing not only territory, but history and civilization.

It is six o'clock in the morning, when the air is cool and fresh, with the spicy scent peculiar to Attica, compounded of orange and lemon trees, sage, eucalyptus, cypress trees, scents that coexist with the equally pervasive ones of chlorine cleansers, cooking lamb and garlic, and gasoline. Someone on the third floor has been up even earlier, because the hall outside smells like a church this morning from the strong odor of incense. Maybe it's Kyria Maro or Kyria Flora—on feast days, old ladies put incense into the ornate brass censers you can buy for home use (in my neighborhood you can find one of these, or indeed any ecclesiastical object, stole, eternal lamp, six-foot candles, much more easily than you can find a wooden spoon or a pepper mill), and cloud all the corners of their houses and the apartment house corridors with the holy fragrances. I reach for my dream book to see if there is an entry under "metamorphosis." It is a promise of good luck to see this icon in a dream, transferred directly onto your sleep, like a scene transferred onto a set of china. "For those who see this scene, good fortune. They may find glory through their ordinary, daily activities, an ordinary tool they work with may turn out to be an important invention, leading to a new business, for example a housewife's cake may lead to opening a bakery, a mechanic's wrench may lead to some innovation in a car's engine. And those who see this dream will be recognized and win followers. If many people see this dream during the same period of time, some national glory can be expected." Like the gods and goddesses in ancient dreams, who in Artemidorus are dreamed in the form of statues, the Christian god must be dreamed the way he is imagined in art. It is interesting, too, to see how optimistic this prediction is—I know a whole category of transformation dreams from Artemidorus, for whom metamorphosis is potentially more ambiguous. As always in his world, who you are in your waking life affects the outcome of the dream. The same dream affects men and women, free people and slaves, differently. This Christian dream is more about an absolute revelation of power than the ones in Artemidorus, which are concerned with changes in your social condition. The people he talked to dreamed of changing sexes, of their bodies turning into precious metals. If a slave dreamed he was turned into silver or gold, he could expect to be sold. On the other hand, if a rich man had this dream, he could expect to be plotted against, since everything made of silver and gold attracts scheming people. For a man to dream he was changed into a woman was good for a poor man, bad for a rich man: a poor man would gain someone to look after him, but the rich man would lose all authority. On the other hand, it almost always foretold improvements if a woman dreamed she became a man. If unmarried, she would marry. If childless, she would have a son, "and, in this way, she will change into the nature of a man." And it was an excellent dream for a harlot, a prediction that she would never lack for clients.

I hear the sounds of church chants from a radio or television down the hall, celebrating the Metamorphosis with the trancelike vocalizing of Orthodox ceremony, which combines inexhaustible rhythmic repetition with sinuous vocal ornament—the cantor sings like the blood circulates, if only it circulated forever. The pungent rosemary-laden smell of the incense seeps under my door. *Livani,* it is called, from the archaic word for the aromatic incense that used to be burned at sacrifices. The whole floor smells as if it is cooking, but without the scent of the missing meat. I look up incense in my dream book, though I should really be checking to see if I have packed everything I need for my trip to Olympia this morning. "Whoever sees that a priest swings a censer toward him and comes into contact with the fumes is being flattered and deceived." This is a piece of dream technique familiar from Artemidorus, the dream that relies on a play of words for its meaning. The verb *livanizo,* to cense, also means to flatter—he is mad for incense, you say about someone, meaning he adores flattery. But the technique used so skillfully by Artemidorus

also reflected a poignant limitation which he must have recognized—
that you could rarely successfully interpret a dream dreamed in a language you didn't understand.

I wait downstairs for Leda to pick me up—she is guiding a
Cypriot group through Patras and Olympia and has invited me to
join her. I am curious not only to see the towns, but about what it
will be like to see them in the company of people who have a stake
in this heritage instead of people who don't. I look at the tenants'
names by their bells, something I couldn't study at leisure when
everyone is awake. There's a dentist, a journalist, the inevitable
teacher of foreign languages, and a majority sprinkling of Peloponnesians and Cretans, origins detectable from the suffixes of their
surnames. *Poulos* is the common Peloponnesian suffix, meaning
child of, as in Yiannopoulos, Johnson. *Akis* is a diminutive meaning
little, as in Grigorakis, little Gregory, and is the usual Cretan suffix,
though when attached to nouns it can be either affectionate or deri-
sive. Come here, *mikraki,* you hear people calling to toddlers, and
the word makes them not only small but microscopic, Lilliputianly
adorable. The same suffix attached to "American," *Amerikanaki,* is
offered as a provocative insult, to diminish these people, naive and
foolish even if they are tall and come from a big, powerful country.
Along with the *poulos*es and the *akis*es, there is one Alvertos Koen,
who in New York, I think, would be Albert Cohen.

People are on the streets very early in summer, both to outwit
the heat before it conquers them and to marshal the ubiquitous tour
groups on their trips before the traffic worsens. The tourist industry turns out to be as tied to early rising and seasonal fluctuation as
farming ever was—from June to October is harvest season, and a
remarkable proportion of yearly income has to be earned right
now. The Greeks are farmers of people, and the newspapers constantly monitor the size and conditions and vagaries of this year's
crop compared to last.

The Cypriots are staying in a no-frills hotel near Omonia, the
square named Harmony to evoke Paris's Place de la Concorde,

although it is a squalid center for cheap hotels, and at night, drug deals, prostitution, and mugging—Athens is an unusually safe city to walk around in at night, because so much of its life is lived nocturnally, with its late dinner and theater hours, but everyone says sternly, Never go down to Omonia at night, and never never go down to Omonia at night by yourself. Leda puts me on the bus behind the driver, an old friend of hers, and goes to work with luggage and vouchers, shepherding the Cypriots onto the bus. This is a working-class group, tiny, lantern-jawed, with eyes like transplanted olives, and dumfounded expressions. Their bodies have the short height and all-weather stature of prehistoric figurines, and make me newly aware of what an important feature of divinity height was, seeing how rare it is. The monumental freestanding statues of the ancient world reflected this, and the gods appeared in dreams as significantly taller than mortals. And I've been told that the military has to work hard to cull enough tall men to function as the ornamental foustanella'd guards of the presidential residence and parliament. The foustanella, the pleated skirt of nineteenth-century Greek soldiers, is a poor sight on a short man—without a well-muscled luxurious length of leg to fill the tights worn with it, and to balance the fluffy, elaborately pleated skirt, the poor men look like bearded mushrooms.

"*Gaidouria,* donkeys, peasants." The bus driver jerks his head toward the boarding Cypriots, with a joking regional insult. One man hears him, and ripostes, with a warning smile, "*Kalamarades,* scribes, bureaucrats," in the spirit in which an American might say "Philadelphia lawyer." If the Greeks slur the Cypriots as peasants, the Cypriots slur the Greeks as pen-pushers, itinerant letter-writers, bureaucrats recording legal transactions, and lying about facets of them along the way whenever it is profitable. Whatever energy is being squandered on regional chauvinism is being squandered through one of the charming features of the Greek language—the insult belongs to the same family of words as *kalamari,* that delicious squid we eat fried in batter, but also "inkwell," as is

sensibly derived from this ink-squirting fish. It is a charming example of the frank physicality of Greek, the way a noun is drawn dripping from the sea, or pulled from the ground, cleaned off a bit, and
put to use.

Outside of Athens, the road is punctuated with cypresses,
poplars, eucalyptus, palms, olive trees, and pink and white oleanders, known here as bitter laurels, having been roundly cursed by
the Virgin Mary. The Panagia, overcome with grief at her son's crucifixion, had been urged by him to prepare the funeral meal, refresh
herself with some wine, and take something to eat, to comfort herself because he would be resurrected. A lady called Holy Beauty was
passing by at the time, and along with an observing oleander,
taunted the Panagia in the malicious style I heard in my courtyard
yesterday: "Who ever saw the son on the cross and the mother at the
dining table?" The Panagia gave as good as she got, in the recognizable accents of a Greek villager—she willed the oleander to take on
her own bitterness in its sap, and she ruined Holy Beauty's career in
Christianity, telling her she would never be celebrated in any liturgy
or have a Christian feast dedicated to her. In Greek Christian
mythology, both the Panagia and Christ are as vengeful as the American Southern Baptist Jesus is free with damnation.

There is another story I like about the oleander, this one about
Saint Barbara, because it seems to me to be a kind of Christian
counterpart to the story of Apollo's pursuit of Daphne, who
changed into a laurel to escape him. The legend says that Saint Barbara was dazzlingly beautiful, and that her pagan father wanted to
connect himself to a wealthy and influential family by marrying her
to its son. As Daphne ran through the forests, Barbara ran away into
the mountains, and sang as she ran, "Mountains, take my body's elegance, and forests my thick tresses, and you, oleander trees, take my
face's loveliness." Unlike Daphne's, her prayer was not to be saved
in another form as a tree, but to shed altogether her sexuality and
her beauty, her life as a part of nature. The stories show something
of the world as it was cloven between pagan and Christian, and each

has a criticism to make of its social world in the form of refusing to participate in sexual life.

Leda is telling the Cypriots the story of Pelops through the small microphone that is always part of the equipment of tour buses. I am surprised at this, thinking they must know it, but later she tells me that the older members of the group very possibly won't have been taught it, and may not have had much school anyway. The poplars by the side of the road are steady on their steep ground, straight, brave, slim and green as kouroi climbing their cliffs. Yiorgos, the driver, puts on a tape of *skyladika,* "doggish" music, a fierily melodramatic kind of nightclub music, which can be either grossly vulgar or superbly animal. It shows off the distinctive timbre of Greek voices, in any case, the pent-up throaty quality of the men's, the peculiar smoky fleshiness of the women's, which you can trace all the way up into Maria Callas's voice, which has a tinge of this, a magnificent but never ethereal sound. *Skyladika* offers a very different outlet than our nightclub music, which is supposed to sophisticate you, to teach provincials about dry wit and dry champagne, initiated by former provincials who can show you the ropes—*skyladika* offers a chance at wildness, to imagine yourself doing all the things that would scandalize the neighbors on your courtyard, to divorce yourself from the practicality that colors even Greek erotic life, where the tradition of the arranged marriage is still strong. "Twice, twice," the woman on the tape guts her lyric like a hunter does a game animal. "Twice, I made the same mistake."

We pause at a truck stop for cold drinks. Inside there are the Middle Eastern sweets Greeks love, sugary pastes covered with sesame seeds or paved with pistachios—chocolate seems glaringly of the New World in this assortment. And besides, the gastronomic logic of this candy is that it is elastic, it will not dissolve in this heat as chocolate does. There are toys and newspapers, bottles of wine, shelves of the inevitable icons and factory-made wooden stamps for impressing church bread with sacred symbols. Leda is amused because the Cypriot travelers seem bursting with curiosity toward me and at the same time overcome with shyness, and she wonders who will make the first approach. When we get back on the bus, she whispers to me that an oblique attempt was made—someone sat in my place, and was soundly corrected by another passenger—"You can't sit there," said the voluntary policeman of my empty place, "an English girl sits there." The occupant vacated the seat resentfully, but took the opportunity to make a severe countercorrection. "It is not an English girl who sits here," she said haughtily, "it is a Welsh girl." The barrier is finally broken by a ten-year-old boy who is being given the trip as a summer treat by his grandparents. "Who are you?" He slides boldly into the seat behind me. His name is Kharalambos, after one of the eastern saints on the other side of the gulf between East and West. I look him up later, and discover that he was murdered by polytheists in the second century because he would not respect their gods, and that on icons he is often portrayed trampling a flame-breathing female demon, that he protects flocks against disease and is invoked against epidemics. The boy Kharalambos on the bus has the bustling air of someone with a great deal of information to exchange, and already has the national dark shadows that give many Greek eyes their hereditary tragic look. I answer his question, and he makes his own interpretation, "Oh, so you are becoming Greek." He bustles off to tell his grandparents what he has learned and, I see from the pantomime, to ask if he can come forward to sit with me for a while. They examine me with friendly caution. The grand-mother is a sturdy woman with a pleasant but mistrustful face, an expression I am already familiar with, a cautious-eyed smile that promises the security of disinterest but offers nothing else, although it is a face that would blaze for any family member, however despised. Her husband is a different but again already recognizable type: square-built and tubby, his face beaming with promiscuous but shallow hospitality—a demeanor that puts its arm around the world in order to put its hand into the world's pocket, a practical hospital-ity that is the civilized beginning of business. I pass inspection, and Kharalambos hurries up the aisle.

We reach Olympia in time for lunch and file off the bus into a taverna where places are set for us. A farmer, filthy from his morning's work, is just sitting down by himself; the brothers who own the taverna know him well, and before he touches the chair, race toward him with lengths of paper for him to sit and lean on, and a cold beer. The Peloponnesian sun is profoundly undemocratic. You wake up when it is light, it rules your appetite, literally forces you to drink and to sit down in the shade—you take orders from it. Around 3:00 P.M. you take a nap as if you had been drugged, and around 5:00 P.M. you wake up when your western-facing rooms burst into sunset flame. The heat is massed in Olympia as if it came from the force of all the bodies that had ever existed. Leda rushes the Cypriots through the museum, knowing how short a time they will tolerate it, only long enough to take pictures of the colossal statues. What is left of Olympia, and our own modern interpretation of the Olympics, gives us a very partial view of it, particularly of the inseparability of the presence of death from the important Greek festivals of antiquity. Our Olympics concentrates on the rewards for achievement, but the Olympics of antiquity, with its throngs of statues of victorious athletes, those always unsuccessful attempts to outlive one's body, and its altar to Zeus, made of the ashes of the athletes who died at each Olympics, was seemingly filled with unconscious irony. Even its patronage under the mythological Pelops, who founded by engineering the murder of his own would-be murderer the doomed house of Atreus, implies that there are no victors.

There is an odd repressed femininity about the place, where married women couldn't watch the competitions on pain of death; in a relief of Athena, the goddess delicately and tactfully stands behind Heracles, with an enabling hand under the weight he is lifting. And when we walk through the athletes' entry to the stadium, it can only be described as vaginal, this long tunnel leading to an arch, releasing the athletes into daylight, struggle, victory, and defeat. Going into that tunnel and emerging into the sunlit stadium was a birth into the condition of life itself.

Leda gives the boy Kharalambos an expert thrill by asking him to stand on a rock on which a commemorative statue of an athlete had been mounted. Put your feet in the hollow places on the left and right, she tells him, and he does, radiant with being looked at—he holds up both arms in a victory pose, and adores himself as a statue. When she finishes her explanation, she says, "Bravo, Kharalambe," using the vocative, "we thank you." He clambers down from the rock and turns a series of cartwheels on the dusty, pebble-pitted ground of the sacred precinct. While we, laved with heat, drift toward the cold drinks stand, Kharalambos runs ahead, dancing a few steps of a *zembekiko,* looking back to see if we are observing the statue dancing.

Leda, the bus driver, and I steal away to a secret beach during the siesta. It is concealed by railroad tracks, and a modest climb through a forest and over some sand dunes. The piny hill smells almost perfectly like the incense one of the *kyries* burned on the third floor that morning of Metamorphosis, and on the pine-needle-covered trail over the hill are stalks and stalks of velvety wild sage. Wild sea lilies grow out of the sand dunes, and beyond them is the Ionian Sea, warmer than the Aegean, silkier on the skin, with currents washing our legs with sudden surges of cool new water, like ideas changing.

When we meet before dinner, Kharalambos is watching a Greek athlete competing in the Olympic synchronized swimming on television. His grandfather nods to me. "She's a dolphin," he says, "a dolphin." The announcer says that the coverage of the Olympiakes Agones will continue, and I think that to the Western ear, *agones* sounds with an intuition of the special tragedy of athletic competition, in which the skill we see enacted may be unrepeatable, in which an athlete's prowess is slipping away even as the crowds applaud, in which at the moment of victory even the winning athlete is losing. Kharalambos looks up at me, chewing gum. "Are you Greek yet?" he asks.

On the bus next morning, Kharalambos and another boy his age appropriate the seat behind me. He amuses himself by making me

tell him in Greek the names of objects he points to. "What's this?"
he asks, holding out a finger. "*Daktylos,*" I say, good student. "And in
English?" he asks. "Finger," I say. "And what is finger, *vre?*" he asks. I
am wondering how in any language to sum up the phenomenon of
the finger, when Kharalambos says impatiently, "Finger. It means to
sex, to sex, *vre.*" And with scornful disappointment, he turns to his
friend and says, "She doesn't know anything about it."

Patras is a scruffy-looking port with ramshackle offices off the
harbor offering tickets to Italy, the U.S., the Ionian islands, and
painfully, Yugoslavia. This city is the center of the largest Greek pre-
Lenten carnival, and its central avenues are lined with amusement
parks, small-scale Ferris wheels, and the ubiquitous Disney characters painted on various chariots and floats. It is also said to have a
serious unemployment problem, and the skeletal look of the place
makes me sense what a sharp economic necessity is underneath
those festival carnival costumes.

We pull up outside the cathedral of Saint Andrew, the patron
saint of Patras. The cathedral is huge and new, reasonably tasteful,
but too much like a spiritual supermarket, with all the traditional
products supplied in bright new versions. On the steps we are met
by a priest, who in what Leda says is a common arrangement with
various travel agencies receives a fee to meet groups of pilgrims and
conduct small services of blessing for them. The priest has a luxuri-
ant chestnut ponytail and a showmanlike smile of warm condescension, like a Hollywood agent representing an extremely famous and
much-sought-after client. All the group dutifully purchase and light
candles as they follow him to a chapel containing the remains of the
saint, while he explains how the church recovered the saint's head
after its five centuries of exile in Rome. We pass a large, trivial, but
childishly pleasing folkloric painting of the Panagia with outstretched arms embracing the port of Patras, including this very
cathedral of Saint Andrew in which she has been represented. It is a
kind of aesthetic mathematics, creating a presence by multiplying it
into infinity, and placing it in an endless series within itself. We

stand behind a low gate in the chapel next to the reliquary itself, and
the priest sings "Kyrie Eleison," throwing his stole over the heads of
the people nearest him. When he ends the prayer, he begins to speak
about the Turkish occupation of Cyprus, while many of the tourists
begin to sob. He speaks of a monastery dedicated to Saint Andrew,
which is now in Turkish territory. "I will pray for you," he says, "and
for the day you will be free to make pilgrimages to your monastery,
when your saint will no longer be enslaved." It is a remarkable display of the convergence of two kinds of power, the magic and ritual,
that create a romantic, divine yearning, and the political instruction
linked to the magic at the moment of greatest receptivity.

After the speech, the group passes through the gate of the chapel,
kissing the priest's hand and kissing the thickly ornamented head-
shaped gilt case, pulsing with jewels as if they were the ideas of the
dead, that holds the martyr's head. Some pass the priest drachma
notes and pencil names on paper for special blessings. Some of the
Cypriots are still shaken with the emotion of the priest's speech, and
Kharalambos's grandfather shakes his head. "Well, God must find the
solution," he says, "God and the Americans, since it was they after all
who brought this about, they who wanted the Turks to partition the
island so they could have their bases. It's a wonder they left the
Greeks any territory at all." For him, the Turks and Greeks lived
together on Cyprus before the 1974 invasion in a golden age of harmony, but I know that can't be true. I get on the bus for the trip back
to Athens with a deep sense of the futility of getting at a reliable version of what happened, from either the Greek, the Turkish, or the
American side. A family are seated in aluminum garden chairs in
front of their small grocery store, playing backgammon. The game is
briefly interrupted as the priest who blessed the group arrives to buy
a watermelon. Orthodox priests don't cut their hair, and his hangs
down in a long ponytail under his black fez. He gathers his black
skirts in his hand, climbs into an expensive-looking German car, and
goes roaring off down the avenue. A sticker on the back of the car
reads, "Macedonia is only Greek."

I am leaving the trip after the ferry crossing that will set the bus down on its route to Ioannina, an important town where Byron spent a good deal of time, near the Albanian border. At the ferry, there is anarchic shouting and near collision as the cars and tour buses and trucks with beer and produce fight their way on. The man directing the vehicles onto the ferry couldn't care less about the vehicles' schedules; his job is to fit as many as possible onto the vessel, not to worry about who should precede whom. It is an accustomed tense situation for Leda; she has to fight for her bus so that her travelers won't lose their connections on the other side if she isn't aggressive enough to get them on the scheduled ferry. And the restaurant booked to give this group lunch on the other side will have wasted a morning's worth of labor and food if the promised clients don't arrive. I watch my friend, who I know has great reserves of tenderness, mercilessly badger the ferryman on the ground to find a place for her bus. She has an obligation to meet; he does not, and only her will and persistence will make that important to him. It is an ordinary, exhausting circumstance of Greek daily life, in which simple transactions that might elsewhere be understood as reciprocal obligation are here dependent on patronage, permanent or temporary. It is strange to think that the business of getting us on the ferry will be partly the result of Leda's resoluteness, but also of accident—what the ferryman feels like. He continues to wave other vehicles onto the ferry, and she continues to surround him. "My bus is next, my bus has to be next," she says furiously. The ferry attendant glares at her, and says, "What do you think I am doing, playing with the little bird? You think I am masturbating here?" She answers, "I don't know. Please find a place for my bus now." He waves us on, and we sail briskly across the water, parallel to a ferry sailing from the other side, a constant daily traffic, here where seas are genuine highways.

After lunch I say goodbye to Kharalambos and his grandparents take pictures of us. An amorous plumber from Famagusta also begs for them to take a picture of him with me. "Embrace me, embrace me," he cries jovially as they adjust the lens, and I know precisely to what uses this picture will be put in stories of his summer vacation.

I make my way back to Athens, and arrive to pandemonium. Two Greek athletes have unexpectedly taken golds. Both come from politically charged regions of the Greek diaspora. One is a weight lifter from southern Albania, or northern Epirus, as the Greeks call it, who has only recently emigrated to Greece. The other, the first Greek woman to win a gold medal, is Pontian, her family Greeks from the Black Sea region of Pontus. The newspapers can't print enough pictures of them, and all the appliance shops selling TVs play videos of their victories over and over. Pyrros Dimas, the weight lifter, has the naive, pure, handsome face of the ideal Greek son, and like the perfect Greek son who worships his mother, he calls out at the moment of maximum effort, when he strainingly hoists the barbell overhead, "For Greece! *Yia tin Ellada!*" His is the idealized victory. But it is the counterpart phrase shouted by Voula Patoulidou, the runner, that enters indelibly into the language, is repeated in revues, shows up in political cartoons, becomes the refrain of a pop song, and will clearly never be forgotten. It is another reminder that Greece is the country of the double, that the famous Greek light has an eternal twin in the Greek shadow. When Voula Patoulidou astonished herself and the other competitors, breaking through the tape on the track to win her gold, she shouted in a voice strangled for breath, but audible, "For Greece, for fucking Greece!"

THE LIFE-GIVING WELLSPRING

Mail in Greek apartment buildings is set out by the deliverer on a communal table in the lobby. Mine has been freely opened while I was away, and a CD someone mentions in his letter to me is missing from his package. It is a common complaint among people I know, who have often failed to receive packages I sent them, and it seems not to be felt here as theft, but more as the seizing of an opportunity—"I saw it first."

The floor just beyond the front door of my apartment is thick with leaflets and advertisements, those wellsprings of modern national mythologies. I pick up one with a drawing of an olive-laden branch, in which the olives have been subtly reshaped so that they now have nipple-like tips. "As necessary for our children as mother's milk," the ad reads, "the Olive the honored one." *Timi,* honor, prestige, public recognition, is as crucial a Greek word as *fthonos,* and I read on, realizing that this scrap of paper promoting olive oil is a miniature dissertation on ideal national values. "Nothing can be compared with olive oil," it proclaims, and there again is the popular Platonism, for which to be incomparable is a condition for perfection. "Liquid treasure, Homer called it, Hippocrates described it as healing medicine. Today all doctors declare unanimously that olive oil is a spring of health and life for the young and the old." There the eternal wisdom of the ancients is confirmed by modern science, whose technological powers are seen in their turn to be neither novel nor challenging, but comfortably rooted in antiquity, both elements present in the olive, which, it is hinted, is a source of immortal life. There is a subliminal reminder here of the use of olive oil in Greek baptismal rites, in which the godparents and priest wear aprons to protect themselves from water splashes and oil stains—and baptism, of course, is the first requirement of the modern method for attaining immortality.

The other leaflet that catches my eye is one for a *paidikos stathmos,* a day-care center—in literal Greek, a children's station, as one would use the term "first-aid station." Buildings with signs identifying them as children's centers are ubiquitous, since now that Greek women often have salaried jobs outside their homes, nearly one in eight Greek children are looked after by either private or state-run child-care centers. This one is a school, with credentials from the Department of Education, and its assurances are revealing, and touching. The rarity and value of parks and gardens in Athens underlies the eager declaration, "Our two buildings are immediately opposite a garden—they are sun-drenched because they are not adjacent to tall apartment buildings, and we have yards with real earth and sand!" The school asserts that it possesses a wealth of contemporary educational material for children, an important claim in a country where some schools are so overcrowded and badly equipped that their students go to school in shifts, and often rely on *frondisteria,* private schools offering lessons in special subjects, for their most intensive academic training. And finally, this school offers English, to be learned, it asserts, within games, and not in formal lessons. "In no case," the school guarantees, "will the English language function at the expense of or to the detriment of Greek." Reading these claims makes me think of the bittersweet nature of promising. How defensive these promises

are—against overcrowded urban life, against irresponsible unqual-
ified centers that mishandle and exploit children, against encroachments on national identity. There can be abundance and joy in
making promises, but there is also an element of tragedy in a
promise, a gate locked against some threat or danger. The mixed
elements are acutely present in the common form of the Western
marriage service: the great inner freedom and generosity of the
promise to love, which is however made in the face of danger, the
external threat of death.

I run down Spyro Merkouri street for a downtown trolley—I
am to meet Leda at Mignon, the signature department store of
downtown Athens, and then keep an appointment for lunch, via letters of introduction, with a journalist. It is amusing to be running
down a street named for the actress Melina Mercouri's grandfather,
who was a beloved mayor of Athens, or "mayor of the Athenians," as
the office was known in the early years of the century. Her own
international fame as an actress and spokesman for Greece obscures
for outsiders how deliberately she is sustaining a legacy, a legacy
with modern roots, not antique ones. Reminiscences of Spyros
Merkouri give a tinge of color to the monochrome picture outsiders have of Athens as it entered the twentieth century. His office
was run like a reception room—hung with portraits of War of
Independence heroes in foustanella kilts, and populated with peasants in regional costumes and Europeanized businessmen swelter-
ing in black coats, communally following the Greek-Ottoman
tradition of doing business through personal petition. Spyros Merkouri christened babies all over Attica, as modern Greek politicians
continue to do, where the godfather relationship is a canal of trade
and mutual advantage, and a stronger method of vote getting than
bribery. Mayor Merkouri was said to be keenly conscious of his
position as an advocate of Hellenism, *ellenismos,* that mysterious
sense of national mission whose essence is a source of conflict to any
table full of Greeks; and he had the modern Greek's sense of the
work of archaeology as patriotism, convincing the Athenian citizens

to fund the restoration of the famous "Treasury of the Athenians" at Delphi.

Mignon reminds me of nothing so strongly at first as of local department stores in southern towns like Jackson, Mississippi, or Mobile, Alabama. It must have once seemed a high-storied proof of urban sophistication, a place where people would come in from the country to buy winter coats and have city outings—it even has a floor with a book department, tables piled with coffee-table books about Macedonia, and many-volumed collections of the lyrics of the Greek *rembetika* songs, a fusion of Turkish and Greek music and themes something like the blues, that came to life here when the Ottoman Greeks were driven out of Turkey in the twenties. There are illustrated children's books with stories from Herodotus and Aesop, and a book about the Gulf War, an imaginary letter written by a dead Iraqi child to "George Bush, Chief Zionist."

On the way to the appliances section, we pass a cafeteria where high school students come after school to hang out and play computer games. The whole place has an old-fashioned feel—in the dress department again, I am reminded of the rural South—what is impressive about the clothes is the racks of them, the glamorous abundance of the factory-made, industrial milk and honey. The dresses try at once to be appealing, through flowered prints, and chaste, through sheer ugliness of cut. When we get to the appliance floor, Leda tells me she will buy a hair dryer for me, since civil servants and their families and students get automatic fifteen percent discounts here. As the saleslady writes up the purchase, Leda fumbles in her wallet. "I have the wrong set of cards," she tells the saleslady. "My brother is a policeman, but I don't have the card with me." The saleslady shrugs and subtracts the discount anyway. I am curious to see everything, so we wander down to the floor for personal and corporate gifts—all icons, for a range of possible namesakes, as heavily ornamented with silver and gilt as if they were Byzantine royalty, and shelves and shelves of good luck charms, brass evil-eye charms, gleaming horseshoes, blue glass cloves of garlic, plaques embossed with the images of sailing ships, papier-mâché pomegranates dangling from strings of blue beads, a world of wishes made visible, ropes of beads to cling to in a world of accident, stacks of lucky icons to be dealt like handfuls of cards in a sacred game of chance.

THE TRUE LIGHT

Trucks equipped with loudspeakers are roaming around the neighborhood of the journalist I am to have lunch with, Kyrios Angellopaidi, whose name translates to Mr. Angelchild. Many Greek surnames grew out of village nicknames and contain buried fragments of village lore, local reputations, or local mockery. You come across people named Mr. Been to India, Mrs. Adopted Child, Mr. Little Fairy Tale. As I skimmed the newspaper this morning, a wedding announcement for Penelope the Barefoot caught my eye. The trucks are portable shops, advertising their wares over loudspeakers, selling fish, firewood, chairs for children and adults, flowerpots and furniture for the ubiquitous Greek balcony. I have arrived during the vacation of the neighborhood electricity, and Mr. Angelchild greets me downstairs, carrying a candle wrapped in tinfoil, and apologizing that we will have to climb five flights up because of the stilled elevator. His two clear-eyed children arrive home from school for lunch before our ascent, and they clamber after us, blushing excruciatedly over their father's proudly goading them into displays of school English. Upstairs, Mrs. Angelchild has been interrupted in the preparation of our three-course lunch, but

she assures me we only have ten minutes to go until the strike
moves over to the next neighborhood. When the lights come back
on, I find that I am sitting on a red velvet sofa covered with plastic
tarping, facing an enormous glass coffee table resting on the supports of four huge brass mermaids, four brass Barbies with fishtails.
There are various diplomas and certificates hanging on the walls, an
icon representing Constantine, the emperor who made Byzantium
the capital of the eastern Roman Empire, and his mother Helena,
and a lithograph of Kolokotronis, "the old man of the Morea," who
fought the Turks in 1821, and was a son of Mr. Angelchild's own
region. Mrs. Angelchild goes off to the kitchen, refusing all offers of
help, and her husband brings out a bottle of wine. "You see what
wine I am giving you?" he asks. It is a Macedonian rosé. "Come and
look at the view," he says, and I obediently go to the window. The
neighborhood is a dusty outskirt, now frantically turning into a suburb. There are a few villas down the road, and an unfinished high-
rise across the way. "And yet there is traffic, constant traffic, even
here"——Dora Bakoyiannis, the prime minister's daughter and a cabinet member, lives down the way, with an entourage of bodyguards
and a flow of famous visitors. "I see many celebrities," he says in a
taxed tone, as if he is barely able to fulfill this responsibility along
with his many others. He pours me a glass of wine. "That is a pretty
necklace you have——it is Greek?"

"It is from New York."

"I thought it must be Greek because of the finesse of the gold
work. Because, I will tell you, since you are here to learn about our
manners and traditions, the most important thing about us is that
we are light——Hellenism, *ellenismos,* is light, like spiritual gold. We
know that terrible antihellenic propaganda is spreading now both in
the West and in the East, that the West wants us to be inferior, and
the Muslims are surrounding us like a noose in the East, and want us
again to be their slaves. The West has no culture or history without
us, yet we know they now denigrate classical Greece, just as they
have abandoned Christianity and now worship Science. But they

will realize too late they need our light to exist, as they always have. And we know that in the East, they are lusting to say that their cultures were superior to ancient Greece, that we imitated them. But let me show you something all Greek children learn in school." He tears a piece of paper from a legal pad and draws on it an Egyptian-style column and a Doric column. "Look. You see how top-heavy the Egyptians' columns were, how elaborate the capitals? Now look at the Greek column. What supports it has the mass and the power, not what is on top of it—their columns were the architectural expressions of monarchy, ours of democracy. They made mummies, we made statues. Their culture was preoccupied with death, their art an art of death, but ours is of life, our statues with their kinesis surge up from the world of the dead into life—theirs is the art of slavery, ours of freedom!" Mr. Angelchild has made it clear that only a hater of Greece, a tool of vicious international propaganda, would remember that classical Greece is considered the first true slave society in the West. I have read that one in three inhabitants of classical Athens was a slave; in fact, there is evidence from various sources, including vase paintings, that slaves staffed the workshops of the master carvers who produced the magnificent Greek sculptures. To say nothing of women, whose free labor and lack of legal status was more insidious, considered an organic rather than a political condition. Since no legislation was required to enforce their subjection, it was unalterable. They were not people, as male slaves were, but elements of men's lives, like hands or feet. Slaves could be freed, women could not—the dispositions of men were taken to be the fates of women, rather in the way that in the 1970s, American federal judges rejected claims of hostile sexual harassment in a case called *Corne v. Bausch & Lomb Inc.*, on the grounds that the supervisor's handling of his female staff "satisfied a personal urge."

In fact, to call classical Greece, an ethnically based androcracy, a "democracy" is just a little more meaningful than calling China a "people's republic." The word "democracy" in classical Greece has the air of a demagogue's coinage, a persuasive flattery of the governed by their governors. However, it is Kyrios Angellopaidi's passionate stake in idealizing the legend of classical Greece that interests me—it is sacred to him, a holy precinct where any but worshipful approaches defile. It is sacred as even his own children are not, since he could not do the crucial work of bringing them up if they were; what a different matter it is to be idealized than it is to be loved.

"Theirs is the art of darkness, with their pyramids and tombs, ours is the art of the sculpture, the column, and later, the dome, when the light of classical Greek reasoning joined the radiant light of the Logos, the truth, the absolute, when the Parthenon was revealed in Agia Sofia of Constantinople. For the word of God came to the world in Greek. It was given to us to create Christian civilization as we had created classical civilization. It is no accident that all of Jesus's teaching was recorded in Greek, but a divine mystery. He only says one Aramaic phrase in all the gospels, and that is an expression of anguish, of betrayal. The Jews say they were chosen by Jehovah, but it is we who were chosen by Christ. Christ is incarnated in Greek.

"Our whole history is a cycle of miracles. It cannot be understood with reason—and I don't say this out of nationalism. Who can explain how the Cyclopean walls of Mycenae were possible, the perfection of the Parthenon, which we built before you had a language, the sublimity of Agia Sofia, so beautiful that it alone converted the savage Russians, the women of Zalongo, who danced off cliffs to their deaths so the Turks could not capture them, or 1940, when we almost with our bare hands defeated Mussolini's soldiers with their beef and their overcoats and their imitation civilization? Greece will never die, no matter how much people who hate our light would like to snuff us out."

Kyrios Angellopaidi has written some poems about Greece, and he reads me one while his wife is setting the *mezedes* on the table. They are full of golden suns, and crystalline architecture and motion in marble and perfect truth.

Lunch is ready. This is still, particularly in summer, the most substantial Greek meal, whose heaviness acts as a pre-siesta hypnotic, and I don't linger long afterwards, since it is clear that the Angelchilds are longing for their nap. It seems to me that Greeks are not truly at peace with the enterprise of sleep unless they can fall asleep and wake up while it is still light. The whole nation seems to resist going to sleep in the dark, as if they are afraid they won't wake up. Before I leave, Mr. Angelchild gives me a book by Fotis Kondoglou, a modern neo-Byzantine painter whose work I can see in various churches and buildings in downtown Athens. It will help me understand Byzantine art, he says, and he also gives me a little book which he says has a great deal to say about Hellenism. It is called *Greece, Light of the World, Go Forward!* and is written by a monk who seems to be associated with the monastery on Mount Pendeli, the mountain known in antiquity for its marble. On the cover of the book, under a garishly blazing sun, is a photograph of the famous Hellenistic bronze sculpture of a boy jockey riding a horse galloping full-tilt, a statue that was recovered from the sea off Cape Artemision in 1926. "That," Mr. Angelchild says, "is the spirit of Greece, never in stasis, in eternal motion, racing forward." I wonder if he realizes that the boy urging the horse forward has long since been identified by scholars as a portrait of a black African.

I SEE ELVIS

I leaf through the monk's book while keeping an eye on the clock, since I am going to walk over to the Marble Stadium, the 1896 Olympic site, to see the reception for the Greek gold-medal winners, a ceremony to which all Athens has been invited. My eye is caught by an admonition. "Three things the modern Greek must get clear: First: There was illumination not only in ancient Greece, but afterwards, also in Byzantium, in 1921 and 1940, and in contemporary times, with Greece's Nobel Prizes, her shipping, and the Greek colonies all over the world. Second: New archaeological researches and other historical evidence are bringing to light that Greece was advanced for a long period of time before all other civilized peoples through her immediate pre-Hellenic Aegean ancestors. Third: The current geographical borders of Greece do not represent the country. The great powers have pinned us down. The recovery of the lost fatherlands is and will be the perpetual goal of Greece." I flip to the last page—there is a faint photograph of a map with the caption "And our Cyprus, like our northern Epirus and our Asia Minor, is Greece." It is the old claim of the Great Idea, the dream of a Greece as it had momentarily been under Alexander, the idea that so many

Greeks died for in the twenties, appearing again in a book published in the nineties. It was never an idea, though, but a dream, beyond the reach of thought. No matter where I travel here, I am traveling in dreams.

At the stadium, on this hot late-summer night, the Greek policemen on duty for the event wear short-sleeved pale blue shirts. Two large video screens are placed in the center of the stadium, flanking a dais draped in the Greek colors, Aegean blue and white. The dais is crowded with ten or so chairs for the athletes and dignitaries who have yet to arrive. The screens are playing again and again the triumph of Pyrros Dimas, the weight lifter, raising his barbell to its full extension and shouting "*Yia tin Ellada!* For Greece!" Every time the video reaches this point, the crowd bursts into applause. Braziers where vendors are selling grilled corn are set up at the entrances to the stadium, and vendors clamber up and down the aisles selling small Greek flags and *pasatempo*, the time passer, which are pumpkin seeds in small bags. "*Pasatempo, paidia,*" the vendors shout out, habitually addressing groups of Greeks as "children," as is the custom here. "*Oriste, paidia, pasatempo.*" Across the stadium, a huge banner draped over the railing reads "Northern Epirus is Greece." The national anthem is struck up to fill the time, and a tiny girl on her father's shoulder waves her flag in time to it. At intervals during the wait for the limousines, the anthem, the "Ode to Liberty," is sung at least four times, the gentle nineteenth-century melancholy of its melody conflicting with the violence of its lyrics, in which the figure of Liberty is recognized by the terrible edge of its sword, and is drawn from the sacred bones of the Greeks. The words are the words of the national poet, Solomos, a contemporary of Byron's. Byron of course is the model of the heroic foreign philhellene, a district of Athens is given the Greek version of his name, Vyronas, and there is a monumental romantic nineteenth-century statue of him downtown, dying in the arms of Mother Greece. Oddly, I can call to mind a bust of Solomos in Athens, but no full-length statue. The image of Byron overshadows Solomos, the stories of Byron's adventures and last days in Greece are familiar as Solomos is not. And yet, Solomos made an epitaph for Byron in what for me is one of the exemplary scenes of nineteenth-century romanticism. When he heard in 1824 of Byron's death at Missolonghi, he is supposed to have leapt onto a table in a taverna and improvised a new stanza for the poem I have just heard sung as the national anthem: "Liberty, for a moment, leave the battle, drop your sword, / Come to this place now and mourn / on the dead body of Lord Byron." There always seems to be an imbalance of memory here, whether the angle of vision is from inside or outside—Greece distorts memory, like a flawed telescope.

Children wearing sashes in the Greek colors chase each other through the tiers of seats, as the athletes arrive and are conducted to the dais, where a gold-robed priest blesses them, and politicians make speeches about their achievements. A video of the actress Irene Papas dressed in white classical robes standing in front of the Acropolis plays, and more parallels are drawn between these athletes and the great Olympians of Greek antiquity. They kneel on the steps of the dais and are crowned with green wreaths, which have, I think, been made larger to be visible to the crowd, and have a saladlike overtone. Groups of dancers draw the athletes into dances from the Pontus and Epirus. In the morning when I pass by the stadium, the grounds will be littered with the green husks of corn.

I have decided to take an accelerated conversation class for a few weeks, before I go to the islands of Thasos and Naxos to write a magazine story—a few days ago I received an obscene phone call and decided that my halting response was less than effective. The telephone had rung, and a man had said that he was calling from the local police station, and that he was making a routine check to obtain certain pieces of information about new residents in the neighborhood. So I started out in the spirit of polite cooperation, and by the time the shade of his questions changed, and I figured out that this was not the standard practice of neighborhood police, I was flailing. It must have been as strange for him in a way, like trying to make an obscene telephone call to an extraterrestrial, whose delayed responses and careful searching for correct vocabulary and grammar across the intergalactic borders of language must not have been what he had in mind.

The makeup of the class is amusing. A French girl engaged to a Greek boy, a half-Greek Swede, a half-Greek German, a Spanish classicist, a wealthy Mexican who spends part of every year here on romantic homosexual pilgrimages. This is a phenomenon so familiar that it is frequently satirized on Greek comedy shows—I saw one the other night in which an actor Kostas knows played an Englishman with dyed golden hair who flirts with a Greek policeman—"Which way to Mykonos, darling?" he asks, and failing with Greek men, tries his luck with Greek women as a last resort.

The door opens and everyone falls silent for the teacher, but Elvis Presley walks in, with sideburns, tight jeans, boots, and a white T-shirt. His eyes are red-rimmed as if he'd had a long *tavernaki* evening the night before, and when he introduces himself his Greek is a fantastic hybrid, its great polysyllabic mouthfuls lapping up and down in the slow currents of a Georgia accent. "*Con su permiso,*" the Mexican mutters appreciatively under his breath.

Elvis tells us he is from Savannah, but has no time for details because our teacher arrives with copies of the newspaper article we are to discuss. Her mouth is set sardonically as she slides photocopies of an advertisement for Coca-Cola down the table. The picture shows the Parthenon propped on Coke bottles instead of columns, an ad which has run in Italian newspapers and been reproduced here, to cries of indignation. She has invited an advertising businessman she knows to participate in the discussion, and it is clear that this morning's instruction will not only be in language, but in politics.

"What do you think of this?" she asks the group, and outlines for us the reaction of the Greek government. The minister of culture will be asked by the Central Archaeological Council to raise the issue with the EEC. The mayor of Athens has commented that the ad is unacceptable and must be withdrawn. Melina Mercouri has

remarked that Coca-Cola bought the Olympics, so now it is trying
to buy the Parthenon as well. There are demands that the Coca-Cola
Company publicly apologize. "Do you think," the teacher asks, "that
such an ad shows the proper respect for our ancient heritage?" The
advertising man answers coolly that the ad is part of a series that has
shown the landmark buildings of other nations, including the
Empire State Building, with Coke bottles forming some element of
their architecture. No one else objected, he says. "Besides, is that
image any worse than these?" He passes around an assortment of
ads—the Aphrodite of Milos is posed next to a washing machine,
and groans, "I'm jealous." A computer is juxtaposed against the
columns of the Acropolis to show how durable it is. Another one,
he says, provoked a similar scandal: it is an ad for shoes, showing a
model stepping freely away from the marble women upholding the
Porch of the Maidens—presumably they can't come to life or leave
their work of supporting the temple because they aren't wearing
the brand of sandals she is. But it is hard to work out why one ad is
offensive and another is not. Why was this ad withdrawn on the initiative of the Union of Advertising Companies in Greece but some
of these others ignored? "We must not vulgarize the symbols of
antiquity," the teacher says. "It is for us to set an example for the
younger Western cultures which are based on ours." The advertising man tells us that the company that made the sandal ad defended
it on the grounds that it served to remind the Greek people of the
missing caryatid, stolen away from the Parthenon, that it was an
image that evoked appropriately patriotic feelings. The teacher calls
on different students and asks them to explain their opinions of
such advertisements. I am glad not to be called on, and glad to see
from the wall clock how close we are to the end of the class. The
teacher reads a section of the Greek code of advertising from a
Xerox she is holding. "An advertisement must not trade on subjects
of national importance, sacred objects, the national, cultural and
spiritual heritage, national failings, religious doctrines . . ." The
notion of *filotimo,* the hunger for honor and prestige, reaches even

into advertising, whose very practice, some might say, is evidence of national failings. And there are those who would say that *filotimo* itself, which acts as a kind of unofficial national and personal censorship of critical thought, is a national failing. I notice the teacher is wearing a small gold charm of the Parthenon on a bracelet. She looks challengingly in the direction of the advertising man, who stares back with a look of affected dissipation and pulls his trump card out of his brief case, a bottle of ouzo in the shape of a classical temple. "Which you can buy duty-free at the Athens airport," he says mockingly. "Many would say we have nothing else to sell with. I say, let's all have an *ouzaki* before lunch."

Elvis has a small car and is in the mood to run up to Mount Pendeli for lunch. He is clearly homesick, and his eyes light up when I offer him one of the boxes of grits I brought. "That would be great," he says, "they just have *koulouria,* the sesame bread, and coffee for breakfast, and I can't live on that until lunch." We head first for the monastery of Kaisariani, on Mount Hymettus, and the traffic is not so bad, because the city has emptied for the death and funeral of the Virgin, the second great festival of the Greek year, in its way as important as Easter. As at Easter, people try to go home for August 15, *dekapende Augustou,* to their villages or islands, or to make special pilgrimages to churches associated with the Virgin, a lady who has often been sighted here, although she also never set foot on Greek soil. The neighborhood of Kaisariani is still known as a leftist, working-class neighborhood, and there is a Communist Party office with a prominent banner in its central square. It was a heroic center of anti-Nazi resistance, and its streets were named nostalgically after towns in Asia Minor by the refugees who settled it in the twenties. The monastery of the same name (and as is often the case in Greece, nobody knows the provenance of the name, so folklore is free to breed its own origins) is a popular Sunday refreshment for Athenians, the urban equivalent of a country outing—on the grassy plateaus of the mountains, Athenians picnic, play soccer, and gather the olives the signs strictly forbid them to pick. The Kaisariani monastery made such a cherished Athenian expedition that it was nicknamed "Seriani"—stroll—and found a place in a couplet about the three monasteries on the edge of Athens that all Athenians can repeat: "In Seriani, strolling—and in Pendeli, honey—and cold water that angels drink flows in Dafni."

On the walk up the slopes to the monastery, an eleventh-century foundation, I try to imagine the *nyfopazaro,* the "bride bazaar" that was set here well into the 1930s and maybe beyond, depending on whether the person you talk to finds the memory embarrassing. Eligible young women would be strolled up and down the green paths by their parents, getting together afterward to discuss whose eyes met whose with the most significance. That bride bazaar, as many women of refugee descent will tell you, was not just an offshoot of sexual conservatism, but an arena for desperate maneuvers. The refugees were in an odd social position to begin with, often held in contempt by the "autochthonous" Greeks, who had in their turn felt held in contempt as provincials by the Asia Minor Greeks, who viewed themselves as cosmopolitan. Many of the refugees too were in the schizophrenic position of blaming the government which was giving them shelter for the disaster which had brought them here to begin with. The refugees were considered suspicious, possibly disloyal to Greece, undesirable social connections; and to complete the chaos, the dowry system on which marriage was based was completely shattered because the refugees had lost all their property in Turkey, burned or appropriated, while their prospects for compensation were indefinite. In a world in which marriage was the only future for a woman, and a woman without property was virtually unmarriageable, the situation of the refugee girls was abysmal. Kostas sent me in the mail the other day copies of two popular songs from that era, from a collection a friend of his of refugee descent has made. They are tragic pop songs, in a way you get used to in Greece, where people dance and sing for pain as much as for pleasure. In one, a rich boy marries a *prosfigoula,* a little refugee girl, and his mother is so angry that she fries two snakes and feeds them to the girl, poisoning her. The second one is the most nakedly cruel song about marriage I have ever encountered, sung by a potential bridegroom—"If your mother doesn't give me promissory notes and cash, then we'll have clashes," he sings in one verse. "If your mother doesn't give me a house and a car, you'll never have me for a husband. If your mother doesn't give up her own house to me, I'll marry someone else." And if her mother succeeded in bringing off the marriage? I wondered on this beautiful late-summer afternoon, in this serene oasis overlooking the mass of Athens out to the Saronic Gulf. These landscapes are as full of hidden events as people's daily lives are full of hidden dreams.

"*To teras*," Elvis says, "the monster," looking out over the jumbled white buildings of the city—it looks like something breeding under a microscope, chains of molecules making unpredictable new connections. Exactly as if the city didn't exist, a donkey is standing impassively in front of the view, while a man loads the baskets on its back with olives. Elvis and I look at the monastery kitchen and baths, and listen to the finale of a tour group's lecture inside the church—a group of retirees who have different outings every month, they smilingly tell us. "So you see," the guide concludes, gesturing toward a fresco showing the *myrrofores,* the three women bringing aromatic oils to anoint the dead body of Christ, "Byzantine art is just as good as Renaissance art, only different. I hope you will remember that as you continue to learn more about the treasures of Byzantine art, which is the true fruit of the ancient Greek heritage." The group applauds. I see a striking icon of a scene I don't recognize. It is a picture of the Virgin Mary holding the baby Jesus, sitting in a womb-shaped fountain raised on a column. The fountain is pierced so that four streams of water flow into a kind of pool below her—it is an icon of a type which represents Mary as the Zoodokhos Pygi, the Life-Giving Fountain. There is a special feast day to celebrate this aspect of the Virgin, and apparently this kind of image is linked to a particular medicinal spring outside the walls of Constantinople, and often with other healing waters too. It is a jarring image, this Christian Aphrodite, who is not rising from the sea but is enclosed in a cramped basin she can't even stretch out full-length in, in water to which she has no physical relation—she is not rising in naked splendor from infinite water, but squatting in a kind of birdbath. And she perches in her water fully clothed, so heavily draped and veiled that her only visible flesh is her sober face.

"Let's go on up to Drosia, where they make good *peinerli,*" Elvis says, adding more ragged edges to the world by talking Turkish (*peinerli,* Turkish for bread and cheese, is a kind of French bread pizza, brought here by Asia Minor refugees) and Savannah at the same time. I want to have a long look at the Pendeli monastery, with its exhibit of materials from a "secret school" which operated inter-mittently under Ottoman rule, teaching Greek and the principles of Orthodoxy, often under cover of darkness. Depending on who is telling you, they were either the stratagems through which the Turkish aim to render the Greeks illiterate slaves was outwitted, or hotbeds of sacralized nationalism—the view of them probably dif-fers from region to region, too, since the relationship between the local Turkish and the Greek populations differed from place to place. But in any case the folklore image of the secret school, with its tender-faced boys tracing Greek letters by candlelight under the tutelage of a wise priest, is the one conjured up when people say the phrase, and matches the famous Greek children's song about them: "My dear little glowing moon, shine so I can walk and find my way to school, so I can learn my alphabet, the letters and the other lessons, and things about God." I heard two famous Greek poets, both known for their wit and the number of their lovers, launch into this once after a winy dinner, both in startlingly piping boyish voices, as if they had recovered their childhood pitches, both chang-ing the last line so it ran "and how to kiss girls."

Elvis is starving and hurries me out of the monastery into the car—on the way out, I notice stacks of books for sale by Mr. Angelchild's hellenizing monk. We find a restaurant with a pine-scented garden and *peinerli* and Elvis tells me why he is here. "It's kind of surreal," he says. His father is Greek and divorced his mother when Elvis was a teenager. His mother was devastated and lost custody of her son when she started drinking too much. He stayed with his father, but when his father married a French tourist passing through Savannah, and they began to have babies, Elvis was shipped off to his Theia Eleftheria—his Aunt Freedom—in Greece, who was overjoyed that her brother's marriage had failed, but furious that she was saddled with Elvis. Elvis hoped his Greek blood would make him wanted here, that the whole nation would turn out to be a family, but he came back as a teenager when adolescent social structure is as highly organized as insects', and he couldn't find friends comfortably, with his poor Greek and strange childhood, so his poor Greek took much longer to improve. His girlfriends have been older women, friendlier to him than the teenage girls who don't want to take romantic risks with a boy who has no clear prospects. "Theia Eleftheria curses me every day to my face, and has since I was fifteen. I'm a *tembelis*, a lazy bastard, I go with older women, I drink too much wine. I'm a pervert—anomalous, she says in Greek, which sounds pretty funny when you're drunk. But nobody could live with her and not get drunk. Every day I say please don't give me potatoes with dinner, and every day like clockwork I get them. So I don't eat them. Because I hate them. Then even more, it's pervert, ungrateful shit, stinking drunk, stray dog. The neighbors can hear her fine. Last night she screamed at me, 'When will you go to work, you drunken scum? You can't dye Easter eggs with farts! You have to have money for the colors!' She rapes me—that's how women rape you, with words, they rape your whole life. And she knows I have nowhere else to go. I'm thinking of joining the Greek army—they have like divisions or something for diaspora boys with not great Greek, and afterwards you get a passport, and maybe the connections for some kind of job."

I ask him if he thinks about going back to the States.

"I'm scared to," he says. "I've been here seven years now, and I don't have anyone there at all. It's too big there not to have anyone at

all. Here at least there is someone who hates me. Do you like poetry?"
he asks me.

'   I tell him I do, and he pulls out a clipping he cut out of the newspaper about Cavafy, a reminiscence by someone who knew him in
Alexandria. "When he got older, he used to have visitors come by
candlelight so they wouldn't see his wrinkles. And he served *raki* in
pink glasses. And always held a sprig of jasmine to smell. That's
something I like about here. That this would be in the newspaper,
just a human interest item. I saw another one the other day, a little
headline that said 'Persian poet in traffic accident; condition stable.'
That's something nice. In America they have journalism; here the
newspapers are more like personal letters about what happens. I
think about doing that, if I can get my Greek good enough. Or
maybe I'll join the army and then be a poet. I'm in the ideal situation—like Solomos. Or Cavafy. His first language was English. It's
practically a requirement here that Greek be a second language for
the national poets. It's like they have to make themselves into
Greeks. So maybe I'll end up a poet. And a Greek."

A DREAM OF THE VIRGIN

I would have liked to go to the island of Tinos, the Cycladic island known for its ferocious summer winds and its miraculous icon, for the Virgin Mary's festival. But you need to secure a place to stay months in advance for this most elaborate of the pilgrimages, since some seventeen thousand or more people make the pilgrimage, and I was too busy with the arrangements I was making to settle in here and for my trips to Thasos and Naxos. Still, it is a disappointment, even though Kostas tells me some of the ceremonies from Tinos are broadcast on national television. Tinos is sometimes called Greece's Lourdes, although it is another dramatic measure of the separation between the eastern and western Roman Empires that Tinos is a local pilgrimage, not an international one, and that while many westerners could dredge up the name of Saint Bernadette, partly thanks to the syrupy movie with Jennifer Jones, few would know the Greek nun Pelagia who was inspired to find the Virgin's icon. It would be impossible to call Lourdes "France's Tinos." Greece is so far in sensibility from western Europe that it traditionally has not been included by the West in the geographical grouping "eastern Europe," and just barely in the Balkans, thanks to the Balkan Wars of 1812–13. Greece is neither western nor eastern Europe, but oriental Europe, where Europe and the Middle East live together, although they may pretend they have never met. In Lourdes the vision of the Virgin was the icon itself rather than a guide to a material icon, a physicalized demonstration of theological difference, of a thoroughly different imagining of what incarnation means, of different images of power, even different political ambitions.

Unlike the Lourdes Virgin, Panagia Tiniaka does not teach and offers no message to the world. What she does is perform miracles in exchange for offerings. There is a folk votive verse that people repeat when she is beseeched, varying the person prayed over: "Oh Panagia Tiniaka of the many lamps/watch over the sailor and I will give you thousands more." The Lourdes Virgin is a shimmering apparition who appears like a sudden reflection of heaven on the face of the world; the Tinos Virgin, like so many Greek icons, comes from the underworld, buried in the earth or the sea—she does not descend to earth, but is resurrected from out of its dark depths, evidence of Greece's eternity, and of its divine genealogy, of the mysterious presence of gods under its earthy surface. She is in some way Greece's modern dream of coming back to life, since she was discovered in 1822, just one year after the Greeks rebelled against Ottoman rule and fought to make themselves what they had never been even in antiquity, a nation. Saint Pelagia, who was canonized in 1971, dreamed of a beautiful woman, dressed like a queen, who ordered her imperiously to dig for a miraculous icon of the Annunciation in a certain place on the island, and to build a church to house it. That it was an icon of the Annunciation linked it to the War of Independence, whose outbreak is celebrated on Annunciation Day. The festival here became even more politically charged in 1940, when an Italian submarine torpedoed the Greek battleship *Elli* in the Tinos harbor on August 15, the Virgin's festival, an event which is commemorated in Tinos on this day as Pearl Harbor is by the Americans. What it touched off in the Greek imagination, this prelude to the Italian attempt to conquer Greece for the Axis powers, appears in the many popular songs that commemorated the event, in which the attack is a reliving of the struggle between the Greeks and the Romans to dominate civilization, in its modern version an attempt by the Roman Catholics to possess the Orthodox Virgin, the true goddess of Christianity, who despises them for desecrating her feast, and proves her contempt by guiding the ill-equipped Greeks to their miraculous victory over the invading Italian army.

I would have liked to have seen the Panagia Tiniaka, the icon that emerged from a dream, as so many icons did after the theological victory over the iconoclasts, when images that had been buried or concealed in caves suddenly surged back into consciousness, like so many repressed dreams. This dream of the Virgin Mary is one of the most common dreams of modern Greece; all over the islands and the mountains, tiny chapels and imposing churches have emerged from this vision of the Virgin's ordering the building of a house for her image, architecture of the dreamworld. I would have liked to see the great silver harvest of the *tamata,* the votive offerings hanging from the golden lamps in the church—they have something to teach about modern Greek art. There are silver ships and plaques decorated with silver grapevines, heavy with grapes, dedicated by sailors and vineyardists. There is a silver miner's lamp with a message thanking the Virgin for saving a miner who was lost in the silver mines of Lavrio, those mines that in antiquity helped fund the Peloponnesian War. There is a silver bucket draped with silver leeches, given by a pharmacist whom the Virgin told in a dream to use the leeches in treatments. There is a model of the public market of Athens, built in the 1880s, with a message of thanks from someone who survived the collapse of an upper floor of one of the market buildings. There is a silver house marked *Chios 1881,* probably from a family who survived the devastating earthquake of that year. There are silver cows and sheep; and according to records, there was a silver model of a wineshop donated by wine merchants whose building was saved from a fire, a silver plaque

from a butcher, sculpted with animal entrails and butchers' implements, a silver pistachio nut from someone who nearly choked on
one, and even a silver fountain from a Cretan Turk named Mustafa
Aga, who was cured from paralysis in 1845 after a vow to the Virgin, and left his own version of a thank-you note to divinity. They
are all part of a very Greek notion of art, art as propitiation, and as
magic charm.

The television coverage of the feast is very full, three or four
hours, followed by a program of folk songs and dances from all
over the country, specifically celebrating the Panagia. The bishop
celebrating the liturgy is dressed regally, swathed in satin, holding
a golden staff. The presence of the navy is strongly marked, with
close-ups of lines of sailors kissing the miraculous icon, and crisply
jacketed (rare in this climate) officers. The icon has even made
occasional trips, most recently being taken on a ship across to
Athens to work a cure on the dying King Paul, father of the
deposed Constantine.

It is odd, this convergence of the miraculous technology of the
television camera close-up with the delicately bitter features of the
miracle-making face of the Panagia. Ships in the harbor, like life-
sized votary offerings, flutter with blue-and-white-striped Greek
flags. The television commentator mentions the political and business notables at the service and the camera lingers on them. The
minister of trade, the minister of the merchant marine, the under-
secretary for the Aegean . . . Andreas Papandreou and particularly,
I hear, the voluptuous third Mrs. Papandreou, buxom Dimitra
Liani-Papandreou, favor the Assumption festival on Tinos—Mrs.
Papandreou during Papandreou's worst health and political crises is
said to have pleaded with the Virgin for his recovery.

The icon is borne down the church steps in a miniature jeweled
pavilion, carried by an honor guard of the Greek navy, while the
television commentator recites some of the miracles that have been
ascribed to it: cures for blindness, lameness, madness. A military
band begins to play a thumpy march during the recession from the

church, while the bells make their lovely music, like children's voices heard over some limitless playground. The festival is a glimpse of the survival of an element of medieval economy, and even of the economy of the antique world, in which public cults of gods, and discovery of artifacts connected with them, brought tremendous infusions of cash and prestige to insignificant little towns.

As the icon passes on its route through the crowds, pilgrims struggle to get close enough to touch the pavilion, running their hands ardently over its sides. Women walk toward it on their knees. Hundreds of these pilgrims have waited all night in the courtyard of the church, hoping for dreams of the Virgin. Families who want a favor from the Virgin often designate a female member to come to Tinos and crawl to the church on her knees up the main street, while motorcycles and cars speed around her. The shots of the women performing this act make them look like amputees, as if the logic of this beseeching forces them to impersonate the disabled in order to be healed.

After the liturgy, the dignitaries board one of the navy ships and sail out of the harbor to throw a wreath on the spot where the *Elli* sank. Tinos is a fascinating theater where different aspects of power enact the drama of their relations to each other—politicians always haunt places associated with sacred symbols, to show themselves as incorporated into some ultimate, final power structure, to evoke a sense of their wills and their acts as part of a supreme moral authority, the most elaborate of the costumes with which naked power comes onstage. Just before I left Greece altogether, after Papandreou was elected prime minister again, there was a chance to see the baroque political masque of his pilgrimage to Tinos, in which the power relations between church and state, official and party, man and woman, public figure and journalist were all touched on, although with different emphases by some of the players. Unlike ordinary pilgrims, the Papandreous were specially greeted by the presiding archimandrite, who chanted their particular supplications to the Megalokhari, the Lady Great in Grace, acting as a kind of personal interpreter. The couple and their entourage were conducted to the miraculous icon to make their reverences, and afterward taken to a small reception room behind the church for refreshments of water and the famous *loukoumi* (known in certain circles as Turkish delight) from the nearby island of Syros. After the prime-ministerial couple left the church, teams of members from his Pasok Party cheered them vigorously while he applauded them in turn. The Papandreous made statements to the crowds. He said: "We came to beautiful Tinos to make a pilgrimage to the Megalokhari as we do every year, because she gives us vitality and faith." She said: "A time-honored and never to be neglected obligation to the First Lady of the Universe, the Holy Virgin." The Papandreous departed by helicopter, the First Lady clutching bottles of holy oil and water from the church, in an effective display of folkish solidarity and exclusive power, whose contradictions are in themselves an evocation of power. Even what is considered opportune to photograph by the Greek press on occasions like this is revealing: the newspapers ran a picture of Mrs. Papandreou with intricately coiffed blond hair, kneeling in a sexy summer dress before the miraculous icon, while Papandreou stood beside her, looking as if there were nothing he found more moving than a blonde kneeling at his feet.

I switch channels on the television and find the evening news. The announcer begins the broadcast by wishing many years and a happy name day to all Marias and Panayiotis, names associated with the Virgin. There is coverage of the gold-medal runner Voula Patoulidou being presented with an exact copy of a miraculous icon of the Virgin of Soumela, the Virgin sacred to Pontian Greeks, whose picture was transported from Turkey to Greece in 1951, when masses of Pontian Greeks were uprooted. There are Pontians from Greece, America, Canada, Sweden, Australia, Georgia, playing the Pontian lyre, dancing, and wrestling—they are a people famous for athletes and wrestlers. Voula has dedicated a candle of her own height to the Virgin of Soumela, and looks solemn when she is presented with the icon and told she is an incarnation of the Pontian soul. The people of Pontian descent speak different languages, they are scattered, they change places and costumes, they die, but their athlete Voula has been entrusted with an image they must always keep the same. The announcer reads the tally of the traffic accidents, always intently followed in Greece, celebrated in Europe for its high-risk driving: 112 wounded, 27 dead so far over the weekend of the Dormition of the Virgin.

Idly, I let the television stay on while I write letters and bring my journal up to date. A dating game show begins, and the hostess, a sixtyish woman with Rapunzel-like curls and the shortest skirt I have seen here so far, emerges to the theme song, stretches her arms out in a symbolic embrace of the audience, and wishes everyone a Happy Panagia Day. "May the Virgin grant the prayers of every one of you," she says. The Virgin strikes me as an odd patroness if the object is to meet a lover, but when the bachelor who will ask questions of the three possible dates comes on stage, he kisses the hostess on both cheeks and hands her a wrapped package—an icon of the Virgin. I am fascinated by the distinctive patois of the hostess, who melds a dizzying number of English, Italian, and French phrases onto a Greek substructure. When she is greeting the girl contestants, she touches the hair of one of them and says, "*Agapi mou,* your hair is so *dama,* so *femme fatale,* so *plaka,* yes do it do it." There is an undercurrent of complaint always in public discussions about the xenomania of the Greeks, their craze for the imported manners and phrases and objects, the glamour of foreignness to them. But the hostess's hybrid patter reminds me uncannily of nineteenth-century descriptions of the speech of people from Smyrna—it is the speech of a shipping people, dealing in imports and exports and in constant contact with a transient foreign population. Rural Greek doesn't have this magpie quality, but it is exciting to think this speech has roots, not in xenomania, but in a way of using words natural to a busy port and a trading people.

The bachelor perches on his stool behind the wall that keeps him from seeing the three girls. The hostess asks him what his professional goals are, and he tells her his ambition is to be a biomechanical engineer. She crosses herself. "May the Panagia grant it to you," she says.

He begins asking the contestants his questions. "Girl number two," he asks, "if you had to choose between being Penelope or Circe, who would you be?"

COLD SHOULDER

I seem to have hurt my shoulder shifting furniture or boxes. The pain has been more than impressive and worsening over several days, bad enough, I have to admit, to need a doctor. Besides, I need to be able to carry my suitcase when I travel, and I am going to the islands in a few days. So I call a friend of mine who like me is stuck in Athens over the holiday period and ask if he could refer me to a doctor. "What's the problem?" he wants to know, and after my description, he is satisfied that I don't need a doctor. "You don't want a doctor," he says firmly, "you have a cold. A cold in your shoulder. Probably it got chilled when you were driving in a car with open windows. Just put hot compresses on it, and it will be fine. You don't want a doctor."

I wish I didn't, but I do. The pain is severe enough to be occupying nearly all my attention now, and nothing eases it. Kostas is in Brussels, Leda and her fiancé are on Andros, no one I know well enough is in town to ask, so I decide to call on the couple downstairs who collect the common fees of the tenants, and are for the time being the chairmen of the building. They invite me in and give me coffee, and Mr. Mylonas, whom I had run into at the celebration for the Olympic athletes, waxes eloquent about the ceremony. "You know," he says, "I had begun not to care about the Olympics after we lost the hundredth-anniversary games. It just seemed big business and dirty politics to me. But when Voula and Pyrros won, suddenly the Olympics existed again. The ancient Greek spirit was resurrected for us Greeks. And the feeling that we will one day be what we were again, that miracles are still with us. And that it should be done by a little Pontian girl, and a boy from northern Epirus, where the Greeks live like slaves in the so-called Albania. And the ceremony, didn't you find it moving? You know when the ancient Greek athletes won great victories at the Olympic games, their towns would tear down their walls when the victors returned. I tell you I had tears in my eyes, and I'm not ashamed to say so, when they gave our children their crowns, just like the ancient athletes got. It must have been a wonderful sight for a foreigner like yourself to see, coming from a place with so little history."

I agreed that it was, already knowing from the process of paying my rent, which requires roughly two hours of preliminary conversation, that you don't go directly to the question here. But I find the moment, and ask if the Mylonases know a doctor who could have a look at my shoulder.

"You don't need a doctor, my love," says Mrs. Mylonas. "You have a cold in your shoulder. Don't go to a doctor."

"She's right," says Mr. Mylonas. "The doctors here fatten themselves off of the sick. You must give them an envelope under the table after the examination, in addition to the fee they say they are charging. And our hospitals are infernos. If you get sick here, you get on a plane and go to England or Switzerland if you can afford it. I will personally drive you to the airport. You don't know what chaos is until you have seen a public hospital here. Dogs and cats roam unchecked through the corridors, begging from the patients at mealtimes. Clean sheets aren't supplied—that is the patient's responsibility. There may be no oxygen, they may be out of rubbing alcohol. Treatment orders may not find their way to the staff. Treat-

ment happens wherever there is space for it—I read a newspaper
article not long ago that said that chemotherapy in one hospital was
being given in a staff office, because there was no other place to put
the equipment. Sometimes you can't even get into a room unless
you pay the nurse or doctor; there are even wings whose space is
controlled by political parties. Of course I can't prove it; where is
there a witness when a sick person lying on a stretcher is told to pay
thousands of drachmas or lie in the hall? Even I, who believe there
would be no world at all without my country, must warn you about
our hospitals. We are cruel to sick people." Listening to him, I
remember an anecdote from William Miller, one of the best social
historians of modern Greece, who lived in Greece during the Belle
Epoque. He told a story about the queen of Greece, who asked that
a bed be found in a Piraeus hospital for some acquaintance who
needed care. She was, according to Miller, "informed that the bed in
question formed part of the private preserve of that local political
party to which the patient did not happen to belong . . . the two
parties had made a compact, dividing the hospital between them."

"And the scenes." Mrs. Mylonas shook her head. "The sick people
pushing and hitting each other to reach the doctors first, their relatives screaming. My love, you are too quiet, no one would take care
of you. Anyway, you don't need doctoring for a cold in the shoulder."

I ask for the name of a doctor anyway, just in case, but promise
to use the ointments they solicitously give me to cure my shoulder's
cold. Climbing back upstairs as I habitually do instead of taking the
elevator, I am trying to trace the feeling of déjà vu the popular diagnosis is giving me. This mosaic sense of the body as broken into
guilds, not so much a unified organism, but a collection of tes-
serae fitted together, which have independent vulnerabilities and
strengths, seems to me to be pushing me beyond the borders I am
used to, into medieval territories, that medieval world of intense
stratification in which specific angels guarded churches, altars,
cities, individuals, nations, and even the intellect functioned in
strict division—students studying literature had to perform sepa-

rate exercises in comparison, in character sketches, in the proposal of a law, in the descriptions of places and objects. Kostas has often told me how profoundly he feels the West was formed by the Renaissance and how profoundly Greece has been separated from Europe by not experiencing it, but it occurs to me for the first time that what he means by this is not just abstract, but a direct shaping part of daily experience. I have caught a glimpse of it oddly, in taverna evenings, where the diners share food from central dishes brought to the table. You can see this pattern of eating in Byzantine medieval paintings of the Last Supper, where there are fewer bowls and glasses on the Apostles' table because the guests ate from them together. The individual place setting is a development from the Renaissance, and sitting in tavernas with friends, I am eating in a past remoter than I am used to. And now, I have been having to struggle to get a referral to a doctor, because my body is being perceived through a medieval prism. Perhaps this sharpens the sense here of being in the Middle East, where popular culture preserves great intact fragments of medieval ways of thinking and feeling. It is a strange sensation to feel your body transported to an era which you thought was populated by no living bodies at all. In traveling here, I seem to have discovered there is a gravity of time as well as of space, and I am coping with the effects of weightlessness in time, as astronauts cope with weightlessness in space. In order to get medical treatment, I am going to have to find someone who can approach my body with a twentieth-century imagination.

Upstairs, I call the doctor and make an afternoon appointment. Staring absently at my bookshelf, I have a sudden enlightenment about the source of the déjà vu. It comes from the twelfth-century chronicle of the life of the Byzantine emperor Alexius Comnenus. His niece Anna, who wrote the history, recorded that he fell gravely ill after a horse race, "and as a result of the strong wind which was blowing at the time the humours [of his body] subsided, as it were, left his extremities and settled in one of his shoulders."

THE SISTER
OF ALEXANDER THE GREAT

The taverna is in the poet Palamas's old neighborhood. Palamas has something of the position for the twentieth century that Solomos had for the nineteenth—not necessarily for his art, but as a figure for the nation, an incarnation of the country, since this is the land of the Logos, where what exists must first be spoken into being, and where what is threatened can survive in the underwater of speech alone until it is safe to come back to the surface. It is hard to use the word "poet" in American English without there being a kind of automatic recoil of unpleasant associations, affectation, fancy doublespeak, hypocrisy, constriction, compulsory Sunday school culture when you would rather be outside playing. It is an example of a word which is cognate in both languages, but is actually barely translatable because it has such different connotations. In America, if you conjure up memories of statues in Washington and New York, they are of Lincoln, Washington, General Sherman, but it is hard to find a memory of one of Walt Whitman. I don't know of a street named for him in New York or Washington, much less a town. But all over Greece there are villages with streets or squares named for Palamas and for other poets. It is not necessarily that people like poetry any better here, but that the figure of the poet represents something different. One equivalent might be someone like Arthur Ashe, an artist who was an exemplary figure, whose genius revealed the connections between tennis courts and courts of justice, whose game was brilliant and exciting because it described the world, and who performed the ultimate athletic feat of living what he thought.

All over Greece, but particularly in Athens, the ideal taverna recreates a miniature, perfect dream village in a state of feast, the tables set out in a plaza under shady thick-trunked old plane trees, the moon if possible shining peacefully through their branches, the wine flowing from barrels, the kitchen abundant with home cooking, long tables crammed with families drinking, singing, joking, not struggling to earn the money for this abundance, not preoccupied with the latest village slander, not fighting over an inheritance, not leaping up with an unsheathed knife or ready gun to settle a new chapter of a family feud. It is the village as the village never was, and as I walk through the door that opens off the city street full of parked motorcycles, *periptera,* and small neighborhood grocery stores, I enter exactly this dream of a village square. I pause for a moment before I go in, to look at a newspaper story. The Greek Olympians, Voula and Pyrros, have been awarded the highest Greek decoration by President Karamanlis—the Golden Cross of the Order of Honor. It evokes the crucial modern Greek symbol of the golden baptismal cross, as if these two are baptized by the state and have now become the nation's godchildren. And it also uses that charged word in the Greek vocabulary, honor, a word for which many throats have been cut here. In the American equivalent, the highest American civilian decoration, the word is "freedom." A decoration, maybe, must use a costly word, a word people have lived and died for.

It is eleven at night, but wide-eyed babies are dandled at the tables and children run back and forth, true to the elongated Greek sense of time. I see my *parea,* the Greek word for company that has the sense of a kind of momentary family, at a table at the far end of the courtyard. There is Kostas passing through Athens from Brussels, Aura and her Dutch husband, a TV producer friend of theirs, some other people I don't know, a woman and a fairy-tale old man, with white hair, brilliant blue eyes, and an air of sharp wintry vigor. They wave me over and pour me a glass of retsina; this place stakes part of its reputation on its own barreled wine, and while I am not a great retsina drinker, it can be bracing with blunt country food. It is wine's equivalent of seawater, which sounds like an insult but isn't; a breathtaking mouthful of seawater has a dazzling vital bitterness, like retsina's. Kostas hands me a package of French books from Brussels, to take to his mother, an art historian, and his father, a professor of law, on the island of Thasos, where they have a summer house. "So you are on your way to Kavalla and to Thasos," says Marina, who runs two art galleries, a winter one in Athens and a summer one on the island of Skiathos. Her son goes to the island school for half the year and the city school the other half, like many Greek children, and is annoyed to have to be back in the city for September, when the swimming is at its best. "Yes," Marina says, stroking his hair while he glares at her, "we are some of the many Greeks who have eaten the seeds of the pomegranate and live our year in the pattern of Persephone—six months on earth, six months in hell. I hate to be back in Athens, too. *Akhh,* I envy you to be going to an island as beautiful as Thasos." Her *Akhh* reminds me that we can't even sigh the same way—modern Greek has no equivalent to our *h* sound, so what is "Ah" for us is *Akhh* for them. Nor can we laugh the same way—I have a vivid comic memory of the first time I saw a Greek translation of the comic strip "Peanuts." "*Xa, xa, xa,*" said Snoopy in the punch-line frame, laughing in Greek.

"My father is Macedonian," Marina says, and the old man at the table nods to me, "and his village is not so far from Thessaloniki. You are lucky to be going to Macedonia, there you will see real Greeks."

"The only real Greeks," her father says, "are Macedonians. We are not," he whispers, "part Slav or Albanian or Turkish, like these others, we are the pure Greek race descended from the ancients."

"Is that old man telling you that Macedonians are the only true Greeks?" calls out a dark-eyed man from the far end of the table. "Be careful, there is a Cretan at this table."

Someone from a village of Epirus, the region bordering Albania, responds by reciting the names of famous schools and charities and museums founded by wealthy Epirote benefactors—"Without us, the modern Greek nation does not exist. We are the blood of the Byzantines who fled Constantinople after the Franks' Crusades."

The old man pats my hand and mutters, "The Cretans have taken a lot of air into their brains, but the fact is that most of them are descended from Saracen Arabs."

Kostas winks at me and says under his breath, "There are actually no Greeks at this table, with one exception. There are actually no Greeks in Greece, with one exception. Remember my *yiayia,* Anastasia?" I had met her in Athens the summer before, at the wedding of Kostas's oldest sister. Anastasia was brought up in Constantinople, and she had explained the guests to me. "You must not have the impression that these people, my dear, are real Greeks. I look at them and think, Get on your donkey and go home to your little village. I don't know what Greeks these are, who beat their children and don't know how to cook the foods of civilized people. The real Greeks are from Constantinople and from Asia Minor, my dear, we were never Turkified, we remained what we had always been, the creators of Orthodoxy, and the rulers of the eastern Roman Empire." When Kostas steered me away, he said, "You notice that she was dramatizing—but she was not playacting. It's a strong difference." I do remember, and I whisper back that I now know how to neutralize all heated discussions about Papandreou and Mitsotakis and their two parties—surely neither of them is really Greek—and the government itself, how can it represent Greece, if no one in it is truly Greek? "You'd be surprised," Kostas says, "how often just that line of criticism is taken up."

Marina has taken her father's head in her hand, and turned its profile to me. "You see this profile? All true Macedonians can be recognized by this profile—they all have the profile of Alexander the Great. You will see this in Macedonia, and you will see why Macedonia is Greek." She too is dramatizing, but not playacting.

Her father is monitoring my plate and wineglass, with the warmth and absolutism of Greek hospitality. The Greek traditions of *filoxenia* are always written about as something conferred on the guest, but they are also a demonstration of the absolute power of the host; there is an element of force in this hospitality, perhaps shared by all Ottoman peoples, if the Turkish proverb is evidence: "The host is the sultan." In Greece the guest is not asked what he wants, but shares what the host gives.

Greek taverna meals don't come in individual but in communal portions, and are shared out at table. "Patricia," says Marina's father, "do you want onions in your salad?" He holds on the serving spoon chunks of onions, Greek onions that fuse fiery strength and sweetness, like Samson. "No thank you," I answer, "the onions here are very strong unless they're cooked." "Patricia," says the father, with the unwavering unaggressive certainty of someone who has set out to help someone else in sore need, "it's true they're strong, but they are invaluable for the cholesterol count, they help prevent rheumatism, and they are critical for the free healthy circulation of the blood. So I think you must want onions in your salad."

Kostas kicks me under the table. "Yes," I say, masquerading as someone who has made a choice, "I think I will have onions in my salad."

"Thasos, Thasos, Thasos," says Aura. "So you are flying to Kavalla, and then you take the ferry?" I nod. A song has started at another table, a Hadjidakis song called "Let's Take a Walk on the Moon." It is one of the most endearing features of Greek life, this unselfconscious singing that is present in every corner of Greek life. Greek bus drivers travel with stashes of their favorite tapes, and Greek dinners often end with song—in a nation so fraught with verbal argument, song is a way to agree. "Well," says Aura, "in the waters off Thasos, you may very well meet the sister of Alexander the

Great, who is known to frequent them, according to reports. And do you know how to answer her when she asks after her brother's health?"

"I hate to be the bearer of bad news," I say, "but I was under the impression that Alexander the Great was—dead."

"*A pa pa pa!*" cries Marina, and Aura leans forward. "Is Jesus Christ dead?" she asks. "His tomb was empty, no? And Alexander has no tomb, for all the claims people have made that it is found. And I know, because my grandfather worked in a cotton firm in Alexandria, and every office boy spent his weekends digging for the tomb of Alexander the Great. Now, as I say, you may very well encounter members of the Macedonian royal house where you are going. So let me do you a favor and save your life. There is a certain etiquette which is required, since they are a temperamental family.

"The images you must have seen by now of the Gorgona, the giant mermaid, with the magnificent cascades of hair and the beautiful breasts, rising from the sea holding a ship over her head in her two hands? Well, that mermaid is the sister of Alexander the Great." I had seen many of these images painted on wood or on ceramic plaques—the toy and gift store on my street has some hanging in the window—but I had thought as I passed that she was a kind of odd marine counterpart to Saint George, rising up from the sea to rescue a ship in the way he had thrown down his lance to kill a dragon. I hadn't realized her genealogy was so distinguished.

"What happens is this," Aura continued. "She swims up to your ship and grasps the edge of the deck with her hands; then she asks, 'Is great Alexander living?' And you answer, 'He lives and reigns, *zei kai vasilevi.*' Or 'He lives, he reigns, he rules the world.' And then she will take your ship in her hands and take you herself where you want to go, swiftly and safely; she will still the waves, and teach you the music of the sea. Which is why our songwriters when they introduce a new song say 'I learned it from the Gorgona.'

"But if you tell her that Alexander is dead, then she will go into a rage, and pound your ship with her huge fist down onto the floor of the sea. Or she will be grief-stricken, and begin to cry and chant mourning songs, *mirologhia,* the speech of fate, as we call them. And no one will survive, because when the mermaid mourns, everyone drowns. The mermaid's *mirologhia* become powerful typhoons, and she tears out strands of her shining hair, which become bolts of lightning, and her sobs make the huge swells that wash over ships during storms. And speaking of liquid, we need another carafe, don't we?" Marina's father gets up out of his chair to marshal the waiter, and watching his movements, it occurs to me that we don't observe fully if all we see in an aged body is weakness. He moves with a special vigor and force belonging to age, which is not an energy drawn from the shreds of youth, but of accomplished will, a strength coming from an expert judgment of the relation between him and his object, a calibration of just how much force it will take to get something or someone to do as he wills them to do. His aged body is a kind of physical philosopher, the components of motion are wordlessly analyzed as knowledge and practice come to play a role in his getting out of a chair.

The waiter brings us more wine, and when everyone's glasses are filled, Kostas lifts his glass to Aura and says, "Well told. You are doing a great service for our guest by teaching her this story. Because the story teaches that if you are Greek you have to learn to lie in order to live. Because we all know that Alexander is in fact dead, but we are doomed to keep saying he is not in order to survive. And the only Greek who doesn't know he is dead is the Gorgona, and she is mad. That is in another part of the story, the part you haven't told, Aura, about how it happens that Alexander the Great's sister is a mermaid.

"After Alexander the Great had conquered all the countries he knew of in the world and taken all their treasures, he called together the magicians and astrologers and interpreters of dreams who advised him, because as Patricia knows, Alexander never went on a campaign without a dream interpreter, and said to them: 'Where can I find the library where the Fates store the scrolls of all the destinies of all living beings? I have conquered every kingdom on earth, but I have not yet conquered the Empire of Time, and only with that conquest will I live to enjoy what I have achieved.' And a great dream interpreter said to him, 'Your Majesty, you are the most powerful mortal on earth, but what the Fates, those great poets, write cannot be unwritten, only a little edited, its grammar corrected, a phrase polished. There is only one thing I know of that you can do to be sure that you will live to rejoice in your kingdom and your glory—if you want to live as long a life as the mountains have lived, you must become immortal. And that is a difficult thing to do, very very difficult.' Alexander the conqueror said to the dream interpreter, 'I didn't ask you if it would be difficult, I asked you if it would be possible.' His adviser replied, 'Well, then, Your Majesty, within the borders of Greece, your own kingdom, exists the immortal water, and whoever drinks it need fear death no longer. But you must risk your life in order to obtain it. You must pass between two mountains that clash together and pulverize whoever tries to escape. Many athletes and aristocrats have been crushed there in their quest for the immortal water. And if you clear the passage between the mountains, you must descend under the world of Greece itself, where you will find a sleepless dragon who guards the immortal water day and night. You must kill the dragon and take the water and pass again through the grinding mountains.'

"Immediately Alexander mounted his horse Bucephalus, the horse who could fly although he did not have wings. Together they overcame the trials and Alexander took the glass carafe with the immortal water and brought it back to his palace in Macedonia. But the great hero forgot that having the immortal water was one thing, and guarding it was another. He gave the carafe to his sister while he rested from his arduous feats, and she tripped as she was taking it inside the palace and spilled the immortal water. By chance some drops fell on a hill full of wild onions, and that is why onions have such great keeping powers, and can be kept all winter without rotting.

"After Alexander had rested, he called for his sister to bring him the immortal water to drink. She, having thought the carafe held ordinary water, told him that she had tripped and spilled it, but would bring him a fresh carafe. The great Alexander went nearly mad with rage, and he cursed his sister for depriving him of immortal life. He cursed her to live forever a half life, half woman, half fish, able to live fully neither on the earth nor in the sea. God heard him and changed her into a mermaid that people on ships see swimming through the waves. And she is so crazed with guilt because she caused the death of her brother that she compulsively stops ships to ask them if Alexander is living and will destroy anyone who says he is not.

"So now you know, Patricia, that in Greece when you hear a story, you must expect to hear its shadow, the simultaneous counterstory. Because as you said, Marina, we have eaten the six pomegranate seeds here, and all our stories come in two versions, and the story that is told in hell will sound different from the same story as they tell it in heaven. And you know that in Greece you must never use the past tense when you are speaking of Alexander the Great, although you also know that he is dead. We are telling different stories at the same time. So if you see the mad mermaid, what will you say?"

"He lives and reigns." We overhear the strains of another familiar song starting at a table, one of the loveliest and most elegiac of modern Greek songs, set to a poem of Seferis's called "Denial," everyone here knows because the Theodorakis melody is so treasured. "We were thirsty at noon, but the water was brackish . . ." Once begun, this song is irresistibly taken up. Sophisticated Marina and her white-haired father are singing it with their heads close together, as if in intimate conversation: "With what heart and spirit/ what desire and passion/we lived our life . . ." There are ghosts in this haunted language, there is a ghost in this song, in the form of the word for desire, *pothos.* The ghost is the ghost of Alexander, whose association with the word *pothos,* irresistible longing, is so strong that classical scholars have written monographs about it. Alexander's urge to cross the Danube, and his urge to make the pilgrimage to the oracle of Zeus-Ammon in Egypt to be formally proclaimed a son of Zeus, are both described with the word *pothos*. It is Alexander's word, the logos of Alexander. The song is ending: "With what heart and spirit/what desire and passion/we lived our life. A mistake!/So we changed our life."

Pothos, Alexander's word, has a special nuance, almost as if desire and ambition were fused together, as if a lover had an ambition as well as a desire for his object, a nuance which makes sense in a world in which the very ambitious, like Alexander's mother, declared that their children had been conceived in lovemaking with gods. I imagine I can feel Alexander trying to escape his word, like a firefly in a glass jar. But the dead are in such different conditions than we are that the boundaries of a word are enough to contain them. It was a coincidence hearing this word sung after the dinner-table stories, and a coincidence that I, through accidents of reading and childhood accidents of experience that began this journey, am here tonight to recognize it. I have a mental glimpse of the kind of connect-the-dot drawings that show you the shape of a constellation in books that teach you how to recognize them. The Greeks made their constellations out of myths and immortalities, but I am not Greek, so I trace my own out of history and mortality. I draw my imaginary line between two fireflies who have traveled an immense distance, a firefly conqueror audible for a moment in a word it was in his character to speak, and a temporary firefly consciousness who recognizes it. Mine is a constellation of fireflies.

Mirrors as Biographers

Off Constitution Square downtown, the police are beating demonstrators who are protesting against the privatization of the buses. It is impossible to judge from the footage on the morning news how the beatings began, but the scene of at least fifteen policemen attacking one demonstrator and beating him to his knees with nightsticks, the tear gas masks on policemen's faces, the threatening of the television reporter and chasing of the cameraman following him were unambiguous images, whatever their origins.

One of the worst fires recorded in Attica, which started last Saturday, so fierce that it had a twenty-kilometer blazing front, closing down the highways between Athens and northern Greece, seems to have been set deliberately. A government spokesman and several local government and environmental officials blame the fire on an organized plan by arsonists who work for land developers and real estate speculators. The mayor of a town called Kalamos turned in an arson device with a full gas cylinder found near a gas station to the local fire squad.

Arson is one of the ugliest traditions of modern Greece—nineteenth-century travelers' accounts almost uniformly record

the Greek use of arson to settle property claims, to clear land for
farming, and the indifferent, almost contemptuous Greek attitude
toward trees, produced in part by the scarcity of fertile farmland,
and by the centrality of cultivable land to the marriage dowry.
Even William Miller, a profoundly philhellenic historian and resi-
dent of Greece at the turn of the century, wrote exasperatedly
that the expatriate Greek millionaires ought to turn their attention to reforesting Greece and reeducating the Greeks about
forests rather than building the grand urban monuments they
often favored. In the Greece of the 1980s and '90s, the protection
of forest land is still regarded ambivalently—over forty percent of
forest land in Attica is involved in contested claims, and the state's
own commitment to protect the land is as ambivalent as the citizens'. Sometimes the ambivalence extends even to the people
hired to protect the forests. I was told about one part-time forest
fighter who set fire to a forest in Akhaia; he explained to the judge
that he was afraid the new government plans for forest management would eliminate his job.

Forest ranger posts are understaffed and fire roads are often
neglected, while the government rarely defies the builders and
developers who seem to start construction on sites almost as soon
as fires have died down. Whole towns have risen up on land
acquired by arson. And the claims on protected land, which because
they are rarely based on solid documentation can be neither effec-
tively refuted nor proved, are an unexpected demonstration of the
enormous force of myth as a political weapon. Perhaps the most
familiar and the first full account of the power of the imagination
over political action in the matter of appropriating land is in the Old
Testament, in which the Hebrew people destroy communities and
attack the gods of other peoples living on land which they believe
belongs to them, according to a story God has told them, a story
into whose maw bodies continue to be thrown. In fact, following a
tangled skein of irony, one of the classics of Zionism, Yehuda Alka-
lai's *The Third Redemption,* published in 1843, which helped inspire

the resettlement of modern Israel by the Jews, itself drew inspiration and practical ideas from the Greek Revolution of 1821, an effect the Greek revolutionary leaders, Christian nationalists who had uneasy relations with the Ottoman Jews and who often spoke disparagingly of them, can hardly have intended. And the Jews, whose Hanukkah is, among other things, a feast celebrating the rejection of Greek culture, in opposition to a royal successor of one of Alexander's generals, Antiochus IV Epiphanes ("Greeks gathered against me," runs one line in the Hanukkah prayers), seem to have formed their modern nation, at least in part, on a modern Greek example, in an ironic convergence of Zionism and Hellenism. Stories that seem perfect strangers to each other often intersect unexpectedly, like those couples whose chance encounters destine them to marry. And it may be that we should approach stories with more caution; many of them live longer than we do. I have read that in some areas of Greece, the claims on forest land by people who assert it is situated on ancestral property amount to more acreage than actually exists. "We also have ancestral claims on the many mansions in heaven," Kostas told me during one dinner in Athens. "Where the standard language is the koine Greek of the New Testament. Just think what the consequences would be if Christ had spoken Latin."

I watch another news story as I am getting dressed to run errands before I catch the afternoon plane to Kavalla. There are shots of foreign dignitaries being greeted in front of the presidential palace. My eye is jarred when I am faced with this world in which the images of authority are so different, and would only become recognizable by living here. The building that here evokes jeers, or affection, or anxiety, is delicately scaled, to my American eye, looking like a substantial Mediterranean summer vacation villa. I walk past it at least twice a week, and it shocks me to pass so close to it, close enough to see in full detail the faces of the heads of state as they shake hands for the camera. There are always TV camera vans and cars parked across the street from the palace, their doors open as the reporters and cameramen lounge with one foot on the sidewalk, radios playing, cigarettes lit.

As I watch the television producing images that correspond to the ones already in the viewers' experience, I realize that television is a technological extension of the mirror—every time I turn on a Greek program, with its different manners and inflections, symbols and conventions, it is like looking into a mirror and seeing not myself but a complete unsuspected world of other beings, like having dreams that belong to someone else's life. I have been thinking about mirrors, second-century mirrors and twentieth-century mirrors. Artemidorus's second-century clients dreamed of them, and so do the twentieth-century dreamers in my *oneirokrites.* The difference is in what they expect to see in the mirrors. The twentieth-century mirrors show unexpected reflections, images of other people, or of animals, or of landscapes, worlds within faces—our mirrors have been tutored by surrealist painters. The twentieth-century mirrors are themselves unstable; the dreamer may be looking for his reflection in a shattered mirror, something the second-century dreamers don't seem to do. Artemidorus's mirrors are more obedient and static, as are the faces of his dreamers, which seem to remain their own, although their reflections can be distorted, or can seem uglier than they really are. "Standing in front of a mirror and seeing one's reflection in the glass as it actually is means good luck," he writes, but I suspect him here of one of the flashes of deadpan irony I think I recognize in him. A philosopher of dreams, above all, knows that no mirror shows us as we are, since, like Snow White's stepmother, we never look into them without a wish. We can only hope to catch a partial glimpse of our true reflections in the responsive expressions on another person's face, and only then on the condition that we recognize that another person's face is not a mirror.

I pick up my dry cleaning before I go downtown for a haircut— I have had to change cleaners because the man whose shop I had

been using asked persistently for a date with me, although he displayed on his wall not only a picture of General Plastiras, a prominent Greek military figure and politician of the twenties, but a color
shot of his wife and two little girls. I asked him the last time to tell
me the names of his wife and children, but his campaign carried on,
and although there are certain kinds of men I find irresistible, my
temptations don't include married Greek dry cleaners. But the
price of virtue is as always a high price—the white-haired dry
cleaner I chose because he looked safely decrepit through his front
window is charging me significantly higher rates.

I try to flag down a taxi to take me downtown for my haircut,
but the driver throws his head back like a horse refusing a bit, rolls
his eyes, and clicks his tongue against his front teeth. It is the word-
less no the Greeks share with the Turks—he is not going in my
direction. The Athenian taxi system is, I think in some moods, one
of the great arguments against the city. You can only get your ride if
it fits the driver's preference, and this involves you in shouting out
your destination as he drives by, something you may not want all the
world to hear. It is a terrible system for the discreet, the shy, or anyone sensitive to rejection. Still, I find a consenting driver, and am on
time for my appointment with O Kyrios Emmanuel, as the master
hairdresser is reverently called by his staff.

The retention of the "Kyrios" and the formal definite article O
has a certain drama in an environment where the title is usually so
quickly dropped, and where newspapers and magazines routinely
call former prime minister Papandreou "Andreas." O Kyrios
Emmanuel is artistic, "as a gift of nature, since I am from Alexandria," he tells me, "and like many children of the city chosen by
Alexander, I am a very old soul, both artistic and not easily
impressed. I think I am now on my last incarnation, there is so little
I have not seen. You, I think, must be a very young soul, in your first
incarnation—I can tell by the way your eyes light up with joyful
surprise at each new thing you hear, like a newborn who cannot
believe the world is so beautiful." I resign myself to the fact that O

Kyrios Emmanuel has decided to give me a metaphysical haircut. I had been thinking this morning about mirrors, and now I am one. It may be that O Kyrios Emmanuel helplessly possesses the kind of brutal sentimentality that runs from antiquity through Christianity, that sees a face that shows its suffering as a wise face, probably a good face. But it is also true that wisdom is not only won through an appetite for suffering. O Kyrios Emmanuel believes I am transparent in the way an icon is—I may have seen people so corrupt that their lives could best be described as decompositions; it may be that I don't choose to make my face a theater of pain; I may have fought as hard as a guerrilla soldier to keep a route to joyfulness open in my face—but for O Kyrios Emmanuel, I am a looking glass, in which he sees the image of his own honed judgment and the ancient wisdom he has acquired.

While he is cutting my hair, O Kyrios Emmanuel gives me a portfolio to leaf through, of newly developed photographs he took on his summer vacation at Monemvasia, a famously picturesque town of the Peloponnesus, restored under the patronage of millionaires. They are elegant, a boat with a geometrized Mondrian-like reflection of itself in the water, a crashingly romantic shot of waves breaking over the rocks, but they are inane—Greece is often too beautiful to be a good subject for the cameras of amateur photographers, who capture its beauty only as decor, and miss what makes the best still photographs, the sense that they are moments out of a continuing story. O Kyrios Emmanuel tells me he is taking *zembekiko* lessons, learning the famous Greek dance you see mostly men dancing, with dramatic improvised solos. "We didn't do this so much in Alexandria," he says, "we had more of the *tsifteteli*," the belly dance the Greeks took up from the Turks, whose arm movements are the signal of a dance in an erotic mood, even among teenagers at discos. I ask him to tell me about Alexandria, which lost the last mass of its Greek population in the 1960s, when Nasser set out to ensure that it would be Egyptians who profited from Egypt's resources. "Perhaps it takes an old soul to feel it, but there you can feel the presence of Alexander as nowhere else, not even in Macedonia, which after all was only the country of his boyhood, not of his manhood. But Alexandria was a city that came to him in a dream, when he was given the omen that he had chosen the right site, through certain verses of Homer's that were quoted by a white-haired man in the dream. And it was in Egypt that it was confirmed that Alexander was a god and the true son of Zeus. Oh, yes, there are proofs of it in his life story. You know, for instance, about the sign that occurred just before Alexander fought the Persian king Darius at the battle of Gaugamela? Alexander was addressing the troops, and inspiring them to victory over the barbarians. He raised his right hand and prayed that if he were the true son of Zeus the Greeks should be protected and should win this battle. There had been some debate about the right moment to attack the enemy, but at that instant an eagle, the bird of Zeus, flew down and hovered over Alexander's head, then the bird itself led the Greek troops into the battle, which they won. You don't believe this? There were eyewitnesses." It is the first time that I have been told a story out of Plutarch while my hair is being blow-dried. He seems a person who would enjoy the small erudition of knowing the source, so I guess, since he hasn't mentioned it, that he may not know it is from Plutarch—or that it is a story.

When I pay the bill, I discover that I am ten dollars short. So far, it seems that all bills in Greece are paid in cash. I go to the bank to get cash for my rent, I pay utilities at either the post office or their headquarters in cash. Checks seem not to be accepted, and my landlady tells me, although I can't verify it, that it is actually illegal to send a check in payment through the mail. I tell O Kyrios Emmanuel that I will go to the bank for the extra cash, because I will be away for the month, but he waves me out airily, saying, "Bring the money whenever you remember it."

I stop on the way to the airport at one of the Alpha-Beta supermarkets, grand-scale food palaces with products imported from all over Europe that are said to have revolutionized the Greek diet, a mark of Greece's membership in the EEC. I want to buy a particular brand of Swiss chocolate for Kostas's parents, who can find it easily in Thessaloniki, but not on the island of Thasos. Though the selection is luxurious, there is still a core of the foods that declare you are on Greek territory—olives, feta, *loukaniko* sausage, octopus, fresh capers, stuffed vine leaves, *pastourma,* the cured meat that in Turkey is still made with camel, tahini, the special Greek pastas, *manestra, kritharaki, trakhana.* As I am getting into the car with my purchases, I see a sign with the market's slogan, *"kai tou pouliou to gala,"* a proverbial Greek phrase for recherché luxury, "there is even bird's milk," that dates back at least to the poet Menander, who wrote of Samos, a famously fertile island, that life was so abundant there that even the birds gave milk.

At the airline terminal, a sign at the check-in counter tells passengers: "Macedonia is Greek and has been for centuries. Read history." Tape-recorded bells announce the departure of flights for Rhodes, Kefallonia, Crete, Zakinthos, like a choice of dreams. But I board the plane for Kavalla, decorated inside with a bestiary of fish with wings, and fly over the Saronic Gulf at sunset, the water like blue space beneath me, into blue space above me. I pass the flight reading a men's magazine with the young Marlon Brando on the cover, a kind of equivalent of *Esquire,* which presents itself with self-assured virility, and has had various staff members in and out of the government, I am told. This is one of the less considered consequences, maybe, of living in a small country—the web is very tight, and the relations between press and business and government almost inevitably more close-knit. I turn to the cover article on the Greek man and his mother, which leads off with macabre double-page color spreads of well-known TV and show business personalities and their mothers. Four plump, sixtyish mothers are pictured punishing their fortyish sons, pulling the men's hair and boxing their ears. One is shown pretending to diaper her muscular son, his hairy belly dramatized by the white cloth, and the outlines of his adult testicles visible through his diapers. In another spread, a hefty comedian with a heavy beard and dark-ringed, exhausted eyes is sprawled across the lap of his mother, who wears a ladylike shirt-waist dress and carefully waved gray hair, as she lifts her hand to spank his half-bared buttocks. Each of the mothers describes the high points of her childbirth and describes what her son means to her. "He is all. He is everything," says one; "He is more than everything," says another, "he is above my life."

The feature continues with a questionnaire which matches a man with the movie archetype of the Greek mother that fits him best. There are, it seems, more movie archetypes of Greek mothers than of Greek wives, and it is surprising to see how developed this mythology of the mother is. You choose from the questionnaire alternate responses by your mother to a variety of situations, in themselves an amusing partial guide to the fantasy lives of Greek men. What kind of house do you live in with your mother, what kind of father do you have, what pet name do you like her to call you ("my darling golden one," "my boy," "my pasha"), what profession does your mother want you to take up, what kind of wife does she want for you, how does she behave toward your girlfriends, how does she act when you enter your obligatory military service ("She kisses me, makes the sign of the cross over me, and says to me: 'Keep three women always in your mind, my son—the All-Holy Virgin, Greece, and your mother!' "), when you go to war with the Turks, when you conquer Constantinople and become involved with a Turkish girl. Among the possible responses to this scenario: one mother curses her son; another says, "A Turkish girl, of all things! Is she at least Christian?" and a third says with considerable schadenfreude, "What should I say, my pasha? . . . You are a man, now make her understand that, the Turkish bitch!"

The five movie archetypes are as local in flavor as farm produce. They hone my sense of the profound effect of being surrounded by icons from childhood on, images with strictly prescribed poses and costumes that classify and stabilize, a taxonomy of the sacred. Like icons, these images of women are caught between power and incapacity, the inanimate and the superhuman. One is a plump, impeccably bourgeois lady in a hat, who interferes in her son's personal and professional life, and dominates him by mercilessly feeding him, putting herself beyond suspicion of mixed motives by always having a favorite dish on hand to stifle his protests. The second is a cat-eyed, hawk-nosed woman with a cruel glamour, the sadistic mother, who bullies and slaps her son capriciously, and tries to drive away his girlfriends by paying them off. The third choice is a woman self-absorbed to the point of madness, who sees her child more as a character in an ongoing story she is acting out. Four is a terrifyingly hatchet-faced woman, with a twisted bitter mouth, who shouts "you anathematized one" when she wants her son to do chores, and teaches him from childhood that life is hellish and stony and that he has to face it as brutally as it faces him. This fantasy mother curses her son, brandishing a knife, when he moves out, and when she meets his girlfriend, threatens to kill herself if he marries that slut. The final choice is the sentimental favorite, the *laiki* mother, the mother of the son of the people, her pride and the pride of the village, who is good-hearted, ignorant, "poor like our poor country Greece," who taught her boy to be "a good Christian, good man, and good Greek," knowing nothing beyond the world of custom and common sense that shaped her, "the unfortunate one," an object both of tenderness and condescension.

When I next have the courage to look out the window again, we seem to be flying straight into the sea for landing. We fly directly over a boat, then some marshy patches of land floating in the water like carnival masks, and drop onto a runway, land abruptly substituted for water.

I clamber onto the airport bus marked "Kavalla" and head off into the northern Greek night, feeling oddly between worlds, since the lonely freedom of a bus on a highway is for me a quintessentially American feeling. A song called "I'm a Man" is playing, which I recognize because I have it on this same tape, an anthology called *Classical Popular Songs*. We pass a village whose lights are glowing with an almost desperate-seeming brilliance in the first fullness of night. Each house or taverna we pass is glowingly illuminated, as if it were emitting its own inner self. There is a *kafeneio* on the main street where shadowy old men with intent faces are drinking and playing cards, and then an *ouzeri* where the glasses of the drinking men glitter in the strangely isolating glare, as if they are being filmed in close-up. This sharpness of gesture is not just in my personal vision, but is a consequence of being born into the world of TV and movies, with a secret, ever-present expectation that the camera will be there, that this is all being filmed, that in a moment the star will make an entrance. Here it would have to be a pop icon, an old rock star, so out of his element he was back in it. I look out onto the blank darkness of the highway, now that we have left the village, dreaming one of the most common twentieth-century dreams, one Artemidorus's people couldn't have had—I am dreaming up the credits of a movie. Little Richard would be good for the old rock star. He and a band with instruments would be on a bus marked "Drama," going to give a concert near where I am going tomorrow, to Philippi, where Cassius and Brutus killed themselves. The cleverly designed titles appear floating over the backdrop of the mountainous landscape, and you hear a pop song expertly setting the mood.

We are pulling into Kavalla, a city set on a curved harbor, built up into the hills behind it. At night it looks like a reclining lamb hung with the white flowers of lights. A fortress and church are floodlit on the heights, and the town is walking its *corso,* its evening promenade, *pano-kato, kato-pano,* on the waterfront. I check into the grim but functional little hotel facing the harbor, and prepare to carry my suitcase to the elevator, but a man in a baseball cap steps forward and offers to help. "You're not from Athens, Greece, are you?" he says in a strong Texas accent, grinning a chipped-tooth grin. "No," I say. "You're not from Athens, Texas, are you?" "No," he says delightedly, "Beaumont, not Athens. They have us out here working on offshore rigs, and if you don't mind, I would love to talk to somebody I can understand for an hour." I put my suitcase in my ugly room, which has an icon of Jesus over the bed, and a fine view of the harbor where the ferry from Thasos is coming in, festively ablaze with lights, and meet the homesick Texan downstairs to walk the *corso*, which runs along the harbor, from a group of fish restaurants on the left to a disco and small-scale amusement park on the right. One wrinkled old man is grilling corn over a brazier, and another presides over a kind of counter on wheels which has partitions for chickpeas, pumpkin seeds, pistachios, the fiddly snacks the Greeks love, the edible equivalents of worry beads. A teenage boy in front of us is eating a whole rosary of pumpkin seeds, counting and fingering and clutching, without which care and exercise of the hands he threatens to go wild. It is a hot September night, but regardless of the iced lemonades they are drinking, the conventional farewell to any kind of meeting at this time of year is "*Kalo himona*," Have a good winter.

Since the night is young, parents and children populate the miniature carnival, so small that you can see all its components from the wooden benches that form its boundaries and provide a place for the parents to sit while their offspring go up in rockets, ride beribboned mechanical ponies, drive toy motorboats. Each section is neatly partitioned according to age—tots in the area of rainbow-colored vehicles that bob gently up and down—here the emphasis is on gentle prettiness and maximum choice. Even the rocket ship is anthropomorphized, and would not look unnatural with a pair of eyelashes—and no pony or buggy is repeated, so any imminent tears about wanting what someone else has are cleverly forestalled. In the older children's section, there are the bumper cars. Here imagery matters less than skill and daring, as the children guide their cars to total destruction, and all miraculously survive. In the teenagers' section, the theme is controlled aggression, with a portable boxing machine, and a booth for hitting targets with rifles. And for parents and children together, a tilting car ride, with the cars set in the hoopskirt of a dancing lady, whose swiveling hips determine the speed and direction of the passengers. In Greece, you are never far away from an outbreak of dance. I was walking past my local elementary school on the way back from paying bills at the post office, just this morning, when I saw a heavyset ten-year-old leap up onto the stone ledge that runs around the front of the building, raise his arms like torches, and begin to dance the *zembekiko* without music. Passersby stopped to watch him, smiling with admiration, and his audience drew a style from him, the schoolboy's dance gained a dignity.

We buy ears of corn, smoky and salty, and sit for a while watching a two-year-old in a lace dress galloping on a white-maned pony with an expression poised between pleasure and anxiety. She keeps looking at her parents, to calculate from them the degree to which she ought to be afraid. If they had showed the slightest alarm, she would have burst into tears.

We eat at one of the harborside fish tavernas, which in classic taverna geography nearly adjoin the daily fish market, and drink a bottle of Saint Panteleimon wine—Agios Panteleimon is the patron saint of bakers, so it is good to know that he has wine to go with his bread. The nearest table is occupied by a group of high school couples, just old enough so that eating out on Friday night without their parents is a heady pleasure. Everyone is dressed up, and the table looks like the ideal Greek taverna table which is a standard tableau in movies—a table littered with plates and bottles is an archetypal scene of largesse and enjoyment. The boys smoke, rocking back in their chairs with their hands in their pockets, à la *mangas,* a key noun in the Greek poetry of masculinity—it can have negative connotations, but it always implies being unconquerable, and a largesse that expresses daring and power, a kind of macho equivalent of the quality of charity more often associated with women; but the largesse of the *mangas* is less freely given than conferred. The *mangas* character is most vividly associated with the experience of the Asia Minor catastrophe, and is a measure of the event's impact on Greece, as well as a masculine archetype. The *mangas* was often a displaced Asia

Minor Greek who had lost his property and supported himself by
day labor and robbery, though he may once have been wealthy. He
fell between classes, neither peasant nor middle-class, and so made
his own laws: the Greek masculine ideal. Certain postures and facial
expressions were associated with the *mangas*—swagger, threat, dangerous sexuality, cigarette dangling from one corner of the mouth,
readiness to dance or kill—the original *mangas* was supposed to
wear a black mourning band around his hat, in memory of the people he had killed in fights, a generosity based on the power of being
the survivor.

The *mangas* is an essential figure of modern Greek mythology,
and I tell Jerry from Beaumont what I know about it. Myth extends
a modern figure or characteristic backward, in the direction of
infinity, so that a historical figure is made to exemplify timelessness,
and in the body of modern Greek myth, becomes a proof of the all-
important continuity between ancient and modern Greece. It is a
sleight-of-hand that comes to seem quintessentially Hellenic, the
magic illusion of eternity. And myth must work to seem true while
destroying as much history as possible, which is why it is the kind of
story that tells the lives of gods, and why truly concrete historical
information about gods must be unavailable—if we saw a god as a
truly historical figure, it would be difficult to see the god as immortal. It is, in a way, a contradiction in terms to speak of ancient myth,
since myth does its work by eroding the sense of the past in favor of
an eternal present.

"So can you guess the archetypal *mangas*?" I ask him, but he
prefers to be told. "It's Alexander the Great." I take out my notebook and read him a quote Aura copied for me: "No one was such a
mangas as to accomplish what he did then. To conquer all the East
and to behave as he behaved! *E,* this was the essence of being a
mangas."

Jerry takes what I can see is a speculative Texan slug of the saint's
wine. "One thing about being here—you sure as hell hear a lot
about Mr. Great and his Macedonians."

Especially here in a part of the world so ambivalent about its identity as Macedonia. Just a glimpse at a small selection of pamphlets and books about the "Macedonia question" at the turn of the century and preceding the Balkan Wars makes me understand better the seemingly hysterical sense of threat the Greeks display over Macedonia now. The region had been home to Greeks, Bulgars, Albanians, Jews, Serbs, Vlachs, and Turks, and there are books arguing the justice of each country's actions there in nearly all Balkan languages. So kaleidoscopic were the claims and counterclaims put forward by all parties that you find one of the most philhellene writers of the period, who wrote a worshipful book about the Greek politician Venizelos, stating that he was forced to conclude that the majority population of Macedonia was Bulgarian. The Greek view of him would probably be that on this issue he had succumbed to Bulgarian propaganda, with the inordinate Balkan faith in the political efficacy of mythmaking. Other anecdotes are told of people declaring unshakeable loyalty to their homeland, Greece, in Albanian and Slav dialects. The status of Kavalla itself was uncertain enough that Venizelos, the politician who led Greece through the 1912 and 1913 struggles over Macedonia, held it as a possible bargaining chip to be handed over to Bulgaria in exchange for other concessions during all the early-twentieth-century negotiations of Greece's borders. The complicated motives and resolutions of the imperfect claims of all the interested parties to this territory make up one of the most disheartening episodes in human history, thick with the murdered bodies of people who always seem to lose their lives when eternity is invoked, and territorial claims sacralized beyond compromise.

Melons and the rich September grapes of Greece are brought to the teenagers' table. They begin to sing a recent hit, swaying to its joyful assertive rhythm—"I have accepted both life and death, and I have nothing more to fear . . ."

In the morning, I go to the modest childhood house of Mehmet Ali, the nineteenth-century viceroy of Egypt, responsible for plant-

ing cotton in the Nile valley, sending Queen Victoria the present of
the obelisk known as Cleopatra's Needle, and executing a political
mass murder on a scale unmatched even by Hitler's Night of the
Long Knives, by slaughtering in 1811 some five hundred of the ruling Mameluke faction of Egypt, his guests at a feast in honor of his
son. The house, despite its small scale, preserves the radioactive
eastern division between men and women, with special secured
rooms for the women, and a dumbwaiter for the women to send
along the food they prepared for the men, while remaining invisible. It is perhaps some measure of the Ottoman presence in Macedonia that both Mehmet Ali and Atatürk himself were born here.

I get on the bus marked "Drama" to go to the site of Philippi,
where the Roman Republic was struck its deathblow by the forces
of the future Augustus Caesar. Walking away from Philippi's Acropolis overlooking the desolate-seeming Macedonian plains, toward
the baptistery of Lydia, which celebrates the conversion of the first
European woman to Christianity, through Saint Paul's missionary
work here, I think how unlikely that so many world-altering events
will ever be concentrated again in one region. There are people who
claim that this density of history is due to some inexplicable magnetism of place and sensibility, and it may be true, but the unavoidable fact is that Brutus and Cassius and Saint Paul couldn't travel
very far. Their theater of action was confined to the space that bad
roads, limited funds, unpredictable seas, and primitive modes of
transportation would allow them, and the intense philosophical fer-
ment of this world was also in part a result of how geographically
cramped it was. What a different sense it must have given even to
the idea of coincidence—which must have had more the force of
overlay and repetition than it does in our world, where it has,
appropriate to the way we travel, more the drama of things coming
together from vast distances to meet. Without airplanes and hydro-
foils and ferries and gasoline-powered buses and paved roads and
highway signs, I think, I would not be walking into the bapistery of
Saint Lydia this morning, and admiring the rich purple-red color of

the garment she is always represented as wearing, since she was a
well-off seller of dyes, one of the wealthy widows who gave an economic base to the early church. The lady who runs the gift shop
closes it for a moment to come into the church with me. Ten or
eleven children, she tells me, are baptized here every Sunday, and it
is an enormously popular site for the baptisms of people being
received into the Orthodox Church. "You are Orthodox," the lady
says, and when I shake my head she says, "But you must be, since you
speak Greek." Again I say no, and she seems sincerely disappointed.
"Well, at least you behave well. So many people come here who are
not Orthodox and they behave in such ugly ways." She tells me I
must see the river where Lydia was baptized, a fast shining river
fringed with thick greenery and two splendid trees on the opposite
bank. The modern speed I was thinking of leaves me more than
enough time to see more of Kavalla before I catch the ferry to Thasos. I have a dish of late tomatoes stuffed with rice and mint for
lunch, and stop in the small archaeological museum. In a case with
treasures from a tomb excavated near by, a third-century-B.C. silver
mirror is ingeniously displayed so I can look at it from both sides. I
look at my reflection. My face in the old silver wavers like a faraway
dream, like something either dissolving or forming. It is like meeting my own future, or my own ghost.

THE GODFATHER

A cluster of men, all wearing naval captains' caps, swarm in front of the ferry to Thasos. Streams of cars, motorcycles, trucks carrying cases of beer and wine, and refrigerated trucks full of freshly butchered meat are being waved onto the ferry. I ask one of the group where to show my ticket. "You must give your ticket to that beautiful man," he says, and giggles at his joke, since it is embarrassingly evident that the man he means is in fact the handsomest of the group.

Inside the big public room of the ferry there is a refreshment counter selling greasy snacks, fruit juices, beer, and bottles of a white wine named for the Via Egnatia, the road the Romans built to link the eastern and western empires that ran through Macedonia and Thrace, from Rome to Constantinople. The ubiquitous ferry TVs, suspended in corners, are playing an ad for a TV series about Jacqueline Onassis, called *Jackie i Agapimeni,* Jackie the Beloved. I go out on deck to watch Kavalla recede, and pass on my way the control room from where the ship is being steered, a room that contains not only the ship's wheel but a well-tended nursery of hanging baskets of flowers spilling from the ceiling onto the deck, and the fresh perfume of basil, for no self-respecting Greek ship seems to sail without its protective pots of basil, nor without its icon of Saint Nicholas, patron saint of sailors and merchants, and formerly known as Poseidon, according to some.

Basil is *vasiliko,* the royal plant, honored since the emperor Constantine's mother Helena found it growing at the site in Jerusalem where by legend she found the true cross. Sadly, the reverence Greeks have for basil means they rarely cook with it, although it is used in various church ceremonies, and the Greek school year starts with a first-day benediction from a priest, who blesses the schoolchildren with basil dipped in holy water. A Greek-American child of a family here for the year, after encountering the custom for the first time, reporting to his parents on the day's events, announced, "The priest beat me with parsley."

I settle on deck to read guidebooks, which are always worth a look in Greece, either because they are informative or because they are anthologies of brilliantly Samuel Goldwyn-esque English. One outlines the chief treasures of the archaeological museum, promising that a kouros bearing a ram is "exposed" there. A second tells of a Christian basilica built in the fifth century B.C.

The Greek islands are lessons in the sheer lack of uniformity and the discontinuity of Greek history, ancient and modern. The islands often weave themselves into relation with Hellenes and Hellenism through those founding myths that bury political history as surely as successions of new towns built on old sites. Thasos was supposed to have been a Phoenician prince, a relative of the Asian princess Europa—he landed on the island while searching for her after her abduction by the Greek god Zeus. The island was prominently and stably settled in the seventh century B.C. by colonists from the island of Paros, although there is evidence of prehistoric settlement. The poet Archilochus, first to use the iambic meter, was one of those colonists—in one of the telegraphic fragments which make up the bulk of his surviving verse he describes Thasos as "an island crowned with forests and lying in the sea like the backbone of an

ass." On Thasos, he courted a rich man's daughter, and when her
father broke his promise that they could marry he is said to have
written such excoriating verses that the whole family ended in suicide. But for me he is most interesting as a verse diarist of the life of
a professional soldier, courageous and cynical, brutally conscious of
all that he has to simplify in his view of the world in order to
sharpen himself to kill, measuring the failure of his aging body with
a trained eye, mercilessly aware of the constant presence of misfor-
tune, of all that can go wrong between one engagement and the
next, one hour and the next. I knew Thasos would put me in the
mood to read him, but I didn't bring a volume, because I thought I
would surely find one on the island. Of course I was wrong. Thasos
exists in Archilochus's verse, but at the moment I was there,
Archilochus did not exist on modern Thasos. To be fair, I found
hardly any more recent Greek writing either.

Thasos's history, like the biographies of most of the islands, is a
story of alternating invaders and governments, and a reminder that
in Greece, neighbors can have profoundly different histories. Some
of the patterns may be similar—all the islands were targets for
pirate raids, one reason the coasts remained so undeveloped, on
some islands well into the 1970s. Inland towns on most islands were
more heavily populated than coastal ones, much safer from the
threat of raids, and in the island treasuries of Christian folklore
miraculous rescues from pirates are the miracles most often retold.
Between pirates and occupiers, you could hardly ask for a more
unstable political life. Thasos was occupied by European crusaders,
the Genoese, the Turks, the Venetians (several times), the Russians,
who exploited the richly forested island for shipbuilding, and Egyptian overseers, representatives of Mehmet Ali, who had spent part
of his childhood on the island and is said to have demonstrated his
affection for it by giving the island substantial tax breaks.

We land on the side of the island which lost some twenty-five
thousand acres of forest in 1989, after a devastating fire which was
said to be set by arsonists. The murdered slopes and hills the bus

drives past are still covered with charred stumps. When I settle in a hotel in the main port, I call Kostas's parents, Kimon and Elpida, who have a summer house in a fishing village here, and they say they will pick me up tomorrow and take me for an exquisite swim, a promise I take seriously, since they and many other Greeks study and describe the characters of beaches with the nuance of wine connoisseurs talking vintages.

I set out for the archaeological museum, that official link to the past which, like a legitimate birth certificate, is the pride of many cities and islands here. The range of woolens, sweaters, blankets, and mittens you can buy warn that in this northernmost Aegean island, winter will be sharp and Macedonian. The houses are not Cycladic houses, but structured to take serious cold, with smaller windows and slanting roofs to dispose of snow. The stores offer, besides the woolens, the odd mix of trash, quality, and unmatched kitsch and sheer flotsam and jetsam that makes shopping here an experience of fate as much as intention. There are insanely grinning poodles made entirely of seashells, Aphrodites in faintly porno-graphic vaudeville poses, magic tricks and surprises; one package is labeled "The Horror Ax—makes horrible sound"—which I like for the sheer benevolence of the threat. There are painted china plates with popular Greek proverbs, which you can use to send messages and veiled hints in the form of souvenirs. "If you don't know the Dance of Isaiah, I will teach it to you," reads one painted plate with a dancing couple, a reference to the part of the Greek Orthodox marriage service when the bride and groom circle the altar three times in what is known as the Dance of Isaiah.

The archaeological museum is small-scale and familial, just a few rooms washed with milky blue paint, and the treasures of Thasos— barring some fine works that were appropriated by French archaeol-ogists in the nineteenth century and taken to the Louvre—arranged with a clear eye for drama. The enormous ram-bearing kouros is what you see as you enter, the boy dominating the room with his massive stature, but startlingly similar to the limp helpless animal he holds in his capacity to die. In another room, a Hellenistic Aphrodite perches sidesaddle on a dolphin, her pretty breasts exposed, drapery clinging to her promising belly, while her baby son Eros rides on the dolphin's tail. They show another facet of immortality—the immortals don't suffer loss or change from love any more than they die. On their dolphin, the two love deities sail sportively through the sea of love, beyond its gravity, enjoying its dangers and passions as a form of play.

I sit down for lunch at a restaurant overlooking the harbor; indoors there is a room with an open kitchen, a glass-globed lamp suspended from the ceiling, and a television sharing its shelf with a hookah, but I choose an outdoor table, watching the movements of fishing boats and ferries, and the sun glowing on the water, lulled by the last of summer, that great hypnotist of the seasons. "Welcome to our restaurant," says the man who conducts me to my table. "My name is Steve. I am from Bulgaria." He wears horn-rimmed glasses and has a cheerfully neurotic air. "Where are you from?" I say the United States, and he says that is rare up here, where most of the visitors are German. "Can you talk the real American English?" he asks me. "Can you talk like Eddie Murphy?" Probably not, I say, and he is crestfallen. "Consequently," he says, "your Greek is better than your English. I love the language of Eddie Murphy. I hope someday to hear it really spoken."

Kimon and Elpida pick me up from the hotel for an early breakfast. Elpida is writing the text of a catalogue for an exhibition of paintings in Paris, and has the slightly splintered stare of someone facing an imminent deadline, but she would not be deterred from having at least one day together despite the pressure. "Welcome, welcome," Kimon says, and Elpida adds laughingly, "and a very happy Saint Evfemia's Day," and answering my unspoken question, explains, "Saint Evfemia is the patron saint of dressmakers, a seamstress who was martyred during the Roman emperor Diocletian's persecutions. Her bones are in Constantinople, in the Patriarchate, I think—my grandmother remembered from her childhood going to mass on Evfemia's day, and that afterwards, blessed needles would be distributed to the women in the congregation. I spoke to my mother just yesterday, and she sends you greetings, which is what made me think about the needles."

"Still," says Kimon, "there is a better saint for Patricia in the City." The City was what Byzantine Greeks called Istanbul when it was their capital, and it is what most Greeks I know still call it. Several different dishes of Ottoman Greek cooking are suffixed "in the style of the City," and it is frequently explained that the Turkish name Istanbul is a transcription of the Greek *eis tin Poli,* into the City. And although Constantinople has been Istanbul since the fifteenth century, I've noticed that when there is a TV news report from a correspondent in Turkey, the titles identifying place and reporter read "So-and-so, reporting from Constantinople." "Patricia is a poet, not a dressmaker, so maybe her patron saint is Saint Kosmas the Poet. When you go to the City, you must make a special trip to the Khora church to see the mosaics and the portrait of Kosmas with his pen and manuscript."

"I think, as many people do, that Khora is more beautiful than Agia Sofia," Elpida says. "But perhaps at this particular moment, the most interesting saint to you is the patron saint of breakfast. We'll stop at an interesting little hotel run by a mixed Greek and German family, a mixture that the Greek *Gastarbeiter*s in Germany have made more common, and have something to eat. And then, if you don't mind, we have a few household errands to run, which I fear will involve us in a series of coffees and gossips. But finally we'll have the beach."

We drive through stands of pine and poplars, trees heavy with figs at this time of year, and pomegranate trees, which look like the natural archetype of Christmas trees, with the brilliant red globes of the pomegranates dangling like living Christmas ornaments from their branches. The hotel, all clean marble and glass, is set on a hill dense with trees, like an alpine lodge on the beach. Behind the reception desk is a library of paperback German novels, and break-

fast is uncannily silent; the voices of the German clientele are mod-
ulated as Greek voices never are. One of the children of the owners
knows Kimon and Elpida, and puts us at a table overlooking the
trees. He and Kimon fall into a discussion of whether or not the
upcoming Maastrict agreement to European union is a good or bad
idea, a hot debate this summer. Interestingly, the boy's response to
it is divided, like his heritage. He feels it will be good for the
Greeks, who as one of the lower-income nations of Europe will
benefit, but bad for the Germans, who will end up disproportionately supporting the poorer nations. Kimon feels that the assent to
the idea of the union is inevitable, but that the fact of union will not
be accomplished in his lifetime, or perhaps ever. And he is not sure
that in the end the Germans won't profit even more from Greece
than the Greeks will from the Germans. "Now that Greece is a
member of the EEC, no one can prohibit the sale of Greek land or
houses to foreigners under the broader European laws we have
agreed to. And what this means, perhaps particularly in Greece,
with our labyrinthine laws and taxes on property inheritance, is that
it is often more advantageous to a Greek owner to sell his house
than to leave it in the family. The heirs often stand to profit more
from the proceeds of a sale, and it also spares them the considerable
expense of restoring traditional houses to the standards now codi-
fied by the Greek government." It is ironic to hear that the word
that would be the equivalent of our "preservation" is *anapaleosi,*
which in its literal meaning is not restoration at all, but making
something old again, reinfusing a house with antiquity, the architectural equivalent in a way of Katharevousa, the "purified" Greek
which was conceived in the eighteenth century, and which was
designed to reinfuse spoken modern Greek with classical Greek, in
the broad effort to make the new nation of Greece a neoclassical
nation.

"You cannot yet imagine—I cannot yet imagine," Kimon says,
pouring himself more coffee, "what impact this will have on the
country. Even now, there are whole villages on Thasos which are

virtually German, always prime real estate with beautiful settings and traditional houses. And this is also true on other particularly picturesque islands, like Santorini and Crete. And Chios, whose mastic villages, with their unique houses, are coveted by foreigners. So here you have enormous shifts occurring—there are organized foreign networks that actually comb islands for properties, cultivate local politicians, and then bring in their own construction workers to restore properties, whipping up bad feeling locally. Then of course, what happens if our islands end up being Floridas, retirement communities for Europe, with foreign populations who are also aged, and may not have much interest in local communities and problems which are in any case outside their own roots? And what is most extraordinary, and unpredictable, to me, is that the whole tax structure of the country will change shape, since so many houses must then be owned by people not subject to Greek income tax, and since real estate values have altered so dramatically with tourism. We could, if we don't think this through and find the balance, end up with a situation in which Greeks can't afford to live in Greece. Can't live on their own islands. You cannot imagine how this preoccupies me—it is so central to our history, this problem of how you earn your living through foreigners, which we always have, whether as colonists or emigrants, but without relinquishing the ownership of your assets and properties to them—it is a problem we have never solved, not in antiquity, not in modernity."

We drive to a village called Theologos, named for the evangelist Saint John, where a couple live who supply Kimon and Elpida with eggs and produce. In the nineteenth century, this was a principal town of Thasos—the Turkish quarter is still an identifiable part of town, despite the cycle of mutual massacres visited on each other by Turks and Greeks. The houses strongly resemble the houses on the Macedonian mainland, with their tweedy stone walls, slate roofs, and the arched doorways peculiar to Thasos. These are houses built for the severe cold of the Macedonian winter, the roofs pitched to release their burdens of snow.

The farmer and his wife are sitting on their first-floor terrace, chickens pecking in the small orchard beyond the wall, large marmalade cat sunning himself at their feet. They are eating string beans cooked in garlic, oil, and tomato, along with bread, cheese, and wine. The farmer's wife, dressed in the sacklike flower-print housedress that is the daily uniform of village wives of her generation, stands when she sees us, and greets us with the traditional phrase of welcome. Her husband remains seated and nods his head at us. They work like a team producing two effects—she shows deference to the visitors, he shows benign indifference. When she moves to bring extra chairs, I see she is wearing socks but not shoes, and an ace bandage around her left knee. Her husband pops a whole clove of raw garlic into his mouth, and satirically offers me one. I say no thank you, as he knows I will, and he downs another clove like an aspirin tablet. His wife brings in a silver tray with three crystal dishes of the local sweet made of Thasos walnuts in sugar syrup, while her husband and Kimon discuss the Maastrict agreement. "It will only benefit the capitalists," says Yiannis the farmer, "the people will gain nothing. We must get rid of Mitsotakis and put Andreas back in. Andreas is the only one who cares about the people." I ask what in his lifetime has been the best Greek government. "Not one time, not ever, has there been a good government in Greece," he answers. He asks me what he can tell me about the island. I want to know if there are reminders of Mehmet Ali's childhood time here. Yiannis says, "Was he brought up here? I hadn't heard. But I am *agrammatos,* unlettered. You are educated. If you read it in your books, that's how it was. But whether or not you find Mehmet Ali's village, at least you will swim today at Aliki. And you will see the way the burned side of the island once was. It was sabotage, you know." I ask if the arsonists had ever been found. "No," he says. "They were professionals. But it was the Turks. Or maybe the Italians, to destroy tourism." It is a traditional Greek analysis, the rival in the East or the rival in the West.

Elpida and I go into the kitchen to help pack up the eggs Elpida buys here every week. On the wall hangs a picture of Jesus walking through wheat fields, and on the floor are huge barrels of oil from the family trees. Yiannis's wife offers to sell me a container of this private stock, and funnels it into a plastic bottle for me. "You are of Greek descent," she says, and I say I am not. "No, no," she says, "I can tell because of your Greek. It is always the women who keep the language—I have a nephew and niece who were raised in Zimbabwe—he doesn't speak a word of Greek, she speaks well. The language the women keep like *prika,* like the furniture and linen we inherit to take into our houses when we marry. A part of you is Greek, or you would not have held the language." It is an impeccably antique Greek piece of popular belief, shared by Plato. I can and do find it later in my notebook, a line from the *Dialogue of Cratylus* 74: "It is the women who retain the old forms of speech."

Yiannis loads us with figs and pomegranates from his trees, and we drive off through shady secretive hamlets, one on the verge of restoration, with goats roaming through the foundations of the stone mountain houses, magnificent views of both sea and mountains, and a pretty marble fountain in its square. The interior villages are hidden enclaves that reveal themselves to you unexpectedly, often built on sharp slopes, and designed to be as invisible and inaccessible as possible to marauders and probably to Ottoman tax collectors as well. We stop for a minute in one where the mimosa-and-pine-scented air has a cakelike sweetness. An old lady comes down the path accompanied by five goats. She tells us that only five families live in this village in winter. In summer, the foreigners come who own many of the houses, but in winter, the goats outnumber the people. We wish her "Good winter," and drive on through the heat to the cove at Aliki, divided as so much in Greece seems to be. On one side there is a site with the ruins of a classical temple, where a fury of waves lashes the rocks, a site for propitiation. You can see blocks of marble in the sea, possibly scheduled for transport in the seventh century, since Aliki was a center for marble export to ports all over the Mediterranean. On the other, the water smiles, smooth as a porcelain platter. The swimming is dreamlike, in a bay with the serene texture of lake water combined with the salty originality of ocean water. "It is *pétillant,* isn't it," says Kimon, surfacing from a dive, "gentle, but vital and festive like a *blanc de blancs.*"

We walk afterwards along the small roads behind the cove, through what seem to be clouds of wine-scented air, and find the answer when an old woman beckons to us from a walled garden above the road. Wait there, she says, and we do, until she comes to the fence to hand us bunches of wine grapes from her harvest. They are the absolute inch away from being wine that genius is from being wisdom. "This month is called the Vintager," says Elpida. "Have you ever noticed the profusion of the religious holidays and saints' days during important agricultural months? I mean in September, the month of the vintage, and of the fruit harvest, there are one or two or more every week. We farm the supernatural in proportion to how much we are farming the natural." We stop at another beach at sunset, and walk it for a while. A grandmother in black knits under a tree, while her grandchild stares meditatively at the sea. We walk past brilliant blue gallon olive oil tins planted with red geraniums, and tables in little pavilions and under trees where families eat watching the shore until it gets cold. A seagull runs clumsily away as we advance—he makes us feel untrustworthy, with his seeming idée fixe that we are determined to struggle with him over the fish he has caught. "When I walk here," Kimon says, "I see something invisible. And astonishing. A complete reversal of fortune, an economic change so profound that the whole social structure is changing with it. As we walk past these families, who now own prime coastal property, realize that until the first waves of tourism in the sixties, this was the poorest land you could own. Rich farmland was desirable, but sand? The daughters of these families had to be either nice-looking or cunning, because they had no property of value to bring to marriage if this was what they brought. And now these undesirables are potential millionaires." "Like the oil booms in

Texas," I say. "Yes. Just think of it," says Kimon, "people who were once despised courted, new members of parliament, peasants suddenly the parents of *jeunesse dorée*."

When we drive back to their house, in a fishing village as compact as a quatrain, Kostas calls in high spirits over an interview he has read in the paper with a prominent classicist. Classicists appear regularly in the pages of newspapers and journals, partly because the kind and degree of teaching of ancient Greek in the schools is constantly debated here, and alters according to which party is in power. It is an issue that seems to divide fairly evenly along right- and left-wing lines, with the right wing favoring the compulsory teaching of classical Greek, and the left wing preferring that it be elective, proposing that the presence of classical Greek in modern Greek, if the language is intelligently taught, is itself an education in ancient Greek, adequate for people who are not going to be professional classicists, getting a full knowledge of the ancient language through its different dialects and periods. The right wing on the other hand seems to believe that the meaning of being Greek is held in the amber of fifth-century Attic Greek.

The special urgency of Kostas's call, though, is because he knows I will enjoy the professor's response to a request to find a classical equivalent for the refrain of a pop song hit of the summer, "I feel high when you're near by." The classicist suggests a line from section 536b of the Platonic dialogue called *Ion*. "And listen to the end." Kostas reads the question, " 'Is ancient Greek a living language?' And the answer comes, 'Not exactly living, but immortal.' I knew you'd like it. What are you going to do tomorrow?"

What we are doing is climbing up to the theater of Dionysus, placed with especially brilliant intuition, since the ring of marble benches of the theater slopes down toward the stage, resembling the cliff beyond, which itself slopes gently toward the larger circle of the sea, so that the landscape continues the theater. "There is a theater made by men and one by nature," I say to Kimon. The audience sitting in the theater of Dionysus, looking beyond the stage to the corresponding sea, realizes that this theater is for the drama of art, but the sea, the theater beyond, is for the drama of life.

We buy a cold drink from an enterprising man poised on the path with an ice chest, and walk back down to a panoramic site overlooking the Aegean. A clean white chapel with a red tiled roof has been built here, shadowed by pine trees. Two ferryboats are crossing in opposite directions, one for Thasos, one for a mainland port called Keramoti. A man is line fishing from a craggy rock wrinkled like the poet W. H. Auden's aged, drink-raddled face. The waters from here are all possible blues, milky, washed with emerald, blue black, aquamarine.

It was recently the name day of my new baby goddaughter in New York, so I show Kimon pictures. Name days are still important here, though I notice that the bakery shop windows, in Athens at least, make a point of displaying birthday cakes. "Choosing a godparent is still a complicated business here," says Kimon. "For a politician, it means almost a guaranteed vote in exchange for protection, still. You would want to choose the strongest person whose power connected to your interests—let's say a shipbuilder would choose a man who owned a forest. But you would also have to calculate that your children couldn't marry each other according to church law, so the one alliance ruled the other out. But who do you think the best godfather would be, Patricia, if you were choosing?"

"I don't know—the prime minister? Elias Lalaounis, your Tiffany?"

"Maybe. But there is a famous fairy tale, a *paramythi* as we call them, about the search for the ideal godfather, that says that even picks like yours are unstable. Would you like to hear it?"

"Please." Kimon lights another of the endless cycle of cigarettes he smokes—they seem to be an alternative for many Greeks to the worry beads which are becoming too nostalgic to make use of; the sheer self-consciousness of carrying them defeats the purpose of relieving tension. I look out over the brilliant blue-green anarchy of waters, a symbol since antiquity of the unreliability of patronage, from Odysseus, whom Poseidon hated and sea nymphs unexpectedly pitied, to Onassis, whose vast fortune and dynasty was founded on water.

"There was once a villager, a farmer who had a few acres of olive trees and a patch of vineyard, but barely eked out a living. So when his son was born, he was naturally anxious to find the most influential of all godfathers for the boy. For what a dowry is to a girl, a godfather is to a boy. 'Ask the head of the village,' said his father-in-law, 'he will not refuse you, and he is not only the most powerful man here, but knows officials in Constantinople.'

" 'No,' the farmer said respectfully but decidedly, 'I want a godfather for my boy who is both more influential, with broader connections, but is also completely reliable. You and I know the head of the village can be bought for the right price. I want someone absolutely just, so my child will never be cheated at the moment when he needs sponsorship most. Tomorrow, I will set out on a journey to find the perfect godfather for my son. I ask you to oversee the planting while I am gone.'

"The next morning, the farmer set out on foot, carrying on his back a bottle of the wine from his own grapes, and the cold lamb and pie of wild greens that his wife had made for him. Have you had *hortopitta*, Patricia? I will ask Elpida to make us one—it is a pie made of fresh-picked wild greens and sheep's cheese, the most elegant of dishes of the cuisine of poverty. We learned our wild greens especially well during sieges. Well, anyway, you will like *hortopitta*. So the farmer was walking along the coast road, thinking about the godfather problem, when he overtook a royal procession, horsemen and bearers carrying a sedan chair draped with velvet curtains and jewels and hanging silver lanterns, like the sultans used for short trips. A tall old man with a massive head, pure white hair, and a long white beard stepped out onto the ground, towering over the farmer. 'Where are you going so far from your acres?' the old man asked the farmer. 'Your worship, I have just had a son, and I am going in search of the perfect godfather, because I want my boy to have every advantage.'

" 'I offer myself as your new son's godfather,' said the old man.

" 'But I am looking for a godfather who is perfectly just, and who will have my boy's welfare at heart.'

" 'I am the man you are searching for,' said the magnificent old aristocrat.

" 'What is your name, sir?' the farmer asked.

" 'I am God,' said the old man.

" 'Then, with respect, you are not the person I would choose for my son's godfather.'

" 'Why not?' the old man asked. 'Isn't the name God the synonym for justice?'

" 'No, my Lord. You give riches and pleasures to the evil, and hardship and pain to the good. You accept bribes. Just look at your velvet and your silver lamps. You are unpredictable. And you have influence only in certain circles. You are not the right godfather for my little son.' And the peasant went on his way, leaving God standing with His retinue on the coastal road. He ate some of the lamb and drank some of the wine from home, and spent the night in a field under the open sky. The next day, he continued his journey, and his path crossed the path of a tall, athletic man wearing a coarse homespun tunic. 'Where are you going, countryman?' asked the man in the tunic. 'I am going to seek a godfather for my newborn son, a godfather who is perfectly just and will not fail him.'

" 'Then you have found that man in me,' said the traveler in the tunic. 'Take me to your house and I will sponsor your son.'

" 'What is your name?' asked the peasant.

" 'I am Saint Peter,' said the man in the tunic.

" 'Then I cannot accept your kind offer,' said the farmer. 'Everyone knows you guard the gates of Paradise, and everyone knows you play favorites. You love sinners more than you love the good. The drunkards, the avaricious, the evil-hearted are the ones you sponsor, but the struggling decent folk you abandon. If a murderer builds you a church, the gates to Paradise are open. But if a good man can't afford to light you a candle, to hell he goes. You are not the right godfather for my child.' The farmer walked on, leaving Saint Peter speechless in the road; that night he found a cave and slept in it. When morning came, and he emerged, he saw three beautiful women with baskets on their arms filling them with wild greens. 'Where are you going, Christian?' asked the most beautiful one. 'I am going to look for a godparent for my child, someone perfectly just to give my son protection.'

" 'I will be the godparent and protectress,' said the lady.

" 'And your name, sister?' asked the farmer.

" 'I am the Virgin Mary,' she replied.

" 'Then I must respectfully refuse,' said the farmer. 'You consented to give your child up to a dreadful death, as if his life was yours to give, without knowing whether this fate came from God or the Devil. You did not protect your child, sister, and besides, you are known to demand buildings and candles and jewelry. Your icon in my church is hung with gold and diamonds, sister, while people's children go barefoot. I will look elsewhere for a godparent.'

"The farmer continued on his road, while salty breezes blew from the distant sea. He saw coming toward him another farmer, who had been doing the hard work of harvesting, since he was sweating and carrying a sickle. 'Where are you going?' the sweating farmer asked. 'I have been traveling for three days now, looking for a godfather for my child. But I have not found him yet, because I am looking for a man of supreme justice.'

" 'It is lucky that you have met me, then,' said the thresher. 'I am a supremely just man, and I am willing to stand godfather to your child.'

" 'On the road so far,' said the farmer, 'I have met and refused God, Saint Peter, and the Virgin Mary. You call yourself more just than they are?'

" 'I am more just than God, more just than the rock on which He built His church, more just than the Queen of Heaven, who yields to persuasion.'

" 'And who are you?' the farmer asked.

" 'I am Death,' said the thresher.

" 'Then you are telling the truth. You favor neither the rich nor the poor, the ugly or the beautiful, the man or the woman. You take the child sucking the nipple and the blind woman limping with a cane. You are supremely just. Will you stand godfather to my son?'

" 'I will,' said Death, and accompanied the farmer back to his home. Kharos himself held the infant over the font and smoothed the wriggling baby with the holy oil. Death himself handed sugared almonds to the guests, lifted his wineglass to the company at the baptismal feast, and led them in the Greek songs he knew so well, since himself is present in so many of them. At the end of the day, he thanked his host, and said, 'It is not often I am invited to a feast, and have the chance to sing and dance with the living. It is an honor to be *nonos* to your boy, and I would like to honor you in return. I would like my godson to benefit from his *nonos,* so if you like, I will put you on the road to riches and a great reputation. From now on you will be a doctor, and you will become the most eminent doctor in the world.'

" 'How can that be, your excellency?' asked the peasant nervously. 'I am *agrammatos,* unlettered, I can barely read the initials of Christ on the holy bread in church.'

"Death shrugged. 'The rich bey in the town is sick, but I know he will not die yet. Go to him, prescribe something, no matter what, and tell him he will recover. You will instantly become famous for your medical wisdom. And when you are called to diagnose other patients, look for me. If I am standing at the patient's feet, prescribe whatever herb that comes to mind, the patient will survive. If I am standing at the patient's head, you will say the case is hopeless, and you will never be wrong.'

"So the farmer went to the bey and cured him, and became famous throughout the country for the perfect accuracy of his diagnoses. He became one of the richest men in the country, doctor to the government officials, the diplomats, the judges, the shipowners, the sultan himself, and his son was brought up in luxury and sent to fine schools. Every day, the former peasant blessed Death, his *koum-*

baros, for his largesse. He prospered and grew old. One day he was smoking his narghile under a leafy plane tree in his garden, and he saw a stranger coming toward him.

" 'Who are you?' he asked.

" 'Don't you recognize me?' said the stranger.

" 'My eyesight is not what it used to be,' the doctor said apologetically.

" 'But you can still recognize me when we are at a sickbed,' said the visitor.

" 'Oh, my apologies, *koumbare,*' said the doctor. 'I feel so light-headed this afternoon, and everything looks hazy. What can I do for you?'

" 'You can come with me to die,' said Kharos. 'It is your time, now.'

"The doctor trembled and threw himself at the feet of Death. 'Have mercy, *koumbare,* give me a little time more for the sake of your godson. I beg you to let me stay until he is married, until I see his own son born.'

" 'I cannot wait for you, kinsman,' Death answered. 'We have lakes and seas and mountains and plains to cross, and you must come with me.' So they traveled together, over islands and mountains and water, over Greece, through Greece, under Greece, until they came to a great palace hidden in a cave, a palace as huge as the sky, with as many windows as there are stars in all the galaxies. Some of the windows were brilliantly lit, some softly lit, some altogether dark. 'We have come to the end of our journey,' said Death. Kharos led the way into one of the lighted rooms, where many banks of candles were burning, some strongly, some weakly, and one an inch away from going out. Death stood the doctor in front of that candle and told him, 'This is the candle of your life. Do you see how the flame is going out?'

" 'But here is a whole supply of fresh candles, burning strongly,' said the doctor. 'Let me replace mine with one of these.'

" 'They are the lives of your kin,' said Death.

" 'What about this one, it has a steady flame,' the doctor pointed to a tall candle.

" 'It is the life of your son, my godson,' said Death.

" 'What does that matter?' said the desperate doctor.

" 'I am the just godfather,' said Death, and blew out the flickering flame of the doctor's candle. The doctor fell dead at the feet of Kharos, who is at the center of the most intricate network of relationships, but who cannot be influenced."

It is the most skeptical fairy tale I have ever heard, and I tell Kimon so. He laughs, and says, "Naturally. We are profoundly skeptical, like all truly superstitious peoples. Privately, I think this is why we are so disturbed by infidels, by the beliefs of other peoples. Because we are afraid what they believe gives them some advantage we are being cheated of. Because we don't believe anything we say ourselves. Because as the story tells, we wouldn't take even God's word at face value. You are aware of course, that we have two verbs meaning 'to love'? Now the standard explanation for this is to say that one has the nuance of to love with the heart, to give love, the other is to desire with the body, to want love. But I think we have two because when we fail at one, we can always claim we meant the other. Shall we walk back down slowly and have an ice cream?"

We stop at a patisserie whose menu features full-colored eight-by-ten glossy photographs of possible sundaes, each one with a name out of mythology: the Aphrodite, the Danae, the Adonis, names from the old gods. Kimon leafs through the booklet and comments that it is perhaps a mark of the change in religious sensibility that these voluptuous temptations could not be called after Saints Cecelia and Catherine and Stephen, despite the fact that Danae and Adonis had similar violent deaths.

"I hope you don't mind ancient goddesses and so forth with your ice cream, Patricia," he says and winks at me. I smile back. It seems to me they've instinctively got it right, that eating ice cream, the sweetness that disappears even as you pursue it, is about as close as you can come to the classical idea of pleasure.

I order the Persephone, a scoop of ice cream decorated with pomegranate seeds. Kimon orders the Leda, two scoops of vanilla covered with rosettes of whipped cream and studded with tiny paper Greek flags that is set before him in a swan-shaped dish. Persephone and Leda melt quickly in the late-afternoon sun, vanishing into milky pools before we have a chance to finish our immortal ice creams.

WISHES AS HISTORIANS

"Guide them into the harbor of salvation," I read while on the ferry to Naxos, in the prayer against storm winds and tempests at sea. A couple who have no language in common are communicating solely through kissing. They pause to grip each other's thighs, stare out to sea, and kiss again. In the prayers of a people are their longings and their fears—at least those they are allowed to voice publicly. The prayers for special occasions in the Greek Orthodox prayer book are also atoms of social, political, and economic history, at least until the Second World War—it is one of the ironic results of the bitter Greek experience of four hundred years of Ottoman occupation that it seems to have preserved well into the 1970s a sense of continuity with the medieval world that the Renaissance ended in the West, but here has only recently begun to be disturbed. It is an even more dazzling piece of historic irony that an element of the Greek sense of eternity, of world without end, may be drawn from the economic and social immobility of the Ottoman years, as well as from the unchanging agricultural challenges of this region. And of course, from the Christian translation of Platonism, so poignant in these prayers which see this world as a damaged version of a perfect prototype. "Would the ancient Greeks be proud of us and our Athens today?" is a question often posed to schoolchildren, and according to Kostas, has become a standard filler human-interest story that appears at least once a year in some newspaper or magazine. He sent me a sample when I was on Thasos, with a newsprint photograph of cherubic children visiting the Parthenon with their teacher, measuring their modern distance from the perfect Greeks, the ancient ones.

What do they pray for, what did they need, what were they afraid of? They pray that new-dug wells be blessed, that their water be pure and drinkable, here in this part of the world where water is a precious commodity still, and later this year will be so strictly rationed that exceeding your limit carries threats of fines and even imprisonment. They pray against harm that might come to vineyards, fields, and gardens. They pray to bless fruit, wine, olives, seeds, at planting and harvest, and vintage time when the grapes are pressed. They pray to exorcise evil spirits from the things they are trying to grow, and they pray with tragic regularity against each other, against ruin that might come from human malice. They pray against their old gods who threaten them as demons that need to be exorcised from the streams, trees, and rivers over which they used to preside, and need to be driven out of the human bodies they can still possess. They pray against deadly illnesses of cattle, swine, horses, goats, sheep, mules, and donkeys and bees. There is a prayer over silk making, which was once an important Greek craft—the Peloponnesus is sometimes called the Morea, in memory of the abundant mulberry trees that grew there. They pray that the little silkworm will survive unharmed and will grow and multiply in the name of the god who promised to father Abraham that his seed would multiply as the stars of heaven and as the sands on the seashore. The prayers over food are reminders of the constant hunger of this world; as one historian, Peter Brown, has written, "Food was the most precious commodity in the ancient Mediterranean." A traditional fillip of the Karaghiozis shadow puppet plays the Greeks adapted from the Turks was Karaghiozis's merry promise that "tonight we'll eat, we'll drink, and again we'll go to bed hungry!" During the German occupation of 1941–44, when the Germans requisitioned Greek produce to send to Germany, so that more Greek citizens died than in any other occupied country, one famous Karaghiozis master cut plays that referred to food from his repertoire, because he would not torture the audience. There are prayers over cheese, and God, the true nourishment, is asked to bless meat, and salt, that preservative cornerstone of the stored foods that meant survival. There are prayers against the rotting and spoilage of flour, honey, olive oil, wine. They pray with poignant specificity, at all contacts with water, the building of all kinds of ships, the moment of voyage, the completion of fishing nets. They pray over the foundation of a house, so important that dowry houses were often the critical factors in whether or not a girl could marry, and they pray over the moment when the members of a family enter a new house. They pray to welcome someone who has worshipped as a Roman Catholic back to Orthodoxy. I remember that I have yet to see a church dedicated to Saint Peter, and will not see one during my time here, although they may exist. But Peter seems primarily identified as the putative progenitor of the Roman church—and of course, Western churches dedicated to Constantine, the founder of the Eastern church, are also rare.

They pray, having lost Constantinople, first to the European Christian crusaders, and later to the Turks, and having seen the swastika flying from the Parthenon, against invasion by "other races of people"; they pray against civil war, still so traumatized by the last one ending in the early fifties that most people cannot bring themselves to speak of it; they pray against plague, starvation, fire, sword—they pray not to experience what they have experienced, their prayers pit them against the very world they live in.

Being here has taught me to be conscious of the metaphors which words are often built from, expressions at the same time of the brilliance and the limitations of each of our perceptions. The word for government, from which our own word derives, is a marine metaphor, connected to the ancient Greek vocabulary for rudder, ship's pilot, and the verb "to steer." I have read on the other hand that the Arab word for politics descends from an ancient Middle Eastern word for horse training. And prayer? The metaphor at the heart of our English word is from the Latin *precarius,* something obtained by entreaty, also the source of the word "precarious." The Greek word for prayer, on the other hand, means "a wish."

White gulls fly alongside the ferry, beautiful inscrutable scavengers. I look again at the couple caressing each other, their hands touching faces and thighs in a passion of wishing. Naxos is quiet on this late Sunday afternoon as we sail into its harbor with a view of the Portara, the monumental gate in the square shape of a Greek letter *pi* that was part of a temple of Apollo. The Venetians who took Naxos as a victory prize after the Fourth Crusade were said to have used remnants of the temple to build the fortress castle which was the nucleus of Naxos town. It is their presence that is most marked here, in the Venetian colonial architecture scattered through the countryside, in the small-scale medieval town they built and lived in as seigneurs, establishing a feudal system that was ended only after the Turkish conquest, in the Roman Catholic cathedral and uneasy Catholic coexistence with the Greek Orthodox. The Cretan novelist Kazantzakis was sent to the school operated by Roman friars here in what is now the island archaeological museum, although his father harbored dark suspicions that the friars were trying to convert him.

The Portara was also supposed to have been where Dionysus, born on Naxos, appeared to claim the abandoned Ariadne. Or at least one of them, since in the Greek world of relentless dualisms, there seem to have been two Ariadnes, one of whom died when abandoned by Theseus, and was worshipped with funeral liturgies and mourning chants, and another who survived the abandonment and was married to Dionysus, celebrated with wedding songs and dances.

The passage from the ferry through the screaming, shoving swarms of room renters, who fight you for your suitcases and press your face into photographs of their rooms, is like something out of Alfred Hitchcock's *The Birds*. The fortress town is superbly beautiful, with views of the sea that are almost shocking in their inexhaustibility and brilliant color. The town is laid out on the amoeba plan, with houses radiating from each other via communal walls, and forming a common defensive outer wall. It combines defensive necessity with religious sensibility, a maze of tunnel-like streets and low gates and sudden forks that lead into unknown passageways, and would either stymie an invader or confront a visitor with revelations, like the unexpected angel I am facing now, standing in a carved niche over a doorway I never meant to find. Here you find your way by being lost. Still, although the sun sets as dramatically as a great lover makes love, the streets resound with tapes of cheap beach holiday music and the restaurants offer the kind of "international" cooking that is quintessentially provincial. Kimon and Elpida have given me a letter to a friend of theirs who is the president of an inland village, and I am glad to be going tomorrow to look him up.

I set out early so that I can stop at villages on the way. It is easy to see, as I drive, why Naxos was Byron's favorite of the Greek islands, with its confluences of romance. There is the romance of legend, the romance of aristocracy, the romance of desolation in the uneasy, agitated-looking brown mountains that climb and fall as sharply as a heart patient's cardiogram, and the romance of fertility in the interior, all terraced vineyards, olive trees, fruit orchards, potato fields, houses swathed in bougainvillea and jasmine, like rich women in furs. Naxos is the largest Cycladic island, and there is something palatial about its scale, the way the terraced farmland makes a grand formal descent into the valleys, like the impressive staircase of a grand house. I stop to look at a Venetian lord's tower, with a small stone chapel curled against it like a house cat. The little chapel has a dual identity: one aisle is consecrated for Greek Orthodox worship, the other for Roman Catholic.

The village of Apiranthos is a world of marble, even nicknamed *marmarino,* "made of marble"—it must have once been a wealthy village, as the elaborate marble plaques, carved with names and dates over many of the doorways, suggest. Now, though, the crusty proprietor of a museum grumbles that all the money goes to Naxos town. "Apiranthos doesn't make any money during the season, and look around you, even with our views, we don't have a hotel, only a few rooms to rent." He strolls me down to the museum of village life, past a small penned flock of goats, two of them lying odalisque style on a wooden table. The house is ordered and charming as only uninhabited houses are. Even in this village house on Naxos, the new ideal of the photograph shapes the arrangements inside, just as our idea of the beauty of a face is now the camera's ideal, the photogenic face. Our eyes are used to conceiving the perfect interior as one about to be photographed, nothing spilled, smudged, disarranged, scattered. This "village" house mirrors the ideal; even though its furnishings have been painstakingly collected, it cannot really look like a village house looked. The kitchen especially has an unearthly order, with its earthenware *pithoi* for olive oil and wine neatly displayed, and its stunningly clean paddles for sliding bread into the oven. In the bedroom, a *stefanothiki,* a carved wooden box holding the imaginary couple's wedding crowns, hangs on the wall, and a colorful embroidered hammock is slung between posts of the parents' bed, so the mother could tend to it and rock it without having to get up—without a baby the arrangement seems ingenious. But none of the babies I know would be cooperative enough to accept this neat packaging. The house poses the mirror problem again—when do we see what we are looking at?

"You must come again," the museum proprietor says as I get into the car. "You can rent a room in my house. It is a museum."

"A museum of what?" I ask. "A museum of me," he answers.

I drive on, searching for the comfortably prosperous village of the man who is expecting me, whose name translates to Basil the Rifle, a name given to some ancestor, maybe because of good marksmanship, or the lucky acquisition of an impressive gun, or simply because of a reputation for bad temper. It is a mark of the enormous power of public opinion and community relations, and the martial force of Greek gossip, that in Greece so many people carry surnames their neighbors gave them, distinguished permanently by a moment of local reputation. No wonder there is a prayer against the evil eye, and that one of the striking features of the prayers I read on the ferry was the tense mistrust and suspicion of other people—it is a companion tradition to the tradition of Greek hospitality.

The world of Naxos is of a different scale and color than bright, gemlike Thasos; Naxos is coppery, its vistas farther away from the viewer, as if you are there and not there at the same time. When I arrive at the village, Mr. Rifle, his three daughters, and their grandfather, all wearing high rubber boots, are making wine. Cascades of grapes are stacked against the wall. They have already trod the grapes, Mr. Rifle tells me, and now they are finishing the pressing by machine. He throws great shovelfuls of pressed grapes into the machine, while the three daughters, their eyes purple-black as grapes, ladle the juice from a well that catches the runoff into buckets. The oldest girl passes the buckets to their grandfather for barreling. "When you harvest grapes for wine," Mr. Rifle says to me, "you are practicing a kind of agriculture in which time is as important an element as sun and soil. So I think it is not only practical, but a kind of *gouri,* a good luck talisman, to have three generations pressing the grapes together. How can my wine not be good to drink?" I sit on a stone wall and watch the family, this living votive image, making their wine, until Basil and Maria, his shy teenager, are ready to drive with me to the seaside village of Apollonas for lunch. In a field, a tiny newborn donkey looks like a toy animal, and we pass men riding sidesaddle on donkeys on the highway. Donkeys are still the most efficient way to reach farm plots cut out of sharp terraces, and rural Greece is crisscrossed with well-trafficked mule paths. When we reach Apollonas, we make the local pilgrimage to the gigantic kouros who has been lying on his back overlooking the rich blue sea since the sixth century B.C., when his maker seems to have judged him a failure and left him here. "Don't you want to take a picture?" Basil asks me, and I hold out the notebook and pen I am carrying. "That's your camera?" he says skeptically, and shrugs at my lost opportunity. But this is exactly the kind of tableau that makes me think that in Greece, the adage that a picture is worth a thousand words is exactly reversed. The light and scenery seem to turn photographs into symbols, not even images, of a kind of general sublime; only words will make experience of being here specific— even glorious photographs seem to take on a curious embalmed quality here, where a word is worth a thousand pictures.

We settle at a table overlooking the sea at a taverna called the Little Dolphin and eat local sheep's cheese, the proprietress's chicken in tomato and cinnamon sauce, salad with tomatoes she takes me into her garden to pick, and wine from the barrel. Basil will not be happy until I abandon my knife and fork. He leans forward and says, "Do you know the saying?" I say I don't know the saying. "Well," he smiles, "the proverb says women and chicken both need to be picked up in the hands." The proprietress is watching our glasses and brings us another carafe and more bread—I recognize this vigilance and custodial tenderness in her cooking, her well-tended garden, her well-tended clients. She looks to me to be one of those people who think their way into the world through a skill, who develop the personal excellence of a gift into a principle, a successful balance of herbs and meat leading to a carefully nurtured garden and animals, leading to nourishing people, leading to thoughts about conserving the fertility of the soil, and on to an awareness of the meaning of being a part of a community, all consequences maybe of experimenting with oregano and cinnamon. I wish we could do something less cold than paying her—give her a gift, something she wanted, not something she earned—but open admiration of her beautiful cooking and beautiful manners will have to serve. "We have always been famous on Naxos for our wine,"

Basil says, taking an appreciative sip. "You know wine was discovered here by Dionysus? There is a story about how it happened, that
everyone hears at some point, at any rate, any one who grows up
here, though of course we have large emigrant communities, like all
the Aegean islands—our mothers and grandmothers, the women of
the islands, were the domestic servants, the baby nurses and child
caretakers and seamstresses and cooks of the wealthy families on the
mainland and in Asia Minor and Egypt. They would work for a family for a set number of years with the agreement that the family
would then provide them with *prika*."

"Well, at least the *prika* part is over," I say. Demanding and offering *prika* in exchange for marriage was made illegal in 1983, and if
you look in a Greek glossy wedding magazine, under the cheerfully
efficient checklist that in an American counterpart would be called
something like "Wedding Do's and Don'ts" (Do remember that the
bride's parents pay for the rehearsal dinner, etc.) you will find the
admonition "Do remember that the dowry has been illegal since
1983."

"*E*," he says to me, using a sound that is as distinctively Greek and
as untranslatable as "uh" or "uhm-hmm," sounds you don't hear on
these shores, "the *prika* part is over like sheep stealing, which is also
against the law, is over. And we have a patron saint of sheep stealing,
Saint Mamas. We had a lot of practice under the Turks in appearing
to obey laws. With us, men obey some laws and women obey men.
Maybe *prika* will disappear, but right now it has only changed its
shape. Now the ideal is a girl who has a civil service job, because
they can't be fired. Or a job with a multinational; prime real estate
is always attractive. But there are changes, too. The boy now has to
offer something; he should show he can earn a decent living, or have
a good degree, or at least be a *kalo paidi,* a decent guy, whereas
before, all he really had to do was have a pair of balls. You'll see if
you stay here that *prika* is still around. But it's more fun to talk about
Dionysus, who took Ariadne without *prika*. Do you want to hear the
story?" I nod that I do.

"When Dionysus was still an adolescent, he set out on a journey towards Naxos. Since it was a long way away from where he was, he needed to break the monotony of the journey and sat down on a boulder to relax. From the boulder as he looked down at his feet, he saw a plant beginning to grow directly in front of him, and the shape of its leaves and stems was so beautiful that he decided to take the plant with him and transplant it when he reached Naxos. So he uprooted it and carried it along with him. But the sun was burning hot and he was afraid that the plant would wither before he reached the island. He stumbled on the bone of a bird in the road, and got the idea to put the plant inside the hollow of the bone to protect it from the sun. Then he went further on his way. But held in his divine hands, the plant continued to grow, and it flourished so quickly that it spilled out below and above the bird's bone. So he had the same worry that the plant would wither and pondered what to do next. Then he happened upon the bone of a lion, broader of course than the bird's bone, and he fit inside it the bird's bone with the green plant. In a little while his divine force made the tendrils of the plant spill out of the lion's bone. He caught sight of the bone of a donkey, even larger than the lion's bone, and he sheltered the two other bones and the plant inside it. Holding the three bones with the plant growing as rapidly as a river rushes, he arrived in Naxos. When he was ready to put the plant into the good dark soil of our island, he observed that the roots of the plant were tightly bound around the bones, and he could not separate the plant from them without destroying its roots. So he replanted it, leaves, bones, and all, just as it was. In just a little time the plant took root and flourished and became a vine that put forth grapes. From these vines, the god made the first wine and gave it to the people to drink. And the mir-acle of the drink came from the way the god had brought it to Naxos. Because when people drink wine, at first they sing and rejoice like birds. And when they drink more, they become as strong as lions, and as ready to fight, and when they drink still more, they act exactly like asses." Basil hits the table with his fist, loving his punch line. I think it is funny too, but more because it seems comic to hear such a moralizing Christian story about that outstandingly amoral god, Dionysus. The god of frenzied inspiration is here used to convey the village equivalent of a message against drunk driving. The god's gift of wine here is received with admonitory folk proverbs and wry skepticism, and he is admired as villagers would most admire him, for his magical fertility, divine agricultural powers.

We pay, and drive on to the church of Panagia Drossiani, the Dewy Virgin, the Virgin of Refreshment, probably named for the soft coolness of the glade where the chapel is built on its hill. Inside, there are two pictures of Christ as the Pantokrator, ruler of all, painted in the apse, and so two Saint Georges and two Saint Dimitris accompany them. The picture of the Panagia is unusually expressive. She looks surprised to be here at all in this position of prominence, her eyes wide, brave, and a little frightened. I wander into a dark chapel at the back of the church, looking around by the light of a candle. Against the wall are discarded silver icon casings, a stiff silver costume, an empty brocade some saint has abandoned. And there is a round, freestanding church candelabra, some of its candleholders bent and broken, lying against the wall, as if someone had fought with it. When we come out of the church, the old woman in black clothes who is caretaking it urges me to look at her embroidery. Her white pieces are as fine as stitched snow, but I don't very much like the Greek fashion of throwing squares of ornamental cloth over every possible undraped surface, as if the furniture were naked and needed aprons of fig leaves. Basil calls out from the foot of the steps, "You'll need at least one piece for your *prika*," teasing me into the purchase. All the talk about *prika* made me curious about the other world, the dreamworld of alternate phenomena that accompanies all the realities of Greek life, and I looked up *prika* later, in Angeliki's, Kostas's sister's, dream book, which dates from the fifties at least, since it was her mother's. There is a mix of interpretations—if you dream of getting *prika*, the dream is unlucky, and you will be deceived in some financial dealing. If you are giving *prika,* expect money from a relative abroad, while marrying without *prika* is worst of all, meaning some enemy will step in to destroy a cherished hope. If you dream of any of the many fasts ordered by the church, the dream foretells that you will marry without a dowry. I wonder what happened after 1983, after *prika* was made illegal as a part of a marriage transaction. My own dream books were published then, and when I look up the dream, I can't find it. As it has been removed from the legal code, it has lost its status as a dream.

We stop for a coffee at a village in the Melanes Valley, the site of another monumental kouros, who sleeps like a king of fertility waiting to wake up in the spring and impregnate the world. The kouros at Apollonas was austere, broken, his site made him tragic, but this one's pastoral setting, reigning over the marvelous garden just below him, rich with pear trees, lemons, planes, cypresses, sunflowers and marigolds, turns the atmosphere pleasantly ribald. "Does your boyfriend wish he were this big?" Basil grins at me, gesturing toward the endless stone body of the kouros. "Perhaps he does," I say drily. "And do you also wish that he were?" Basil persists with mock scholarly interest. "How can I not wish for him what he wishes for himself?" I say with pious obedience, and we climb down to drink coffee in the flowery shade.

Back in Khora, the generic name for so many of the main towns on Greek islands, I walk back to my hotel to call Kostas, which I have promised to do at least once a week when I am on the road. "Succulent, very tasty, *akhh,* my little mother," one man says as I walk by, confident that I hear things only in my own language, whatever that might be; he uses an adjective that descends from the ancient Greek word for homecoming, *nostos,* used of Odysseus's return to his motherland; someone fancifully told me that the meaning of the modern word evolved because homecoming was for Odysseus as sweet as the savor of home-cooked food. Homecoming is invoked often as one of the sensations Greek men yearn for erotically—whatever Greek women might yearn for, it is not this, since home cannot yearn for itself, food can have no appetite for itself. In the collections of modern Greek ballads of *xenitia*, exile from the homeland, in the voices of the men who have had to earn their livings outside Greek territory, I have naturally not found one in which the singer is a woman, among other reasons because Greek women did not vote until 1956 (remarkably, Turkish women could vote in the 1930s), and until 1983, lived under legal disabilities that evoke the status of women in certain Islamic countries. As late as 1890, Greek women were forbidden by law to become scientists, merchants, or civil servants. And until 1983, a husband exercised an absolute authority within the family; a young person could not be issued a passport without the written permission of a male who held paternal authority, and in the event that the father of a family was incapacitated in some way, decision-making power was not transferred to the wife, but controlled by a "family council" acting in conjunction with a court of law. The husband was also entitled to choose where his wife would live. So the women in *xenitia* ballads either long for their men to come home, or ask for permission to accompany them and are refused. "There where I'm going, my girl," says one song, "women cannot journey. / You would meet there unmarried Turks and married men from Europe / who would ravish you and murder me."

As I travel here, I am losing the illusion that I know where I am. Words are like the facets of diamonds, showing only the shades of meaning in a language that history and experience, prejudice, ideology, politics, myth, desire, have cut out of them. It seems there is something poignantly and fruitfully incomplete in each language; each has its partial brilliances and inadequacies, each is a dream of the truth.

English and Greek have words for east, west, man, woman, but they don't mean the same things or produce the same sensations. Even in translation, we often are not saying the same things, as the trouble over the Christian creed, which ultimately split the churches, demonstrated. Key Greek words and Latin words simply could not be made to render the same nuance. This can be true within Greek itself, where Greeks pray in Christ's Greek prayer for *artos,* their daily bread, but they eat *psomi.* And the home Greeks yearn for is not the mystical better world of true freedom and dignity across the Jordan of African-American gospel music. Nor is it the storybook Jerusalem of the Jews, the place in which the Old Testament stories are perpetually relived and therefore true, nor is it the transfigured cottages of Jerusalem in England's green and pleasant land. It is not the home of the pioneers of the American West, which must be sought through the hardships of a physical and spiritual journey, and in the end be created, since it can be found in no other way. The home of the Greek ballads is a literal place, the familiar place where you grew up, where your mother and father were, where you were known as a boy, your childhood, your neighborhood. Perhaps it is also the place where you don't have to be a hero, the place where you are always a boy. "Buy shoes from your own neighborhood, even if they are patched," runs one popular Greek proverb. The *xenitia* songs also give wonderful through-the-looking-glass glimpses of America seen from the other side—there are the grim ballads about the stormy ship's passage to New York, the loneliness of wandering New York like scattered birds, not knowing anyone, the comic defiance of the son who declares to his mother that he will fall down and die before he will consent to go to Chicago, the son who pleads that he doesn't want to die in America, the jealous songs of local youths who have to compete for girls with wealthy gray-haired men who have returned from America to choose, at last, young brides, spending freely, sporting dyed mustaches, and playing the *pallikari.*

"Oh, look what a pretty blouse she has on," says one housewifely-looking woman to another as I climb the staircased streets typical of a fortress town like this to get to my hotel. This must be what people mean when they say they wish they could attend their own wakes, this power to overhear whatever is said about yourself while remaining invisible. When I call Kostas, he sounds depressed, so I tell him the Christian fable I heard about Dionysus today at lunch. He knows it but not anything about its origins. "Sometimes these stories, which in our cultural politics are supposed to prove our direct descent from the ancient Greeks, 'the greatest people in history,' as the voice of the son et lumière at the Parthenon says, actually came to us through the European travelers from the eighteenth and nineteenth centuries. They would be astonished as they passed through villages that villagers knew nothing of the ancient mythology they them- selves were brought up on, and would tell them stories out of ancient Greek literature, which would then evolve into folk tales, or be grafted onto them. I remember an anecdote about a Philhellene fighter during the 1821 War of Independence, who told some klepht leader that he reminded him of Achilles, or some such compliment. And the klepht said to him, 'Who was Achilles? Did the musket of Achilles kill many?' But we will never know the proportions of import and export in these stories, because, and often by design, we are poor historians and great fabulists. We accuse you of having no grasp of history; Greeks have even less sense of history than Ameri- cans, only a kind of imperialism with regard to the stories of the past. Who else would be so blindly possessive of antiquity that they would call their air force academy the School of Icarus, invoking a patron who after all couldn't fly and falls to his death because of faulty equipment? We never realize how inadvertently comic this makes us, like a nouveau riche showing off the correct acquisitions that are supposed to make him seem cultivated. When I was in the States, I laughed whenever I was reminded that the Greek-American men's association calls itself 'The Sons of Pericles,' a magnificent faux pas if you remember your *Protagoras.* The legitimate sons of Per- icles were such duds that Plato uses them as examples to prove virtue cannot be inherited. And I am tired of us today."

"What makes you tired?" I ask.

"Because the police are beating the transportation demonstra- tors here, and now, apparently with the approval of higher-ups, have taken to removing their badges so no one will be able to identify them in complaints. And the minister who should be responsible gave one press conference to say this was all right, that policemen should not be required to wear badges 'in order for their job to be easier,' and then reversed himself after the outcry to say they would after all wear badge numbers, that he originally hadn't had enough information. But what's most depressing is that getting beaten up is taken for granted here. I've been beaten up, for God's sake. I was just looking at an interview with a former government minister who was asked if he'd ever been beaten by the police. Of course, he said, during the struggles for union with Cyprus in the sixties. But then the police wore badges. Children in schools are slapped and punched and hit with belts. In the nineteenth century, they were actually tortured. Have you read *Patoukhas?*" I say I haven't. "It's a turn-of-the-century comic novel by a Cretan writer in which the hero runs away from school after being tortured by the monk who runs the school with *falanga,* a method in which the soles of the feet are beaten which was used elsewhere by the Greek communists who tortured Nicholas Gage's mother Eleni during the civil war. Here's a Greek proverb, knowing your fondness for them: 'Beating comes from paradise.' In which case, God is a sadist. I'm sorry, but it drives me wild to see this as an accepted part of civil life here, no matter what party is in power and closing their eyes to it. And of course I would rather that you not see it."

"I know. And I wish you hadn't seen the tapes of Rodney King." I had been in Greece when the videotape of that beating was first broadcast. "But we can't stop corruption we won't see," I say, struggling for a grip on this rock face.

"I know," he says. But I can tell he doesn't feel better. "In any case, there's a bon mot circulating that you'll enjoy. Someone recently asked a clever political cartoonist whether the country has a future. Well, he said, we have a past. You can't ask for everything."

I go out for a sunset walk along the harbor, to see who is represented by the two modern statues—I hadn't recognized either of their features when I'd passed them before. On the base of one statue is a relief of Shakespeare—this is a scholar of English, Michaeli Damiralis, who spent part of his life (1857–1917) translating Shakespeare into modern Greek. The lateness of these dates is one measure of how intermittent the contact has been between Greece and the West, as is the introduction of the first piano on mainland Greece, also in the nineteenth century. It is hard to imagine Mozart, Bach, Haydn, Beethoven, Chopin all arriving together at the same moment along with the renewed consciousness of the classics of Greek antiquity, all seen through the prism of romanticism.

The other statue is of a government minister named Protopapadakis, executed in 1922 along with five others for criminal, even treasonable, mismanagement of the Asia Minor campaign. The meaning of the statue is unreadable—does it mean that Naxos is in agreement with the substantial number of both Greeks and foreign diplomats who saw the executed men as scapegoats and their deaths as shallow vengefulness? Or does it mean that Naxos views its native sons on the Greek mother principle, as the best boys in the world no matter what their failings? I won't ever know. I wander back through the bazaarlike jumble of patisseries, tavernas, and jumble shops— "We buy gold, silver, used books," one tantalizes. I walk upstairs to the common salon of the hotel, where a group of people, some Greek, some foreign tourists, are watching a music program—a Rubensesque Turkish man, dressed in spangles, is rolling his hips in the motion of the belly dance, and licking his lower lip with a suggestive tongue between lyrics. *Pousti,* someone says, using the Turkish word for passive homosexual, which is the standard Greek term too. It strikes me, hearing the word, and watching the man's feminine movements, that the scandal of this act is its violation not of the sexuality of the individual but of the culture. In these two cultures with their deification of masculinity, the most illicit desire a man could have would be not to desire a woman but to desire to be like a woman. The daring is in the suggestion that a man might have a desire to be feminine, something that is forced here to be inadmissible, through popular imagery, and behavior and religion—it is terrifying to think there might be freedom as well as subjection in being a woman. The same man who said *pousti,* confident that nobody but his neighbor hears him, jokes, "What they call Greek, we call Ottoman love."

"Yes, but there's a difference," says the other man, mesmerized by the performance. "The Greeks use vaseline, the Turks use spit."

As soon as you are aware of the light in the mornings on the waterfront of a Greek island, you hear the wet slaps of the fishermen beating octopus against the rocks to tenderize it, an act that is the source of many sexual double entendres, since "to beat" is also slang for "to fuck." "What needs to be pounded to be made tender? An octopus and a woman," says one riddle. I sit down for breakfast at one of the seaside tavernas—the chairs of the table next to me are draped with the drying bodies of octopus, as is the railing across from me. The octopus legs stir slowly in the morning breeze, a skull with eight weaving crossbones swaying beneath it. Passengers are beginning to board the ferryboat to Athens. A group of Greeks bearing gifts has just surged aboard: bags of fruits, island flowers, Naxos Gruyère and the Naxos yogurt, the dairy equivalent of pâté, all probably destined for relatives in Athens tonight. Some of the passengers may have doctors' appointments; while there is a small hospital on Naxos, anything chronic or serious has to be handled in Athens—if it's really serious, a helicopter or plane takes you from the island. The doctors write out a prescription for you to go to Athens just as they would for Darvon—and the government medical plan is supposed to pay if the doctor sends you to Athens. On the deck, I watch the Scandinavian and German tourists, their faces blank in repose. But the convention of the Greek face is different; it is the norm to show a face worked with emotion, like the faces of actors and actresses, even in repose. An obviously Greek man standing at the railing shows animated features, his eyes widening, his forehead wrinkling, even distorted by his responses to what he is looking at. Greeks, with their strong eyebrows and thickly modeled features, look like theater actors trained to project emotions to even the back rows, with their open expressions a kind of makeup, a concealment through dramatization of their private thoughts, as effective as the blank tabula of the northern European face.

I look toward the Protopapadakis statue, and think how often in Greece the mental path into the past seems wide and paved, while the path flowing in the opposite direction is unmarked or simply disappears. The Naxos guidebooks focus on antiquity and on village traditions such as trying to provoke a dream image of your future husband by eating salty food on certain feast days; the man who offers the sleeper water will be her husband. But of the history of Naxos from medieval to modern times there is virtually nothing, not even a mention of that intriguing figure Joseph Nasi, the Sephardic Jew who was made duke of Naxos by a Turkish sultan in 1566. Appropriately for Dionysus's island, the appointing sultan was such a great wine lover that he was known as Selim the Sot, while the future duke of Naxos's fortune was founded in part on a kind of bootlegging—he supplied the sultan with wine, and controlled the wine trade in Turkey, where imports of alcohol were nominally banned by the sultan, in keeping with Islamic law. But he and Naxos seem to have found each other mutually repulsive, since he only spent a brief time here in the Venetian fortress before returning to Constantinople.

I walk aimlessly inside the medieval town walls, where the houses are joined together like segments of one vast dwelling. I relish the green and blue painted doors, and the coats of arms on marble pediments. A woman stops a young mother on the street to examine her new baby. She gives it no compliments, careful not to risk the evil eye, but calls after mother and child, "May it live for you." For us, wishes are *niaiserie,* the "Wish you were here" scribbled on postcards is a code with us of insincerity, as the "Best wishes" closing a business letter can be. But here, a wish brings you even for a short time into a relationship of intimacy with someone, the intimacy of common humanity, of being at risk in a world of lucky or terrible events. When I bought a cassette player in Athens, its façade gleaming black with silvery buttons for sophisticated commands, the machine was handed to me with the wish *"Kaloriziko,"* may it be well fated (or well rooted, since *riziko*, the word for fate, is related to *riza*, the word for root), as new acquisitions are wished into place. I pause outside a shop where a handsome carved wooden mirror and a cleanly made painted chest have been placed on the edge of the narrow sidewalk. Inside, more furniture and mirrors are strewn around in various stages of development, a carved leaf here, the beginning of a spray of wheat there, pieces of the world the craftsman is transferring into wood, onto chests for household storage and mirrors for faces to look into. The man offers to show me the chest I am admiring, but I tell him I cannot buy it. He is hoping that my hesitation means I want to bring down the price, while I wish that it were a ploy. But it isn't. Misunderstanding, he tells me the price, which is high. Instinctively, I mutter *"po po po,"* the Greek "oh dear, oh dear," which you helplessly pick up if you live here more than a month. "Not *po po po,"* he says, offended. "It is worth that price and more." Nothing destroys fluency faster than the presence of anger—only the truly native speaker or linguist of long standing can manage both anger and grammar, and I am upset, too, that he thinks I meant my head-shaking at the price as a comment on his work rather than my checkbook. We resolve the moment of hurt in the Greek way, with a wish. I ask shyly if he himself made everything I see. Yes, he answers gruffly, I do it all by myself, every piece. And I lose my stammer and say, *"Yia sta kheria sas,"* health to your hands, which means health to your gift, may your talent flourish. He looks at me with surprise at this sudden homecoming in his language. His cheeks flush with pleasure, and he nods at me warmly, thanking me. "Your Greek was broken, but your heart is whole," he says. I have made the right wish, which is all I have to give, and as it turns out, all that is necessary.

THE PAST AS THE FUTURE

A thick Albanian-Greek dictionary is displayed in the window of the local school textbook and supply store, I notice as I pass. It is an acknowledgment of some tacit kind of the growing population of illegal alien Albanians, who surge over the border in the hundreds every day, and whom the Greek police round up and return by the busload. And another Balkan knot—the Greeks and the Albanians would like to be differentiated from each other absolutely, but there are parts of Greece, for example, the island of Hydra, that were populated largely by Albanians. There are villages in what is now Albania that are largely Greek. Albanians served as Turkish henchmen during the Ottoman years, but a number of Greek revolutionary war heroes were of Albanian descent. And the foustanella, the famous Greek kilt, is said by many to be a version of the Albanian warrior's costume, and is sometimes called the Albanian kilt. The Balkans did not and still do not seem to have the Western notion of national borders; villages dominated by different ethnic groups intricately veined the region, and the Balkan notion of borders seems based on the notion of the ethnic enclave of the village—which, if this is true, explains why nationhood here has been

wrought through three predominant patterns: federation, coloniza-
tion, or genocidal slaughter.

I am on my way to pay my electric bill, which now comes in an
envelope stamped with the Star of Vergina and the legend "Macedonia—The Eternal Greek Light," and my rent, which is an event
requiring an entire afternoon—Leda tells me that that is nothing;
paying her monthly rent needs a full-scale evening visit, with a bottle of wine and sometimes a card game. I am back on schedule, after
a bout of flu—or of nothing, according to the Greek diagnosis. I had
canceled a dinner since I was sick, and the hostess asked me, "What
are your symptoms?" Coughing, body aches, sore throat, clogged
nasal passages, fever. "How many degrees?" she said. A hundred and
one, I answered. "And what is normal on a Fahrenheit thermome-
ter?" Ninety-eight-point-six, I said, feeling too feverish for all this
medical inquiry. "Oh, then you don't have a fever," she said. "Don't
I?" I said weakly. "No," she said, "fever would be much higher, a hundred four, or a hundred five." So I learned that in order for fever to
qualify as Greek fever, you must in fact be dying, your brain cells on
the point of being comfortably medium rare. In fact, i'm not
entirely sure there is such a thing as illness in Greece. Illness is what
has killed someone. Life is suffering, illness is death.

Cooped up in the house, and feverish, at least by my standards, I
watched a Greek TV melodrama called *Nemesis,* about a Greek émigré who has made a vast fortune abroad, and returns to revenge himself on the family responsible for his father's death. There is the
conventional, almost obligatory scene of a woman being slapped or
punched, here by her husband, which is repeated daily in so many
variations that it has come to seem that Greeks have an appetite for
this kind of scene, as Americans do for high-speed car chases and
gunfights. The style of acting too is utterly different. A Greek actor
never tries to give the illusion of not acting, the hallmark of the
American style, embodied in someone like Spencer Tracy. He conveys first of all that he is playing a role, that characters who are acted
out are people who are represented because they have a special fate,

a distinction. If anything, a Greek actor or actress constantly shows the way in which his character is singled out, through gestures or speech, through a sense that a unique destiny is a kind of stardom.

My landlady, Kyria Ioanna, is a terrifyingly good housekeeper: her parquet floors are polished to daunting perfection, the hang of the fussy lace embroideries on her furniture is straight as a marine's spine, the fussy crystal knicknacks everywhere are translucent, and the wooden tables gleam, free of dust, a condition almost impossible to achieve in Athens. The odd little functionless squares and pennants of cloth like oversized napkins hung on the backs and arms of furniture are taken very seriously at Kyria Ioanna's, and in other middle-class Greek living rooms. I am guessing that this is a middle-class memory of the great importance and value of fine fabric in late antiquity and the Middle Ages. Perhaps these are tapestries and silk tunics, which were so valuable that the Goths who sacked Rome demanded them as part of the booty, evoked on a smaller scale, as silver-plate place settings evoke grander silver services. One reason the ceremonial vestments of priests and altar cloths, stiff with gold and landscapes of embroidery, are so elaborate here is not just that they are decorative, but that they were once immensely valuable, they were part of the church's financial treasures, and evidence of its powerful patronage.

"Wait just a minute," she says before she comes to the door. "I am boiling *horta,*" an archetypal housewifely activity, these wild leaves braised with olive oil and garlic being the Greek equivalent of greens and pot likker. Kyria Ioanna has the mistrusting, tense look of many Greek adults, their eyes ever bright with vigilance. She also has the familiar short, square middle-aged body without curves, a solid mass with no dip or indent, a *doulapa* they call them, like the squat wooden wardrobes that substitute for built-in closets here. During our first meetings, although her face would relax slightly when she saw me, I was struck by the absence of the convention of the American smile of greeting. Here the initial glance is harsh, probing, prolonged; a smile has to be earned, there is no assumption that just your existence can be valued by a smile. There may be no reason to smile at your existence. This is true even of people you are not destined to meet, the frank assessing stare on the street, of which the stare of sexual invitation is only one variant. As you pass by a *kafeneio* at eleven in the morning, populated by men reading newspapers and drinking coffee, a mosquito net of stares drops over you, a world of unarticulated judgments.

Kyria Ioanna, though, and I have come to enjoy each other. She is a thoughtful, funny, strong, kind woman, with distinctively Greek manners, a combination of consideration, bluntness, and impulsive warmth, as well as keen estimation of the person opposite her. Greek courtesy has a fascination like no other. It is not a magnificent construction, a formal garden, like French courtesy, or a social contest following Marquis of Queensberry rules, like British courtesy, but a volatile fusion of refinement and passion, a tough but breakable ceramic fired at high temperatures.

I hand her the envelope, thick with drachma notes, which she counts in front of me, apologizing, and then she sweetens our transaction by pulling up a small table and setting on it a sweet, a glass of water, and a napkin. Today it is a piece of elegant chocolate *tourta*, left over from her son's thirty-second birthday party. The cake is voluptuous without being blowsy, and has the fine calibration of bitter and sweet that is the mark of good confectionary. She likes to hear an account of my month, where I have traveled, what I have read, and enjoys measuring the progress of my Greek. I have just read a novel set in Greece during the German occupation, and Kyria Ioanna, who was a child then, says she remembers the October day in 1944 when the Nazi flag was lowered on the Acropolis, and the Greek flag raised. She remembers, too, the savage moral dilemmas of the war, the neighbors starving on the street while people indoors listened, barely able to sustain their own lives. And the black marketeers who profited and the endless cunning thefts of anything valuable to sell, chaos and random death, followed not by peace but by the Greek civil war, sniper battles and midnight knocks on doors on the streets of our own neighborhood. I ask her if she remembers the funeral of the poet Palamas, one of the emblematic scenes of Greece's modern history, retold in histories and novels and children's books of Greece's World War II, and a familiar image through the photograph of the poet Angelos Sikelianos delivering the famous eulogy with an anguished expression on his theatrically handsome face. "In this coffin lies Greece," he began, and when he finished the crowd sang the forbidden national anthem, defying the German soldiers poised to shoot at demonstrating crowds. But it is not so much the literal event that makes this an emblematic modern Greek scene, but the different intensities of the details. It is a scene enacted by poets for many disparate reasons. Palamas is central because he was a demoticist, and the poet par excellence of modern Greece, not necessarily because of the aesthetic value of his poetry, but because of the role it played in inventing and defining modern Greek life, language, culture, and national identity. His work, like my modern dream books, is an encyclopedia of the key symbols, the icons of modern Greece. He, along with the other members of his circle, invented a way for modern Greece to proceed, finding parents, a house, and a heritage for this abandoned orphan. The history of modern Greece is above all the history of the forming of a nation. Knowing something of Palamas and his generation dramatizes what a cultural frontier Greece was, and how consciously they set about to settle it. It was not that there was no past, or that the Greeks were not its legitimate heirs because of ethnic dilution, as the nineteenth-century German scholar Fallmerayer, who asserted that the "race of Greeks" had died out due to invasions and intermarriage, claimed, but that the nation had not shaped the claims it would make on the past. It was there, but also beyond them, like my own heredity. The past was the Greek frontier, and the modern Greek sense of the past grows, above all, out of the invention and composition of their relation to that past. It was a task that had also faced the Christian Byzantines, who never worked out a consistent or satisfactory solution to the problem of their relationship to the polytheistic classical past. And it is a task still confronting the present-day Greeks, and Turks as well, whose cultures are intricately permeated by each other in still unacknowledged ways, regardless of their history of mutual hostility, like the "black" and "white" populations of the United States.

And poetry figures in this scene, not only because of Palamas, but because of the customary usefulness of poetry and song as coded free speech during periods of occupation—during the Ottoman period, Greece was a country that existed only in poetry and song lyrics; Greece itself was no more and perhaps no less than poetry. In this scene there is also the Greek mysticism toward the Greek language, which Greeks are taught to regard as sacred—in the Greek drama of revelation, the Hebrew father god abandons the stage to his Greek-speaking son, the Logos, the Greek word, Greek speech, the chosen expression of the Christian divinity. But perhaps the most tellingly Greek detail of all in this scene is that it is a funeral, like Easter, the signal Greek holiday, the trauma that acts as a trigger to the wild Greek appetite for and insistence on resurrection. Funerals hold a special place in both community and national ritual. They are moments of resolution, as in the many village stories of peace among feuding families accomplished over coffins, and moments of defiant calls for new life, like the funeral of George Papandreou during the junta years of military dictatorship (1967–74), when someone cried out, "Get up from your coffin, old man, and see what we have become," and, in 1994, shortly after I left Greece, the funeral of Melina Mercouri, surely the largest public funeral of modern Greece, which received a full day's television coverage, from the procession of the coffin through the streets of Athens, while rose petals rained down from balconies along the way, to the burial itself.

"You are reading more Greek literature than most Greek students I know," Kyria Ioanna is saying. "And I think that is so partly because of the war. We who lived through the occupation and the war have spoiled our children and grandchildren—we were so horrified at our own deprivations that we gave our children a dream of what we would have liked to have had ourselves. But some deprivation is no bad thing. Downstairs lives a widower and three children, all together in two rooms. The oldest boy is a lawyer, the girl is a teacher, the youngest boy just now in university. The older children help with the younger's expenses. My son, on the other hand, lives with us, for which he pays nothing. His meals are free, he contributes nothing to buying the food or cooking it, his laundry is done, I clean his room, we pay his medical bills. He has a big car, we have a small car. He has a CD player, a VCR. He has no idea of what it would mean to have a household of his own. He will be shocked when he is married, unless he marries a wife like me. But at least we haven't had the trouble with him that my sister-in-law Mimi has had with her Stavros. He insisted on going to university in London, but he doesn't work hard there. Because he is alone and has no help. I told Mimi she would have to go to him if she wants good grades."

"Go to him?" I ask, weighing the possibility she is joking, because of her speech on the values of adversity. "Yes," she says. "Go to him, like I did with my Elias—she should find him a good place to live, not something so uncomfortable as a dormitory, and when he has exams, she should be there to clean house and do his laundry and cook for him, and sharpen the pencils, so he can study more. Yes, Mimi doesn't do what she should for the boy, she should go to him."

THE *PLANETARKHIS*

"The ruler of the planet," Greeks call the American president, and I spent much of election night in the ballroom of a hotel off Syngrou Avenue in Athens, an avenue that runs from the temple of Olympian Zeus to the sea that was made famous by a George Seferis poem: "When you let your heart and thought become one/with the blackish river that stretches, stiffens and goes away;/Break Ariadne's thread and look!/The blue body of the mermaid," which, although Syngrou Avenue is now most famous as the marketplace for Athenian transvestites, is still a stirring description of how it feels to find the sea at the edge of tangled Athens.

The election night party is sponsored by the American embassy and the Hellenic-American chamber of commerce. In order to get into the ballroom, we must run a gauntlet of security checks, bags examined and bodies X-rayed as if we were boarding a plane. The crush is spectacular, some three thousand people are vying for breath here, since, the security man tells us, the two organizations failed to coordinate their RSVP lists. Inside, miniature Greek and American flags decorate the tables; the Republican table is watched over by a nearly life-sized poster of Dan Quayle; junior government ministers are working the crowds surrounded by burly bodyguards. The active anarchist organization "November 17" targets not only politicians, but prominent businessmen, so this crowd is dense with possible victims. "Wise men say only fools rush in," sings the middle-aged bandleader, in the accents of the island of Kefallonia, "but I can't help falling in love with you." Greece has followed this election with the special intensity of a country which has a large population of Greek-Americans, often employees of American companies, or retired people who have returned to their birthplaces, who live and cast their votes from here. Greece's absorption of American culture has a distinctive cast because American culture comes to Greece, not so much from the outside, but transmitted through relatives. The returning émigré, the taverna singer who risks her soul for a record contract with an American company, the attempt to arrange a marriage with an affluent American relative, all are staples of Greek literature, songs, and movies. I recently saw a comedy in which a young American woman on a ship was slapped onto a bed by a Greek man (which, in the film, she enjoyed, having at last encountered a real man), while the hero said, "At last, Greece on top of America."

The strong ties of the Greek and Greek-American communities, not to mention the presence of George Stephanopoulos at Clinton's side, ensures that the major Greek television channels will provide all-night coverage and commentary. A panel of experts, including one of the Papandreou sons, who has just returned from a month at the Harvard School of International Affairs, is emphasizing the importance of the African-American vote. A usually impassive news anchor cannot conceal a small ironic smile when he translates Little Rock—Mikros Lithos—into Greek. "Who will be the new *plane-tarkhis?*" someone murmurs, helplessly changing vantage points in the throng, while cameramen and Greek TV reporters trample militantly over us. I am struck by the faces in the crowd, the difference between the appearance of the Americans and their Greek guests. The Greeks have a national face, features recur, there is a striking current of physical relationship alive between these faces and these bodies. The Americans have some common expressions, but rarely common features. When you see them in contrast to an ethnically related people, you realize how synthetic this nation is; under the coarse overhead lights, the group of people sitting behind the long Democratic Party table remind me of an Edward Hopper painting, with their patchwork of features and lack of physical resemblance, the wakeful look of people who must find ways and reasons to be together by choice.

In the morning, the front-page photographs of Clinton in the papers share space with shots of Stephanopoulos, who will, if anything, dominate the news of the new administration for a time, as Greece reverts to a village in relation to him. His aunt from Evia is photographed leaving for America, with the hopeful text "Maybe she will bring us news"; and in the national style of Greece, his mother gives interviews to the glossy magazines to discuss her George. An editorial cartoon this morning shows a man in a foustanella holding a newspaper marked "Clinton's promises" and warning his wife, who wears a classical tunic, with a Greek proverb, "When you hear about many cherries, bring just a small basket." The wife replies, "I'm holding only a thimble."

LUST FOR A SAINT

"*Ti oraia mera,* what a beautiful day," echoes around me on this brilliantly sunny early November morning, on the island of Aegina, the feast of Saint Nektarios, which is the last truly out-of-doors feast until spring, and unofficially marks that we are now to perceive ourselves as entering fall and winter, even though I did swim just a day ago. The ceremonies for Nektarios go on all night, from about 5:00 P.M. the previous day, all-night vigils being a mark of spiritual merit here. People have already gotten up at dawn to kiss the saint's tomb, and the bus on the way to the church has standing room only. I wedge in, just behind the driver. The passengers cross themselves, elaborating the cross three times as they pass the town cemetery. The men wear sprigs of basil in their buttonholes, a common sight on Greek Orthodox feast days. The monastery is built on one of those hills whose overhang makes the roads of island Greece so narrow. A small homely taverna faces it—the site asks for a building that will live within the folds of this land that looks like dough kneaded by a god, while the walls should be of some earth color that will not argue with the lion-colored landscape. Instead, the furious and distinctively retroactive Greek ambition came into

play, and the architect apparently attempted to copy Istanbul's Saint
Sofia; Agios Nektarios is still unfinished, but the driver tells me that
it is nevertheless the largest church in Greece. The walls are a gar-
ish orangey-yellow, windows outlined in red, and the building sits
bulbously on its site like a raw onion someone tossed on the ground
realizing it had a bad center. The taverna across the way is filled with
people drinking beers on the outdoor veranda, having completed
their obligations to the saint. *"Khronia polla,* many years to you," says
the policeman directing traffic, greeting us with the standard Greek
festival wish. A golden crozier rests on the ledge under one car's
rear windshield. People are thronging the parking lot and the path
spiraling up to the monastery entrance, dressed in various styles.
One woman is wearing a sequin-covered jacket and brocade skirt,
as if she had just come from a nightclub. And there are clusters of
either widows or pious women wearing black dresses, scarves, and
stockings. There are no little black dresses in Greece; it is not the
same color as in Paris or New York, where its purpose is to give a
sculptural line to the body. In the Byzantine world these women's
ideas of clothes descend from, rich colors were the privileges of the
royal and the wealthy—black, which did not show stains or dirt,
was the cloth of those without status, the abased, likely to do dirty
work, and unable to pay for the service of maintaining stain-free
clothes, which must have been a mighty labor, as you can see from
catching occasional glimpses in the countryside of women doing
laundry in rivers. That white should have been the baptismal color
is not evidence of universal abstract symbolism, but of recognition
of the sheer physical difficulty of keeping it clean.

The crowd is of all ages, although teenagers are the least represented, and the elderly dominate. But there are parents with young
children in their arms, some young couples, some mothers with
ten- and eleven-year-olds. There are also the political pilgrims,
high-ranking military officials, well-dressed women and men in
suits, whose hairstyles and publicly graceful carriage show them
used to leading processions and being photographed as they are led

into the monastery through a separate entrance from the crowds that the police herd through the narrow main entrance. Streamers striped in Greek blue and white and Greek flags flutter in the breeze, and booths are set up at the foot of the huge monastery. One sells dolls hanging from their curly blond hair off ropes criss-crossing the booth, pacifiers in their mouths. Other booths hawk radios and cameras, coarse cut-glass vases, round trays of halva and baklava scored into individual pieces. You can hear the amplified singing of the liturgy all the way down in the parking lot. On the path up to the monastery, people are sitting on the ground, their crutches beside them, while pilgrims who are obviously mentally troubled are led up the paths by brothers, sisters, or parents. This practice is a living demonstration of a Greek idiom for madness, dating at least from the Byzantine era, "He is for the *panegyri*," when the mentally ill were brought to medieval fairs probably very much like this one, in hopes of a magical cure. A man who is bearded and dirty, with a heroically stony hermit's face, sits on a portable stool—I overhear him telling a schoolteacher who has paused to talk with him that he spends his life going from *panegyri* to *panegyri;* as the teacher descends the path, the old man calls out, "Many years to you, Mr. Teacher, Mr. Teacher and Catechumen." Just before the monastery entrance a woman is camped, selling candles, incense, and evil-eye charms.

The line to go into the church, the special goal being to kiss Nektarios's tomb, is enormous, at least an hour and a half's wait. I catch phrases from the Sermon on the Mount, powerfully loud, but violently garbled by the audio system. In the liturgy, people hunger and thirst, people are meek. In this least selfless of crowds, how-ever, I am the closest thing available to someone meek. With an instinct for creating suffering where none needs to exist, and then exalting it, the crowd pushes, shoves, stamps on, and makes all its members as uncomfortable and claustrophobic as possible. Old ladies aggressively push each other back and forth, and every time there is a tiny movement ahead, there is a violent surge in the crowd, nearly knocking people off their feet. When I reach the entrance to the monastery church itself, decorated with palm fronds, bouquets of carnations wrapped in foil, and a plastic Greek flag, I am nearly pushed down the stairs, falling apologetically onto a woman in front of me. She is holding a foil-wrapped bottle of olive oil as an offering to the saint, who needs an ample supply for the hundreds of gilt lamps that drop tears of light from the ceilings of his church. If anyone fell or felt sick, he would be trampled, and any accident under these circumstances would produce an enormous death toll. Once we are inside, the crowd becomes even more frantic, obdurately trampling on each other in order to snatch lustfully at the holy bread a priest is handing out, to lay flowers and money on Nektarios's tomb, and to kiss the tomb as passionately as if it were a husband. I smell that off-key smell of singed cloth, and put out the beginnings of a fire lit by a pilgrim's candle on the elbow of my sweater. I walk off, picking hot wax off the wool. Auto-da-fé, *actus de fides,* an act done from faith.

A Nymph's Temple

"You bitch, you betrayed C. C. Capwell!" I hear as I set out for the Aegina harbor from the house of the brilliant poet where I am a guest. She is one of the world's great talkers, a coloratura teller of jokes in many languages, and the only true mystic I have ever known, since her mysticism emerges from a sense that the divine is unknowable, and is uncorrupted by the secret certainties of underlying dogmatism that make so many mystics seem like spiritual pornographers, covering with a transparent black negligee an anatomy they know in advance is naked. She is also a connoisseur of soap operas, and rails joyfully in Spanish, French, Greek, Russian, and English, against whoever plots against her preferred characters, such as C. C. Capwell.

All along the way to the harbor, I am congratulated with golden smiles on the election of Clinton. "It is good for the world that you have such a clever, sincere, youthful president," someone says to me. I stop for a coffee, which comes accompanied by paper sugar packets stamped with images of Delphi and the theater at Epidaurus. Moored at the harbor's edge are rows of cleanly painted blue-and-white boats, some with the general talismanic names of Greek

boats, *Tria Adelphia,* Three Brothers, *Zoodokhos Pygi,* Life-Giving
Spring, named after the icon of the Virgin Mary sitting in her fountain, and *Agios Nikolaos,* after the patron saint of sailors. Local names
crop up too, like *Agios Nektarios,* and *Aphaia,* the daughter of Zeus,
whose temple I am going to visit today. I can't find my waiter, preoccupied probably with the late coffee-and-newspaper crowd, so I
go inside to see if I can order a spinach pie to go with my coffee. A
thin, flat-faced man gets up from behind the bar. Is anyone cooking
yet, I ask, but he only looks alarmed. I try English and nothing happens. "*Alvanos,*" he says, only Albanian, and I see he has the starved
look Albanians here don't seem to lose, even when they gain
weight, the eyes that meet yours as a fish's would, observant, but
without creating a human link. The lives of deprivation and violence
Albanians live in Albania—Tirana is said to be ruled by gangs who
thrive off petty theft and murders—and the mistrust with which
they are regarded here, seen as importing criminality across the
border, have created this distinctive expressionless look. I thank
him, catching sight of a poster behind him of Clark Gable carrying
off Vivian Leigh in *Osa Pernei o Anemos,* and head for the bus to
Aphaia's temple.

The stationmaster is playing cards, but breaks off his game to
wave me toward a bus with two pairs of huge eyes painted on the
right- and left-hand sides of its windshield. A few people are on the
bus, a handful of schoolkids, some old ladies in black with town
marketing, an old man with the unwieldy materials for some car-
pentry project. The driver puts a small boy down at a field across
from a tiny school no bigger than a mountain chapel. A girl of about
twelve is sitting behind the driver, who talks and laughs with her.
When she steps off the bus at her stop, the driver remembers he had
a favor to ask her. He calls out to her, reaching down between his
feet, and hands her a carton of eggs, saying, "Wait just a minute, my
golden one. Would you please drop these off with my wife?" We
drive through groves of pistachio trees with their childlike scale,
Aegina's chief crop, along the steep narrow roads island geography

compels. Near the temple, there is a passage so narrow that cars can only go single file, and eight cars retrace their passage back downhill to give the bus the right-of-way.

Pine trees frame this temple of Zeus's daughter, their blue-gray cones hanging from their branches like votive offerings. A woman is feeding a small colony of hens and roosters at the foot of the temple. My entrance fee is waved aside in President Clinton's honor. It is a mark of the change of seasons that the tourists today, except for me, are all Greek. "Mama," shouts a little boy, racing ahead, "can we go inside the temple?" The chance to linger and circulate, rare at temples during the high tourist season, tempts me to think about what makes this temple seem so brilliantly sited. Height is important—you must have the sense of revelation that height gives to the religious, the sense that you have arrived as a pilgrim at a place where many perspectives meet, where you can come close to seeing everything. Sound is equally important, at every temple site I have visited. A rarefied silence, broken by the powerful secret language of the winds in the pine trees, as there is here, or the grand recitations of the waters, as at the site on Thasos. The gods must always speak at a temple site, in sounds we can hear but not understand, sounds we can only interpret. And finally there must be a sense not only of revelation in the site, but of mystery, of continuation into places you can't see, into unknown worlds. Here the waters of the narrow Saronic Gulf move beyond the mountains of Aegina, between them and the Greek mainland to a destination you can't see; blue water and light stretch to infinity, as soundless boats sail past, backed by immovable cliffs that look like temples themselves, pieces of divine design. This is a place that makes the world seem like a dream, a real world that is also a dream of itself.

A mother and two children who are highly amused with themselves stop to talk to me. "We just jaunted over for the day from Piraeus. I left my husband a note to tell him we would be in Aegina, I just left him a note, American style, American style," the wife says delightedly. The little girl is hungry, so I give her an apple, as she prattles about the horse-drawn carriages on the harbor, pretty little pastiche hansoms, pulled by horses whose bridles are garlanded with flowers, and who look a bit like modern actresses attempting nineteenth-century costumes. In the evening in the streets behind the port you can see them going home to their drivers' small pastures, no longer public, but private horses. The little girl's ambition is to ride in one, just like a blond actress named Aliki, "our national star, *i ethniki mas star*," in her movie called *Holiday in Aegina*. The little boy, wearing the comically adult-looking glasses of Greek children, is cheerfully restless. He darts over and hugs his mother, then rushes off again to dangle from a tree. His mother calls out patiently, "Get down, Bobbi," but he changes his name in midair. "I'm not Bobbis," he says, "I'm Archimedes, I'm Archimedes."

On my way back to Aegina town, I have quite a lot of trouble not getting married in one village, where a lonely taverna keeper announces that he, after years of bachelorhood, may very well be interested in getting married, and has fixed on me as his choice. Having disentangled myself, I am followed through the village by a man on a motorcycle, who says to me, "Here's what I want to do. Let's go for a ride in the mountains and see the scenery and then have sex." I explain I have a *desmos,* a bond elsewhere, and he says, "What, a husband?" No, I say. "Then why not have two? Look how handsome I am," he says, running his hands over his torso. "Don't you find me handsome?" he asks, with the uncanny sophistic skill of the Greek *kamaki,* or harpoon, as these boys are called, for asking questions whose answers can only be interpreted as either insults or assents, and used to achieve the desired result. I walk away from him through the village and take a stand at the bus stop, trying not to laugh, because I am remembering a folk song about the klephts, the idolized Greek bandits, who harried the Ottoman Turks when they were good and harried the Greeks when they weren't. "The klephts are sitting, sitting beneath the plane tree./They wash, they groom themselves, and look at themselves in the mirror./They observe their fine features, they observe their gallantry./Demos takes one look, the *pallikaria* five, and Kostas the proud looks fifteen times./And out of his pride and out of his gallantry/he doesn't go home in the evening, he doesn't go back to his family,/but stayed up in the mountains and high ridges."

When the *kamaki* has given up, I take a path up to the cottage-sized chapel overlooking the sea, knowing I have time before the bus comes. A tiny taverna is perched like a bird's nest on a ledge overlooking this village's dramatic sea, going up in white flames on the rocks. Strange how in one village the sea shows war, in another, peace. A woman is baking bread in an outdoor oven and a very pregnant dog walks up the path with me. The chapel is Saint John's, as its principal icon shows. The door is loosely fastened by wire, and inside, the debris of God's housekeeping that women do here is scattered on a small table—fresh candles, matches, olive oil, and at the foot of the altar, a tiny vase of fresh flowers. Outside there is a small cemetery. The graves are decorated with plastic wreaths of flowers, and set into the tombstones are old photographs of country couples, the men in peaked caps, the women with black shawls draped over their heads. Marble tablets lie flat over the graves, carved with funeral messages, looking as if someone had left a note for the deceased on a memorandum pad. The very banality of the messages—"We think of you far away, and wish you a good journey"; "Though you are gone, you are never out of our thoughts"—is a measure of being alive. Only the living can enact banality, it is out of the range of death. The coffins, I think, must have been brought up here over this rough, hilly track by donkey carts.

In the afternoon, I meet my Aegina hostess and her other guests for the last swim of the season; the water temperature is changing, from the slight champagne chill the Aegean has even on the hottest summer day, to hint at an approaching numbing coldness. We eat cheese pies and drink one of the stony Greek whites, a laconic wine, on a beach known for a single Doric column that overlooks it. This beach was familiar to Samuel Gridley Howe, the husband of the author of the "Battle Hymn of the Republic," who took part in the

Greek War of Independence, and found employment for the hungry in building a mole here, which still does its work. When Howe's project was finished in 1828, he wrote in his diary, "I have enriched the island of Aegina by a beautiful, commodious, and permanent quay, and given support to seven hundred poor." The passing of the afternoon makes a fairy tale for us; as the sun sets, spilling great golden sheaves of light onto the darkening sea, the moon rises, a distillation of pearl, in a perfect balance of day and night—for about a quarter of an hour, we swim between the sun and the moon.

I look around the table at everyone who has just come out of the sea, faces smoothed by the swimming, their lips with the faint unconscious purely physical and private smile that people have when they've just been kissed. We have that involuntary physical intimacy that irradiates a group of people who have just finished a beautiful swim. An outsider could look around at us and know what each person looks like after sex. We all look as if we had just made love.

Polytechnic Night

The morning paper features an ad for a car called the Passat Macedon, photographed against a backdrop of a marble relief of Alexander the Great riding on Bucephalus—"It has all the qualities to conquer you," promises the slogan.

Tonight is the anniversary of the student protest against the junta at the University of Athens, the Athens Polytechnic, on November 17, 1973, when the military drove tanks into the crowds of protesters, and several students were killed. I have seen the grave of one of them, buried with honor at the Protonekrotafeio, the great central cemetery. Many people have told me this was the turning point of the junta years, at least symbolically, that this was the moment the junta was seen by both the right and the left wing as an enemy of Greece itself, killing the Greek future. The memory of this day is such a grave one that it is commemorated by an official nationwide school holiday.

A number of people have also told me to stay at home tonight, and as much as possible today, since it is a day when anti-American feeling runs high, since the United States supported the Greek junta and played a shadowy role in planning the coup that put it in place.

Warnings have come from enough people, both acquaintances and real friends, for me to take them seriously. One well-known student participant in these protests, who is now a radio commentator and author, is interviewed in the paper. When asked if the legacy of the 1973 Polytechnic is still alive, he answers, "Yes . . . like Alexander the Great." An impossible, and sometimes faintly demeaning, comparison is often drawn between the current generation of students, whose moral world is more ambiguous, and the ones of that moment of stark and utter heroism when what was calculated was sheer risk, not the patient estimation of good and evil embedded in each other that the work of peace requires. But it has always been harder to work out how to live a good life than how to die a good death.

I see on the news that people have been laying wreaths since early morning on the site of the Polytechnic building. The youth vote is being courted on all sides; the opposition party is sending representatives to visit the site and make speeches, the majority party has promised a large donation to restore the Polytechnic building, badly in need of repair, partly because of student riots last year.

On my way to see a friend with a new baby, I buy some quinces to make the most magical of Greco-Turkish dishes, quinces stuffed with lamb, cinnamon, and rice. A neighbor stops me, to admire a necklace I am wearing of multicolored stars. "Is it from Macedonia?" she wants to know; the Macedonia issue is at fever pitch, and the stars the Greeks see at the moment are all stars of Vergina, like the ones from King Philip's grave treasures, whose outline has been adopted by the new republic for its flag.

On the corner of Hymettus Street, a men's clothing store offers Yves St. Laurent accessories. In front of the big glass window, a *gria,* an old lady wearing the widow's black dress, stockings, and head scarf, is selling flowers from brightly colored plastic buckets, and from a huge basket on wheels, sesame-coated *koulouria,* the bread rings that are eaten throughout the Near and Middle East, wherever the Ottomans governed. A man walking home with loaves of bread is hailed frantically from a car—"*Yia sou,* my Sotiris, *yia sou.*" Sotiris waves back: "How's it going, mine, how's it going, you great big one?" Greek affection is possessive; a family is often just called something that translates as "my ones."

The baby, who likes to slow dance, will not have a name until he is baptized, a year or maybe two years from now. For the moment, he is called Kourkoumbini, after a popular pastry dusted with powdered sugar. He will be called this exactly as if it were a given name, and I enjoy it so much that I would find it a wrench to give it up for a conventional Yiannis or Constantine. There are different rationales for this practice of the delayed name; in some parts of Greece, it was a safeguard against evil spirits, who might come and take the tender child if they had something as concrete as a name to go by. In Zakinthos, unbaptized babies were called Drakos, or Drakaina, Dragon, something far less appetizing than Kourkoumbini, in order to frighten off evil spirits who might be tempted to interfere. Kourkoumbini, like all Greek babies, lies between East and West even on his changing table. Nicknamed for a Turkish pastry, he sleeps on Mickey Mouse crib sheets, with Winnie the Pooh wallpaper overhead, while on his changing table, the Vaseline and Johnson's baby powder share the surface with an icon of the Archangel Michael. My friends fiddle with their television set, which gives information in Russian, Greek, French, Czech, Italian, and Magyar. A game show is playing—when the male contestant calls out the right answer, the host shouts, "Triumph! Triumph!" and they kiss each other on both cheeks. My friends invite me to stay for supper and tell me there's a *drakulariko* (after Dracula), a monster movie, on television, but I am nervous about Polytechnic night, and go home, where I amuse myself by reading an advice column in a women's magazine. A sixteen-year-old wonders whether to sleep with her boyfriend. If they break up, and she is no longer a *parthena,* who will marry her? Another asks how to stop her boyfriend from making so much noise during sex—her neighbors come to their windows and call out, "Shame to you, we all have children at home."

The adviser tells her, apparently following Greek convention, that men are usually more rowdy during sex than women. Another woman of thirty-two, who has had a series of bitter experiences in love, asks whether or not to accept a proposal that has come her way through a matchmaker, and to make the kind of marriage her grandmother did.

The morning news makes me glad I chose to stay in—Polytechnic night was full of violence. Some five hundred self-styled "anarchists" ran through the city center, smashing shop windows and throwing Molotov cocktails into the central post offices and various banks. They bombed shops, bus-ticket kiosks, and a New Democracy (conservative) Party office building. Twenty-six people have been arrested and riot police are posted outside the Polytechnic until further notice.

Newspapers here could offer a daily schedule of demonstrations, as they do television programs. The week's protests go on— Greek farmers demonstrate against the government's agricultural policies, blocking the Athens-Lamia highway, spilling milk in the streets of Thessaloniki, and blocking entrances to that city. Schoolteachers demonstrate outside the Ministry of Education, in a "severe confrontation" between them and the deputy minister of education. The medical school students demonstrate, ending in a fight between them and the riot police. According to one newspaper, a student leader called police officials to say that the police were obstructing a peaceful demonstration and threatening the students, and the officials replied, "Good," giving the special squads implicit permission to start the beatings—women demonstrators said the police especially singled them out. I look in Artemidorus to see how beatings were imagined in the second century—the dreams of beating are favorable, he writes, if you strike only people you rule, with the exception of your wife. To dream of beating her is a sure sign that she is committing adultery.

I am going out for a drink with a neighbor's relative, a computer programmer who lives a few streets over. He was born and raised in

this neighborhood, went to the local school, and has lived his entire
adult life on the next street over, though he keeps his father's house
in a Peloponnesian village for weekends. I seize the opportunity to
ask him about the names of some of the streets we are walking
through to the café; it is profoundly disorienting to move through
streets named for cities and historical events you know nothing
about, as if space itself were full of conversation and references you
can never grasp. But Christos doesn't know what the streets com-
memorate either, or why the district is called Pangrati, or how to
translate into Greek the café's Italian name. They just are what they
are. We stop to look at the headlines of the afternoon newspapers
displayed on poles at the news kiosk—there is still a drama here in
the changing headlines of the newspapers, an urgency expressed
like the old-fashioned newsboys' cries of "Extra, Extra!," a sense
that fates can alter absolutely between morning and afternoon.
These are full of pictures of the Patriarch of Constantinople, who
has been on a twenty-day trip to Greece, based on a yacht owned by
the billionaire London-based shipping owner John Latsis. I have
some letters to mail, so we stop outside the post office, where the
domestic and international boxes are marked, to my permanent
pleasure, *esoterico* and *exoterico*.

We settle at a table inside the smoke-filled café, and order *mezedes*
and a Cypriot red wine called Othello. Preparations are under way
for a day of national demonstration about the issue of the name of
Macedonia, and Christos is livid about the new republic's declaration
of its name. "They are robbers, they are thieves," he says. "Suppose I
just camped in your apartment and said it was my apartment." "But,"
I say, "that is not what they are doing, that is what you are worried
that they will do."

"We will go to war if they keep the name, we will fight them,"
Christos says, hitting the table with his palm. "Do you really think a
war would be more fruitful than a political solution?" I want to
know. "The European Community does not support Greece's abso-
lutist stand on the name, and Greece is straining its relationship

with valuable allies. This doctrinal insistence on the name seems to me to be trying to practice politics as if the world were ideal, and not one of imperfect compromise. If their using the name Macedonia seems to you to constitute a territorial claim, then isn't this the moment to get them to show their professed good will, to search together for a compromise name, and to firmly establish the borders with a treaty signed by all the European Community?"

"Pay attention, pay attention," Christos hisses, jabbing his forefinger in the air. "Macedonia is Greek. Do you think Alexander the Great was a Slav? What good will a treaty do; everyone knows where the borders are, and borders won't stop their aggression. They want Thessaloniki."

"But if they do," I say, "the name is not a piece of magic that will magically secure the borders. You will just keep yourselves shouting across the borders like children having tantrums, 'Is not Macedonia.' 'Is too.' " But of course in this part of the world, I think to myself, names are treated as magic, personal names, place names. A person's name is a territorial matter, makes a claim to patronage, or states a claim on some property, attribute, or ambition. The Ottoman Turks for a long period wouldn't permit any Greeks but the wealthy, and often pro-Turkish, Phanariot Greeks to name their sons Alexander. Some Byzantine Greeks took it as an evil premonition that the imperial family had "run out of names" and that a Constantine's coming to the throne again in 1449 was the signal of the fall of what a Constantine had founded. And of course, Greece has itself made territorial claims through names. Maps published at the turn of the century, when the Ottoman Empire was tottering, identified great swatches of Turkey as Greece. And there is the case of the Greek border with southern Albania, which, whatever you think about the crude resolution of the border dispute, is a case in which Greece makes its territorial claim through a name. "Do you think that Skopje is using the name Macedonia in the same way that right-wing Israelis call the West Bank 'Judaea and Samaria' and that Greece uses the name 'northern Epirus'?" I ask with tactless curiosity. "It is not the same at all," he answers. "Macedonia is Greek. And so is northern Epirus. It has always been so, and will always be, whatever the usurpers of our history may claim."

We find a way to change the subject, but Christos gives me another glimpse of the politics of the Greek *moyen homme*. He is talking about Polytechnic night, and offers his solution to the disorder. The reason these anarchists run wild through the streets on November 17, he says, is that the Greek public is not yet ready to face the real solution, which is to have the MAT (literally, unit for the "restoration of order") riot police surround the Polytechnic and without interference, beat some of the perpetrators to death. It is a surprise to hear the tone of the junta in the voice of a young man, but the junta could not have been simply imposed from outside, but represented one genuine political impulse in a country which has an authoritarian tradition, at times paternalistic, and at others dictatorial.

"You must," says Christos, walking back with me through the series of tiny squares that make little villages and definite sections of all Athens neighborhoods, where even now that the nights are chilly, people prefer to sit outside, "as a poet, scatter flowers on the paths of people's difficult lives." As he waxes lyrical, he is pushing me against the wall of an apartment building. "It would be hard for me to judge," I say. "You'd probably have to read some of my poems." "No," he says, "I'm sure of it. We must all be grateful to the poets for the rose petals they leave on our rocky roads." I am doing my best to convey disinterest, but he is much more interested in what he is doing than what I am doing.

A series of rather mercantile compliments is produced, like putting coins in a jukebox. He arrives at "You are beautiful." "Especially," he says, "I like your hair. It is the kind of hair I myself would have, if I were a woman."

How It Always Is

"Naive English-speaking girl wanted for lessons," says one leaflet in the current new crop on the telephone pole that stands on one edge of the little squares that make *quartiers* of Athens neighborhoods. Leaflets are everywhere, ingeniously pasted on bank building pillars and on street lamps, advertising the openings of new clubs, benefits to save the Greek foxes, phone sex—"Choose from these story options: 'The Mermaid's Secret,' 'Naked Crete,' 'Sensual Days on Mykonos.'" There are black-bordered leaflets announcing funerals or memorial services for the dead: "Our much-loved and adored husband, father, grandfather, brother and uncle, lawyer, MP of Akhaia, and minister. We are burying him tomorrow at the Holy Church of the Sleep of the Virgin. Wife: Alexandra. The children. The grandchildren. Sister. The nephews and nieces. The rest of the relatives."

The dead are remembered nine days, then forty days after their deaths, then in cyclical ceremonies, all for the rest of the departed soul, whom Greeks seem to expect to be restless—the dead legitimately return to earth during the forty-day period between Easter and Pentecost, and unlawfully and unpredictably as vampires. There is a whole range of vampire lore, anecdotes, remedies, curses. One of the most feared curses used to be "May the earth not eat you." Vampires seem to function as a kind of underworld, criminal class of the resurrected—a body that hasn't decomposed could be a sign of sainthood, but also that the deceased has become a vampire. They also seem to be an underbelly version of the much idealized Greek family, since their principal victims in the stories I've been told are family members, and since they often seem to be people who died with unresolved family quarrels. Vampirism here is a brilliantly simple metaphor for the tragic side of the blood tie.

While I am reading the new crop of leaflets, I feel myself being handled from the waist. I look down and to the left and see a charming middle-class lady running the fabric of my knit sweater between her hands. "Marvelous sweater," she says, turning me to an angle more convenient for her, "is it made in China?" "No," I say, as she outlines the design. "Flowers," she says, "a panel of flowers. It looks easy to clean. How much did you pay for it?"

"Not much," I say. "And where did you buy it?" "New York," I say. "Well, I like it. Simple. And sexy. Have a good week," she says, strolling off with one of the many variations of Greek benedictions on time, which are made for days, weeks, months, and seasons.

I skid on something underfoot as I reach the corner—a late fig that had fallen onto the pavement from the tree above. A new building is going up on this street, next to a pretty neoclassical with a substantial courtyard, which is being punished for its refusal to be part of a big apartment block by having one built loudly next door, the right-hand balconies leaning menacingly over its defiant little roof. The streets are in a constant process of repair even when buildings are not going up—soil and stony rubble, exactly as on the edges of cleared fields, obstruct your passage on your block. You need to be nimble to live in Athens, compact and nimble. The city is always aspiring to be a village again, always veined with ruins, ancient and modern. On the sidewalks of the small streets, grandmothers are having friendly chats, wearing bathrobes and slippers.

At a *kafeneio,* the men are wearing pullovers now as they drink their coffee and read the papers. A radio is playing, and I hear as I pass a broadcast of the elderly novelist Dido Sotiriou, reading from her popular memorial novel about the Greek community in Turkey during the Asia Minor conflict, *Blood-soaked Earth.* Many people whose taste I respect have told me that they dislike the book, for its florid style and the simple-minded political analysis undertaken by the narrator. But for an outsider, it records not only an event but a popular way of remembering the event—and the popular way of remembering an event, the style in which imagination acts on remembered events, is part of the structure of political policy. Sotiriou's way of remembering is like looking through one of those overwrought turn-of-the-century photograph albums, covered with velvet, marked with living dead scent of dried lavender, too sumptuous, but containing real images. And she reads in the same innocently florid style, as if her words were a kind of mourning jewelry, onyx brooches a little gross in their deliberate elegy, but containing real strands of the lost beloved's hair. Outside our local police station stand the usual covey of officers on guard duty, holding machine guns. I take a shortcut through the small park in front of the Evangelismos, Annunciation, Hospital. A man is sleeping on a bench, one hairy muscular arm dangling to the ground, the other flung across his eyes to shield them from the light. He is wearing a dress printed with yellow roses and a pair of high heels.

At a hotel near the restaurant where I am meeting Marina and her father for lunch, an old lady is looking for a taxi. She refuses to move out of the way when a minibus from the hotel drives up to the corner to park. "You'll drive foreigners," she says, and spits, "but not your own people. I won't move for you." The driver leans out of the window and asks her sweetly to move out of his path. "I'm laughing at whatever you say," she retorts bitterly.

Marina and her father are drinking ouzo at a table in the sunshine. They are arguing over a proposed change in the law that would allow Greek stores to stay open on Sundays. Her father is vehemently for it—"It will be good for business," he says, "and besides, the merchants should be free to choose what they will do. Why should they be interfered with?" The church is violently opposed, and so is Marina. "And if a merchant doesn't want to open on Sundays, but everyone else does? How can he compete? Anyway, we should not let business rule our lives, and take a place that culture and music and food and conversation should occupy, we don't want lives like the Americans who do nothing but work, freedom is everything to Greeks." "And I say we are not free when we are told when we may open our own businesses and when we may not."

It is chilly, but Greeks prefer to sit outside unless it is actually snowing. All around are cries of *Khronia polla,* many years, because today is the name day of all the men named Nicholas, who are being congratulated by their lunch companions. Nicholas is the patron saint of the Greek navy; sailors and ships receive special blessings today. "Were you afraid during the earthquake the other night?" her father asks me. There had been an earthquake measuring 6 on the Richter scale. I had been reading a novel when the room began gently but firmly to elongate and compress, as if it were made of elastic someone was stretching. I could see the room's disproportionately large chandelier swaying, my laptop computer sliding a bit on its table, but the rocking had been gentle and stopped before I understood enough to be afraid.

"*Akhh,*" Marina says, turning the pages of a newspaper, "murders. Here is a man who thought his upstairs neighbor was making too much noise and went up in the elevator and killed him. And here is a man in Kavalla, who shot his mother to death and then killed himself. He was unmarried, and the authorities say he was afraid he would be the first to die, so his mother would be left alone in the world. *Akhh.* Well, at least Clinton is good news. He has Greeks around him, so he cannot hate the Greeks, like everyone else, because we refuse to let another race usurp our heritage, because we are not fooled by the tricks of people who are not Europeans but pretend to be. Here, we know who is who. I am Greek—I am Europe."

"And Clinton will not want war in the Balkans," says her father. "Or anywhere. He is a pacifist, you know. He would not fight in Vietnam." Very carefully, as you would replace an egg in a bird's nest, I say that he is not a pacifist. "What, you didn't know?" says Marina's father. "He is of the Baptist faith, and it is against their religion to go to war. This has always been against their religion." I dissent again, having done adequate time at youth crusades and revivals in the South to have known a number of fairly bloodthirsty Baptists, not to mention some who would be insulted by the suggestion that they preached pacifism; but my experience is as nothing to the man's belief in his belief, to the doctrinal national refrain, *panda einai etsi,* it is always this way.

Marina gives me a letter of introduction to an icon painter she knows on the island of Andros, where I am going for the weekend, and asks if I will be back in Athens for the nationwide day of Macedonia demonstrations. "Be back before then, you will never be able to travel on that day, and besides, it will give an interesting impression to you. The whole nation will be together, like villagers around a central square—even children's teachers will take them to the demonstrations." "It will be a national holiday?" I ask. "It doesn't have to be declared. It is a day for history itself, not stories about history. Anyway, my sister is a teacher, and there are many days when she doesn't have class, the teachers strike, the students strike. You know what she says is the motto of the Greek school? 'We also give lessons.' "

Later I meet Aura, who is taking me to a benefit reading given by a famous actress named Dandoulaki. She is waiting for me outside the theater, gloating with mischievous delight over the recently published results of a study of Greek sexuality. "One out of two women have at least one extramarital affair," she shouts like a joyous gospel, to the bemusement of passersby. "They must, my dear, they must. I did. Of course, then I married my affair. The study doesn't say about that. But the best of the study is this: Two out of six couples will develop affairs with people in their 'immediate family environment.'

I cannot tell you how many people I know who divorced to marry their sisters-in-law, and things like that. My dear, the Greek family is even closer than its reputation boasts. It's delicious."

Inside, she tells me, there are several generations of Greek art and thought, actresses and actors, singers, directors, dancers, writers. She introduces me to a famous woman novelist, author of a best-seller that made her considered a spokeswoman for her generation—the woman is thin and dark, wearing an expensive coat, projecting an air of important pessimism. I meet an actor appearing in a production of *Hamlet,* which conjures up unpredictable private images, since the Greeks pronounce it "Omelet," and a heavy-bearded essayist wearing a beautiful ring made of a Byzantine coin. There is a good deal of laughter over a recent interview with one of the handsomest of the new crop of actors, a promising romantic lead, who responded when asked a question in the past tense about Alexander the Great, "Who dares to speak of great Alexander in this tense?" A crush of television cameras and magazine photographers record the scene—many of the conversations I overhear are decorated with ornamental phrases in English, in a way that reminds me of E. M. Forster's British intelligentsia in novels like *A Room With a View,* setting Italian expressions into English conversations. The men stare sternly, almost confrontationally, when they are introduced, but this style no longer unnerves me. They don't follow the convention of smiling during the introduction—instead they look at you with an accusing expression, and say they rejoice to meet you, if they are older, or *yia sas,* if they are younger or bohemian. But the smile doesn't accompany the meeting—military installations don't smile. The women, on the other hand, are frenetic, aggressive laughers, who make the room flash with inscrutable and unpunishable mockeries.

It is striking that there is no outside to this gathering, no meetings, only reunions, another reminder of the dramatic difference in scale between a country this size and America. "Everyone here has slept with everyone else," Aura whispers to me wickedly. The actress Katia Dandoulaki, who wears jewelry magnificently, as if the pieces were decorations for heroism, begins to read from a volume of poetry. Like all Greek actors and actresses, she has to work constantly to make a living, doing television and film work at the same time she is starring in a play. Even important figures in Greek theater regularly appear in TV soap operas, as does Dandoulaki. It must create a completely different set of problems for these performers, whose faces are ubiquitous here, who are never out of the public eye, not so much in their private but in their professional lives. Dandoulaki has a superb voice, with a landscape of variation in the timbre and inflection: she is reading an elegiac poem, and is making full use of the language's sense of radical separation between past and present; Greek verbs are accented differently and change forms in the present and the past tense. She shapes the planes of her cheeks and the muscles at the corners of her mouth the way a coloratura shapes every note, and she has a distinctive way of crafting a facial expression so that it lingers for a moment, almost separate from her own features, before it disappears into another invisible but ongoing existence. It is another lesson in the different quality of the Greek school of acting. Aura's husband, a Dutch cinematographer, tells me he is constantly aware of the peculiarity I perceive. There is a sense less of communicating individual personality than of revealing a concealed divinity; the player doesn't seem to develop a character through time from the interaction of event and personality, but instead to incarnate, to be the vehicle for the presence of something timeless. I think back to the Feast of the Metamorphosis in August. For us, heirs of the western Romans, the idea of metamorphosis comes through Ovid, and conjures up change, permeability, transformation. But the Greek image is in the repeated icons of the metamorphosis of the human Jesus, revealed as eternal god—perhaps the model for this acting style, the ultimate feat of theater.

A Dream of a Bodiless One

"The Garden of the Mad," reads a taverna sign just outside the port of Rafina, a place made familiar to people who haven't been here through a song by Vasilis Tsitsanis, a songwriter so beloved that many rank him with General Makriyiannis and the painter Theophilos, or the anonymous composers of the "demotic" folk song, as one of the wellsprings of modern Greek art. Tsitsanis, considered perhaps the greatest master of the bouzouki, was also the great witness in song of the German occupation, the *katokhi*. There may be Greeks who cannot sing four or five of the most famous Tsitsanis songs, but I didn't meet them; he is still such a presence in Greek music that a journalist conducted an interview with him in 1993, though he died in 1963. The Rafina song tells lightheartedly of a crab family broken up by a seductive bream, who takes Mrs. Crab to Rafina while her little crabs cry on the beach. In a way, the crab husband, who limps awkwardly to Rafina to retrieve his wife, and the pleasure-loving she-crab, who stays up all night and plays in the shallow waters with her new love, are like the lame Hephaestus and faithless Aphrodite, reduced to the scale of toys. Two can always play that game of puppet and master, even in mod-

ern Greek theogony; intense bargaining with saints can be overheard in churches, even with Christ and his mother—*Panayitsa mou,*
someone will preface a prayer, my darling little Virgin, and *Khris-
touli mou,* my dear little Christ, grant me this. I find the ferry for
Andros, and the ticket taker waves me into the first-class salon,
though I have only a second-class ticket. "I am the only Greek who
keeps his smile in the winter, everyone else will make a *moutra,* a
sulky frown, until the spring. But I smile, because we have Greece
all to ourselves now until spring, and I say, let us take the opportunity to see for ourselves what the first-class salon is like to sit in."

We dock at Gavrion, a listless, bored-looking port, lined with
cheap harbor-view restaurants, and one pretty dovecote, a characteristic building of Andros and neighboring Tinos. The coastal road
is the usual Greek meander, the kind of road that always reminds
me of the pattern we call "Greek key." The bus is filled with grandchildren coming for the weekend, a number of whom are dropped
off at their front doors, before it continues, pulled up and down and
through the loops and curves like an embroidery needle. When I
visited Paros, I saw an island made of marble, but Andros is made of
stone and silk. It is a piece of gray rock, veined with three fertile
valleys, famous for its stone walls, medieval defense towers, and
silky perfect spring waters, the famous Sariza waters of the village
of Arikia. It was also, literally, an island of silk, since from the
eleventh century to the eighteenth it was a center of silk production. The prayer I had read on the ferry to Naxos, exhorting the little silkworm to multiply like the descendants of Abraham, would
have been heard here, where silk cocoons were suspended from
grilles inside the rooms of Andriote houses, and a New Year's wish
for luck on Andros, I have heard, was once "May you have your
weight in silk." In the nineteenth century, the shipping industry
made Andros a wealthy island, and created fortunes for families like
the Goulandrises, the great museum makers of twentieth-century
Greece. Andros town has a prosperous provincial handsomeness,
with houses that incorporate Venetian architectural traditions like

the arcade, a memory of the long Venetian domination of the island, which here created a true feudal system, practiced with Greek overlords over a Greek tenant peasantry when the Ottomans forced the Venetians out. Andros was a privileged island, a profitable nest egg, under the Ottoman Turks, who seem to have had no wish to disrupt its smooth functioning. There is an air of public-spiritedness in the town, with a long main street for evening *voltoules,* the communal strolls still popular here; the intelligently organized museums, library, and old-age home give a sense of common endeavor and confidence to the place. I stop in the library, in an elegant bourgeois house given to the town by an important nineteenth-century benefactor named Kairis. The librarian allows me to go into the small room that holds Kairis's own books, the core of the library collection—books in French, German, and Greek, encyclopedias, poetry, medical books. An island library, with knowledge brought by boat to furnish this world, it makes me think of Prospero's treasured volumes in *The Tempest.* As I walk around the town, I see some workmen restoring a grand house near the main square. One beckons me inside, where they are putting vulgar plaster ornamentation on the ceiling, and painting the walls teeth-gritting lime green and swooning blue. One of the painters grins a gap-toothed grin, wipes his forehead, and says cheerfully, "Sickening colors, aren't they? But that's our commission." Outside again, I pause at an imposing church, which reveals another facet of this public-spiritedness: carved in marble next to the entrance are a list of names, many recognizably famous shipping owners' names, with the amounts of their contributions carved irrevocably beside them.

Out in the country, I am in a world of rock, houses and walls and bridges made of rock piled high, the building blocks of children turned into fortresses and farms. Boulders sit on the soil like saddles on a horse's back, and rear up into thick tall square medieval structures that have something like the atmosphere of missile silos. Their ground floors were one huge room, with an enormous fireplace, called a *tzaki,* from the Turkish word *ocak*—a common phrase still in use to express an aristocratic origin is that someone "comes from a hearth." Walking around one of these stone towers is to walk around a building that is constructed out of the fullest possible imagination of danger, the architecture of vendetta. There are no doors or windows—you could enter by a removable ladder—only indentations at the top for pouring boiling oil or water on invaders, and slits in the stone made later for firing rifles. Indoors were spaces devoted to food storage, and subterranean passages for possible escapes or for bringing in more ammunition. Noticing the empty space over the main door where the marble relief escutcheon would have been placed with the family symbol or coat of arms, I am face-to-face with a notion of the family as a hostile, bloody enclave, the source of some privilege, but also of conflict and enemies, and of a future obligation to kill, incurred just as a result of being born into a particular clan. There is a drastic unbridgeable abyss between this and the ideal of the family as the seed of community, or of the holy family held up as a model to the inhabitants of these towers. This tower is well on its way to ruin, but the idea of family it demonstrates is still alive, in the vendetta traditions of Crete and Mani, and in the Sicilian Mafia. The interplay in this landscape is between raw, naked rock and rock broken into structure, but it is hard to say which is really more habitable.

I drive up to Menites, a village caught in a green grotto like light in an emerald, where inexhaustible spring waters rush into a central fountain from a marble lion's head, a village like a resurrection after a sojourn in the underworld. It occurs to me poignantly that when Persephone made her bargain with Hades to spend her six months each year away from the underworld, it was not Olympus she chose to return to, not heaven, but earth. Lambros, the icon painter to whom Marina is introducing me, is expecting me for lunch, but first we drink a coffee under the trees. He is a good-looking man, with a full lower lip like a wave coming to crest, and a glance known here as the *satiriko vlemma,* the satyr's tragicomic gaze, a glance which is insatiable, but which can change registers, becoming a gaze not of insatiability but of tragic and unsatisfiable longing. I understand now why Athens is littered with his former wives and their children.

"It's good you find me here," Lambros says, "the life of an iconographer is a nomadic one. Few churches can afford one of us to paint them all at once, so I must do piecework from place to place. And I must also take commissions to live—I did a chapel on a ship last month—while the official church committee approves the sketches I submit, and makes sure that the hierarchical order of the saints in the proposed design is correct. Because our pictures, the pictures in the Byzantine tradition, are *dogmatismena,* they are incarnations of theology, they are God's fingerprints. And they are the legacy of the greatest empire the world has known, the Byzantine Empire, which fixed its ambition on the supernatural and the eternal. As I do when I paint, I decorporealize, I dematerialize the saint; the painting becomes prayer, the saint's body not an earthly body but a heavenly one. Byzantine art fulfills the meditation on the body begun in classical Greece. Christ, you see, brought a new eroticism into the world. The classical Greeks expressed perfect earthly beauty, and we complete them by expressing perfect divine beauty. For the classical Greeks, the perfect body was the athlete's body, but for Christians, the perfect body is the angel's spirit—we call angels 'the bodiless ones.' Not like your vulgar Western painting, with its gross fat Christs, and magi dressed in gold clothes, and Panagias in designer dresses, which as a great modern Orthodox artist called Kondoglou wrote, is nothing more than painted opera, and has no relation to either the letter or the spirit of the gospel, the gospel which is so simple that it confounds the labyrinths of the philosophers. Even our holy city is bodiless—your Pope is the Pope of Rome, a secular city. But our leader, the first among equals, is the patriarch of Constantinople. And you will say, but there is no Constantinople; this patriarch lives in Istanbul. But our Constantinople, like an angel, is a bodiless city, the leading city of a bodiless angelic empire.

"You should read Kondoglou, he wrote many books, and while he was perhaps not a great artist, he was a great sage of Greekness,

Romiosyni. If you read him, you will understand that you westerners make only tableaux, but we make sacraments. Ours is true
Christian art, yours is nothing but decorated egotism. Like your
repulsive Gothic churches, which are the essence of your entrap-
ment in the material world. They are like rockets, in which man
spares no expense to search for God, insists on Him. But Byzantine
architecture is on a human scale, with the exception of Agia Sofia,
God surrounds man, God sees man, whether he wills it or not.
Unfortunately, now that we have sold our souls for the EEC to pave
our roads and air-condition our museums, this animal Western
influence is polluting the Greek soul. And that is a tragedy, because
if you know us and study our history, you will realize that we are not
a local culture but a universal one, the acts of our holy people are
the acts of the fourteenth apostle of Christ."

"Who was the thirteenth?" I ask.

"Constantine, of course. Our people have followed the path that
Alexander laid down for them in the pre-Christian world and Constantine in the fulfilled world—of becoming gods. This is a part of
our Orthodox theology, not like your 'salvation,' which puts a piece
of virtue in a bank and gets back divine grace as interest. To understand us, you must understand the concept of theosis. Our church
teaches that the goal of each Christian is deification—Saint Athana-
sius wrote that Christ says to us, 'In my kingdom, I shall be God
with you as gods.' "

Lambros steers me up the path to his house. "And not by moralizing, something we imported from the West, whose moral rules
are a form of spiritual capitalism. No. I was never a good man, I am
not a good man, I will never be a good man. Marina probably told
you I have my appetites, I have had some wives, I abandoned a wife
and child in Germany, I have had many love affairs, very intense. We
don't have this Western thing you have, these relationships, this bargaining. We don't have good relationships, we have great loves."
Eleni, his wife, comes out to greet us, followed by a toddling boy of
sixteen months. She has blue-green eyes, and a nose and mouth cut

like jewels. "She looks like a virgin, don't you think? Like what we mean by a virgin, which is not a woman who has never known a man, but a woman of fresh inexhaustible beauty that renews itself timelessly." As we pass through the living room, the little boy suddenly catches sight of an icon of the Virgin, veiled in gold leaf, propped on an easel in a corner of the room, and he sets up a clamor. Eleni brings the picture down for a moment, and holds it to his lips. "Kiss Mommy," she says, and after he does, she takes us outside to a table set for lunch in their garden. She brings us a plump loaf of bread, "like the baby Christ in His swaddling clothes," Lambros says, cutting me a slice, and she sets down a plate of *froutalia,* a potato and sausage omelet that Andros is known for, but she does not eat with us, or talk to us as she moves back and forth between the house and the garden, bringing us fried potatoes and a bottle of wine, and a salad. I watch her, her eyelids lowered and her lips closed in almost stern repose, as she sets down plates and glasses without looking at us, or the little boy who intermittently clings to her leg, and I think, she is an icon. Lambros has made an icon and married it.

"To our health," he says, and shows me the bottle—it is *agioritiko,* wine from the vineyards of the holy mountain, Mount Athos, the peninsula of Greece closed to women, the prohibition extending to female animals. "The vineyards of the holy mountain produce wonderful wines, because so few vehicles are allowed there that air pollution is unknown. It was a pilgrimage there that made me embrace Orthodoxy, and made me understand something of God's plan for my life. Of course, you can't really understand unless you go there and feel it for yourself. And you will never go. No woman will ever go there." He smiles a smile I have seen, even on the faces of friends who have just come from Athos pilgrimages, a smug smile not unlike the bureaucrat's smile I saw recently on the face of a civil servant, who was gratuitously causing a visa problem, though all my papers, proof of employment, and bank account were in order. There was the same petty thrill of exclusion, the same emotional masquerade which justifies a dubious claim of privilege by feeling it as a mark of virtue.

"A man who truly gives himself to God must give up all relation to earthly love. But if you saw this landscape you would see a Dionysian world, it is a landscape made for ecstasy, to be in love with Christ. So when I went there on this pilgrimage, I was leaving behind a love affair. I simply walked and meditated and prayed and stayed in a monastery. And one night I had a dream that I was standing on the shore and out of the foam of the waves beating against the rocks, a bodiless angel formed itself and stood upright on the water. And this angel looked at me, and began to weep tears of gold, which rolled very slowly off its face. And when the tears fell onto the sea, they became women, that is, women were enclosed like beautiful prisoners in these golden tears, and I saw that they were my wives and my lovers. And when I woke up I understood that these women were a gift of tears that God was granting me, that He had planned that all my relationships would be lacking, all would be failures so I would give myself utterly to Him, see through the tears to perfect love." Eleni's clean laundry is drying on a line stretched between two trees beyond the table. A butterfly settles on a towel printed with bright multicolored flowers, which ripple as a breeze stirs the clothesline. The butterfly opens and closes its wings, thinking it has settled in a garden.

Macedonia Day

Today is the great demonstration on the Pedion Areos, the old military parade grounds that are called the Field of Mars, held in hope of influencing the EEC to adhere to Greece's position that the name Macedonia is inadmissible for the new republic, until recently a part of Yugoslavia. There is continuous coverage on the news of the parallel demonstrations in Thessaloniki, even more fervent, since Thessaloniki is a symbol of Greek Macedonia, acquired in the Balkan Wars by a hair's breadth, when the Greek army marched in and occupied the town just ahead of the Bulgarians. The demonstration is also more fervent in Thessaloniki because documents from ultranationalist organizations of the new Republic of Macedonia have turned up printed with images of Thessaloniki's White Tower, making the possession of this important port seem an implicit ambition of the new state. Accusations against Bulgaria, traditionally Greece's chief European rival for possession of this area, are murmured from many corners—many Greeks believe Bulgaria wants to challenge the boundaries settled by the Balkan Wars of 1912–13, and is using the Macedonia issue as the first act of its campaign. Others worry that the new republic intends to stir up the Slav-speaking minority population of Greek Macedonia, kindling an ambition to forge a state with an independent "Macedonian" identity, and others speak apprehensively of what the Turks might have to gain in disputes over Balkan borders. School is canceled throughout Greece today so that teachers and students can attend their regional demonstrations; Greek schools have demonstration days instead of snow days.

The Pedion Areos is crammed with people waving flags bearing the Star of Vergina. From the temporary raised wooden platform that has been constructed, someone is speaking: ". . . The sun of Vergina is the light of Greek consciousness . . ." The speeches are punctuated by Greek Macedonian folk songs and dances; some of the male dancers are wearing the foustanella of the Makedonomakhi, the guerrilla warriors who defended Greek villages in the region and tried to drive out the Bulgarians and the Turks, in the period before the Balkan Wars. The crowd chants, "Macedonia is unique, always and forever Greek," and someone galvanizes a cluster of people near me, shouting that Greece has been betrayed by Europe for the last time. A historian takes the microphone and talks about Alexander the Great, and the unmistakable Hellenic character of Macedonia in antiquity. "Macedonia is Greek! Read History!" a cry goes up from a few other knots of people.

But the more I look at the old men dancing in their fathers' Balkan war uniforms, and the more prayerfully the quasi-mythical Alexander is invoked, the more powerfully I realize that the appeals to sacred and inarguable antiquity are masking the real concerns of the Greeks over the status of this region, the real ambiguity through which Macedonia was won for Greece, and the Greek anxiety that the settlement of these territorial issues was satisfactory to no one but the Greeks, and perhaps the Serbs. The claims to Macedonia were not settled with references to Alexander, but by guerrilla warfare and terrorism on the part of all the nations involved, and frantic building of nationalistic schools and reinforcing of ethnic enclaves by all interested parties. In fact, if you read history as his-

tory rather than as creed, you recognize that this rhetoric has everything to do with the period before the Balkan Wars leading up to the
Greek annexation of Thessaloniki and neighboring territory, and
very little to do with Alexander, whose identity in any case was elastic and strategic—Greek, Macedonian, or Olympian, the son of
Philip or the son of Zeus, as advantage required. The response on
the Pedion Areos today has much more contemporary roots, in the
Megali Idea, the "Great Idea," formulated in the new Greek state
almost immediately after its birth, the dream of replacing the
Ottoman Empire with a new Byzantium, the Greece "of two continents," as it was called, a Greek empire that would include Epiros,
Macedonia, Thrace, Crete, and the Aegean islands, then collectively
referred to as enslaved Greece, all under a reborn capital city in
Constantinople. Macedonia was a crucial element of the Panhel-
lenic ambition. The Serbs too had ambitions in Macedonia, but it
was the Bulgarians, backed by the Russian Empire, who were
Greece's chief challenger in the region, with some parties staking
ethnic claims to the territory and others favoring an autonomous
Macedonia, with Thessaloniki as its capital.

From roughly the 1870s on, educational societies in Greece
published handbooks and tracts invoking the medieval rivalry
between the Bulgarians and the Byzantines, which culminated in the
Bulgarian defeat by Emperor "Basil the Bulgar-Slayer," and sometimes portraying the Turks not only as infidels but as a largely black
race. Societies founded to promote Hellenism sent representatives
to speak to prominent Europeans, and missionaries to Greek communities in Turkey. According to the philhellene observer William
Miller, writing in 1912, Greek elementary school geography maps
labeled the region between the Danube and the Aegean not as the
"Balkan" but the "Hellenic" peninsula. "On the Macedonian question," Miller wrote, "most Greeks are chauvinists; they are only
willing to hear their own side of that difficult racial problem, and
they are, with rare exceptions, so strongly prejudiced against the
Bulgarians, that argument is hopeless, and the philosophic politician

who thinks that there may be something to be said on both sides is apt to find himself labelled as a Bulgarophil. . . . You will hear politicians talk about Alexander the Great, and base arguments on his Macedonian realm, as if he were a contemporary of M. Deliyiannis [the prime minister at that time], and I once listened to a very hard-headed currant merchant from Patras solemnly denouncing Demosthenes as a bad patriot and a traitor to Greece, because he had called Philip of Macedon a 'barbarian' and thereby injured the Greek argument that all, or most, of the Macedonians are Greeks."

The modern nation of Greece was made up of painstakingly expanded borders, a process that continued for roughly a century, while the population continued to experience sudden shifts, like the arrival of many Egyptian Greeks as a consequence of President Nasser's efforts in the 1960s to bring Egyptian business under Egyptian control. Issues that concern borders, as a result, send Greece into frenzies. The issue of Macedonia is so fraught that both Greek and foreign university scholars have received death threats from within Greece for publishing history papers that were perceived as challenging the nationally acceptable view of Macedonia.

Television reporters are questioning groups of schoolchildren and their teachers near me. "What do you think of today's demonstration?" one asks a ten-year-old. "It shows that Greece is united and proves that Macedonia is always and forever Greek," he says, and his classmates wave their plastic flags. The teacher adds, "It is important for all Greeks to take part on this historic day." What is unnerving, though, is that there is no possibility for any kind of critical assessment of the occasion, much less dissent. The schools were closed for the very purpose of being here, and the teachers presiding over their flocks, with television reporters expressing avuncular approval of the patriotic answers, are disturbing. I can't imagine what would happen to a teacher—or a child—who said something like, yes, the borders must remain stable, but the rhetoric is offensive, or who suggested that a compromise on the name might be possible, or said that the purpose of schools was to foster a climate of intellectual inquiry. Here where schools are tightly controlled by government and church—the state, teachers tell me, determines the material to be taught in each class, down to the number of pages covered per lesson, while the official title of the minister of educa- tion is "the minister of education and religion"—the social and professional consequences could be severe. It is ironic that this demonstration, while fervently supported by many of the partici- pants, is also functioning as a form of social and academic censor- ship. I remember another passage from William Miller, written during the period before the Balkan Wars, when the fate of Mace- donia was still undecided. Miller wrote about the University of Athens that one third of its undergraduates came from "enslaved Greece." "It is this factor," he said, "which gives the University its real importance, and which makes it the spoiled darling of the Greek governments. For every Greek from beyond the present frontiers of the kingdom who has studied at Athens goes back to his native town or village imbued with the 'Great Greek Idea'. . . . We can scarcely wonder that no punishments are meted out to students who indulge in political demonstrations, or that the Prime Minister turns a sympathetic ear to the Macedonian alumni, who ask to be relieved from all fees, on the ground that their homes have been devastated by the Bulgarian bands." This matches perfectly fears I have heard Greeks express about the consequences if the Skopje republic is accepted with the name Macedonia—the geography textbooks in the new state's elementary schools will be printed with maps incorporating Greek Macedonia, and the children will be taught that the name is proof of an ancient historic claim to lost territory they must recover.

WEDDING

"Be careful no one takes you for a transvestite in that neighbor-hood—it's their *agora*," Kostas said jokingly when I told him I was going to a wedding reception at a hotel on Syngrou Avenue. "If you wear your gold lamé, then I can't answer for the conse-quences—a woman who looks glamorous on Syngrou Avenue is in all probability a man. Have fourteen eyes when you are in that neighborhood," he says, telling me to be cautious in an idiom he particularly likes, because it reminds him of Argos, the many-eyed guardian of Io.

Shattered bricks, broken concrete, fragments of glass, and iron pipes big enough for people to hide in block the entrance of the lux-ury hotel where the wedding reception for a publisher's daughter and a shipping tycoon's son is being held. The heels of my gold evening slippers sink into the quicksand of the street debris after the taxi lets me out across the highway from the hotel. A small party of explorers has formed from a fragment of the thirteen hundred invited guests to make an attempt to find the hotel entrance, which was hidden by the litter of construction materials. A chauffeured Mercedes discharges another group of elegantly dressed lost people. Someone sights a way in, and reports to the band of searchers, who follow him following a child in a silver satin flower girl dress, down two flights of escalators, past posted security guards, and through the receiving line. Waiters hover with glasses of champagne; the guests are symmetrically divided by gender. On one side of the room, a fortress of black-suited men smoke and transact; on the other, women whose hair has been braided and souffléed by craftspersons who obviously have a taste for baroque fountains wear brocades and sequins that are eerily like the festival ceremonial robes of priests, which in Greece are glittering landscapes of gold thread, jewels, and brocade. Huge bars, surrounded by guests, anchor the room, and the entire length of the far wall, which I estimate to be a quarter of a mile long, is lined with linked buffet tables. Monumental floral arrangements, which include tags at their bases with the name and telephone number of the florist, are placed like perishable sculptures at the corners of the dance floor. In the middle of the dance floor, as if on an altar, is a nine-tiered cake, roughly eight feet tall.

The weddings of wealthy Greeks are extraordinarily drawn-out affairs, since time is made between ceremony and reception for the wedding party and guests to change from their grand church clothes to grand evening clothes. And since the ceremony itself proceeds at a stately pace, with the repetitive chanting and actions performed in the triple patterns that are emblems of eternity here, a wedding can be an all-day business. For this and for other reasons, my friend Aura doesn't want to drive out to the green glade of Agia Filothei, probably the most popular wedding church in Athens, booked months in advance. "I simply cannot feel comfortable listening to a ceremony which is founded on an insistence that women are inferior to men. I don't even like to say I am married in Greek. I am happy to say it in French or in English, but in Greek, I feel the twinge of etymology—*pandremeni,* married, descends from the ancient Greek *ip-andros,* to be under a man, to be subject to him. So in Greek, I can't be married, since I don't agree to this. But you go—it is a marvelous opportunity for you to observe the precise moment when social ideology is transformed, by the alchemy of the liturgy, into divine commandment."

I am struck, as Aura promised, by the almost badgering emphasis on the wife's secondary position, both with her husband and in creation itself, the constant admonition that she must obey her husband in all things, that he is her head. As the bride and groom stand at the altar, both wearing wreaths of small white flowers that are linked together by a satin ribbon, as if it is a new umbilical cord, the groom is exhorted to love his wife as if she were his own body, and the bride to fear the man, to stand in awe and even in dread of him, at which point this bride stamps firmly on her groom's foot, in a traditional gesture of defiance. An image of an old embroidered wedding coverlet I saw on a visit to Crete with Kostas makes me momentarily lose the thread of the ceremony.

The quilt was bordered with square after square of tiny churches embroidered in colored thread; they proceeded inexorably as armored tanks around the bedcover. I could tell from his face that the aggressive coverlet made Kostas nervous, with its endless triumphant repetition that legitimate marriage had been achieved. The power hidden in those toylike churches declared that lovemaking in this bed might have been, without this quilt, romantic adventure, but was now, for good or ill, destiny. Kostas had joked about the admonition in the marriage service to woman to fear the man; "They don't have to warn us to fear the woman, you see; it goes without saying." But no matter who fears whom, I thought, this moment introduces a power struggle into the very heart of a ceremony that should celebrate the mutual love and mutual respect of the partners. And as I watch the bride and groom make their ritual three circles around the altar while we pelt them with rose petals, sugared almonds, and rice, I realize that, for me, the strangest element of the ceremony was that no pledges were made by the bride and groom, who do not speak. Our ceremony is based on the asking and answering of questions, this one on exhortation. It occurs to me on the way to the reception that the absence of questions may reflect the tradition of arranged marriage here, evading the issue of the bride's and groom's consent.

At the hotel, I catch sight of the friends I am meeting, and join their table while we wait for the bride and groom to make their entrance. Two Americans who introduce themselves as Tweedledum and Tweedledee sit down with us; Dum looks like an expensively dressed Woody Allen; he wears a costly gold watch, and carefully chosen Italian glasses, which magnify his tiny dead eyes, the eyes of a flesh-eating fish, with neither scruple nor bitterness over lack of scruple, eyes in which nothing is left but will. Dee is a particularly late-twentieth-century American character, with a boyish face achieved as if through a kind of plastic surgery of the soul: he is an artist whose art has been to create an audience and sustain his own celebrity, specializing in pornographic pictures of himself with his wife. He tells me he lives part of the year in Munich, and I ask why. "Because the sex is good in Munich," he answers. "Did you hear what I just told her?" He nudges Dum. "I told her I live in Munich because the sex is better there." Dum nods with distracted admiration and beckons for another glass of champagne. "It's very fertile in Munich," Dee says. "Even the cows are dripping with milk. That's why the sex is so good. In Africa, the cows are dry and bony, but in Munich they are fat and luscious and full of milk." He nudges Dum again. "Did you hear what I just said? About the cows in Munich?" He urges me to go to an exhibition of his work in Athens. "You'll really be surprised. Just go. I promise, you'll get a big surprise."

Suddenly the strains of Mendelssohn's wedding recessional, in an arrangement so dictatorial and pompous that it sounds like the music radios play after military coups, strike up. The bride and groom walk on a white carpet through the throng to the cake—the groom is stalwartly dark and handsome, and solicitous of the bride, like a danseur presenting the prima. She is wearing the most artful dress I have ever seen, arranged on a series of wire hoops, covered with net studded with brilliants. It looks as if she is dressed in galaxies, stars draping her breasts and bare rich shoulders. Dee leans over to Dum. "Do you think Romeo fitted the dress himself?" Dum replies, as the couple cut the cake in every kind of photograph, and begin to do the work of their wedding, moving around the room. "If he knows how important Ari is in the art world, he must have knelt at her feet with pins stuck through his tongue."

On both sides of the room waiters wheel up rounds of ice six feet in circumference, some holding beds of oysters, others bottles of vodka and aquavit; waiters circulate with trays of caviar on toast. Every luxury from other climates and other countries that is most unattainable in Greece is offered. The room breaks up into different *pareas,* close-knit circles—the tycoon's *parea,* the grandparents' *parea,* the *parea* from Athens College, the most prestigious school of Greece, which routinely turns out not only future prime ministers but future opposition leaders. A band begins to play: "I like to be in America, everything free in America," sings the leader, moving on to an Elton John song, and some Latin numbers, popular for dancing here. Quadrilingual buffet tables begin to function, offering smoked salmon, pâté, tender rare beef, almost impossible to find in Greece, asparagus—not one Greek dish or wine is offered, although the scene calls up images of the outsized festal cooking equipment, vast cauldrons and enormous trays used for public celebrations that I have seen in some villages. Ari, I think, is feasting the village. There are no toasts, no speeches; the whole occasion is the display of abundance, which seems all at once heroically generous, aggressive, and panic-stricken. Even the *koufeta,* the sugared almonds given as favors at Near and Middle Eastern weddings, are not wrapped in the usual tulle and satin ribbon here, but offered in monogrammed crystal boxes.

When we leave, the dance floor is crowded; many of the dancers are mouthing the English words to the tune the band is playing: "This land is your land, this land is my land, from California to the New York island . . ." In Athens, they are dancing at lavish weddings to American protest songs from the Depression.

POMEGRANATES

As Christmas, or I should say New Year's, approaches—since Protokhronia is more like our Christmas celebration, and Christmas is a foreign fruit grafted on the Greek tree—the small, cell-like empty storefronts in my neighborhood, which are inhabited only by perpetually renewed populations of wild kittens, old cardboard boxes, and stray wine bottles, turn into magical chambers glittering with Christmas ornaments. The street cats are an insoluble Greek problem, since the Greeks disapprove of sterilizing animals—I heard a distinguished teacher of mine, educated at the Sorbonne, and known throughout Athens for the skill and imagination with which she teaches this difficult language, agonizing with her father over the decision to sterilize a beloved male cat named Achilles. Her apartment was at that point overrun with Achilles's children, who barely left a corner for her, but her father pleaded with her, "Don't ruin him." The alternative, though, is this, streets full of hungry, scavenging stray animals breeding new stray animals, who are often given poisoned food, or killed in other ways, or driven, like the storefront kittens, to some unnameable elsewhere.

I am glad to be walking outside, since I am always cold in my apartment. This is not a severe winter in southern Greece, although northern Greek villages are snowed in; but southern Greek houses are sensibly built to capture as much cool air as possible against the summer heat, and mine is very successful. And in my building, as is common, the heat is only turned on three times a day, so I shiver indoors and sleep in an embryonic tuck. I stop to look at the gift book offerings for children in a shop window—it features a book displayed in many windows and catalogues this year: *I, Alexander: King of Macedonia, Son of Zeus, Conqueror of the World*. The cover is in lurid blood and earth colors, and shows Alexander in girlish-boyish beauty, a reddish fringe of beard contrasting with his blond curls, perhaps to make his sex less ambiguous, his eyes staring with furious determination. A label is fixed to the book, a breathlessly worded reminder that a free poster of Alexander of Macedonia comes with each book.

I go in, to buy a translation of *Little Women* (Mikres Kyries) for a friend's daughter, and leaf through it, relishing the Greek version. Amy, accused of being an affected niminy-piminy chit in American, in Greek is criticized for her use of high-toned Katharevousa words. The saleswoman asks, "Is it a gift?" and when I say yes, wraps it with genius. It is something that moves me about life here, this love of anything to do with gifts—you are invariably asked when you make a purchase here if it is a gift, and it will be wrapped in glory if it is, with a characteristic "second gift" fastened to the package—a wand with a tiny gold rose, an evil-eye charm, a tiny ship. My package is fastened with a tiny ceramic pomegranate, the key image of this season here, and a measure of the emotional difference between the Eastern and Western holidays. The fruit sellers at the farmer's markets display pomegranates dyed gold on their tables, along with branches of gold- and silver-dyed leaves. Flower sellers offer pomegranates wrapped in silver foil for you to smash against your threshold with all your force on New Year's Eve, to spread the seeds of good luck, and to have an abundant year, and gift shop tables are covered with brilliant red candles in the shape of pomegranates. In jewelry shop windows, there are pomegranate-shaped pendants, and silver pomegranates to give as gifts, cast open to show their abundant silver seeds. Again, I am reminded that the world of the unconscious is different here than in Scandinavia, in Mexico, in Benin, as is the imagery of daily life that we take with us into our dreams and bring back with us transformed, to change the world of reality.

Modern Greek dream books always catalogue pomegranate dreams, as Artemidorus did in the second century. And other divinities are present at this feast which now celebrates the birth of the baby boy Christian god: the pomegranate is a symbol of the promise that the Queen of the Dead will return to earth, bringing spring with her, before she retreats again into the underworld. Persephone's pomegranate means nothing in the West as a mark of this season, but in this part of the world the pomegranate has a long history as a charm that mediates between life and death. In Egypt, a wall painting of Pharaoh Seti, the father of Rameses II, shows him offering to Osiris, the first god of the Egyptian pantheon to die and return to life, a tray holding bread, wine, and pomegranates. Here of course, the pomegranate is the fruit of Persephone, or at least, I realize, in this dual-natured country, half of it is. The other half belongs to Hades, since this fruit is also the King of the Dead's, which he offers in order to ensure that she will remain with him in the kingdom of the dead—the pomegranate is a fruit neither of death nor life, but of the inseparability of the two. And perhaps, in a way impossible to document, since the art of myth is in part the art of shredding documents, the pomegranate came to memorialize the end of women's sharing in divinity, which the various monotheisms chose to personify as exclusively male. Perhaps Demeter mourns, in the form of her daughter assigned to the underworld, her own lost publicly acknowledged divinity—the ambiguous figure of Mary reflects this loss, an underground divinity, with the constant official assertion that she is not a goddess, and the constant private invocation of her in popular worship. Or perhaps not, depending on which six seeds preoccupy you, the six Persephone ate or the six she did not. Myths are malleable, molded utterly by how we interpret them, unlike literature, with its changing but indissoluble links to history and to social life.

The dream pomegranate of both the Greeks of antiquity and the modern Greeks is an ambiguous fruit. It is not a good omen for Artemidorus, meaning "wounds because of their color, tortures because of their prickles, slavery and submission because of the Eleusinian legend." The modern dream books differ—some foretell, for those who see pomegranates in their sleep, charming and pleasant erotic adventures, because it is a symbol of the return of spring and fertility. Others interpret it as a symbol of danger, that if you see someone offer you a pomegranate, it is a sign that your life is in danger, that some underworld force may be reaching out to seize you, as Hades did Persephone. One says that an open or broken pomegranate foretells wealth, but without joy, and that a pomegranate full of seeds foretells a powerful love that will not end in marriage. But the modern dream books, even when they present a pomegranate as a sign of warning, present this old dream as a symbol of a new reality—the idea of an erotic relationship, the idea of an erotic marriage, the idea of erotic choice, militantly discouraged for both men and women under the system of arranged marriage and profound social and professional segregation in place in Greece until recently. The pomegranate may foretell relationships that fail, or charming adventures, but either way it suggests the existence both of erotic pleasure and erotic married love inconceivable under the old system. There are dreams that change, and the world changes with them; the world changes, and the dreams the old world inspired become untranslatable.

I walk on to Plaka, the old quarter, lovely without tourists as I've never seen it, on a chilly winter day, with its trees studded with bright flame-colored clementines, thinking about the pomegranates, about the irony of the presence of the old gods at the feast of a god whose champions tried to destroy them. I pass a demonstration by a group holding a huge red banner and chanting—this one seems to be against fascism, but I don't stay to find out who they are, because there seem to be as many police as there are demonstrators, and I am aware now of their notorious readiness to "make you eat wood," in the Greek idiom for beating. I stop at a magazine stand to look at the holiday issues—the cooking pages of the women's magazines are a regular anthology of EEC country recipes and customs, *bûche de Noël,* Christmas pudding, *pfeffernusse.* New images in Greek eyes, the primitive beginnings of new dreams. One of them reprints a twentieth-century classic, a popular Christmas story called "Christmas at Missolonghi," by a woman who virtually invented children's literature in this country, Penelope Delta, the daughter of the extraordinarily wealthy Emmanuel Benaki, whose cotton-based fortune is enshrined in monuments like the famous Benaki Museum in central Athens, and Benaki Hall, at the Athens College preparatory school.

I buy the magazine, curious about the story, and turn around at a tug on my arm to see Eleftheria, a girl I run into from time to time at my gym, when I go for a workout and a steam in the *hamam,* as the steam baths here are called. She shows off a pair of Versace leather trousers she found on sale while visiting her Marine boyfriend in the States. "Four women cursed me on the way down here today," she says proudly. "I think my new pants must look nice. You know how it works here, half of the people are going '*Ftou, ftou,* may the evil eye not see you,' and the other half are going '*Katara mou,* you have my curse for all eternity.' " We walk together out of Plaka, while Eleftheria riffles through my magazine, discoursing like a wine connoisseur on the qualities of Lancôme, Estée Lauder, Cover Girl, and Chanel makeups. She shows me a new palette of eye shadows she got for her name day last week. "Saint Eleftherios—Saint Freedom, Saint Deliverance—the patron saint of pregnant women and of prisoners." She smiles. "If you go to a maternity hospital, you will see his icon everywhere, and when you make a wish for a pregnant woman, you wish her a good liberation." We wander toward Hermes Street, a name that reflects the neoclassicism of the new Greek state—in both substantial and provincial towns, the major commercial street will often be called after Hermes, the ancient patron god of commerce, reflecting the determination to revive a consciousness of ancient Greece, to regain a place in Europe through classicism, eluding the impossibility of being reintegrated through the awkward symbols of Byzantium: Byzantium and western Europe had, after all, evolved into political and religious enemies; the Greek Orthodox prayer book has a special prayer for a ceremony marking the return to Orthodoxy from the errors of Roman Catholicism, a circumstance that periodic control of Greek territory by Catholic powers, and the frequent education of Greek boys in Roman Catholic schools and universities, must have created often.

"Are you Christmas shopping?" Eleftheria asks. "Yes," I say, and she says, "I have a bit more time—we still exchange our gifts on January 1. And we do something that will be gone in another generation. We give the men the women's gifts and the women the men's gifts, and then swap afterwards. So when my brother's name is called out, he gets, let's say, a pair of earrings, but I get a tie. I don't know why, maybe because Protokhronia leads up to carnival, when everyone masquerades. Lots of people used to do it. But I am having trouble with gifts at all this year. I am saving for another trip to the States, and besides, we girls have so many expenses, don't we? You have your lipsticks, your tights, your sanitary pads, and then your light-days pantiliners." Eleftheria has just finished a course in manicures, pedicures, and face masks, and she tells me she spent the weekend practicing on her mother, and while she was resting with a Chinese hair-nourishing treatment on her head, her boyfriend called from the U.S. "I told him, 'I miss you,' and asked 'Do you miss me?' And he said he did. When I put down the phone, I bounced up and down on the bed, and I was shouting, 'Thank you, *Panayitsa mou,*' and my mother came in to see what was going on."

We pass a temporary Christmas store which features in its front window a huge ceramic music box which lights up to show a scene of three blond children revolving in a snowy landscape, while a selection of Western Christmas carols plays. The base is marked "Made in China." There are tables full of matchbox-sized calendars for the new year, which offer poems, or recipes, or extracts from the lives of unfamiliar Orthodox saints, on the back of each tear-off sheet. And there is one of the many editions of a kind of almanac sold at this time of year, not only in the stores but on the trolleys and buses. The one offered here is a very homely, farmer's and housewife's version. "Who Were the Real Greeks?" reads the title of one article. Stacked high on another table are Christmas books for children, blending the three names in use for the seasonal bringer of gifts. Greek children used to have gifts only at New Year's from Saint Basil of Caesarea, a thin, ascetic-looking man from Asia Minor who is a patron saint of education, and is often shown in icons carrying a pen and writing tablet. But now he is part of a holy trinity of gift givers, with Europe's Saint Nicholas and America's Santa Claus. A fat stuffed toy looking like the American Santa Claus I know is sprawled across a tower of Christmas books. He has a string at the back of his neck, and I pull it to hear his greeting. "Merry Christmas," he says, "Agios Vasilis is coming. *Xa, xa, xa.*"

I say goodbye to Eleftheria and walk to the theater where I am meeting Aura and her husband, in a crumbling district with boarded-up neoclassical houses, without any sign of domestic life, waiting for their inheritors to negotiate them into high-rises. Hans points out a ramshackle neoclassical cottage, which he tells me is a famous brothel. The whole neighborhood has a doomed and painful loveliness, the air of Violetta in *La Traviata,* especially bleak because rescue seems so possible. After the play, we go to the Les Halles of Athens, to a restaurant in the central meat market that opens around midnight and closes around six in the morning, a place for truckers and market employees and intellectuals. Aura is talking about the recent remarks of a magisterial elderly actor named Dimitri Horn; the surname sounds German, and I am reminded that there are a handful of well-known Greek families with transliterated German surnames, some of whom are said to have been part of the retinue that accompanied the Bavarian prince Otto who was assigned the monarchy of Greece shortly after the War of Independence, as the choice of the great powers of the period. "I remember it for you because his mood and tone were so Greek. He was asked about his future plans, and he replied, 'At my age people have no future.' Can you imagine an American actor saying that, there where you are trained to say death is not death, it's just a new opportunity to live without breath? We have a sense of the irrevocable that you don't. Maybe because our lives are more controlled than yours are, surely because we lost a world. The last question they asked him was if there was anything he would like to forget. And what did he say? 'Everything, forever.' "

HEADS OR TAILS

The bell rings at 8:15 in the morning on New Year's Eve, and when I open the door, a group of children shout, "Can we tell them?" the traditional introduction to the New Year's carols, the *kalanda,* whose name comes from the Roman Calends, the feast of the first of the month, even more powerful when Julius Caesar's solar calendar made January 1 the beginning of the year as well as the month. The children make a glorious din, one holding a wooden ship with a burning candle projecting from it like a mast. They beat their triangles, and sing: "Saint Basil is coming from Caesarea, holding an icon and paper, paper and pen . . . the pen wrote a fate and the paper spoke it . . ." This is a delicately melancholy song you hear in many variants at this time of year, a song that has something in it of the weariness of traveling for long distances on foot, and some of the sweetness and expectation of meeting that is part of walking far. It is in the melody itself, which has, with its particular turns and sudden vocal vistas, a feeling both of physical effort and of sudden perspective, a glimpse of the sea. I give the children coins and candy that are the traditional reward for the songs, and hear them beginning the cycle down the hall, before I have shut the door.

Saint Basil is a patron saint of education, but the pen he carries that writes fates makes him a double-edged figure appropriate to this month, which was named in honor of the two-faced Roman god Janus, god of endings and beginnings, of peace and of war. Basil comes bearing the fortunes of the year, a figure poised, too, between worlds and different ways of perceiving fate—in the antique world, fate was something spun out of threads held by three frightening women, but by the time of this carol, set in the world of the intricate holy bureaucracy created by bishop-administrators, it had become what is written. The two conceptions coexist in the language's words for fate, *mira*, the name for the women who wove destinies, and *to grafto*, the written, what is recorded for each person. Saint Basil's feast, New Year's, is here a feast of luck: everywhere you walk the shop windows are full of good luck charms, gold coins marked with the year to bake into your Saint Basil's bread, the sweet cakey bread served on New Year's Day; medallions with raised reliefs of ships, for the voyage of a new year, or with houses, or keys, which Janus often held in Roman statues, entwined with evil-eye charms; coins that this year carry the portrait of Alexander the Great, for luck with Macedonia—the world around you becomes a double of itself, multiplied into votive talismans, the planet itself seems hung in the heavens as an offering to secure a better world than itself. My United States preconception of this holiday is erotic, images of men in black tie and women in glittering dresses, champagne, dancing all night into the dawn of the new year, love songs punctuated occasionally by noisemakers that make the sound of a baby wailing, a holiday of couples, in a way, conceiving the new year. When people complain, as they often do, that New Year's was a disappointment, or as you hear occasionally, that New Year's is always a disappointment, the tone is one of erotic disillusionment. Here, as I make my way in a taxi to the airport to pick up Kostas, there is a sense of the transition from one year to another as a moment of pure risk—the neighborhood shop windows tremble with good luck charms, precarious existence dangles from glittering chains and brilliant scarlet ribbons. Along with the medallions and coins are displays of cards, dice games, small roulette wheels, and toy slot machines—everyone is supposed to participate in a ritual gamble on New Year's, as a way of inviting luck to come into their lives, and card playing was mentioned as a central feature of the three New Year's parties I was asked to.

We drive past a damaged tax office on the way to one of them—the government is promising tax crackdowns in the new year, since a recent study estimated that the combined income from Greece's black market and envelopes-under-the-table economy and widely practiced tax evasion equals some thirty-one percent of the country's gross domestic product. In the past few weeks, four city tax offices have been bombed, partly, I suppose, to destroy records as well as to help subvert the stricter policy the government wants to put in place. "It will be difficult to enforce tax collection," Kostas says. "We have a well-rooted double economy, in which people are used to being paid twice, once the official taxable salary, and again in the envelope under the table. We even have a patron saint of tax evasion, you know."

"Who is that?" I ask. "Saint Mamas. The patron saint of sheep-stealers, and of the Greek criminal world, who are said to invoke him before bank robberies, which as you know are nearly everyday occurrences here." It's true that there seems to have been a rash of bank robberies during my stay here, the most recent involving a bank that found a hole in its vault and discovered that over three hundred safe deposit boxes had been broken into.

We wind up at Aura's, carrying a *vasilopitta* made by Kostas's mother, whose Asia Minor roots are a special gastronomic credential in the making of this cake-bread supposed to have originated in the saint's Caesarea. Already hanging at the front door is a large onion wrapped in silver foil, for this year's luck, since an onion, even if it is uprooted, continues to put out shoots, and is thought of as an immortal plant, I remember from the stories about Alexander the Great. The room is thick with cigarette smoke and the noise of card shuffling and rattling dice, players priming their luck, "for the good of the year." An aunt of Aura's is telling fortunes with coffee cups, and the technique makes me wonder about the ethnic origins of Rorschach, since the reader sees a picture in the shape the grounds make at the bottom of the cup, and the interpretation tells the meaning of the picture. The room quiets for Aura to cut the *vasilopitta*—another dream image in my modern *oneirokrites,* which agree that it is good luck to get the coin in your dream, as long as the dream takes place during the season of the feast. I would be helpless to have this dream, and wonder if that means I couldn't have this particular kind of luck. But we don't have the custom, so we don't have the dream. I wonder, too, if that means my fortune cannot be told here. The world of external experience is one of the wellsprings of the unconscious, and maybe the images of the coffee cup will be too local to map the delicate intersections between the alien icons of my experience, and my imagination, the capacity to have new experience, there where people's fortunes begin to take form.

The first slices of the *vasilopitta* are dedicated in different ways by the person sharing them out—Aura cuts one for the poor, one for the house, one for the theater, one for Amnesty International. "No one really knows where this custom comes from, as far as I can make out," she says. "And of course it has a set of separate mythical origins—it may have been associated with the worship of the sun god, a sun-shaped cake made for a festival to coax the sun to return light and warmth to the world. December 25 was, after all, the feast of the Persian Mithras, the god of light, whose holiday was adopted by the Romans as the Feast of Invincible Light. This is how the Persian magi get incorporated into the Christian myth, it works the same way as the Zeus and Europa story—the Greek god Zeus takes Asia in the form of the Asian princess Europa, and breeds with her; both plots have figures who represent the concealed origins of the myth.

"The Christian myth I know about *vasilopitta* is that the citizens of Caesarea, which is now, of course, Kayseri, in Turkey, were mercilessly overtaxed by the Byzantine emperor's representatives, so they went to Basil, their bishop, to argue the case on their behalf. Basil asked them to bring him jewelry and treasure in case he had to offer the government officials bribes. But he was successful and they refused the treasures in the end. When he tried to return the jewelry to the lenders, however, many dubious claims were made, and so he had pies baked and put precious objects in each one. And by a miracle, each family received the pie that held its own particular treasure. But the Christians had to work hard to appropriate this season for themselves. The church fathers did their best to destroy the Roman January festivals—a first-century bishop was martyred for trying to suppress the festivals, which shows how popular they were, and John Chrysostom, one of the three hierarchs of Orthodoxy, and a singularly nasty man, preached viciously against the celebration of Calends, in the fourth century. There used to be transvestite masquerades, and street drama, especially interesting to me, of course. And church canons were made against the celebrations, quite late—it was a struggle that went on into the tenth century. You see, we are told that the Romans and Greeks spontaneously embraced Christianity, but only some did. The fact is that the state imposed this religion on its citizens—Theodosius, after all, declared officially that anyone who refused Christianity was to be considered insane—and Byzantium was full of conversos, people forced to declare a public faith they didn't share, or were simply indifferent to, like the Jews in the period before the Spanish Inquisition.

" 'No man,' " she recited, " 'is to put on feminine dress, nor any woman, the dress proper to men, nor yet are masks, whether comic, satyric, or tragic, to be worn'—for this, the good fathers would excommunicate you, that is to say destroy you socially and economically, since no one would do business with you as an excommunicate or marry the children you needed to settle. Later, the masquerades were clearly used as veiled protests against the church, with mock church ceremonies and people dressed as monks carrying huge wooden penises, which helps explain the church's frenzy over the festivities. Someone has told you, I'm sure, about the *kalikantzari,* the hairy demons who especially emerge at this time of year, and are only driven away on January 6? Well, it seems clear to me that they are part of the Christian program to demonize the people who stubbornly celebrated their traditional January festivals, parading in goatskins or other animal costumes."

I think to myself that some of this hostility to the state-sponsored religion may have crept into the portraits of the saints, some of whom behave very much like household demons—like Saint Spyridion, who if you don't celebrate his holiday will give you acne. He will also spoil sewing and weaving, as a legendary lady who wanted to finish her weaving found out. "Little Saint Spyridion doesn't need a holiday," she said, finished her task, and went to bed. There she dreamed of an angry monk, who said to her, "Since I am so little, you will see how many little holes I can make," and when she woke up, she found her work motheaten. And there is my own favorite holy mischief-maker, Saint Andrew the Frying Pan Piercer, who will make holes in your frying pan if you don't make him pancakes in it on his day.

After the cake is cut, the guests return to their pursuits of their fortunes, playing their preferred games of chance, or hearing their fortunes, while one of the myriad holiday music programs plays on television. Linked-arm dancing breaks out in one corner and winds its way from room to room when a favorite song in the sexy melancholy voice of the singer Mitropanos is overheard: "I love you like sin, I hate you like prison . . ." I brave the coffee-cup reading, which is meaninglessly general. To compare, I draw tarot cards, for a woman with a muse's name to read. They envision something so specific, and so ridiculous, that I dismiss it, so by the time it happens the following September, I have completely forgotten about the prediction.

As a treat for New Year's, Kostas rented a famous 1954 Melina Mercouri film called *Stella,* which he tells me was the role that first

made her famous, and is a crucial piece of Greek pop culture, which
is after all, he tells me, "the modern expression of folklore. Anyway," he says, "you cannot proceed without seeing this film. It cap-
tures a modern Greek view of erotic love that is still alive. It is very
melodramatic, but then the Greek idea of erotic love is a melodramatic one." He grins. "It will help you understand why we have one
of the two lowest birthrates in Europe." I am also curious because
Melina has been much in evidence this season, trailing a Belgian film
crew behind her on her many progresses through Athens, declaring
to them that as to Macedonia, "our name is our soul."

Stella, played by Mercouri, is a singer at the Paradise Taverna,
who sings "all the songs of life and love and death." She chooses her
lovers instead of being chosen by them, and deals with them hon-
estly; her idea of a contract between lovers would have a respect for
the other's freedom as its first principle. She wears low-cut dresses
that outline her body neither indifferently nor to provoke: the way
she handles them reminds me of the costumes of women skaters—
she has an athlete's sense of her beauty, that her sensuality and fine
body are an accomplishment, they reflect her skill in being alive,
not enticement; they are a sign of self-respect, not cunning or need.
She is ending an affair with a younger man, who is well-mannered
and gentlemanly with her but is essentially using her to escape his
suffocating family, whose idea of middle-class correctness conceals
brutalities that are completely foreign to Stella, and who are horrified that she loves and respects her work dancing and singing with
the "repulsive bouzoukia." She then meets a soccer player named
Miltos, who courts her by threatening to drive his car over her,
when she initially refuses to go out with him, tearing through the
entrance of the Paradise Taverna. He tells her that when he likes a
woman, it's "like going into a cage with wild beasts," and lights
a stick of dynamite, threatening to throw it at her instead of roses.
He presents himself as her erotic equal, someone who defies conventional social or sexual constraints, but he sees erotic life as violent, a struggle to the death, in which victory, the man's fulfillment,

means that the woman submits utterly to the man's will, or has to die. He cannot tolerate the sense of her as separate from him, and must either force her to fuse with him, so that they seem to be a being with one will, or destroy her. He tells her that he has decided they will marry, and that if she refuses to do what he wants, he'll leave her, he swears on his mother's life. Stella wants him so much that she goes against her misgivings and consents, and he tells her the church and the day he has chosen. Love, she sings at the taverna, in a song you still hear often on the radio or at concerts, is a switch-blade, with a double blade of joy and pain.

The wedding date is set for October 28, "*Okhi*" Day—"No" Day—a serpentine irony, since the day unreservedly commemorates one of the most ambiguous figures of modern Greek history, the dictator General Metaxas. Kostas presses the pause signal on the remote to make sure I know the story of Metaxas, a Nazi sympathizer who tried to make a miniature Germany of Greece, down to the youth organizations for Greek Christian boys only, but when the Fascist Italian allies asked for free passage through Greece to Africa, replied with the famous and fictitious "*Okhi*," no. "So you see," he says, "there are helices of irony here, the ultimate irony being that this is a holiday that in a sense, by heroizing Metaxas, denies the existence of irony, adopts a deliberate national amnesia, says no to everything but myth. In fact, Melina's own father, Stamatis, protested against the Metaxas dictatorship, and was involved in a coup to overthrow Metaxas."

He starts the tape again; the groom's mother, a dumpy little colonel of a woman, calls on Stella, protesting that Stella should have come to her to kiss her hand, and announcing that Stella is too beautiful for her son. She tells Stella bluntly, and with the calm smug schadenfreude of a camp guard addressing an internee, what marriage means—that her job singing is finished, that she will move from her familiar beloved neighborhood to a respectable middle-class house that Miltos has already decided on, that she is no longer Stella, but the wife of Miltos. Stella is horrified by the message and the messenger—she sees her future in the figure of Miltos's mother, who seems to have been destroyed as a woman by marriage—she is monstrously neutered, only her costume of dress and hat, but nothing in her features or bearing, expresses a distinctive femininity. Stella realizes that marrying according to this conception will destroy her love and her humanity—that, ironically, the sanctified convention is immoral—although she wants Miltos so much that the only way she can not marry him is by not going to the church, losing herself in the Okhi Day parades, and dancing until dawn for the last time, since she knows that Miltos will come hunting soon to kill her. As she reaches her own street at dawn, she sees him coming toward her with a knife, and stands her ground. "Run away, Stella," he says to her, "I'm holding a knife," but she walks freely toward him, in a magnificent piece of acting, struggling with her fear and her knowledge that she is about to be murdered. He warns her again to run away, but she continues to walk toward him; at this moment, she is "the man, the hero" he is not, the gallant *pallikari,* proceeding in the full consciousness of what lies ahead, while he, despite his muscled strength and the honed knife he drives into her, is helpless, compulsive, too weak not to kill her.

"Some people say it's the Greek *Carmen,*" Kostas says, rewinding the tape. "But it's not like Carmen at all," I say. "In the last scene when she walks toward him, she is pitting love against murder, she is offering him a choice of life and love in all its complexity. And he says, '*Okhi.*' This is not the Greek *Carmen,* it's the Greek *Psycho,* as if Miltos and his mother, fused together, kill Stella. Except in Hitchcock, it was treated as a psychological aberration, and in *Stella,* as a social norm."

A few days later, I stopped at the *laiki* in Melina's neighborhood to buy some potatoes—Greek shops open and close in different time patterns according to the day of the week, and the shops in my neighborhood would be closed by the time I got back there. Melina suddenly appeared, in full coiffure and handsome heavy gold jewelry, trailing an entourage of cameras, while the *laiki* merchants called affectionate greetings to her. As she passed by a booth selling tableware and kitchen utensils, the gold-toothed, gray-haired proprietor grinned with delight, seized a knife from one of the boxes, and waved it in her direction. "Run away, Stella," he shouted to her joyfully, "I'm holding a knife."

THE RULE OF WOMEN

Magic water in great vats is set up in the forecourts of the churches in my neighborhood for the January 6 feast of Theofania, a feast with many themes, the baptism of Christ, whose divine presence purifies the waters, and who is always shown in icons of this scene with "the personification" of the river Jordan crouched at his feet in a corner, a river deity miniaturized by the power of the divine mortal. The celebration of the return of light is continued in this feast also known as Ta Fota, The Lights, here allegorized as the light of Christ coming into the world. It is also the day of the blessing of the waters, a day when drops of the water blessed in church are flung in spots where the *kalikantzari* demons lurk, in corners of the house, on the fields and vineyards, in wells. Icons are taken outside to be washed in the sea or in blessed rivers and fountains, reminiscent, as many friends have pointed out to me, of the annual sacred cleansing of Athens's cult statue of Athena in the sea.

Women crowd around the vat after the liturgy, carrying pitchers, teapots, and plain drinking glasses to get supplies of the holy water, "the holiest of the year," one says to me. A man and a boy ladle the water into the containers, busy as short-order cooks. The sea is also being blessed today; a neighbor of mine tells me that the ceremony of diving into the water to retrieve the cross helps bring the beginning of calm weather, and hurries the process of breaking up the ice. All over the country, men who have made special vows are performing the feat of diving into the waters to bring to the surface the cross their bishop or priest has thrown. In northern Greece, where the rivers and lakes are full of ice, the feat is especially painful, and the evening papers are full of pictures of shivering men with hard-won smiles of pride. The main Athens ceremony, the friend who is taking me to lunch claims, is held at a heated swimming pool—the bishop, she says, has the cross on a kind of leash, so it doesn't sink to the bottom. I can't tell if she is teasing.

We head for Glyfada, a seaside suburb of Athens, for lunch, parking her car once to run down the beach to dip our hands in the cold, steely sea for luck. The restaurant, a well-known seaside dive, has moved, and is now, it turns out, on the highway. Inside, we eat mussels stuffed with rice and currants at a table facing a huge poster showing a quadrant of views of the Swiss Alps and Swiss villages. A mirror over the bar is inscribed in bright blue paint with the Greek word for tradition, in Roman letters. A bearded priest in a long black cassock, with his hair in the Orthodox ponytail, reels his way to the bar, carrying a carafe he wants refilled. "They are all traitors," he shouts over the noise of the crowd. "All traitors. They have all betrayed us." He looks around the room, as if he expects a challenge, and finding none, lurches unevenly toward the door, pausing to support himself at intervals with the backs of strangers' chairs.

Next morning, I am on my way to Thessaloniki, planning to go to a curious yearly celebration in a Macedonian village called the Yinaikokratia, the Rule of Women. Thessaloniki is hemmed in with fog, as it often is, I am told, in winter, so I wait for hours in the airport while a businessman who has just come in from Russia tells me about his wheat trade, and entertains me with his racy version of Mrs. Papandreou's sexual biography. "Her breasts," he says, "are phenomenal, they are like engineering feats. Have you been to

Istanbul?" No, I say, I haven't. "Well, Dimitra's breasts, they are like the dome of Agia Sofia."

Yiannis, a friend who is a brilliant painter, drives with me through the dove-colored gray and brown winter countryside to the small, pleasant, nondescript village of Monoklissia, where the festival is held. The usual archaeological layers of myth have settled over this holiday, which some say came here from eastern Thrace, as a vague festival celebrating a female god: some call it Saint Domna's Day, a Christian festival honoring midwives and female fertility, which of course is a dead giveaway of its pre-Christian origins, because of the Christian idealization of celibacy and condemnation of sexuality; some say it was brought here by Greek refugees from Turkey after the 1923 population exchange. I was told by a Macedonian specialist that there was a similar holiday celebrated by the Bulgarians of Macedonia when the region had a mixed ethnic population, a January holiday called "Matron's Day," with festivities very like this one. And although everyone has told me, in odd tones of reassurance, that this holiday, like the January holidays, and like carnival approaching, is dedicated to fertility magic, it is clear from the moment we reach the village that, like the other holidays, this one carries strong social messages— a huge banner is arched over the entrance to the village, reading "Yinaikokratia," and an orchestra of men wearing long skirts greets us as we enter the town. I can pass freely through the entrance, but Yiannis is restricted, and must be given a kind of permission to enter by the women controlling the visitors. The transvestism here is a social, even a political transvestism—the men are not just dressing like women, but being treated like women by women mocking men's behavior. A woman comes forward carrying a bowl of water and a sprig of basil, and with gleeful malice splashes Yiannis with the drops clinging to her plant, in a deadpan parody of a typical Orthodox priest's blessing and assumption of moral authority. "Why do you splash me?" Yiannis asks, a shade of hurt in his expression. "Because you are a man, *vre,* polluted," she says, "and you must be purified to enter." She winks at me, having a high time mocking the theology which defines women as physically and morally imperfect, and evoking in particular the prohibition against women entering a church during their menstrual periods, a routine prohibition for a woman of her generation. As a girl baby, she would not have been baptized close to the sanctuary as a boy baby could be. When Yiannis has met the standards of the ruling women, he is allowed to follow me past the houses where men wearing long aprons and holding brooms are shut up for the day. He accompanies me to the edge of the village square, but he is not allowed to set foot in it, a community transvestism, since a village *plateia* is usually a male preserve. Someone points out the mayor to me, standing theatrically at a window in the *dimarkheio,* the mayoralty overlooking the square, peering mournfully out, like a harem woman. Women and girls are dancing round dances on the square, many of the older women swigging from open bottles of wine and ouzo. A lone television reporter and cameraman follow the leader, a magnificent *yiayia* with long gray braids, who must be at least eighty, and is leading the dances, holding a bottle of brandy in one hand and a carved wooden cane in the other. She takes a superbly stagy gulp of brandy, composes her face into a hilarious caricature of a manly leer of authority, and issues her edict: "None of us will be going home tonight, *vre!*"

On the way back to the city, we pass a sign showing the route to a city named Florina. This city is ruled, Yiannis tells me, by an old archbishop named Augustinos, who has been a power here since the sixties, the junta days. In Florina, he says, dead people remain unburied if the records show them as having had a civil marriage ceremony instead of a church one. A well-known movie director named Angelopoulos has been threatened by locals while on location in Florina and his movies cannot be shown here because the bishop has anathematized him. The archbishop is nostalgic for the sixties, when he issued a directive that women must remain standing throughout church services, while men were permitted to use pews and chairs, if they felt tired. He also forbade celebrations of the pre-Lenten carnival, because, I am told, he feared the festivities would bring about a religious revival of the twelve Olympian gods.

PREGNANT MEN

The half-hearted Valentine's displays, since Saint Valentine belongs to Rome, and this is a thoroughly imported holiday, are overshadowed by the glittering masks and costumes that mark the overlapping three weeks of carnival. On the way downtown, the few Valentine's offerings I see have neither hearts nor flowers. Instead, there is a gigantic baby's rattle with the legend "You're my baby," and a thick green felt cucumber, inscribed "I'm very juicy, do you want some?" In a window a few blocks down, I do see hearts decorating a pair of red and white boxing gloves tied together with a red ribbon. One glove reads, "If you don't love me . . . ," and the other continues, "I will make you eat wood," the idiom for "beat you up."

In Cathedral Square, between the Little Cathedral and the Great Cathedral, I wait for Kostas to take me to see the famous Zographos paintings commemorating the Greek revolution that were commissioned by General Makriyiannis himself. The alternative cathedrals themselves are witnesses to the meandering patterns of Greek history. The Little Cathedral, also known as "The Virgin Who Grants Requests Quickly," of uncertain date, but probably twelfth or thirteenth century, was the cathedral of Athens under Turkish rule in

the eighteenth century; its size, smaller than a one-room frontier
school, tells something about the status of the city itself during the
Tourkokratia, and during the Byzantine era too, when Athens was
considered a backwater, a memory of a great city. What is riveting
about the Little Metropolis is that its builders made use of ancient
marble reliefs that were to hand, just as the Christian emperor Constantine's statue in Byzantium was constructed of his massive head
set onto the decapitated body of a statue of the sun god. Some of
the marbles are carved with signs of the zodiac, and personified festivals of the classical year, including the Panathenaic ship which carried the newly made garment used to dress Athena every year, and
whose procession figures in the Parthenon marbles, as they are
called here, never the Elgin marbles. In Byzantine days, when the
countryside was covered with Greek and Roman antiquities, marbles were often thought to harbor demons, and a Christian folklore
grew up about the old gods, whom Christ had revealed to be
demons, some of whom, like Artemis, were said to roam the land
with demonic followers. Scholars say that so many carved marble
sarcophagi survived intact because people often left them un-
touched, afraid of the demons they harbored, although other, prag-
matic, villagers put them to use as troughs or fountain basins. The
builders who made use of these might have thought they were neutralizing the demonic powers that permeated them—now these
marbles are infused with a different dream, a different kind of
magic. I have come to this church many times, or passed it with different companions, who pointed it out to me as a perfect example
of a magical unbroken continuity of Greek culture, a belief as strong
here now as the belief in demons was in the twelfth century.

The big nineteenth-century cathedral, a monument to the tangled collaboration between the European powers and the Greeks
which produced this state, was founded by King Otto and his
Queen Amalia, neither of them Greek nor Orthodox. From 1863
to 1964 the German-Danish Glucksberg kings were crowned here,
until the Greeks voted against further monarchy in 1973; and inside

lie the bones of Orthodox martyrs, the remains of the unofficial patron saint of the Greek revolution, Gregory the Fifth, a patriarch of Constantinople hanged by the Turks shortly after the outbreak of the rebellion, and the sixteenth-century martyr Filothei, whose bones are always carried in procession on February 19 by one of her descendants. Her stinging remarks about Athenians have made more than one modern-day Athenian speculate about who exactly it was that martyred her: "They cannot stand firm, these Athenians. They are . . . irresolute, faithless, shameless, abominable, desperate, their mouths always open in mockery and complaint, speaking a barbarous language, eager to blame, loving strife, cavilling, pusillanimous, gossiping, arrogant, lawless, guileful, snooping, eternally on the lookout for the disasters of others."

I look at my watch, and sit down on a bench. Kostas is fifteen minutes late, but I am used to Greek timekeeping, which is utterly flexible in a way I find very pleasant: clocks seem to be perceived as representatives of a cosmic bureaucracy, which may nominally rule us but to which we will never submit. A man sits down on the bench next to me, ready for a chat. He tells me that he is originally from Chios, and about his navy days and how a saint named Agia Markella saved him from a coma after a shipboard accident that left him unconscious. He gave a lamp to her church in Chios to thank her, and tells me if there is anything I want, a child, for instance, I must pray to her to make me worthy of getting my wish, and to help me. He puts his hand on my knee, and I politely remove it, and tell him that I come from a place where the customs are more austere than in Crete. He says he is surprised, that he didn't know such places existed in America, and asks me one of those ingenious *kamaki* questions to which there is no safe reply. "Have you ever been with a Greek man?" I run through my menu of options. "Yes" will mean to him there is no reason to turn him down. "No" will mean you don't know what you're missing, let me show you. I briefly consider "I don't remember," but consider national *filotimo*; this would possibly be grounds for deportation. I settle on "Why do you ask?" and he tells me that in all the ports, the ladies of the harbor request Greeks. "The Americans get drunk, they are only good for a short time, but with the Greeks, my girl, eight times a night is what you can expect. I remember a time in Tokyo when I went back and forth between two girls all night, and satisfied them both, like a rooster does with the hens. Eight times a night! Do you want to go somewhere with me and find out?" Luckily, Kostas arrives, and we set off to the museum. "I'll think of you," the old sailor calls, waving good-bye to me.

On the way to the National Historical Museum in the old parliament building, we walk past the statue of the revolutionary leader Kolokotronis, whose raised arm, Kostas says, points to Constantinople. I was very curious to see the Zographos paintings, since they crystallize another split between Greece as East and West. Originally, General Makriyiannis had commissioned a European painter to paint scenes from the revolution as he described them, but the French painter's work could not translate the images as he wanted them to exist, and Makriyiannis fired him and hired a Greek instead. At many of the little souvenir postcard stands, you can find a reproduction of a popular folk picture that represents General Makriyiannis decisively showing the European painter, who slinks off, in his un-Greek frock coat and top hat, the way back to Europe. I saw some of the drama in the division between the nineteenth- and twentieth-century Greek paintings in an earlier visit to the National Gallery's collection. The nineteenth-century Greek painters seem to have been mostly schooled in Munich, the city that strongly influenced modern Athens, because of its Bavarian king and courtiers. Despite the academic realism of the paintings' style, though, the subjects are often unintelligible. It is unnerving to look at paintings so conventional in style and so unreadable in subject: an old woman who incomprehensibly kneels on a mountain is making a *tama,* a religious vow; a peasant girl, with furtive misery, watches another woman dandling a baby—this turns out to be a scene of natural and adoptive mothers; some men dressed as fanciful monstrous animals burst into a dining room, a scene as it turns out from carnival; an old man in a turban is about to lead a small child away from its mother, who is kissing the child on the forehead—this is a scene of the *paidomazoma,* the Ottoman Turkish practice of culling non-Turkish boys for the Janissary regiment, while girl children were chosen for harems. And a scene of festively dressed beaming adults and tiny children in a cottage room, which turns out to be not only a picture of everyday domestic enjoyment, but the children's engagement party. Even your eyes couldn't tell you what was happening in the pictures—it was like seeing Chinese genre scenes done in Western style. The twentieth-century pictures by and large evaded realism, and many had returned to the Byzantine rejection of perspective.

Marble busts of Greek patriots and self-consciously grim portraits of Independence warriors, cases of axes and rifles and fatally curved swords, make this seem a museum of rage. One room displays a case of Kolokotronis's belongings, the famous plumed helmet marked with a cross, and weapons. A guard comes up to us, and asks Kostas, "She's French?" "No," he says, "American." "I thought American girls only wore trousers," says the guard, "but she's wearing a skirt." "They wear what they like," says Kostas. "And why do you bring her here?" "She wants to learn about Greek history," he says, and the guard takes my arm. "What, she wants to learn about Aliki?" he says, referring to a Kewpie-doll-like blond actress of uncertain age, who is always referred to as "our national star," and whose comedies are the bread-and-butter films of Greek TV. Kostas says, "She knows all about Aliki, she's seen *Holiday in Aegina* and *Aliki in the Navy,* and I read her the critic who said that there were two timeless phenomena in Greece, Aliki and stupidity."

"Then let me show her a picture of Athens in Otto's time," the guard replies, and we go into another room. "Look how poor Athens was, like a village." "But beautiful," I say, and the guard looks at me with irony and regret, and Kostas says, "Yes, sometimes we seem crucified between hopeless poverty and hopeless prosperity." "Now she must see the American doctor," the guard says, and con-

ducts us to a painting of a foustanella-wearing Samuel Howe, the
husband of Julia Ward Howe. The guard begins to tell the story of
Howe's service here during the Greek War of Independence, but
some of his lower teeth loosen during the telling. He spits them into
his hand, and calmly replaces them; "I can't finish the story without
my teeth," he says, his fever to tell his story so great that he treats
the teeth simply as instruments in its service.

Kostas has to be in Brussels later this evening for EEC work,
so we pass hurriedly through a gallery of traditional women's costumes, and a room full of intriguing patriotic posters from the Second World War, one of which shows the Virgin Mary hovering in a
cloud above a battle, next to a newspaper which has a headline
about the Panagia's presence, declaring in smaller print that this was
no fantastic story or legend.

The Zographos paintings are a kind of history of the birth of the
new Greek state, from the fall of Constantinople in 1453 to a
painting that had to be destroyed, showing a Bavarian minister
tearing the heart from Greece's body with a bloody hand. There is
a picture of Greece crowning the Philhellenes—Europeans and
Americans who fought alongside the Greeks—and one of God
addressing Greece, telling the country, "I shall set you up to be
ruled over by Othon and Amalia." God floats on a cloud, wearing a
white beard. On one side of the picture, the European powers,
wearing European military uniforms, decorations, and nineteenth-
century ballgowns, accompanied by foustanella-wearing Greek
soldiers, observe as an angel drops laurel wreaths onto the heads of
Otto and Amalia. Makriyiannis commissioned twenty-five paintings, and described in detail the battle scenes for the painter, who
was himself a veteran from Sparta, taking him to the sites of some
of the battles. With their sense of the human figure as symbolic,
their sense that time is continuous, that time is the perspective,
rather than space, so that scenes occurring at different times occur
on the same plane, these paintings are profoundly different from
what the French painter must have shown Makriyiannis. This

painter's idea of what an image was was formed on different models, Byzantine icons obviously, but also eighteenth- and nineteenth-century Greek and Turkish embroidery; cloth forces just this magical floating sense of space and these doll-like human figures—and I am stunned, finally, by their resemblance to Turkish Ottoman miniatures.

"How could we not be part of each other's art?" asks Kostas. "We are part of each other's music, each other's languages, each other's traditions. Like you blacks and whites in the South, we may be hostile to each other, but we are fused; we each are the unconscious of the other. And at the time of Makriyiannis, not so very long ago, the people we fought were much closer to us in our customs and way of life than our allies. Makriyiannis was a man for whom images were full of symbolic meaning, and I doubt the French painter understood this. The general tells a story about another set of decorations he commissioned after Zographos had finished his pictures. He set aside part of his garden to be laid out in mosaics of black and white pebbles taken from the seashore, *krokalia,* we call it. He had the mosaicist lay out a circle with spears around it, to symbolize Greece surrounded for centuries by tyrants. Below the circle there was a dog, who was the Greek faithful to his country as to a religion, and the columns of the temple of Olympian Zeus and Hadrian's gate and an owl, to represent the classical past. Then he had the mosaicist show two men dancing, one a man in Greek clothes, one in European clothes, which Makriyiannis called 'Frankish costume.' The two men were struggling to dance in the style of their own native dances, and Makriyiannis wrote that this represented how Europe and Greece would come into conflict, 'for no man can learn another's steps.' "

I stop at one of the downtown kiosks for a newspaper—an attempt was made on the life of an environmental official who had gone to the police with evidence that portions of the local forest were being destroyed by organized real estate speculators. Some fifteen shots were fired into his house, and a family member commented that in Greece people were murdered for earth more often than for narcotics. A married housebuilder has killed his sister-in-law and himself in what seems to have been a crime of passion, in the family's apartment building, where both his and her relatives lived, including her own mother and brother. This typical Greek domestic arrangement is often praised as a demonstration of the exemplary value of keeping families together, but it can also, as I have seen, enclose a family in a kind of insidious theater instead of a house, magnifying and concentrating passions and incompatibilities so sharply that the only denouement possible is one of violence, since the possessiveness of disturbed families is motivated by needs for power and punishment more often than love or mutual concern.

The cover of a lavish weekly television guide shows a popular and witty satirist named Harry Klinn dressed in a strapless orange gown for a carnival special, which reminds me that I am going to a carnival party myself tonight, and the sight of turbaned golden faces covered with glitter and jewelry hanging from wires in a window tempts me inside the store to see if there is anything I can do about a costume, or at least a mask. The season's shows featuring music and political satire, and the displays of costumes themselves, reflect the tradition of carnival in Greece as an outlet for free speech and uncensored social commentary, under the protection of a mask and costume. A London *Times* correspondent circa 1875 remarked that he had seen a local Athenian humorist "reeling drunk" during carnival, "who had put on the classic helmet of the princely Agamemnon, king of Mycenae, making a little fun of Dr. Schliemann's recent discoveries there." He also noticed the other distinctive preoccupation of carnival here, transvestism—not just a sexual transvestism, but a social one, a chance to reveal temporarily what is hidden in you. The reporter remarked that "a tendency to appear in the costumes of foreign countries is strongly manifested . . . the Turk, and at times, his wife, seems to be a favorite character"—still true, I think, looking around at the many mannequins wearing belly dancer costumes and jeweled mouth veils, or fezes and toy curved scimitars. There are costumes in which to metamorphose from European to African, with heavily muscled dark-skinned rubber chests and spears, from adult to baby wearing a goblet-sized pacifier and lace cap, from local working person into European leader, through rubber masks of Mitterrand and Margaret Thatcher, and a supply, stamped "Made in Germany," of Hitler. But the most popular transformations, judging by the variations available, are from male to female. There is practically a whole floor upstairs of enormous portable breasts, some white, some black, some celebrity. Some come with toy babies to suckle. A face and full-breasted torso of Madonna is offered, and there is a range of malleable rubber strap-on pregnant bellies.

Later that night at the party, the room is crammed with whiskey-sipping men, smoking relentlessly, in the Greek style, many in various stages of pregnancy. It is interesting to see that there are few Greek-flavored costumes here—no Olympian gods, no Byzantine empresses, no village dress heavy with embroidery and the portable dowries of jewelry, no one from the Karaghiozis shadow puppet repertoire, except Alexander the Great. The host and hostess, a theater couple, are dressed as Rhett Butler and Scarlett O'Hara. They pour me a glass of wine, and introduce me to other guests in various clusters of conversation, lastly a man who says his name is Stamatis, a name that with its relation to the Greek verb "to stop" was often used as a kind of magical talisman to stop a run of bad luck or deaths in a family, or in one case I know, as a form of magical birth control, since the wife didn't want more children. Stamatis is dressed as Violetta in *La Traviata;* his cleavage is deeper than mine, and his makeup much better applied. Our hostess tells him I am working on a book, and he says he will be happy to talk to me as long as I don't identify him. We agree that I will call him the magically protective name Stamatis. I compliment him on his costume, saying that La Dame aux Caméllias seems to be a kind of traditional transvestite costume here, mentioning that I have seen a famous photograph of the great Greek painter Tsarouchis as Violetta. Tsarouchis, a flamboyant homosexual whose epigrams are so

famous here that they are simply called "Tsarouchia," wrote that
he had made his Violetta costume out of traditionally masculine
materials, using the white undershirt worn ubiquitously by Greek
men, and his grandfather's foustanella. "Of course," says Stamatis,
"you will surely have noticed by now that we are a completely transvestite culture, it is our one real continuity, in history, in sex, in
politics, in religion. For us, the supreme ideal of emotion is a
transvestite ideal, the moment when reality and fantasy fuse and
become the same thing, the moment that gives the sensation of
simultaneity, as in Holy Communion. If you hear our great Lenten
hymn to the Virgin Mary, you will hear her praised as the one
who resolves all contradictions. Our political aspirations, too, are
transvestite: our great modern political experiences, like the
Megali Idea, or the defeat of the Italian attack in 1941, or now, with
Macedonia, are supreme because we feel ourselves transformed
into our own legends, legends that correct what actually occurred;
we wear the drag of Byzantines reconquering Constantinople, ancient Hellenes staving off the Romans, transvestites of time. This is
why myth, the transvestite form of fiction, is our ideal literary
genre. Myth is not, as earnest European scholars have earnestly
written, an attempt to explain reality; it is an attempt to recreate it,
so that story and life are the same thing, so that there is for a time
no painful difference between imagination and reality. That moment
of fusion, central to all religious ritual, is for us what gives the
sensation, even the illusion, of immortality, which we struggle to
reproduce again and again.

"Our transvestism is cut into every facet of Hellenism, some
of it quite literally. Here, in Athens, a city where Ramadan as well
as Easter was celebrated for hundreds of years, we changed our
clothes after the War of Independence, starting when carriages
were introduced in our new European city Athens. The drivers
changed their fezes and foustanellas, garments shared with Albanians and Turks, for top hats and European coats. In our parliament,
some members held out for their fezes, but even the members who

put on the black frock coats accompanied the debates with the music of the clicking beads of the *komboloi* they had taken up from the Turks." I remembered my actress friend, Aura, telling me that her mentors of a generation ago told her that one of the great challenges they faced onstage was in not being distracted by the audience's clicking beads, even at Epidaurus, the classical theater that is to Greek tragedy what Stratford is to Shakespeare.

"To the East," Stamatis says, fanning himself with Violetta's lace-and-mother-of-pearl fan, "we dress as the West, to the West, we dress as the East, and I expect the Turks do a version of the same play. Where else but here would people insist so bitterly that any deviation from the Greek point of view is a betrayal of Western culture, and at the same time claim that the war in Yugoslavia was stirred up by 'Western' warmongers? For the West, we dress as classical Greeks, for the East and the Slav Balkans as their Byzantine Christian superiors. We dress our cultural villains *en travesti;* it is always the Turks who shattered our culture. And yet the great model for the Ottoman Empire was the empire of the Byzantines. I don't excuse the Turks, their rule was full of poor administration and barbaric abuses, but I don't glorify the Byzantines, whose rule was also full of barbaric abuses and poor administration, and who were far less tolerant of any deviation from their state religion than the Ottomans. The Byzantines tried to crush classical culture, although they ended up, as destroyers often do, like the Nazis who wanted to obliterate European Judaism, preserving it in maimed form, or like the Jews, so obsessed with obliterating what they perceived to be idols that they ended up idolizing themselves.

"Even our gods are transvestites, thanks to the willful Byzantine destruction of the religious pluralism the polytheists embraced. And gods that are forced underground will resurface in the strangest places, as Athena, Aphrodite, and Demeter, and Tyche, and many others do in Mary, an utterly pagan goddess, and in Christ himself, whom the Greek councils designed in their creed as a three-personed god, in a common Hellenic pattern, like Hecate and others, and with a dual nature, like Aphrodite, who as Ourania presided over marital generative sex, and as Pandemos presided over erotic sex and prostitution. Even the divinizing of individual mortals is a Greek pattern of worship—the sky is full of our divine mortals, as over our heads in churches hovers Jesus the human Jew whom we made Christ, the Greek god, the thirteenth Olympian. I tell you, transvestism never ends here. Do you watch Lazopoulos?"

I do, although the Greek is difficult for me, and his political humor beyond me, full of inside jokes, rapid and idiomatic. Still, I am sure that Lakis Lazopoulos, although he may never be well-known outside of Greece, is a comedic genius on the order of Chaplin. He appears on television in a show made up of a cast of ten characters, all of whom he plays. The most famous of them is the widow Mitsi, the archetypal Mediterranean mother, whose destructive "nurturing love" is itself a form of transvestism, who disguises her malice, moral narcissism, and domineering drive to power by ascribing all her actions to maternal concern and tenderness, drawing all her distinction and prestige from a motherhood that is ultimately imaginary, a kind of mutual enslavement which it is sacrilege to confront. She is like the kind of Jew or Muslim who deflect any legitimate critical look at their cultures as being anti-Semitic or anti-Islam, insisting that any critical observation or dissent is a form of attack.

Dressed as the widow Mitsi, Lazopoulos turns himself into a busty middle-class matron, her helmeted coiffure a symbol of convention itself, her enormous bosom an aggressive weapon, her anguished made-up eyes gleaming piteously and ferociously behind unfashionable glasses, her lipsticked Cupid's-bow mouth pursed, signaling flirtation, self-righteousness, calculated, coercive, theatrical misery, and real misery. Like many great comic creations, she is utterly humorless. The widow Mitsi is so famous that Lazopoulos has even been interviewed by a newspaper not in his own person, but in hers. Lazopoulos has also done brilliant theater sketches, one of a mother who invades every aspect of her son's life, his career, his orgasms, even his wife's womb, announcing at every conflict that she will die if her wishes are not followed, finally driving her son to suicide. It is a brilliant comic feat, this piece, made out of material that is purely, oppressively tragic.

"And our greatest modern novelist, Taktsis, who was murdered only a few years ago, was a transvestite—I'm sure you've read *The Third Wedding Wreath.*"

I had read his remarkable novel, narrated by its women characters, which for many Greek readers is the consummate picture of post–civil war Greece, but I had not known how he was killed.

"He was found naked in his bed, strangled, on a summer day in 1988. Most nights, his neighbors said, he would get in his car and drive to places that were gathering places for sexual buyers and sellers, and Taktsis would look over the possibilities. Witnesses said Taktsis had gone out three times that night, dressed in women's clothes and wearing a blond wig. He came back three times, each with a different man. The third man killed him. He was described as well-dressed, of average height, and wearing a mustache. You can always rely on your neighbors in Greece to know what your lovers look like and when they visit you. I can guarantee you that yours do too. The police found the house torn apart, with a camera and a video missing, who knows why? In their reconstruction of the murder, they concluded the attack must have come as a surprise, since there were no signs of previous violence, and the police coroner said the killer strangled Taktsis with his right hand. Isn't it strange that they can know the details of a murder down to the murderer's hand, but never find the killer himself? In this small country, in the narrower circles of male prostitutes, no information was ever turned up. Strange, isn't it?"

Stamatis catches sight of a sloe-eyed man with thick dark hair, full lips, and the ideal body more often cultivated here by homosexuals. This ideal seems yet another variety of transvistism, since the mortal anatomy is supposed to cross-dress as marble, looking as much like a classical Greek statue as possible, and displaying the classical profile. "*Ah, fors' è lui,*" Stamatis says, in Violetta's Italian, and I can see he is impatient to move on. He gives me a card from an ornate period card case he is carrying, and tells me to call him if I feel like it, when I am in Athens between trips.

When I get home, all the talk about the widow Mitsi makes me curious to look up the category of mothers in my dream books. *Yiayias* are in my modern dream books, a much idealized dream, in which you are advised to attend to her every word. But only one catalogues dreams of mothers, dreams in which the mother's mood or physical health determines the outcome—if she is as she is in everyday life, it is good luck; if she is dead or sick, you will suffer grief, or be humiliated in some way. I turn to Artemidorus on mothers, where the dreams are stunningly different: "the case of one's mother," he writes, "is both complex and manifold." The dreams are interpreted on the basis of the particular sexual positions the mother assumes during sex with the dreamer. In Artemidorus's world, men dominate the world of dreams as they do the world of waking—each of these particular dreams presents the world as dreamed by a man. Artemidorus discusses first face-to-face intercourse between a dreamer and a living mother, delaying the interpretation of the same position practiced with a dead mother. This dream is bad for someone with a living father, but good for craftsmen, laborers, since a trade is like a mother, and demagogues and public figures, since a mother is a symbol of one's country, and "just as a man who follows the precepts of Aphrodite when he makes love completely governs the body of his obedient and willing partner, the dreamer will control all the affairs of the city." The view of lovemaking as a form of successful political domination of a submissive partner, and as a form of humiliation, is fascinating; dreaming of many different positions with a mother foreshadows bad outcomes, "for it is not right to insult one's mother." And so is the hierarchy of meanings assigned to the positions themselves, which, except for "missionary position" sex, are all the result of "wantonness, licentiousness, and intoxication . . . ," the worst of all being the mother performing fellatio on her son. As for the Christian dream books, there is not one scene of explicit sex in any of them; sex is entirely represented through a veil of symbols, like caves and columns, never through felt experience, its existence charging the world with hidden meanings, codes recognizable to initiates, but carefully hidden away, as if for protection from someone.

CLEAN MONDAY

Instead of flying kites and picnicking on Philopappos Hill, near the Acropolis, while the president of Greece strolls among the crowds, as is traditional for Athenians on Kathari Deftera, Clean Monday, the first day of Lent, I am going for the weekend to Hydra, which a friend has told me is the Greenwich Village of Greece, "bohemian, arty, full of discos and shipping families and vegetarian restaurants. But not Greece." Still, I want to see this island, which has been repeatedly painted by modern Greek painters with much the same kind of erotic attention French impressionists felt for Provence. And besides, no matter where I have traveled in Greece, I have invariably been told that it either is not or is no longer Greece, as if there is an imaginary Greece that exists in perfect intact detail somewhere, much realer than the Greece we live in.

The island, largely settled by Christian Albanians, is almost pure rock, its cliffs ruddy and nicked like the faces of men who spend their days working outdoors and impatiently cut themselves when they shave. The town itself looks like a stage set, the red-tiled houses artfully positioned in negotiation with the cliffs, so that the town is forced to have a visible foreground and clear recession into the distance, with a stage apron formed by the curving harbor; it is easy to see why painters love this island, with the radiant geometry of the houses, and the climactic harbor. I stroll through the many-leveled town, admiring blue iron railings wrought in the shape of enlaced anchors. The houses differ in details, with handsome, even playful entrances, brilliantly colored doors, brass door knockers in the shapes of women's hands, some wearing rings and bracelets; but the buildings themselves are mostly variations on a theme, like domestic icons built to satisfy the strictures of some domestic theology. The steepness and rockiness of the setting they must be built in gives an intensity to the close gathering of the houses, helpless emblems of the compulsory intertwining of this community.

A model in a striped summer dress and white flats leans against a railing on the harbor on this chilly day, while a photographer holds up a white hoop to test the light on her face. A makeup artist wearing a blond braid strokes her cheeks with blusher, while Greek boys settle like pigeons on steps to look at her. The makeup artist brushes the model's hair as if she were a doll, and the model moves her head slowly from side to side, experimenting with smiles of different intensity. The photographer tells her to unbutton her skirt to show more leg, while more local boys and a man in a ship captain's hat flock to the steps, smoking furiously and cupping their chins in their hands, attentive as ideal schoolboys, their legs splayed hopefully. The makeup artist strikes up a conversation with me, telling me about the Athens hotel she was booked in, a place she says where men wearing toupees rent rooms by the hour, and other men who hung out by the clerk's desk offered her jobs teaching English, and pressured her to let them take her picture, a well-known *kamaki* trophy, the album full of alleged conquests to be shown to buddies, the snapshots often more important than sex. She went for a coffee with one, she says, who told her he was a university professor, and confided to her that he chose sexual partners from a pool of his female students. "I don't pressure them," he told her, "it is their choice. Of course if they imagine it will help their grades, that is a

motive. But I say nothing." When he made his offer to the makeup
artist, she refused him, but he warned her, "You should choose a
man soon, soon you will lose your beauty. I might marry you now,
but in two years, I don't think I would."

The dawn comes into Greece with the quality of lightning, suddenly there is absolute, unavoidable light. Roosters crow, a donkey
sounds its anguished wheeze. I have been invited to a pretty seaside
village for Kathari Deftera lunch, a meal which marks the beginning
of meatless Lent and consists of fish salads like taramosalata, a special kind of flat bread studded with sesame baked only once a year
on this day, and the rivers of wine, which anesthetize the fast. I set
out to walk to the village, ascending above the mansions with lemon
trees in their marble courtyards, climbing the steeply cut stone
staircases, marked with a variety of animal droppings, donkey, cat,
dog, and bird, behind Hydra town, which lead to the hill villages.
Some women and children are setting a table on a flat roof looking
out from the cliffs, feeling spring beginning. I walk through brilliant
green terraces of farm and pasture land following a dirt lane; a donkey passes by with a man riding sidesaddle, his wife walking behind
him, exactly like a nineteenth-century genre painting I remember
from the national gallery. To the right there is a dreamily beautiful
farm, in a green valley overlooking the blue Aegean, which is set behind an elaborate door and gate, as if the entrance led directly into
a mansion instead of a tree-lined country lane; and to the left there
are flocks of sheep grazing among starry clusters of periwinkle-
colored flowers and endless oceans of clover, their bells sounding
exactly like church bells, which gives a new concreteness to the
Orthodox prelates' reference to their congregation as flocks—
the very local world of Mediterranean pastoral metamorphosed
into Christian symbolism, the divine, like our dreams, made up of
images we see around us day by day, images that change worship
from place to place as dreams change reality. The path drops down
to the fishing village just above the shore, past a stone bridge in the
shape of a ruined rainbow. Men in sweaters are working on boats,

painting and planing, sipping frappes, cold foamy coffee in glasses. One boat passes on the way to Hydra town, a dog standing poised on its prow like some old salt, the hero of a children's story, his profile revealing a kind of canine *filotimo,* a proud sense of having mastered life at sea. I see my hosts already at a table overlooking the sea, with them a woman, and to my surprise, Lambros, the icon painter I met in Andros. He is painting some frescoes for their weekend house. The lady with the iron-gray cropped hair turns out to be another American, who tells me right away that Greece is her spiritual home, launching into a story about Knossos and how somewhere off the coast of Crete she is sure the lost testaments of Atlantis will be found, that we are on the verge. I reflect, not for the last time, that the romantic classicism which arrived here from the West has done this country little good, and settle down to hear the theology of the world underwater. At another table a fight breaks out between a little boy and his father, who hits him in the face. "You made me eat wood, you hit me," the little boy complains, and the father pulls his head back like a disobedient dog's and threatens him with more. The mother says nothing.

Our conversation has turned to the war in Yugoslavia. Lambros says that he is appalled by the footage shot by Western television journalists, which makes the Serbs look like aggressors. "The Greek coverage will show you who the real victims are, the persecuted Orthodox of Serbia. The other stations that use the Western images give the impression the westerners want people to have. In any case, the Serbs are being hunted down because they don't bow down to the interests of the foreigners who fomented this war," he says. I have seen several stories about young Greek men volunteering for the Bosnian Serb army, to join battle in what they perceive as a religious war. "I know journalists who work for our own national television station," Lambros tells me, "who have reliable information that these skirmishes you see are staged, who say that if you freeze and enlarge the pictures, you can clearly see the hands of the director at work. And as for Sarajevo, my same friend tells me that there is only very confined damage, and that the Western journalists simply shoot the same ruins again and again to give a false impression of devastation." This, too, or variants of it, I have heard before; it is an article of faith in certain circles, believed in fiercely, like the doctrinally settled title Theotokos, God Bearer, given to the Virgin Mary, whose role as the mother of deity is emphasized here, it seems to me, even more than her virginity. Lambros wants someone to argue with him, but no one will. He says threateningly, "It isn't fanaticism. It isn't fanaticism. Orthodoxy is a stain that can never be removed from us by laundering. It is not a religion, it is a way of life, it comes from the depths of man's soul." The waiter brings another carafe of wine, and Lambros quiets, remarking that the sea reminds him of the Panagia. We drink the wine and eat mussels, looking out over the glittering water to a passage to the hidden open sea between the cliffs. The glory of the Greek landscape is how uncannily it seems to enact the processes of thought and perception it inspires, taking the eye on radiant, inconclusive pilgrimages. The bright cold spring sunshine fills the seawater full of orbiting stars flickering.

AT COLONUS

A philosopher is taking me on Cicero's and Pausanius's walk around the precincts of the Academy, where they recorded seeing the tombs of Pericles and other Athenian great men. I stop to buy a paper with a favorite cartoon strip, "The Wild Babies," which today pokes fun at Greek dealings with God. The wild child wants good weather for the traditional kite flying on Kathari Deftera, and shouts into the sky, "Make the wind blow, *re* God, make the wind blow, *re!*" using *re*, a particle that conveys a certain coarse, even at times contemptuous, familiarity; *re* is something you aren't to call your parents. The next drawing shows a downpour of rain drenching the child and his kite, and in the last frame, the child says, using a diminutive endearment, "Okay, *Theouli mou,* my dear little God, I get it! A thousand pardons for the *re!*" The child takes no account of one kind of disrespect, freely dictating to the deity, but concludes that God is upset to be called by the wrong title. He sees it not so much as a breach in his behavior, but as an insult to God's *filotimo*.

The Academy district is now a working-class neighborhood, mostly six- and eight-story apartment buildings, with a crushed little white house and garden occasionally to be seen on a corner, and some poignantly irreparable nineteenth-century neoclassical houses. With their unhinged wrought-iron gates and missing patches of wall covered with the last of their elegant terra-cotta ornaments, they have the air of nineteenth-century opera heroines maddened by unattainable love, like Lucia di Lammermoor. My friend points out to me what is thought to have been the garden of Epicurus—now a squat apartment building with underwear, blue jeans, and bath towels printed with jungle animals hanging from the laundry lines on the ascending balconies. We finish the walk at Colonus, the place where Oedipus entered the earth to die after Theseus granted him sanctuary. It is a park now, with lovely views of Mounts Parnis and Pendeli and the Tourkovounia, the Turkish mountains, as they are called. A handful of children are playing on a swing set, while a group of teenagers in leather jackets set off gunshot-sounding firecrackers that they have left over from the carnival celebrations. A boy of about six runs with a kite to the bench where his heavyset, black-clad grandmother is sitting, to harass her to climb to a higher point on the hill where the kite will fly more impressively. She doesn't want to move from her perch, but he clambers onto her lap and kneels on her heavy thighs, putting his arms around her neck. He whispers and cajoles. She doesn't smile and her eyes do not soften, but stare into his, with implacable acquiescence. He climbs down and pulls her along, like an earthbound kite. She breathes heavily as she follows him higher onto Oedipus's hill at Colonus.

SOUL SATURDAY

An intense energy is exchanged between the living and the dead during the Lenten period before Easter, as if in some ways, the prescribed fasting is a kind of death for the living, making them clairvoyant, and narrowing the boundaries between them and the dead. Soul Saturday is a day especially devoted to the dead, when their graves are tended, and they are fed *kollyva,* the food of the dead. As I walk down heavily trafficked Hymettus Street to the Protonekrotafeio, where I collided when I first arrived with the funeral of the actress Jenny Karezi, I see an unusually heavy concentration of taxis. They are pulling up at the various gates, dropping some families off and picking others up. I walk to the entrance along one wall of the cemetery, staring up at a huge sign with the Playboy logo and the admonition to "Read *Playboy* every month," and smelling over the gasoline fumes the strong perfume of incense wafting from inside. The flower shops outside the gate are doing substantial custom, and a beggar with a crutch stands sentry, asking all the entrants for money. I see no men in the crowd, just a cluster of women wearing black—the departing group are clutching plastic bags of trimmings from the newly pruned and cleaned grave greenery, and from some of the bags, silver edges of the trays on which the food of the dead was served gleam dully. As you enter the main gate, you have a clear view of the Parthenon, a sense of the strange logic of this country, this other world, ruled from here and from there by parallel sets of ghosts. The flower sellers inside the gate are offering bouquets of orange and yellow marigolds, branches of apple blossoms, white carnations. I buy a bunch of tongue-pink hyacinths. It would make me uncomfortable in the presence of people performing private rituals not to have some purpose of my own, so I decide I will walk until I find a grave that seems to call for remembrance; that way my wandering will not be prying, but a quest.

I move through the rows flanked by masses of grave sculpture, a city of stone people. I pass busts of Balkan War soldiers with the generic sternly mustached face you see in sculpture and medallions and even photographs. Beyond is the shrinelike grave of Korais, the advocate of Katharevousa Greek, and a champion in Europe for the creation of the modern state. There is a life-sized sculpture of a girl student in uniform sitting at a worktable, a stele with a relief of a woman in ancient Greek dress clasping hands with a man in a modern suit, a life-sized sculpture of a man lying on his deathbed with two children sitting on either side of the bed. In some rows there is almost no greenery; in others palms and, more beautiful, orange trees covered with golden oranges grow out of the graves. Scattered throughout the cemetery, priests wearing colored silk embroidered stoles over their cassocks are chanting private memorial services. A woman in black stands at the foot of a grave, fork in hand, eating *kollyva* from a china plate, while another, dressed in unfamiliarly formal clothes, puts her hands on her hips to shift her tight girdle. On benches at intervals, impoverished-looking people are selling candles bound together in groups of three to symbolize the trinity. "Go in goodness," a candle seller says to a man who lights them and puts them in a container at the foot of his family's grave. On another bench, a woman is selling small paper bags of *kollyva,* for those who didn't bring it from home. An old *mavrofora,* a black-clad woman with a black kerchief, sits facing her family grave, holding a burning candle, and staring. I am still looking for a grave that looks as if it needs my flowers. I pass a grave with a portrait bust of the woman it holds portrayed as the head of a sphinx, and another with a large goddess-sized sculpture, surrounded by a wrought-iron fence to which a color photograph is attached—an advertisement by the sculpture company, with its address, telephone number, and the name of the sculptor. Among the labyrinth of graves, I notice the memorial of a member of parliament, with a photograph of the man in a smiling pose, smoking a pipe, displayed in a stone casing on the grave. Directly on the marble slab some relative, perhaps, has placed a crystal bowl, with the real wooden pipe the man in the picture is smoking. I turn down an alley and see a tomb inscribed with one name in Roman script between a row of names in Greek script. When I go closer to see what this configuration means, I see it is the name of George Polk, the American journalist who was murdered in Thessaloniki in 1948, and whose cruel death caused so much suffering; an innocent man, experts on the case say, spent his life in prison for it, because the right-wing Greek government authorities and the Americans who backed them during the cold war were determined to assign the blame to a political scapegoat. I had seen the famous photograph of Polk's body after it was recovered from the Thessaloniki harbor, openmouthed, limp as a scarecrow, a picture that forces you to imagine what it must have been like to realize, as he must have, that you were going to die this way. I leave my flowers here, to cover with some tenderness this untender death.

INDEPENDENCE DAY

I wanted to be in Mani for Independence Day, since some of the most famous warlords who fought with their more or less private armies to harry the Turks out of Greece came from here; after independence was won, with so much Maniote blood, it was men from Mani who helped destabilize the new state by assassinating its first prime minister, in the pattern of Greek duality, fighting both for and against Greece.

Peloponnesians, and people from Mani in particular, feel possessive about their role in the Greek uprising, so I wanted to see how the holiday felt there, and signed on for a week's walk led by a talented mountaineer who is reputed to know every trail, hidden or public, in this part of the country. A few days before we set out, I went to the Museum of National History, a museum mostly devoted to the War of Independence.

We set out on a cold and brilliant late-March morning, making our way to the small seaside town of Kardamyli by the usual patchwork method of bus, taxi, legs, and patience. We look as if we will be on schedule for our connections, but a long line of stilled buses and cars on the road to Kalamata brings our smooth progress to an end. Three police officers, having a lovely morning, saunter over to us from where they have been chatting and smoking, and tell us that the road is being dynamited this morning as a safeguard against rockfalls and landslides. It will take three minutes, they tell us, the famous *tria lepta* that are a sure sign that the time they are supposed to define and limit is completely fluid and anarchic. We settle in for a leisurely wait, some of the passengers getting out by the side of the road to smoke. There is the first of a series of crashes, as if monumental dishes were being dropped, and a very old man sitting across from me grins a gap-toothed grin, and says waggishly, "Mystras tumbled down," referring to the crumbling ruins of the last outpost of the Byzantine Empire, which seem unsteadily stacked on their nearby hill, blocks that are the toys of historians. The passengers around him laugh at his joke, an applause he has orchestrated and accepts with pleasure; but when he sees my smile, he waves his hand toward me, and says, almost wonderingly, to the company at large, "She laughed." The superb sensation of understanding and of being unexpectedly understood is just as fresh to me as it is to him, the miracle of our being intelligible to each other. We exchange greetings, and he notices that I am shivering a little and pulls his window farther up. Late March is full spring, but even here in southern Greece, it is also a month of downpours and a scorpion's tail of cold. "I see you're cold," the old man says to me. "Well, March is a month with two faces. And do you know why? Because when all the months got married, March was the one who insisted on having two wives. So he married a Greek wife, but also a *hanoumissa,* a Turkish woman. The Greek wife was beautiful, but she was poor, and the Turkish woman was ugly, but very rich. So when March is spending time with the Greek woman, the day is fine, but there's no profit in it; but when he spends time with the Turkish woman, the day is miserable, but rain pours down like silver coins, and makes the soil rich for the summer harvest."

As we drive into Kalamata, walls and telephone poles are plastered with handbills advertising a play called *Mana . . . Mitera . . .*

Mama, three of the Greek words for mother. The central square is being readied for Independence Day celebrations—bunting in blue and white and Greek flags are being arranged, and microphones are being tested. A group of schoolboys wearing foustanellas begins rehearsing a klephtic ballad, one of the folk ballads about the Greeks who formed bands of both thieves and guerrilla warriors in the mountains during the Ottoman period. Although they are always patriotic heroes in the songs, the tradition of thievery was a serious problem for the new state, and even the countryside around Athens was notoriously dangerous, known for both robberies and kidnapping for ransom. From the square's temporary bleachers, a solo voice sings a passage in the sinuous vinelike oriental scale of Greek folk music, and a British hiker leans forward and asks the leader of the group, "Is that a call to the mosque?" Along the road leading to Kardamyli, there are hotels and tavernas with names like the Sydney and the Melbourne, testimony to the double life of emigration. Bouquets of purple flowers grow out of cliff faces, and a cliff facing the coast forms a great gray wave, as if the mountains were commenting on the ocean. We clamber off at the central square and a bulky man sitting at the central *kafeneio* opposite ambles comfortably over to the car. Without greeting us, he reads our luggage labels, and examines over the leader's shoulder the papers he is going through. He stares at each of our faces, and then saunters back to his table without a word.

After lunch outdoors we walk up a mule path, its sharp twists forced on it by the terrain, toward the villages in the mountains behind Kardamyli. The spring in this harsh rocky countryside is so lavish that everywhere we walk, we walk through a surf of flowers, as if the waves of the sea had metamorphosed into blossoms. Silvery-white star-of-Bethlehem, asphodels, daisies, wild white and porphyry irises, red anemones: a generation of *jeunes filles en fleur.* On a plateau that makes a pocket-sized meadow, we disturb a new calf, which runs from us with horrified wide brown eyes, as if we were housebreakers. High on the mountain is a scattering of houses, one abandoned, with magnificent views to the back of the mountains and woods, and in front, a prospect of the sea, whose distance, uncontainability, and transformation of everything that encounters it, thought, light, color, make it seem like a figure for another world.

Another house with a less definitive view has a turret, the defense turret of the old Mani houses, bullet-marked, and overmatched in height by a television antenna, that marks the house emblematically, like a modern caduceus. Sons in Mani families were referred to as "guns," and the household architecture shows an expectation of life as a permanent state of war. The women, who lived helotlike lives, have the reputation, according to a number of my dream books, of being the most gifted dream interpreters on the mainland, as if their powers of divination had developed in proportion to the unfulfilled dreams that were their real lives.

We emerge into a hidden village, so small it hardly has a square, but there is a tiny plaza, the equivalent of a public porch, shaded by a group of tall, burly plane trees, as imposing as wealthy landowners. Two middle-aged women, with handsome, determined faces, string long, curved green beans, laughing during their work with a keen-eyed older man, who sits on the benchlike rim of a marble fountain, his cane resting against it. "Health to the *pallikaria*," they say, greeting the men, as we come up the path into the square. They have all been laughing at some story, and the blue-eyed woman says, "It's the first afternoon we've had that has been warm enough to enjoy being outdoors. You are on vacation? From where?" We tell her, and she flings her arm out, gesturing beyond the square. "Have you ever seen flowers like we have here?" she wants to know. Paul, the group leader, is in love with a house on the ridge, and wants to know its status. They tell him the family who owns it is in Australia, and hardly ever visits, but still can't stand the idea of selling the property with its angelic view. "Yes, but the view from Leigh Fermor's house is even better," the man with the cane says. "You must know that name, the Englishman who has written books about

Greece and about his life on Crete as a guerrilla during the world war. The war made him a Greek. He wanted to live where he gambled with his life and won. That happens to certain soldiers. He loves it here—one spring I saw him dive into an acre full of daisies and poppies, face-down, and roll over and over in it." The women drop their faces to their work; they look wistful. Two stocky little boys with the bodies of miniature men tear through the square, shooting imaginary rifles. "What are you shooting, Taki?" the gray-haired woman asks wryly. "Turks," he shouts back, panting. "He's Botsaris and I'm Kolokotronis." "Well, come back here and rest when you've won the battle." She winks at us. "These are the only two school-age children in this village," she says. "The young families are in Athens, when they are not in Australia or America." The boys come and sit down, and she cuts an apple into slices for them. "Do you know your poems for the twenty-fifth?" the man asks them, not looking at either of them, but keeping his face turned to the precious new spring sun. Taki holds his toy rifle across his chest and drives his poem out like a racing car. It is a toneless, break-neck recitation, common to Greek schoolchildren. Memorization plays a central role in Greek education, and speed is evidence of the perfection of the memorization; intonation and emphasis could be mistaken for hesitation. Teachers I have met tell me that on exams, Greek children are often supposed to reproduce whole pages of memorized text, down to punctuation; a misplaced comma will lower the grade. This boy hero of 1821 does his feat with the flash of an escaping fish, and Taki leans back, word-perfect, waiting for applause. "Bravo, Taki," the villagers applaud, and so do the strangers. The elders tell the boys, "You are our heroes now. And tomorrow, you will be our heroes at the recital."

We walk on past a pair of graves covered with iron grilles that local myth has dubbed the graves of Castor and Pollux, and on to a private family church with a defensive bell tower, to which a story could be added every time a son was born. Evening is beginning to fall, and the cold challenging the warmth of the late afternoon with the extra pinch illness has if you are in the process of getting well. We begin the walk back to Kardamyli through ravines and valleys in the submarine green light of tree and shadow. In deep Mani, unlike here in outer Mani, Paul says, there are no trees to speak of, just sun, salt, thornbrush, and rock. We meet a man climbing to his house, and Paul asks about a monstrous building under construction on a high bluff overhead, that looks like the embryo of a supermarket or department store. "Sickening," the man says, and tells us a story of bribery, code violations, and family betrayal, since the other members of the family sold this land to a developer while he himself was abroad. He speaks with the clearest diction of any Greek I have heard offstage—Greek is not a voluptuous language, or a lilting one, but stony and earthy, a language full of mud, volcanic rock, and glittering precious stones—this man speaks it with a consciousness of its long compound words and shifting accents, as if he is polishing a gem collection. He looks at the future hotel squatting on its bluff, puts his paper sack of eggs in his left hand, and takes his house key out of his pocket. "I am the last member of my family who will live on this land. The hotel will take my house too, in the end. I don't know what we are supposed to think now about these places where we lived. They were hard to live in, but I can never forget how beautiful this place was to look at. They are still hard to live in, but looking at this tumor on the bluff makes me despair. Good evening to you." It is strange to see this almost deliberate-seeming destructive ugliness here, as if the country resented the fact that its face is, to a large degree, its fortune. We walk on past covered springs, whose water flows under the faded remnants of icons painted on stone covers, casual evidence of the Greek struggle to make the natural and supernatural meet. As we come into sight of the water, the sea near us is clear, and far from us, is merged with a mist; one part can be seen with your eyes, and the other only with imagination.

Some more walkers have arrived, a party of three British sailors, two men and a woman, who tells us that she has brought along a supply of true crime books in case she gets bored, and with cheerful sadism regales us at dinner with tales of severed body parts and ingenious police traps. As we make our way back to our rooms through the dark streets of the town, she begins to whistle Mozart arias, and I ask if she likes opera. It turns out that she doesn't know the pretty fragments are from operas, but has picked them up from a TV show about a musical detective. "They're lovely," she says, "but my favorite song is still"—and she begins to sing, "My name is Jack, I'm a necrophiliac."

In the early morning, the small main street where the bus stop is is already lined with chairs, and men are lounging in them with coffee and newspapers, as if the street were a porch. Nobody could come through the center of Kardamyli unobserved. The ruler of the bus stop is a blond boy of about eleven, a kind of Pickwick, the genial, expansive host of the bus stop, who handles the waiting passengers with relish, as someone older might enjoy a well-stocked wine cellar. He bounces up to me, and asks cheerful rapid questions: "What are you doing in Kardamyli? What bus are you waiting for?" He makes the rounds of the strangers, finishing with the three sailors. "You're in the navy, too?" he asks the woman. "What do you do, sweep the ship?" "No," she says, "I'm an engineer."

"I have a poem to say tomorrow for Independence Day. Do you want to hear it?" he asks, and shows me a scrap of lined paper with a penciled-in quatrain: "The mountains are joyous, / the castles are proud, because the Virgin Mary is celebrating, / and so is the country / When they see deacons with swords and priests with rifles."

"Bravo, Kostaki," the storekeeper across the street calls out after the recitation. He is obviously the irrepressible darling of the town.

While we are still waiting for our own bus, a fiftyish man with a leathery brown face and work clothes, nondescript trousers, and a short-sleeved maroon shirt approaches. He says, "I look for a girl to stay with me, to live in my house." I say I have a job. He say, "Forget your job, your job is finished. In Greece, men only working. Woman sit down here. If I get you, women around here not supposed to work—you sit, I work. You want to come see the house? I live in a village in those hills, a small place. I would have a girl just for the summer if she wants. Maybe I find one for the summer, I find one for sure here. I got a house, you know, I don't pay no rent." He puts his foot on the curb proprietarily. The men in the sweater shop across the street sit in chairs on the sidewalk and listen, as if they are trying to guess whether or not he will succeed. The owner of the grocery store mixes himself a coffee in a glass, and hurries outside to take his seat at the drama. He leans over to another spectator, as if asking whether he's missed anything worth hearing. I say I'm not interested, but the man proceeds, as if I am not a sentient being, with absolute disregard for my own response. "You pay no rent with me. You ever been in Chicago, Boston, New York? My older guy working in Boston." He thrusts one leg out, lights a cigarette, and puts a hand on one hip. Along with his disinterest in a willing part- ner, it has never occurred to him that for a woman with any experi- ence at all, the nuances and rhythms of a man's conversation are a stunningly accurate guide to the way he makes love. "If you decide for me," he says, "I'm here for another fifteen or twenty days more, then I go back to the waterfront, for a long time. And if not this summer, maybe next year you come back again. You live for free with me. You sit. If you come looking for me, my name is Antonis," which in Greek pronunciation sounds exactly like Adonis.

Unlike Aphrodite, I am glad to escape Adonis. The bus transports us to hill country, where we walk between the opposing towers of two clans, each with a family church. The Pantokrator, the portrait of Christ as ruler of all that is the focal point of the dome of Byzantine churches, is here surrounded by signs of the zodiac—a fine mermaid is circled by bright red fish, and the image of a man holding a gorgon's head, with gorgons' heads worked on his sleeves, looms up, the imagery reminding me of how the Maniotes had resisted attempts to convert them to Christianity, holding out until four centuries after the conversion in Ireland. The other site's original church is not pre- served, and the structure there now, by contrast to this one, has linoleum floors, and for an icon, a framed photograph of an image of the Archangel Michael, the military angel who oversees God's legions. Outside, an invisible shepherdess's voice orbits through the afternoon from a nearby valley, with that oriental dissonance that the Western ear hears as tragic, moving in great circulating sweeps up and down its scale, without ever finding a resolution, a new phrase implicit in every pause, both never-ending and never at peace.

At six o'clock next morning, dawn of Independence Day, the bells of the Kardamyli church ring and the chants start. Independence Day is also the feast of the Angel Gabriel's annunciation to Mary; several March dates involving the oath taken by revolutionaries at the monastery of Agia Lavra in the Peloponnesus and the dedicatory mass conducted at Patras on the twenty-fourth of March seem to have been conflated to produce the belief so many Greeks seem to share that these events actually occurred on the twenty-fifth. But historians write that the state fixed the date of the independence celebration on the twenty-fifth, making the identification of the rebirth of the state with the messianic birth of God irresistible. The rosemary-laden scent of incense comes across the square, and we can smell it from our balcony. (I know from experience how the use of rosemary in incense mixtures affects its use in cooking, having once gone to a dinner party on the island of Sifnos given by a Scandinavian who cooked a bird with rosemary and white wine. Her Greek guests all looked sadly at their plates, and said they couldn't eat a chicken that reminded them so much of church.)

All the squares of the small mountain villages we walk through today are hung with blue-and-white-striped Greek flags, and we arrive in one in time to hear the schoolchildren's recitations. At first, the village mistakes us for members of a Dutch film crew working in a nearby village, who are making either a feature, they say, about the Second World War, or a film about the Kurds, which the Turks won't let them film in Turkey.

The small boys are wearing foustanellas, the smallest of all holding a huge flag, planted against it with all his weight to keep it from toppling over. The little girls are in feast day costumes, too, velvet bodices and fezes, and coin necklaces—they sing a song celebrating the gallant *pallikaria* who fought for Greece, and when they finish, the villagers kindly invite us to stand on the church porch with them, even though we are dressed for hiking and they are in holiday clothes, an indication of the gravity of this feast. Some of the women are wearing nineteenth-century costumes bequeathed to them, and others are wearing formal town suits and high heels, serious state-occasion dress for women in mountain villages, who dress to fit work and weather more than art or ceremony. We are handed triangles of an anise-scented bread studded with sesame seeds, then some of the boys perform their recitations of commemorative poems, in the breakneck style we have heard, the speed a demonstration of expertise, like taking a gun apart and putting it back together in seconds.

A sign framed in laurels proclaiming *Zito I Ellas,* Long Live Greece, has been hung on one wall. A cheap colored poster decorates another. Its central image is the Annunciation to Mary, the Evangelismos, and it is surrounded by a constellation of smaller icons of the revolution—Kolokotronis sitting on the rocks in his familiar pose, a famous naval battle, a picture of the oath at the beginning of the siege of Missolonghi, an allegorical portrait of Greece as a mourning woman in a torn gown—curiously, men in the poster exist in time, but women in allegory. I am puzzling over this when a heavyset woman smiles at me and asks if I am married. I say no, and though the convention in these villages is to marry by eighteen or nineteen, she says, "That is wise of you. Make sure you first have your own money, and depend on no one. Then with luck, a good groom. But first, I wish that you have your own money, and second a decent man." I ask after her own husband, not knowing whether her black is for him or another relative, and she tells me she is a widow. I say I am sorry, and she looks at me, leans forward almost imperceptibly, as if she is under surveillance, fixes her eyes on mine, and says, "Long live death." The shock of what she says is greater because of the implicit parody of the Greek wish to parents of a newborn child, "May it live for you." She smiles at me warmly as I am leaving and says, "And a good groom to you. Go in the good."

We climb up to a church with a spectacular view over a deep gorge, a clear aim at the imagery of heaven and hell, the fall into the gorge a deadly, terrible possibility, the church hovering over it like an angel in flight in the clear air. The small chapel is dwarfed by monumental flowering apple trees, each one a world of flowers. My friends take out their cameras, but I am not a skilled photographer. Any picture I take would fossilize these trees, while in my memory they will be growing. My looking at them is my attempt to record them, these wellsprings of flowers so inexhaustible that the bright pink blossoms dropped on the green grass are mere overflow, not loss at all. I look at them as you listen to the talk of someone you love, watch his face, the infinite unphotographable range of his expressions.

We take a trail down into the gorge, walking its dry riverbed, from boulder to boulder. This is exhausting walking, strenuous, and requiring constant judgment, calculating the distance between one boulder and the next, judging balance, strategizing how to save yourself the extra work of climbing all the way down into the riverbed and all the way back up onto the boulders, an important consideration for me, since each descent represents a drop of nearly my full height, so I am not climbing with my feet, but my entire body. In the gorge, it is as if we are in the underworld, with the dense mysterious gray and green shade overhead, yellow butterflies visible and then invisible in this hidden region where there is no sky, and where the ground still turns up bullets and World War II debris. Up again among the villages, everything is startlingly human, tended, the fields like well-made beds, flocks of grazing goats and new baby lambs, who don't have long to live, since Easter is coming, cottages. One group of goats is drinking from the central village fountain, their front hooves poised on its rim. The paved path alongside the cottages is black with crushed olives, and a hoard of olivewood kindling is stacked outside one, with olives still clinging to branches and twigs, like pairs of earrings.

In Kardamyli again, as evening is coming on, I sit on my balcony, watching the water, and feeling the cold sharp night winds starting to come off the sea, night coming to take back everything the sunny spring day promised. The blond boy I met at the bus stop this morning appears, running straight toward my balcony as if he has an urgent message to deliver. He stops in the narrow street just under the balcony, and looks up at me with a beatific expression on his face, a kind of rapturous collision between two states of being, like being awake and asleep at the same time. His eyes are radiant, his arms floating weightlessly by his side. "I've just been kissed for the first time," he says disbelievingly. "Congratulations," I say. "It happened in that car over there, see it?" "The blue one?" I ask, for historical accuracy. "Yes, that's the one. I've only ever been kissed on the cheek before," he says breathlessly. "It was a lot different." "Happy Independence Day," I say to him.

The Invincible Commander

The bus to Sparta shuttles through a swirl of mountains that look like melting candles dripping into valleys. As we left Kardamyli, I saw that someone had written in red Magic Marker on the wall outside the school, "You are all masturbators." My guess is that along with its other implications, this is the grandchild of an old class slur. In paintings on the Greek vases in museums and books that show scenes of masturbation, the people participating seem to be mostly slaves, satyrs, and women, all people of inferior or of no social status. It would make sense if this accusation also meant, "You are so low in the world you can't afford either a prostitute, a schoolboy, or a wife."

I look out the window to three loops of road that coil over each other, like the circles in Dante's hell, each potentially a fatal plunge. The topography of Greece is perilous, you are caught between the danger of height and the danger of depth, the jagged mountains and the sea. You travel in Greece over one abyss or the other, an abyss out of which in spring, trees flower. The bus is full of old Mani faces, sun-cracked so that they look like the time-cracked rock out of which these roads were carved, while the rocks in their turn seem

to mirror human struggle and endurance, slashed and furrowed like
old alcoholics' faces. The bus stops by a stone wall to pick up a
woman with tired blue eyes wearing a cheap print scarf and carrying an overnight satchel; she must have walked down the mountain-
side to get here, through clean small streams running over stones,
through trees not in leaf yet. We drive under an overhang of rock,
which scrapes the bus roof—here you drive through, not in the
mountains.

We are on our way to Mystras, the ghost town which gazes down
on the Spartan plain, perhaps the most significant of medieval sites
on the Greek mainland, remnants which have the direct link to contemporary Greece that the classical sites do not—in these settings,
the never-resolved struggle between Christianity and classical culture, between philosophy and theology, was engaged, the struggle
which is powerfully present, both overtly and covertly, in the living
Greece I am traveling in. The schizophrenia of modern Greek history, as well as thought, is demonstrated here, since this site, which
became one of the last outposts of the Byzantine Empire, was built
by enemies of the Byzantine Empire. Mystras is in a sense a medieval
French town, its famous castle having been built in 1249 by a French
princeling, William II of Villehardouin (a generic Greek term for
Europeans, with a somewhat deprecating overtone, and still in daily
use, is "Franks") to consolidate the French possession of the Peloponnesus, their prize for participation in the European conquest of
Byzantium during the Fourth Crusade of 1204. The city later
became a source of recurring contention among members of conflicting Byzantine dynasties, as the encroachments of the Turks further fragmented the centralized power of the empire. Its last ruler
was a Byzantine prince of the Paleologus family named Demetrius,
who, along with his brother Thomas, the governor of Patras, presided over Mystras's characteristically Greek finale, in their split
allegiances to the Western and Eastern worlds. Demetrius was one
of the powerful Greek party who preferred alliance with the Turks as
more advantageous to the Orthodox Greeks than any connection

with Roman Catholic Europe. He surrendered Mystras to Mehmet II in 1460, seven years after Constantinople fell, and became a vassal of the sultan. His brother Thomas, who favored a degree of reunion between the remnants of the eastern empire and the resurgently powerful western empire, went into exile in Italy.

But Mystras was above all the workplace of the philosopher George Gemistus, the passionate Platonist who taught here and took the additional name of Plethon as a further invocation of his philosophical master, through its play on sound, and whose magnetism at the Council of Florence in 1439 inspired Cosimo di Medici to found Florence's Platonic Academy, contributing to the philosophical underpinnings of the Italian Renaissance. Plethon was another embodiment of the paradoxes of Greek history: although scholars often declare him the supreme philosophical mind of Byzantium, he was a philosopher who had little influence on Greek thought, but a strong impact on its imagination. Plethon was one of the thinkers who, in the twilight of Byzantium, chose to begin again to call themselves Hellenes, a term which the installation of Christianity as state religion had made a slur; it is partly due to the revival of the term in his era that Greeks today call themselves Hellenes. One measure of how controversial the term was, and how conscious the decision to use it, is the opposite choice of Plethon's own student, George Scholarius, who was chosen by the conqueror of Constantinople, Mehmet II, to be the first patriarch of Constantinople under Ottoman rule—in effect the governor of the Greek population. Scholarius said, "I do not call myself a Hellene because I do not believe as the Hellenes believed." He chose, by contrast, to call himself a Christian. Plethon's identification of himself as Hellene reflected a grappling with both national and philosophical perplexities. It must have represented a rejection of the term "Roman"— Rome and the Western church had participated in and sanctioned the brutal sacking of Constantinople during the Fourth Crusade. It also, as an illustration of the collaborative nature of all cultures, probably represented a response to the Italian Renaissance intellectuals' admiration of classical culture, which helped recreate for Byzantines a sense of its value, and a wish to be associated with it. And it also represented a recognition of the fundamental split between Christianity and classicism, for which various solutions had been tried but which could only be glossed over by false syntheses. It had been critical for Christianity to root itself in the empire by taking control of education, which was the province of polytheists and based in part on polytheist myth; but education had been in the hands of people trained in philosophy, which by and large treated human thought (as opposed to social practice) as exploratory, incomplete, reaching for conclusions which may lead to other conclusions. Christian theology, on the other hand, held that absolute and final truth had been revealed, and that thought itself could go no further, but could serve largely as an inspiring and illuminating embodiment of different aspects of the perfect truth. Its involvement in government made its social prescriptions, too, a form of theology, and so unchallengeable. And it tried to solve the problem of how it arrived at perfect truth, given human moral and intellectual limitation, by presenting the inspired illumination by divine revelation as superior to thought. The notion of divine revelation, surprisingly, raised issues concerning political power. What happened when ideas and revelations inspired by divine grace conflicted? Who had had the true revelation; would grace always be in the hands of the establishment then, and divine truth possessed by the people with the power to enforce their revelation and anathematize those who questioned it?

In a way, Byzantine church decoration helps us understand what role philosophical experiment and searching, critical inquiry might play in relation to theology, for Byzantine art is primarily theology, and only secondarily art. It was made to embody, illustrate, celebrate, and repeat doctrinal truths, in patterns that may not deviate, although there is room for inspiration and artistry in the embodiment.

Plethon grappled with the problem of being a classicist and a philosopher under an order which had a fundamentally different idea of the nature of knowledge. He is said to have used the terms

"God" and "Zeus" interchangeably, and to have spoken of the divine with the plural "the gods." But scholars can't know what these terms meant to him—after his death, his former student George Scholarius, the patriarch of Constantinople, had his book *On the Laws* burned.

Mystras floats in the distance crowning its mountain as we approach the town. Through the tearful soft gray light of the rainy afternoon, I make out the softened image of the castle. It is a regal site, whose churches and monasteries themselves have the air of being royal castles. The ground is covered with oranges and lemons that split open as they fell, and the rain dramatically draws out their perfume. A shepherd walking beneath an umbrella drives a small flock of goats through the main street in front of the general store and the central square with its war memorial, one of the few monuments I have seen that memorializes soldiers who died in the Greek civil war, such a controversial topic that among my talkative and abundantly opinioned friends, there is a silence on this subject as on no other. As I walk along the roads of Mystras, I look down on the Spartan plain, covered with the shadows of clouds, and yellow spurge flowers spray out of the stone walls, while geraniums planted in old detergent bottles brighten the doorsteps of houses. The streets are full of "the black-wearers," the widowed and mourning women—if a couturier were to describe the color of their dresses in a catalogue, it would be "shadow of death." I am reminded again that what looks like the same color is different in different countries, just as a sister and brother may have completely different upbringings and experiences in the same family.

I wander around the town on my own, below the medieval ruins; the modern town itself has an odd deserted quality. I stop in the dark little cavern of the local general store, often a good source of conversation in Greek towns. Its shelves offer ready-made béchamel sauce to top moussaka or pastitsio, ouzo, wine, *mastikha tou Khiou,* the Chiote mastic, individually wrapped *kataifi,* a Greco-Turkish pastry of blowtorch sweetness—a fortunate symbol in my manuals for Greek dreamers, which would be an uneasy image in mine. Domestic needs are interpreted so differently from place to place—none of these would be considered staples in America, and even the overlap with other EEC countries is not substantial. A middle-aged man just approaching the borders of elderly strikes up a conversation with me. "This is a place," he says, "almost without young people. They go to Australia, or like me, to Canada. I live half the year in Toronto, where I work for a Jewish factory; we make doors and windows. Then I am here for the other part of the year, this time for Easter. I will retire here, like many of the other emigrants. We come back old to this old world." He launches into a family history, and I learn of his mother's diabetes, and where his aunts and uncles are buried, while my attention wanders a little, and I look through the window with its brassy synthetic orange curtains to the cypress-punctuated medieval castle. The man follows my drifting gaze, and says, "Yes, the castle dwarfs the *plateia*. This is one of the strange Greek towns whose life must always depend on what happened in the fifteenth century. The dead and the living have to share life in Mystras, and maybe the dead have a larger than equal share." I hear more family history, and begin the work of excusing myself, since I want to get a glimpse of the town before I rejoin my *parea*. "I talk too much, I know," he says endearingly, and wishes me good walking in the Taygetus.

As I pass through the orange-tiled stone houses on my way to the hill of Mystras, a white-haired lady with kind blue eyes and a naturally comic shrieking voice calls me over to her wall, and tells me to wait. She climbs a ladder to pick two oranges from her tree, and wishes me happy travels, reminding me of another idyllic moment of Greek generosity. In late January a friend and I were having lunch in Galaxidi, a lovely waterfront town near Delphi, an important port before the advent of steam-powered ships, replete with charming neoclassical houses and fine wrought-iron work, memories of its former prosperity. At one of the taverna tables a man was lunching by himself, and the waiter was just bringing him a plate of delectable-looking olives to go with his noontime ouzo. At our table, the waiter didn't mention olives among the *mezedes,* but our neighbor's beautiful plate had given me an appetite for them. I asked him if we couldn't also have a plate of olives, and he shook his head regretfully, explaining that those olives were the fruit of the customer's own tree. We thanked him, settled on something else, and became absorbed in our conversation. The waiter brought our wine, our appetizer, and a small plate, with six olives on it. The gentleman had set aside a taste from his own plate. He nodded to us, and we raised our glasses to him. They were a breed apart, those olives, opulent and tender, like a kind of tree-growing equivalent of filet of beef.

After a substantial uphill walk, I reach the ruined city, a place of stone façades, hollowed-out buildings, and some functioning churches and convents. Moving between churches, I am struck by their determined avoidance of the column, at least externally, evaded through their amoeba-like bubbling domes, arches, tower-like chapels. The place has a feeling of tremendous precariousness, some of the monasteries seeming ready to slip off the side of their sharply angled positions on the hill. If there is an architecture of impending danger, it is here. In the monastery of the Perivleptos, the All-Seeing, a stony-faced Mary lies on rock with her head turned away from her shrouded newborn child, who lies in a sarcophagus-like crib beside her; it is the most infertile birth imaginable, as if being born to earthly life were death itself. In the fresco of Christ's baptism, five or six figures with human bodies swim at his feet, barely distinguishable from the fishes in their cold insignificant nakedness. I turn to the familiar scene of the Dormition of the Virgin, strongly resembling in its elements scenes of Christ's descent from the cross. Her recumbent figure is surrounded by the keening apostles, who by legend were translated to Jerusalem from wherever they were to attend her death, while behind her Christ holds her soul in his arms in the form of a newborn baby. In the foreground of this version, though, there are figures I do not recognize. Someone is kneeling beside the Virgin's bier with outstretched hands, while a winged angel with a drawn sword is cutting his hands off at the wrists. I shyly ask a nun who is keeping an eye on the visitors who these figures are, explaining that I haven't seen them in other Dormitions. "The person kneeling," she tells me, "is the Jew Iefonia, who wants to profane the body of the Virgin, and to overturn the bier, so the Archangel Michael cuts off his hands as they touch her coverlet and stops him. It isn't in every Dormition, though if you go to the Afendiko monastery here, you will see it there too." I thank her, going outside again onto the green hill. I wish I knew at what period this image had begun to be incorporated into the Dormition scenes—was it somehow associated with the threat of the Turkish conquest, since the Turks were friendly to Jews, and eventually invited the expelled Jews of Spain to settle in Turkey, often in territory that had been largely Greek? I decide that when I get back to Athens, I will call Stamatis, whom I had met at the carnival party, to see if he knows its history.

I walk with no goal in mind until I find a waterfall hidden in the hills behind Mystras, its waters curling in marryings and divorcings like the destinies of lovers; some of its currents meet inevitably, others are inexorably divided, others separated and reunited, all with a common destiny awaiting them in the pool below.

Next morning we taxi to a village where there is access to an unused Roman road, a mule path. As we pass a field of sheep, the taxi driver honks the car horn at them in brotherly greeting. "*Yia sta provata,*" he calls out the window, health to the sheep.

As we climb, Paul points out an almost vertical ascent used by shepherds to reach flocks they shelter in a high cave, as Polyphemus, the man-eating Cyclops, that insult to shepherds everywhere, did in the *Odyssey*. The landscape of Greece is the purest remnant of the classical world, I think, its existence is the most independent element of that world we have often shaped and studied according to what we need to believe about it, resisting our enclosing fantasies. There is nothing of the golden world about this ascent; to take that path every day would mean pure hardship, in rain, snow, heat, struggling footsteps up the steep paths by day, and at night, life by firelight in these damp, camouflaged caves. Paul says that the Taygetus has traditionally been a refuge for the persecuted, including the helots, Spartan slaves. The conversation turns to what surprises him most when he goes abroad—the ease of making arrangements. In Greece, to get a telephone can take five or ten years, not so much in Athens, where lines are established, but outside. To move a telephone from one house to another, he says, can cost eight hundred dollars. Checking accounts are expensive, and in any case, people prefer you to pay with cash, something I know from experience. He tells a joke whose punch line depends on the initials of the Greek telephone and electric companies, and the national tourist organization. DEH, the electric company, is code for "We don't have electricity." OTE, the telephone company, is code for "Neither do we have telephones." But EOT, the tourist organization, stands for "Nevertheless, we have tourism."

It is suddenly a cold day, and the clouds on the mountain are thick, dark, smoky, as if the mountains had been lit with cold fire. The sharpest and least secure-looking of the peaks, covered with stained-looking late snow, is called the Nereidovouno, the nereids' mountain. Paul tells us that on this peak, nymphs would dance naked in the moonlight, and young men would climb toward them; when they reached the top, the nymphs would kick them in the face until they fell into the gorge. We see the form of our own fears, desires, and needs in the landscape itself. I know so few Greek stories of trustworthy beauty, of sexual happiness.

We scramble, cling, climb, leap, and endure, and at last arrive at the small village, a village of mostly red-tiled older houses, built of stone, with wooden balconies overlooking the mountains; there are a few new houses with patios of smooth brick, monuments to a new Greek-Australian, American, Canadian legend of the suburb. Two boys are playing in a brick patio of the tiny dream suburb; they call out to us as we pass—*hello hello hello* follows us into the village like mountain echoes. The small village square is flanked by two general stores, mirror images, with matching merchandise of wine, coffee, hardware, new bread, Coke. I note one is called "Scribe and Son"; one accommodates right-wing clients, one left-wing clients, I'm told. An old man falls into step beside me, and tells me that it will snow here until April, and that in winter, the snow will often be as high as my waist. The wind blows straight down the main street, the upper village connected to the lower village by high stone steps. The place has an air of furtive desperation, suggesting the great fear that motivates such camouflage from the outside world. One of the British boys tells a romantic story about surviving some days of being lost in the wilderness, saying that life is not worth anything until you risk it; but danger often has a different value for the privileged than it does for ordinary people—someone who had been a child in harsher circumstances might feel her life counted for less, precisely because, against her will, it had been risked so much. We walk along a river gorge, overlooking great curtains and swathes of rock and sheer drops that make you feel you have already died just to look down them. Two rough-looking shepherds pass, with dirty curly hair like sheeps', and gray-green eyes, both carrying, instead of crooks, rolled-up raffish Bond Street–looking black umbrellas. We stop in a cave that must have been once used for polytheist worship, as caves almost invariably were; now it is a chapel to the Virgin of the gorge, stalactites dripping water that is sanctified and collected for healing. We find slim green stalks of wild asparagus and add them to our bread and cheese, eating and staring at the chain of peaks before us, gray and savage, through the intimate tender blossoms of cherry trees. The delicate wild shoots have a brilliantly concentrated flavor in comparison to the cultivated, like the difference between attar of roses and the memory of roses in cologne, like the difference between reality and memory. The wind up here has the sound of someone asking anguished questions, of breath sucked in and gasped out with effort. After we have eaten, Paul remembers that he needs to make a telephone call to rearrange a ride tomorrow. He stops at a small house to ask if the family has a telephone he can use. A stocky man with a newspaper under his arm answers the door, and before he responds to Paul's question, he turns slightly toward the interior of the house and snaps his fingers. A thickset woman in a housedress printed with infertile-looking dead-brown flowers, her curly hair in transition between brown and gray, comes to the door. With a furtive glance at us, she kneels down and, like a prehensile dog, she puts slippers on her husband's right foot and left foot as he holds them out for her, without looking at her. When he is shod, he jerks his head, and she retreats silently to the interior.

That evening, we go to the thirteenth-century cathedral on the hill of Mystras to hear the *khairetismi*, the hailings, perhaps the most famous Byzantine hymn chanted to the Virgin on the five Fridays of Lent. The hymn is meant to be listened to standing, which is why it is popularly known as the *akathistos* "standing" hymn, and in its full version of twenty-four verses, one for each letter of the Greek alphabet, with repeated refrains, it is an arduous but extraordinary experience. I last heard it in a recorded version interspersed with canons in which Mary was hailed as the "seashell that dyed the Divine crimson robe for the King of the Heavenly Powers" and as the dripping "dew that extinguished the flame of polytheism." But I have never heard it in a setting like this. Cars and buses of people from neighboring towns are coming to hear tonight's *khairetismi*, and a policeman directs the traffic into a parking lot lit with candles. A flaming torch lights the entranceway to the cathedral, giving the stone arch the absolute detail of a piece of sculpture, and the church itself is lit only by candles; their moving shadows add an otherworldly life to the faces painted in the frescoes on the walls, and the chant begins, the words swaying and trembling on their breathsupported scale like fruit on a vine. At intervals, the congregation join in to sing a seventh-century addition to the hymn, an encomium to the mother of God praising her for saving Constantinople from the attacking Persian fleet, which was terrorized by the gigantic glowing figure of a woman walking on the city's defensive walls: "Unto you . . . Invincible Commander, your city, in thanksgiving, ascribes the victory . . . and having your might unassailable, free me from all dangers . . ." After thirty minutes, many people in the crowded church simply sink down to the stone floor and listen from there. I look down and recognize the white-haired lady who gave me oranges from her tree. Oddly, the poem in English that most reminds me of the structure of this hymn is Christopher Smart's eighteenth song of praise, "For I will consider my cat Geoffrey," with its mass of increasingly wild and magnificent epithets, each surpassing the previous one. But the charged subterranean power of the Greek rhetoric is in its evocation of other goddesses, in language drawn directly from earlier hymns: like Persephone, Mary is a divine bride, like the Demeter of the Orphic hymns, she is the *kourotrofos,* the divine nursing mother, a vine, a field, the source of milk and honey, a laden table. Like Hecate, Athena, and Tyche, she is the defender of a city. She is described as a heavenly ladder, a door, a gate, but she is the gateway in this hymn that opens both forward to Christ, and backward to her divine mothers and sisters. And then in an extraordinary whiplash turn, the hymn contemptuously attacks its own sources, the root and foundation of its own eloquence: "O Theotokos [God Bearer], we see the most eloquent orators mute as fish before you; for they are at a loss to explain . . . Hail! O vessel of God's wisdom . . . Hail! to you who prove the wise to be unwise. Hail! to you, who prove the sophists as foolish. Hail! that the dreaded debaters were rendered fools. Hail! that the inventors of myths have waned. Hail! to you, who broke the word-webs of the Athenians . . ." A woman next to me blows out a candle that has burned down too close to her fingers, eaten by its own flame.

CANDLES

A strange light seems to emanate upward from the valleys of Arcadia, as if the mountains were somehow lit from below, and daisies drift up from the green banks of the road like bubbles in a champagne bottle. It is another utterly different countryside, with softly moulded hills and neat terraced farms descending them, like carefully corrected exercises in a copybook. The bus back to Athens stops suddenly when a group of people standing by the side of the road flag it down. Someone boards the bus to ask if any passenger is a doctor; a man with heart trouble has collapsed outside, and the bus driver radios to the nearest town for an ambulance. While we are waiting for it to arrive, two thirds of the passengers pour outside, chattering to the sick man, encouraging him with jokes, and surrounding him with a cloud of smoke from the cigarettes they immediately light.

In the city now, the shop windows are full of unlit candles, pent-up fire, waiting to be lit at midnight on Easter Saturday. The obligation to be joyful at the beloved holiday, and the poignant misery it brings to those whose suffering exiles them from its rejoicing, make it much more like our Christmas than our Easter. The magazines bring out special Easter numbers, Sunday newspaper supplements print selections of poems on the theme of Easter and reproductions of icons known as the Anastasis, which represent Christ in hell, dragging Adam and sometimes Eve out of their tombs, cracking hell open like an egg. Human interest stories report the plights of people who cannot afford to serve lamb this year or buy gifts for children named Anastasia and Anastasios, whose name day falls at Easter. Jewelers' windows fill with gold and enamel pendants in the shape of eggs marked with the year, as at Christmastime in the West you see the worlds of commerce and popular journalism shaping and marking the holiday. A dizzying synthesis of rebirths is being celebrated: natural, national, cultural, divine; familial in bringing to mind the resurrection of the dead, personal as in an ascent and liberation from any personal hell. Like all successful festivals, it is a sea of history and symbolism, infinitely malleable, changing shape and meaning at each approach. One of the magazine covers fuses a mass of popular symbolism showing a child standing next to a grown-up, both holding candles. The adult is partly concealed, only a hand holding a candle, so that you can see that the light has been passed to the child, who is almost the same thing as her candle, something newly lit. Her face blooms in the perfecting and mysterious light of the candle, emerging from the darkness; here is rebirth, spring, Hellenism, religious salvation, the passing of the light from one generation to another. For Greeks, this is the Eorti Eorton, the Festival of Festivals, the parallel Resurrection of the Lord and the Easter of the Greeks, *i Anastasi tou Kyriou* and *to Paska ton Ellinon,* a treasured national possession which their Turkish overlords were barred from sharing. In folk songs with a rainbow of variations, wealthy Turks offer to adopt or marry Greeks if they will only change religions, while the Greek speaker conventionally replies, "It would be better for you to become Greek, to rejoice in glittering Easter."

Easter is known as Lambri, the Radiance, but it is also has strong filaments that bind it to darkness; it is a time of delicate and ambiguous relations with the dead. Songs warn that the dead in their dark underworld must not find out that the living are celebrating Easter, so as not to grieve them or make them jealous, as if the living were keeping the sad secret from them that rebirth is something only the living can experience. But in this labyrinth, tradition contradicts tradition; another belief holds that the souls of the dead are liberated from the underworld on Great Thursday of Holy Week, permitted to inhabit the spring flowers and commune in secret ways with the living for the fifty days, until Pentecost, when they have to endure another separation. A mournful folk saying is attributed to the dead: "May all Saturdays come and go, but may the Soul Saturday of May never come." The next day, Pentecost Sunday, is the day of their return to the darkness, a day of special prayers for the dead, and oddly, of the first swim of the season, a return for the living to an intense summer physicality, and life lived outdoors, immersed in nature.

In wealthy sections like Kolonaki and Kifissia, silver and china gleam on polished tables in furniture stores, in imagined settings for Easter dinner, a *grande bouffe* after a long fast. A beggar on my trolley home walks down the aisle, saying, "Good people, don't let Easter be my crucifixion. Give me something, or resurrection will come too late for me this year."

In my neighborhood, enormous five-foot-tall red eggs appear outside several toy stores, with *Kalo Paska,* Happy Easter, inscribed on the side. But it is above all the wishes on the street for *Kali Anastasi,* Good Resurrection, and the rows of candles to be lit at the moment when "Christos Anesti," Christ Is Risen, is sung at the midnight service, that fix the season for me. There are lyrical candles wrapped with ribbon and dried flowers; enthusiast candles in the shape of tennis rackets, cameras, paintbrushes, boats tied with fishing net; candles in the shape of ice-cream cones and lightbulbs and magic swords; candles wrapped in the Greek flag, with toy soldiers or bride dolls or Karaghiozis shadow puppets tied to them. There is one in the shape of a hulking wrestler, his massive wax forearms flexed, a banner draping his chest identifying him as "Macho King

Randy Savage." Another looks like an open toy box, but both box and toys are to go up in flames. I buy a candle in the shape of a radio, its wax antenna covered in silver glitter waiting to be lit, for a friend who has an encyclopedic knowledge of popular music. The shop owner wraps the candle carefully and puts it in its own box, stamped with the legend *Christos Anesti,* Christ Is Risen.

Remembering the different flavor of an Easter I spent in Florence, I think about the way ethnicity is a kind of manufactured genetic inheritance, a genetics of sensibility, constructed out of landscape and food and family, history, illusory continuities, coercion, ambition, pleasures, and the terror of death. Easter, I realize, is the most concentrated distillation of Greek ethnicity I have experienced, a holiday commemorating a tortured death becoming an eternal festival, ending as unending joy. It gives that most Greek sensation of simultaneity, of a struggle for simultaneity, of a world felt as desperately divided which struggles to hold itself together between past and present, oriental and European, man and woman, Turk and Greek, death and life, Christian and pagan, divine and human. Even the language has more than one compound yoking together anguish and joy. It is the mental world of a circus rider standing with one foot on two horses, trying to keep them running at the same pace and rhythm. Easter, unlike Christmas, is a time of agony as well as joy, a time when the struggle to keep joy and tragedy from dismembering each other is at its height, when you must mourn and rejoice at the same time, like the myrrh-bearing women who go to Christ's tomb in tears and are told, He is not here. They can never not mourn what has happened, even though they are overjoyed at the Resurrection. The Easter candles in all the windows promise this painful beauty, of light glowing and disappearing. It is like Greece to offer candles of sea blue and pomegranate crimson, decorated with flowers and presents, as if light was a marvelous toy you could hold in your hands and play with; it is like Greece, too, to give, with such universal festivity, gifts as tragic as candles—in the end you have nothing.

I look for a cab since I am meeting teacher friends for dinner. A handful of posters washed down a nearby wall by the afternoon rain lies underfoot. They advertise a weekend party at a gay club, with an image of ten faceless male bodies wearing white jockey shorts, grouped crotch to crotch and crotch to ass. My friends and I are supposed to meet for a drink at a bar which is gallantly attempting a Mexican theme. A leather saddle hangs over the door, and behind the crescent of the bar, bartenders pour drinks with choreographed moves like Tom Cruise's in the movie *Cocktail*. The waitress circulates with complimentary shot glasses of tequila, and Greek boys in the white T-shirts and black leather jackets time-warp fifties getups favored by the under-thirty set, bob their heads and smoke, singing along with a jukebox song, their melancholy Levantine faces unchanging in expression as they join in at the refrain, "Ay Caramba."

Foti and Roula are fuming, not because I am late, but because parliament, which recently raised the issue of making the registration of religion on the national identity cards optional instead of compulsory, has withdrawn the proposal, so that all Greek nationals must continue to be registered by religion. "Of course, Easter is a hopeless time of year to debate this kind of reform," Foti says, "which is precisely why the church-owned MPs wanted to have it now. But it is a violation of our rights. Not to mention a disgrace in an EEC country that vividly remembers the Second World War. No one should be forced to record religion, which is a private matter."

"Not here, it isn't, my *pallikari*," says Roula. "Our constitution says it was drafted 'in the name of the consubstantial and indivisible Holy Trinity.'" They both light cigarettes. "They left it in even when it was revised in the eighties." I am curious about what kinds of points were raised in the debate, since in my country, and I suspect in a number of other EEC countries, this is a clear violation of the constitutional right to religious freedom.

"The favorites of the church said the usual things: that the Holy Mountain demanded obligatory registration, that we would lose our identity without it, that Orthodoxy is not a religion, it is a way of life, that the bones of the heroes of 1821 and Gregory the Fifth would groan if the identification were removed. You see we can't even register as unaffiliated; if you don't declare a denomination, you are recorded as Orthodox, even if you are a devout unbeliever. And as for Gregory the Fifth—you've seen his bones in the cathedral here?" Gregory the Fifth, a nineteenth-century patriarch of Constantinople, was hanged by the Turks at the outbreak of the Greek revolution in 1821, and later canonized by the Orthodox Church; I had been to see his bones in their ornate reliquary, where he is honored as a saint exemplar of the fusion of religion and nationalism. "And as for Gregory the Fifth, if his bones grind, it is not over our identity cards, but over our state. Because Gregory the Fifth published in 1798 a pamphlet praising the Ottoman government as crucial to Orthodoxy, a blessing preserving it free of any taint of heresy. 'Liberty . . . ,' he wrote, 'deprives Christians of worldly and divine blessings.' He exhorted the Greeks to guard the religion of their fathers and the government of the sultans. Frankly, if you want my opinion, the best-preserved fragment of the Ottoman Empire is the Greek Orthodox Church."

It is dizzying, traveling in this perpetual hall of mirrors.

"Even I," Roula says, "as a believer, find this situation dangerous. Because as some of the opposing MPs said, the identification can too easily be used for purposes of discrimination, which it is a simple matter to disguise or deny. I am Orthodox, but other people must not be penalized if they are not. Just in March, a teacher in Thessaloniki was fired because he didn't participate in school prayers or cross himself. Think of the message this sends to other teachers. And the church meddles in teaching; the Ministry of Education here is called the Ministry of National Education and Religion. Greek schoolchildren have compulsory religious teaching at school, and the church has many particular positions on thinkers like Nietzsche and Freud, particular social preferences. If you look at the Christian ethics textbooks, they are coercive, you see very clearly which answers you are supposed to give. This makes the act of questioning meaningless, which along with our emphasis on rote learning in other subjects, sets a pattern in motion—repetition comes to have an emotional meaning for us, of allying ourselves with authority, of never being afraid of a question, because we already know the answer. And all kinds of hidden favoritisms can come into play here, with real consequences for a student's future, not to mention the curtailment of free inquiry, although you will hear differently from many people, who say the church has no power. The fact is, the church affects our intellectual training, the patterns of our thinking, sometimes in barely perceptible ways, even when it is not a question of religious doctrine. We do not learn to think, we memorize, we theologize, we declare unalterable doctrinal positions. We don't think, because we know. And to tell the truth, we also have to be very circumspect discussing this with colleagues. Nor, I'm sorry to say, will you be able to come with either of us to a class. We have both asked our supervisors, and both say that it is against the law for you to visit a class without the permission of the Ministry of National Education and Religion. And my supervisor told me not to trust you, that you would only write bad things about Greek schools. So it's impossible, we would only get in trouble, the suggestion wasn't received well at all, and in any case, I doubt you'll get permission."

"The church also has particular political positions," Foti says, chain-smoking obsessively, and hands me a pamphlet circulating at his school. It is called "A National Concern" and tells a banal story of a Greek high school teacher who shocks his class with the information that the *Harvard Encyclopedia* contains an "anti-Hellenic" essay which suggests that the Macedonians might not have been Greek. The teacher then exclaims, "All this is typical propaganda of Skopje! The so-called Macedonians have secret agents in the United States, Canada, and Australia as well as all over Europe." Proofs that the Macedonians were Greek to the bone are provided, evoking for me early Christian doctrinal arguments between monophysites and diphysites over the dual or single nature of Christ, arguments which seemed themselves to be in part coded political struggles over matters of authority and ethnically related beliefs in the Byzantine Empire.

"I have students who should be encouraged to see political and diplomatic problems in all their complexity, writing essays with jingoistic phrases like 'our enemies the Skopjans,' " Foti says. "And the position on the Yugoslav situation is presented the same way—bishops rail that the Orthodox Serbs are being persecuted at the hands of the Vatican and of Islam, and Karadzic comes here and says in press conferences that he is leading a religious war to defend the true faith. And for the students, it may very well work to their practical advantage to agree with these interpretations for better grades, and good records, and university and careers. It is always better not to rock the boat in laying the foundation for a career. Now turn the pamphlet over." It is a reprint from a magazine for teenagers distributed free of charge by the Orthodox Missionary Association of Saint Basil the Great.

"Even for me, this is terrible," Roula says. "When God takes political positions, people get murdered. So say a prayer that you in America never have a state church. And," she says, with conscious irony, "*Kali Anastasi.*"

THE BUS TO METAMORPHOSIS

While the waiter is writing up the bill for our lunch, Stamatis remembers he has a present for me that I could not appreciate until after Mystras. "Now that you have met our warrior goddess, the Invincible Commander," he says. "These you can buy all over Greece, it's a popular picture, made in the eighties." He hands me a postcard of a painting done in a crude blend of folk, Byzantine, and western European styles, which shows a monumental Mary wearing a traditional Greek dress. She has a dreamy almond-eyed prettiness, looking a bit like the actress Anouk Aimée. The baby Jesus she holds is a tiny full-grown man, dressed in a foustanella, his face almost a miniature copy of hers. She holds him with one hand, and with her other hand steadies on her shoulder a gigantic shotgun, its double barrels ornamented with silver.

"Why did you choose Corfu for Easter?" he asks. "There are much more interesting places to spend the holiday, like Pyrgi on the island of Chios, where they slaughter live lambs and you are up to your elbows in blood. You could understand that there is some dialogue, unacknowledged on both sides, going on between Orthodoxy and Islam. I would like to see their *kurban bairami,* celebrating,

I think, the sacrifice of Abraham——with the same business of bringing the lamb home to make a pet of it, and then slaughtering it for
the feast, both feasts of blood sacrifice. Chrislam." I tell him I chose
Corfu because I was intrigued with how invariably middle-class
Greeks recommended Easter there, out of the hundreds of Easters
of Greece that are like varieties of wildflowers. I was curious, I said,
about what they imagined I would enjoy.

"Well, I wouldn't have sent you there," he said, "you won't feel
the full brunt of Easter, but you will have some of it. I will tell you
the three keys: *cherchez la femme,* look through polytheist eyes, and
don't leap to conclusions about who is being resurrected. Easter is
something accomplished between a woman, a man, and an immortal father. I was reading an excellent book recently by an American
classicist named Laura Slatkin, which I recommend to you. She
looks at the events of the *Iliad* through the triangle between Zeus,
Thetis, and Achilles. Thetis, you remember, rescued Zeus at a
moment when he was about to be overthrown; her reward might
have been to marry the greatest of the gods, but there had been a
prophecy that she was destined to bear a son greater than his father.
So the only way Zeus could survive Thetis's maternity was to see to
it that she would only bear mortal children. Therefore, he forced on
her a marriage with a mortal, with whom she conceived Achilles. As
Miss Slatkin points out, Achilles might otherwise have been the
ruler of the universe, that Zeus's divinity depends on Achilles's
mortality. Very like the Christian triad: Jesus Christ did not die to
save man; he died to save God. There were changes, of course, one
enormous change being the exile of woman from divine status.
Long before Jesus, it was Persephone who descended into hell, and
brought life joyfully back to earth.

"This, my dear, is a punishment for the irresolvable problem of
your sex's fertility. You do this magnificent feat of giving birth,
which we believed made you divine——but you persisted in giving
birth to mortal children. With every divine youth you made a mortal death. So the old Easters, and springtime festivals, which used

pregnancy and childbirth as a symbol and a magic to secure immortality, were given a lesser status, a smaller role in the Christian Easter, which tries another route, abandoning the magic of female sexuality, pregnancy, for the magic of male sexuality, erection. Look at the image of the Anastasis, Christ upright in hell, which is pictured as a cave, an ancient and very particular, in polytheist worship, symbol of the female genitals, Christ lifting the supine from their coffins. And listen to the language of the feast, *anastasis,* standing again, *anastaino,* I rise again—it is even present in your own word, resurrection."

Before I go home to pack for Corfu, I walk through the Athens of Megali Evdomada, the Great Week of Easter. I pass stray roses growing in old Mana olive oil tins, and the inevitable neighborhood religious supplies store, its windows full of silver-plated icons and tin votive plaques stamped with houses, babies, and clasped hands over the raised script of the message I BEG YOU. The uglier buildings are covered with great swaths of the willing Athenian wisteria and lilac, like unattractive women with perfect jewelry. The grand buildings—like the house of the eccentric Duchesse de Plaisance, the French philhellene who was said to have kept her daughter's mummy preserved in her old room at home—all seem to be undergoing repairs at the same time. A giant delivery truck goes by; painted on its cab is a portrait of the Virgin Mary, whose face is framed with the word *Megalokhari,* "great in grace." Between the railings of the National Garden, planted by Queen Amalia as the first queen of independent Greece before she and King Otto were sent back to Bavaria in 1862, a group of seven cats are intently giving themselves synchronized baths. Syntagma Square, once the site of the garden of the philosopher Theophrastus, is almost completely blocked off by subway construction; Athens vanishes even as it speaks to you, a city always in the process of disappearing and persisting. I choose another route for my errand, and as I wait for the traffic light to change, a bus speeds past. The destination lettered above its windshield is a neighborhood called Metamorphosis.

TWIN PEAKS

Corfu, probably best known now in the world outside Greece as a vacation island, within easy swimming distance from Albania and easy sailing distance from Italy, wildly popular with English and German tourists, might also be known as Twin Peaks, thanks to its origin myth. The island is supposed to be the sickle with which Khronos, Saturn, castrated his father Uranus. The twin peaks near the town's old fortress, Koryphai in Greek, are probably the origin of the ancient name Corfu; they are supposed to be Uranus's petrified testicles.

In any case, Corfu was the sickle that destroyed ancient Hellas, as the nominal cause of the Peloponnesian War. Corfu's close proximity to Italy made it a commercial prize, positioned to dominate trade between northern Africa and the Levant and northern Europe, and also made it a passageway to the destruction of the Roman Republic—Mark Antony said his last goodbye to his wife Octavia here, and sailed to join Cleopatra. Corfu backed Antony and Cleopatra against Augustus, and had all its civic monuments destroyed for its unlucky choice. Emperor Nero, acting as both his own impresario and his own vocal protégé, sang to a captive audience here. Corfu's connection with Italy continued in the medieval period, when the island became a Venetian protectorate, which it remained until Napoleon put an end to the Venetian Empire. When the British, in their turn, put an end to Napoleon's empire, Corfu became a British protectorate, from 1815 until 1864, during which time Edward Lear of limerick fame spent time here, painting luminous watercolors of the island and writing an endearing journal of his residence. Corfu, never under Turkish rule, also sent many young men to Italian universities, developing a concentration of Greek intelligentsia, and a homegrown aristocracy, able to acquire, with money, effort, chicanery, or marriage, Italian titles. It also developed a reputation, like other neighboring Ionian islands, for much sharper class distinctions between its monied and peasant populations than existed in other parts of Greece.

The first president of modern Greece, Kapodistrias, who was murdered by Peloponnesians in an assassination that came to symbolize the conflict over the future of the new Greek state between European-influenced Greeks and the Greek warlords who dominated much of the Greek mainland, came from Corfu. Corfu's unique position as Greece's link to Europe was altered dramatically by Greece's acquisition of Macedonia, and by technology. In the days of sea travel, the rest of Greece depended on Corfu even for news of Europe. Belle Epoque Greek newspapers didn't have the capital to pay foreign correspondents, so they kept correspondents on Corfu, since according to William Miller, European papers arrived there first, more than thirty hours before they reached the Greek capital. The correspondents would wait for the papers to arrive and then telegraph their newspaper offices in Athens with the crucial stories.

As I wander through Corfu town, with its cricket-playing Greeks, its Italianate architecture and neighborhoods with a strong Italian flavor, and its Liston, two grandly arcaded apartment buildings begun in the island's brief French period, designed to echo the Parisian rue de Rivoli, I suddenly understand why my coming here for Easter had been so warmly urged by so many middle-class Greeks. Corfu has an air of unusual confidence, confidence in itself as Western; there is something of a respite here from the tension of fragmented identity of so many other places in Greece, a more orderly sense of the past, a relief from the sense of being torn between East and West, buildings that evoke a continuity with Italy and France rather than Anatolia and Istanbul. Along the esplanade in front of the Liston, the *corso* looks very different from the way it did along the harbor in Kavalla. Here there is a different carriage, a flow to the procession, a sense of self-possession due not only to Easter finery, but, I can see following the eyes of the promenaders as they claim the elegant arcades and fine façades, to a sense of possessing themselves as Europeans: they are vacationing from the complexities of being Greek. Men, women, boys, girls, elaborately coiffed poodles, a different conception of dog than I have seen elsewhere in Greece, parade up and down the passage. Three old men in natty suits sit together at a table reading newspapers, stopping to comment with whirlwind Greek hands. Holy Week is a time of sombre gravity, but here there is an air of barely suppressed festivity.

Three angels appear, keeping company on a palm-sized icon in a shop window. The painting shows the angels dressed in ruby-colored caftans, sitting together at a round table covered with a beautiful sea-green tablecloth just the color of the Aegean in certain lights and depths. You can tell they have come a long way; they have the slightly weary, relaxed posture of people who have arrived at their destination after a long flight, and their bare feet are propped on soft cushions. They look cheerfully hungry; on the table are three tiny forks and three golden goblets, the same gold as their wings and halos. They are talking together with delicacy and wit, to judge from the inclinations of their heads and the appreciative smile of the angel on the right. It is obvious that the cool wine in their glowing goblets and the aromatic scent of their dinner cooking is inspiring them. I know they represent the angels who visited Abraham in the desert and that, theologically, they are supposed to prefigure the

Holy Trinity, but I don't care. For me they are the angels of the table, presiding over one of the arts of peace, the arts in which the sensual and the spiritual, both physical and metaphysical love, are fused into one substance, far more difficult to accomplish than any of the arts of war. Inside, the proprietress, a woman whose name is Slavic and translates as Mrs. Gift of God, has the most festive air of any merchant I've ever seen. "Today I am a floating angel," she says, "other days I am very heavy, sometimes I am Dr. Jekyll and Mr. Hyde. But icons are very good luck, for Greek people they are very good luck, and the proof is that you have brought me the first money of the season." She takes the first drachma note I hand her and tapes it to her file cabinet, so it will draw more in after it, and as a parting gift gives me an agate. "When you want something, you must hold it in your right hand and say your wish very clearly. Then transfer it to your left hand and say, 'Now.' "

I take the angels to my hotel room before I walk to the British cemetery, and am in time to answer a serendipitous call from Kostas, who wants to be sure I go to church tonight. I had planned to go to different churches on Thursday, Friday, and Saturday nights, since every Holy Week service has a different character and drama, and I grumblingly ask him whether that isn't enough. "No, no, no," he says, "tonight is the night all intelligent women repent for the sin of their intelligence. So you must be there." I tell him I am flattered he thinks I should participate, and ask him to explain. "Tonight, along with the hymn to Christ the bridegroom, they will sing the great hymn written by a woman named Kassiani. The story is that when the ninth-century Byzantine emperor Theophilus held a gathering of eligible women to choose a wife, he approached Kassiani with a golden apple, the symbol presented to the chosen bride. He offered her the apple, and said with inimitable tactlessness, one of the worst pickup lines in history, something like 'Good evening, from woman flowed corruption and our downfall.' Kassiani, understanding the allusion to Eve, wittily responded with a reference to the Panagia, 'And from woman welled up the highest excellence,

our salvation.' This was too clever by half for Theophilus, who took
his apple elsewhere. Kassiani retreated to a convent, where she
wrote a hymn of lamentation in the voice of Mary Magdalene.
'Lord, she who fell into many sins has recognized your Godhead
and has joined the myrrh-bearing women . . . ,' "he chants. "So she
repents, and joins the women who perfume with their intelligence
the altar of male supremacy over them.

"Now I can hear that you want to ask if the men never repent of
their own intelligence. But the rest of the story, which you won't
hear in church, raises the question of whether men have any intelligence to repent. Because as in all cultures where men's sense of
power and divinity rests on the theologically sanctified intellectual,
moral, and political degradation of women, Theophilus's descendants ultimately had to drink from the river he had poisoned. The
woman Theophilus chose instead of the brilliant Kassiani helped
sponsor what is considered one of the great political missteps of the
Byzantines, which eventually contributed to the destruction of the
empire. After Theophilus's death, his wife Theodora took power
along with an uncle, brother, and adviser. She was an advocate of the
ruthless persecution of a sect of Christians she and her party considered heretical, who were concentrated on the easternmost borders of the empire. An army was sent east, where this colony was
attacked; Christian literally crucified Christian. But the ones who
escaped joined forces with the Saracen Arabs, and the process of
the undermining of the eastern border began, a process which
eventually culminated in the onslaught of the Turks and the fall of
Constantinople. So go hear the hymn, and lament your sins, remembering that Didymus the Blind, an early Christian teacher from
Alexandria, said that women must never be allowed to write books
on their own authority without male supervision."

The British cemetery is, like all of Corfu, startlingly green, since
the island has a higher rate of rainfall than any place I have traveled
yet in Greece. It is as much a garden as a cemetery, and I seem to be
the only visitor without a sketchpad. A German woman intensely

sketching a flower explains to me that she, like some of the other people drawing, is a professional botanist, and that the cemetery is known for its rare wildflowers. The graves are a fragment of the human history of colonialism, a kind of counterpart to the economically exiled Greek emigrants of *xenitia,* who lived their working lives abroad; these graves represent another kind of homesickness, these are the colonials who never returned, never got home. Most of the dates show them to have died extraordinarily young, though there is one Fanny Smilie, "beloved friend and nurse" of a family, who must have ended her life here in their service, at age seventy-five. Here is the ship's cook of Her Majesty's Ship *Devastation,* and a crowd of naval men who died in an accident aboard ship. The tiny coffin of Martha Elizabeth Westcott, who died at the age of six months, rests in a bed of wildflowers; near by is a sculpture of a woman, her head held disconsolately in her hands, as if she can't lift it, her face turned to the side, and cracked straight across, as if the stone grieved. The gardener and proprietor of the cemetery comes up to me, wondering if I am looking for a relative. He walks with me, telling me he was born right here on the cemetery grounds, as were his children, and he points out his house. "Unbelievable," he says in a characteristic Greek phrase, "but true nevertheless. It makes friends shudder; the Orthodox don't like cemeteries, you know. They don't come here to enjoy the garden, they say '*nekrotafeio*' and they make their signs of the cross. But I don't feel that way; I am at home here, the dead don't irritate anyone, they ask for nothing. Only the living come here and ask for special favors and disturb the world—look down, here are some wild pansies." He points out near a tombstone with a snail sitting on it a few stems of a delicate throatlike freesia that has double flowers, each with a pattern of purple marking, and tells me it is rare. A giggling and singing child is riding a tricycle on the dazzling flowered paths behind the graves—"My grandchild," he says.

In the evening, in the narrow streets beyond the church, roosters pick their way over their familiar territory, even though this is the neighborhood of the Ionian University, and of a number of Corfu's hotels. I climb up to the women's gallery, full of heavyset matrons in wool pullovers and three black-clad old women who dominate the front of the gallery, looking exactly like the three fates, with their black scarves, gnarled faces, and ruthless eyes. I hear Kassiani's lament and also the "Bridegroom Hymn," in which Jesus, the man about to die, is celebrated as a bridegroom—if there is any single dream that has held a continuity of interpretation from the second century to this morning in the Greek world, it is the dream of a wedding, which is invariably interpreted as a premonition of death, as dreams of death are often interpreted as a premonition of marriage. The imagery of the one and the other converge, for, as Artemidorus says, "the same things befall a groom and a dead man, as, for example, a procession of friends, both male and female, wreaths, spices, unguents, and written records of their possessions." On the other hand, dreaming of a memorial monument often foretells marriage, "since a tomb, like a wife, has room for entire bodies." The same interpretations, unchanged, are in every generation of dream book that I have looked at, and this deep unconscious substitution of one condition for another is being enacted in this very liturgy. A pudgy ten-year-old boy comes upstairs for a visit—there is a great deal of chatter and movement during many Orthodox services—and his gray-haired mother immediately stands and offers him her seat.

Thursday morning is lyrically beautiful, and I take a bus, jammed with Greeks on Easter holidays from other parts of the country, to Corfu's most famous building, the palace the Hapsburg empress Elizabeth of Austria had built here and called the Achilleion. On the way I read an Eastertime interview with a metropolitan who looks out from his photograph with grim eyes, a set mouth, and an air of implacable spiritual condescension. Holy Scripture, he remarks, confirms the Greekness of Macedonia in seventy-seven passages. Asked his opinion of women, he replies, taking a privilege of omniscience usually associated with God, "Very very many of today's women will not enter Paradise."

The Achilleion is an ugly, vulgar, and foolish palace in one of the most beautiful settings in the world, overlooking a blue bay from so many exquisite prospects that the bay seems to be painting its own portrait. But the palace itself is a dissertation on a fascistic, ruthlessly perfectionist strain in classical art that was one element of Nazi physical and racial idealism, and an underpinning of Nazi art. The tremendous drive for power in using sacred architecture for domestic housing is apparent here, as it often is in the Greek Revival architecture of the American South, where white people often chose to house themselves like gods in temples, as incongruous as it would be if farm owners in the Midwest modeled their farmhouses on the plan of Gothic cathedrals. The empress Elizabeth had grown up in the Bavaria that idealized ancient Greece, and it was her uncle, King Ludwig, who collected classical Greek works and ambitiously renovated Munich to make it the "Athens of the North." It was her relative, Otto, who went to rule over what her mother called the "bandit-subjects" of the new state of Greece. She herself developed a mania for Greek, and hired a Greek tutor named Christomanos in 1891, who later wrote a romantic, overwrought, but revealing account of his acquaintance with her in Austria and on Corfu. For her, Greek seemed to provide another outlet for her persistent imagining of herself as a goddess, an imagining she seemed to encourage in her retinue. Christomanos, meeting her for the first time in an Austrian reception room whose walls were covered with blood-red silk, full of opulent gold furniture, mirrors, and crystal chandeliers, said she reminded him of Persephone, the queen of the underworld. And she herself, in planning her Corfu refuge, some years after her son Rudolf's suicide at Mayerling, decorated the palace to evoke the immortal Thetis and her mortal son Achilles, choosing dolphins, sacred to Thetis, as symbols on all the tableware and glassware, and ordering a monumental painting of the Triumph of Achilles by Franz Matsch.

The place has an atmosphere of suppressed violence, of egotism combined with self-hatred. Statues of Zeus and Hera flank the mar-

ble entrance stairway, while Elizabeth's dressing room features a
head of Medusa, and the sitting room is decorated with demonically
grinning plaster cherubs, whose faces and bodies are so poorly
crafted that art seems to have spun chaotically out of the control of
the artisans. And the friezes of hunting animals—dogs, rabbits, pig-
gish boars—are unnerving in the context of her son Rudolf's obses-
sion with guns and shooting; he was famous for his recklessness
with guns, and had a sequence of accidents that almost seemed to be
experiments leading to his death, at one time shooting himself in
the hand, at another narrowly missing his father, Franz Joseph,
instead wounding the emperor's loader, and finally murdering
Marie Vetsera, one of his girlfriends, and himself. In the gardens, the
Ping-Pong paddle–shaped leaves are scarred with Greek graffiti cut
into them with pocket knives, and five men are posing together in
front of the enormous statue of Achilles placed here by Kaiser Wil-
helm, who bought the villa from the Austrian royal family after Elizabeth tired of it. There is a reclining statue of the dying Achilles that
makes death look like a rapturous moment of the most supreme
self-love. I go close to the bombastic Matsch painting, which shows
a victorious Achilles in a scene of battle pornography, a kind of pre-
cursor to the action movie, dragging Hector's dead body behind his
chariot, while doll-like crowd figures react. And yet there is a chill-
ingly prophetic detail in this vacuous painting—over the stone
entrance to the Trojan city, Matsch has painted a small swastika.

This evening's service commemorates the Crucifixion, with
readings of the Passion story from all the Gospels. In the women's
gallery, we follow the readings by candlelight. I hear Peter deny
acquaintance with Christ. In the Bible, a cock crows, and Peter
rushes off crying bitterly, in a sentence of such simplicity in Greek
that you can feel a childlike sense of shame and failure in his out-
burst. Suddenly all the lights are doused in the church, and the
priest emerges from behind the iconostasis, carrying an enormous
cross with a detachable figure of Jesus laid on it. The priest nails
Jesus's hands and feet to the cross, and candles are lit at his head and
hands, while the *yiayias* in the balcony sob and groan. Then the

priest carries the crucifix around the church three times, and I am again stunned by what seems to be an allusion to wedding ritual, reminded of the three circles called the Dance of Isaiah that an Orthodox bride and groom walk around the altar.

At the hotel later, I read Artemidorus on crucifixion, an image that as something the dreamer might suffer has disappeared from the modern books. But crucifixion was such a common punishment in Artemidorus's world, such a common element of conscious life, that it was also a common dream, with none of the uniqueness it has in our imaginations. It was Constantine who ended crucifixion as a Roman punishment, although he instituted other penalties, like the well-known statute which decrees that boiling lead shall be poured down the throat of anyone who assists her mistress in making a love tryst. Surprisingly, a dream of crucifixion is generally very favorable in Artemidorus. It is good for seafarers, since a cross resembles a ship's mast, and like a ship, is made of nails and wood. It is good for poor men, since a crucified man has been placed in a high position; it signifies wealth since the crucified man provides food for many birds of prey, which gives an idea of what a contemporary of Artemidorus's might have seen if he took a walk near a military prison. For a bachelor crucifixion means marriage, although the bond will not be easy. Oddly, in the modern dream book, there is no crucifixion, only the more removed symbol of the crucifix, a sign of a troubled sexual relationship, one in which any joy will be accompanied by conflict and sorrow. On an impulse, I look up the dream of resurrection in my books—the modern book moralizes, warning that such a dream is often a sign of egotism or conceit. But for Artemidorus it signifies chaos, as an offense against the social order and against logic. "For one must hypothetically imagine the kind of confusion that would result if the dead were to come back to life again. They would naturally demand their possessions back, which would bring about losses."

On the morning of Great Friday (all the days of this week are called "Great"), a black and white lamb suddenly appears, tethered on a strip of grass on a small square in front of the hotel. During breakfast, the music piped in is no longer the cheerfully inane pop music of yesterday, but church chanting. Today is the descent from the cross, and later this evening, Christ's funeral, and on the streets the Greek flag, its blue and white adopted from the Bavarian colors of its postrevolution Bavarian king Otto, flies at half-mast. The candles always available for churchgoers to dedicate are brown and are said to be charged with special powers. I climb up to my now familiar spot in the women's balcony—for this service the church is crowded as I have not seen it before, and the women sitting trade places at intervals, to give those standing a place to rest, an extraordinary sight, since anyone who has been on a Greek bus, trolley, or ferry has seen seats and benches defended to the point of violence. The door of the iconostasis is flung open, and the priest, dressed in a magnificent gold and purple robe, moves to the front of the black-draped altar, takes the detachable figure of Christ from its cross, and wraps it in a white cloth. The priest is playing the role of Joseph of Arimathea, who took Christ's body to its grave, and as he carries the white-wrapped figure around the church, showers of flower petals are thrown at it, exactly as at a wedding. The ancient involvement of drama and resurrection is renewed: drama is, after all, the art in which people outlive their own deaths—after Heracles dies in agony in his shirt of flame, he comes around the curtain unscathed to receive his applause. In literature, all tragedies have happy endings, the sufferings of their characters removed from history, and from us, so that their pain ends. A death in literature is always a resurrection. And we make their misery fertile, using the intimacy and detachment of literature to survive it and redeem it, to see by the light of their grief, using our own minds too like candles in the dark. We have not learned that art with the tragedies of history. The Greeks and Bulgarians of the Balkan Wars, the Byzantines and Turks of the Ottoman Empire, the West and East, the Greeks and Turks of the Asia Minor catastrophe, and of Cyprus, have not repaired what they destroyed for each other; these are the tragedies that have not ended. In today's service, worship is itself a form of drama, in which the congregants and priest themselves are actors, not audience, and through them, Christ dies and is resurrected, borrowing their flesh for incarnation, borrowing their lives for the story to inhabit. I remember that in Artemidorus, the dream of being a god is especially propitious for actors, because actors so often impersonate gods in plays—in fact there was a particular part of theater architecture called a *theologion,* the place above the stage where the actors dressed as gods appeared. You can see the niches in the theater of Herodes Atticus in Athens; the *theologion,* I imagine, must be the ancestor of the iconostasis.

Engaging the congregation as actors shifts the gravity of faith; if they believe in their own lives, at this moment, they believe in God's. The body of Christ is brought to the bier, which is a real bed with a pillow, framed in white carnations, the flower associated with Christ's passion, with an emperor's crown of red carnations at the top. Again I am struck by its eerie resemblance to a wedding bed. Children dressed in scouts' uniforms, carrying wooden staves that represent rifles, present arms and stand to attention. The figure of Christ is covered with a magnificent woven *epitafios,* the grave cloth, covered with scattered carnations, and laid on the bier, as the children move forward to guard the bier, as at a presidential funeral, and the older women sob and light their brown candles. The priest delivers a hectoring sermon, denouncing foreign manners and customs, and threatens those who follow *xenoi tropoi* with the loss of heaven.

Outside, when the service is over, the world has come to life again. Booths are doing brisk business in shards of crockery and cheap clayware to throw out the window on Saturday morning, both to celebrate the shattering of death, and as a heckling of Judas. The street where the butcher shops are concentrated is lined with rows of dead lambs hanging by their heels, their eyes blank and their teeth set in grimaces. At the bus stop, a cluster of people are waiting in a thin silvery rain, holding flowers and wrapped lamb parts to put in their *mayeritsa,* the soup that breaks the Lenten fast after the

Saturday night service. A man heaves the whole dead body of a lamb into the trunk of his car, lined with paper to catch the blood. Other booths are selling candles, and I choose one for the Saturday night service, the most beautiful candle I have ever seen, in the shape of a calla lily with green leaves. The church bells toll ceaselessly today. I buy a paper, and find my way to a square centered around a Venetian well that gives me an amnesiac feeling of being in Italy and not where I am at all. I order *pastitsada,* pasta not boiled in water, but cooked in its sauce—the cooking of Corfu is Italianate, too, rather than Middle Eastern, although there is a comical remnant of the British governors, in the form of ginger beer. There is a report in the paper of an arrest for a particularly cold-blooded murder. The account makes me think again, as I often have here, how specific murders, except possibly self-defense murders, are to a culture. Murder is charged not just with personal but cultural symbolism, as the sight of the crucified body of Christ constantly reminds me this week. There are hidden messages in murders, to people or to people who represent institutions which are felt to have previously attempted to harm or even to have actually murdered the killer. But in order to make the murder the consummate violation the murderer desires, murder has to violate cultural convention as well as the victim. Murder is, in a way, the least individual of acts.

  This killing by a waitress and her boyfriend is a particular outrage to Greeks because of its violation of the honored idea of *filoxenia,* hospitality (literally, love of strangers), the sacred contract between guest and host. These killers murdered their hostess, another waitress whom they asked for help and a place to stay, pleading rough times financially. They killed her the first night of the *filoxenia*—she came home stumblingly tipsy, and after she went to bed, the murderers held her down, easy to do, since she was already incapacitated, and began to hit her in the face. The woman delivered the death blow, stabbing her, a murder by a woman of a woman in her own house. Then they put her body into a cupboard, ate, drank, and set aside what they wanted of her possessions, which they gradually sold to secondhand shops. This murder is a double violation, a kind of rape committed by a woman, in a country where because of the dowry tradition, the house, together with its contents, is a symbol of woman, is itself a symbolic woman.

The parents of the murderer seem almost always to be interviewed in Greece, and here the mother of the murderess gives an account of her childhood. The mother tells the reporter she was married at sixteen, and had two boys and a girl, with a husband who continuously beat her and the children. After sixteen years of marriage, she brought herself to separate from him. She kept the boys and the girl went with her father to live in Crete. At age fifteen, the father put the girl in a reform school, saying she was ungovernable. The mother took her out of the reform school, but the girl, she said, despised her, and wanted to live with her father. At eighteen, the daughter gave birth to a baby boy, which she abandoned to her mother. The mother said she was bewildered by how her daughter had come to feel so much hate, and yet no one raises the question about how it was she chose to keep the boys but allowed the girl to live with a violent man, whom she must have witnessed repeatedly beating her mother. There is, it seems, an anthropology of murder, and it is apparent too in the way murders are reported. The story focuses only on the murderess; there is no biography or information about the murderer. And the headline defines the public, cultural aspect of the murder, the violation of the Greek host and guest relationship—"Her guests killed her," it reads.

In the evening, I go back to church for the funeral of Christ. A *mirologhion,* a traditional Greek dirge of a kind that was common through the fifties and can still be heard in parts of the country, is sung. It is a kind of tribute and lament for the deceased, and can be sung by any acquaintance, although the ones I have read seem most often addressed by mothers to sons. Tonight's dirge is sung by Mary to Christ, and next to me an old lady wearing a white napkinlike headdress joins softly in the refrain: "O my sweet Springtime, my most beloved Son, where has your beauty fled?" It is shocking to hear Mary weep for Christ in words that must have been drawn from Aphrodite's mourning for Adonis, and I suddenly realize what Stamatis meant when he said the Resurrection would surprise me. Christ will be buried tonight and and will rise again tomorrow night, but other tombs will unexpectedly release their dead, Adonis will rise with him, clinging to him through these words that belong to them both, like a brother buried in the same grave. Persephone, who pioneered this journey into hell and back, rises too. And the dead who burst out of the underworld and inhabit the flowers for forty days by the grace of Jesus? Are they only the human dead, or are they the minor deities, the nymphs, river gods, nereids, who in some eerie economy, having left the world when Christ entered it, now rise temporarily in his wake?

The streets tremble with the restless mass of people waiting to join the procession behind the carnation-covered bier. Boys in scout uniforms shoulder their simulated guns, and schoolgirls, the *myrro-fores,* the myrrh-bearing women, carry baskets of flower petals to strew over the body of the dead Christ. The mothers are excitedly brushing the little girls' hair, and the fathers are smoking—the emotional scale has tipped, and the anticipatory joy of tomorrow is already stronger than the ceremony of profound grief we have just completed. Now the atmosphere is like a parade, a Fellini-esque band, all white pith helmets and gleaming gold braid, with the naively cheerful sound of a military band strikes up the Chopin funeral march. We light our brown candles, following the pattern of an everyday Greek funeral, but when the march begins, the funeral train turns to pandemonium. All the downtown church processions confront each other competitively in the narrow streets, while spectators add to the confusion, lining the streets three-deep as they smoke and eat potato chips. The city is full of colliding Christs, a clash of only-begotten Sons.

On Saturday morning, I wake up to the sound of crashing dishes; they are being thrown out of windows onto the street, even from the hotel windows. I want a quiet day, since tonight and tomorrow might be grueling, filled with pentathlons of Greek hospitality. I walk to the center of town to take a bus to a tiny harbor, where boats are moored like dreamed fragments of the sea, all painted in colors drawn from the sea, pale blue, a blue mixed with emerald, blues tinged with blacks and dark crimsons. On the way to the bus, I notice that the black and white lamb that was grazing yesterday outside the hotel has disappeared.

Saint Spyridion is the patron saint of Corfu, with a reputation for healing skin diseases. His body is kept in a case in a church dedicated to him, except when it is carried in procession for festivals, and crowds of people file past to petition him and pay their respects before the Resurrection service chanted over loudspeakers in Corfu's central square. The church is a strange amalgam of Catholic and Orthodox decoration—no Pantokrator or Theotokos overhead, but a bad Italianate painted ceiling with scenes of Christ's life encased in gold, and patterned floors marked with light tinted by stained glass that looks exactly like drops of blood staining the floor, which is strewn with bay leaves, the botany of victory celebrating Christ's resurrection like an ancient Olympic athlete's feat.

A tall man carrying a motorcycle helmet strides in and lights a candle from the bank of tapers at the church entrance. A *yiayia* sits on the steps at the foot of the choir stalls lining the body of the church; wearing a black scarf, black apron, and black stockings, she sits with her legs apart in the stance of someone peeling potatoes. A little girl fingers the bridal-gowned Barbie wrapped to her Easter candle, and a young boy absently swings his long candle rhythmically between his legs. A boy in a brilliant red and a girl in an emerald green sweater who cannot bear to unclasp their hands approach the saint together. Saint Spyridion is upright in his glass case now, whereas earlier this week he reclined. A throng of people are lined up to kiss his casket and to hang *tamata* on it, tin plaques with images of the dream the worshipper hopes the saint will fulfill in exchange for some vow or service. Saint Spyridion is as brown as a mezzotint when I go up to the casket, his head angled at an

uncomfortable-looking tilt. His feet are encased in silver and jeweled boots that remind me of Dorothy of Oz's magic ruby slippers.
A man in front of me videotapes his wife kissing the saint's shoes.
There are *tamata* on the casket with images of houses, cars, babies,
limbs to be healed; someone who wants a degree, or a successful
exam, or college acceptance has left an image of a man clutching a
rolled-up diploma. Someone who wants to get married has left a
plaque stamped with raised linked wedding crowns, the symbol of
the Orthodox wedding. A woman holds her baby up to the corpse,
and dips it for a moment so that the baby and the dead saint are face-
to-face. On the walls, the painted frescoes of saints have faded away,
but the gleaming silver casings remain, framing dissolved faces.

Outside, the crowd picks its way over the broken crockery
tossed this morning; people are gathered on the balconies of hotels
around the square to watch the Resurrection ceremony as they are
on parade routes at Mardi Gras in New Orleans. Vendors threaded
through the square are selling popcorn, cotton candy, and yo-yos
that glow in the dark. A little before midnight, a tiny colony of candles at the edge of the square begins to blaze, as the celebrant calls
out "Come, receive the light." There is a sexual, tender, exalted,
and tragic moment as candle touches candle, brief life kindling brief
life, again and again, like the moment of conception: "Christ is
risen" pours the chant from the loudspeaker; the crowd sings with
him, light being born from candle to candle, and a crash of purple
and green falls from the sky, as with the sounds of hell opening, an
earthquake of graves opening, the fireworks begin. Official fireworks hold the center of the *plateia,* unofficial ones set off by children and teenagers go off at the periphery. Kostas told me that
every year there were casualties and deaths from homemade fireworks, and as he predicted, there was a story in today's paper about
the death of a young boy in Chios making his firecrackers on the eve
of the Resurrection. A particularly loud crash sounds as we weave
our way to the street, and someone says with a thrill of pleasure,
"What happened, what happened?" I pass a popcorn vendor who has
lit a candle and placed it in an empty plastic bottle of salt, to free her

hands to sell the bags of popcorn. It is good luck to keep your candle flame alive until you reach home, or someplace you have declared home, and I and my hosts maneuver our flames away from the wind on the way to the restaurant to break the fast. There is a pandemonium of people running now from the square, holding lit candles, all eager to get places in the restaurants, which are throwing reservations to the wind and placing people at tables first come first served. At my table, the hostess takes a supply of red eggs out of her Fendi handbag and hands them around for us to crack against our neighbors'; she asks a waiter for some empty water glasses to keep our candles in, so they will stay lit all through dinner, and we make a bouquet of them. They look like a new kind of white-stemmed flower in their transparent water glasses, with flames for petals. The discos are just getting under way as we return home.

On Easter Sunday, a couple named Stratis and Jocasta who are invited to the same Easter dinner in the country have offered me a ride. While I am waiting for them, I watch a harangue by an Orthodox monk on an independent TV channel. He accuses the Vatican and the EEC of a covert agreement to divide Greece among the rest of Europe, and shows a map he claims has been secretly produced to show how "the former Greece" will look, comparing it to the dissolution of the former Yugoslavia. He invokes the Asia Minor catastrophe, Cyprus, the civil war, gripped by imaginings of disintegration, shrieking in a feverish rhapsody that the Orthodox Church hates no one, it is filled only with love. Part of what makes Greek politics so undecipherable is its tangle of paranoia and lived experience, the one adhering to the other like a tumor on a healthy organ.

We take an ugly road out of Corfu town, past rows of cheap beach hotels and supermarkets flanked by white plastic versions of classical sculpture and billboard cutouts of slim-waisted men from Minoan frescoes. Next to a half-finished building, amid a pile of iron and concrete rubble, a man turns a lamb on a spit. A wall near him is covered with sprawling graffiti: "Say no to the new Masonic identity cards—no to the new identity 666." "Armenians say no to Pan-

Turkism,""The Albanians are our enemies,""The Turkish people will
win." We pass a video store whose exterior is covered with brightly
colored posters for old movies. Underneath *O Politis Kein,* Citizen
Kane, a woman turns a spit on which a whole lamb is darkening, a
plume of the fragrant cooking smoke the old gods loved to smell
rising from its body. Here and there along the road, a road where
because it winds through cliffs, you can look both up and down,
onto people's houses and shops and below them, you see these
plumes of smoke, or a family gathered around a laden outdoor
table, or a lamb, spit run through its head, roasting on one of the
concrete terraces attached to newer Greek houses. After fifteen
or twenty minutes, the coast becomes the recognizable jewel-like
coast whose beauty was perhaps, in the end, a fatal gift to the island.
The bays curve like beautiful women's cleavage, and are watched by
hideous concrete hotels that hover over them like voyeurs.

Stratis and Jocasta want to drop off a bouquet of Easter flowers
and a bottle of wine for friends. We walk up to their small farm past
a flock of *baa*ing lambs who survived the Resurrection. The farm
couple are roasting their lamb outdoors in a cloud of flies, as their
big brown-eyed dog watches attentively. It is impossible to watch
the lamb turning, with its eyes looking coldly angry and its teeth
bared, and not see a kind of substitute crucifixion. The wife brings
us a bowl of blood red eggs, and sweet wine, like a mead, in the coppery wine pitcher Greeks use for their barrel wine, and watches the
lamb turning. "I can't help thinking about Athanasios Diakos," she
says ruefully, referring to a Greek hero of 1821, who abandoned a
future as a monk to fight for Greek independence. Diakos, whose
presence in ballads and image is as ubiquitous as George Washington's, was famous for his beauty—he is always shown with a
romantic head of shoulder-length curling hair and a magnificent
broad-shouldered body. He was also famous for a hideous death at
the hands of the Turks, by a method of execution used both by Turks
and Greeks at the time: he was run through with a spit and roasted
alive over an open fire.

Her husband sips a beer, and makes the dog do a favorite trick, calling to it "Dig for potatoes." The dog acts out scrabbling for pota- toes, and is rewarded with a chunk of lamb. "It is a very clever dog," they say proudly. They insist on our staying for a first bite of lamb, which they announce is done. The wife runs into the house and brings out a sheet; together they remove the lamb from the spit and wrap it in the sheet, and the wife repeatedly slams the lamb onto the ground, bashing it against the earth with all her strength, so that the lamb will fall off the bone, she explains, and will not need to be carved. Again and again, she raises her arms and hurls the animal violently to the ground, until her husband says, "All right, all right, you've killed it." They carry it to a picnic table, and invite us to take a piece with our fingers, but since they forgot to take the lamb's head off at the end, the carcass is slathered with brains.

Stratis and Jocasta thoughtfully suggest a walk, since we are early and they know I don't know the island. We stop in a small village called the Saintly Servants; we move through its lace of intricate passageways and houses, the edges of the streets newly white- washed for Easter, some with delicate patterns traced in white. On the stone pavement in front of the church, a whitewashed *Khronia polla* has been lettered, partly covered now by the carpet of bay leaves that marked the celebration last night of Christ's victory over death. The place has a Christmas Day–like repose. A mother and three little girls pass, and she has the three stop and make toylike versions of her adult sign of the cross. We follow a path that leads past a house with a grape arbor and a concrete terrace heaped with fallen fruit that has overflowed from an orange and two lemon trees, and we step into the otherworld that now exists, the infinite wildflowers that now hold the souls of the dead. The olive trees here are lush and luxuriant-looking because of this island's rich rain, and the ground around them is covered with black netting that catches the ripe olives as they fall and prevents them from being eaten by birds. We cross a narrow stream that runs behind the trees, and look back at the terraces running straight down to sea. The black netting makes the slim olive trees look like women who have just stepped out of diaphanous black nightgowns that have fallen in a heap around their feet.

When we cross back into the village, we hear accordion music, and on the rise of the street, a group of seven men and women, from *yiayias* to young boys, are dancing, forming an open circle that is not complete, round but not closed. Some other members of their party are sitting at a table nearby, drinking wine and pulling bits of lamb from their roast. They are singing a song to the tune of "Roll Out the Barrel," apparently a legacy of British rule here, and one young man calls out, "*Khronia polla.* Do you want to join our dance?" The fresh-faced young boy plays another tune, and we dance in their circle. One of the older men who has had a legitimate holiday idyll with the wine picks choice bits from the lamb carcass to offer to me, and fixing his sleepy-looking bloodshot eyes on me, tells me I must stay in Greece. "Greek people are the best, you like them the best, you must stay here," he says, while everyone around the table applauds the fresh-faced young boy playing the accordion, and has a turn with a request. He plays a charming Theodorakis love song, all pots of basil and kisses, and a popular anthem called "Greece Will Never Die." Someone else sings a ballad about an accordion player who is shot dead as he plays, by a volley of bullets from a vanful of Nazi soldiers; whenever the singer hears the strains of an accordion, the song says, the memory awakens in him the defiance of fascism, fascism will not be tolerated, he sings. The wine has taken the older man all the way back to his childhood, and he insists we stay for one more song, although it is now seriously time for us to leave. He stands up, swaying slightly with wine, and sings a song he must have heard as a boy: "Hitler, don't boast how you conquered Crete . . ." We all exchange kisses, and as we set out for our third Easter dinner, we hear the man launch into another song: "The Duce puts on his uniform and his elegant hat with all the feathers . . . *Akhh,* Ciano, I will go crazy, Ciano, who told me to try to fight with Greece . . ."

THE DREAM OF LOVE
AFTER THE DANCE

An army barracks housing the soldiers who guard parliament and the presidential palace is set in one corner of the National Garden, and a pedestrian walking down the busy thoroughfare of Vassilis Sofias, or Queen Sofia Avenue, is often startled by the sudden resolution of trees and bushes into the shape of a soldier in camouflage, carrying a huge machine gun. "Ah, I like your earrings," I hear from between the iron railings one evening as I walk past, on my way to a dinner party. This communiqué could only have come from the fierce-looking figure in combat boots on the other side of the fence, whose eyes never stopped scanning the street. The literal-minded might hear that whisper as a breach of discipline, but who could criticize the guard's power of observation, or feel less safe under the protection of a soldier with an appetite for life?

I had noticed the imposing but rather ugly Edwardian Benaki mansion as I walked downtown, as I had many times, with two kinds of frustration, first because the museum it houses, which concentrates on modern Greek life, was closed for renovation, and second because it dramatized for me how poor a sense outsiders have of modern Greek biography, and how this deadens our imagination of the nation's history and character. This plutocrat's mansion, rather like a burgher's overfed mansion in Saint Louis, had begun to be a rebuke to me every time I walked past it, particularly after I realized that one of the Benaki daughters, Penelope Delta, had been something like the Louisa May Alcott of modern Greek letters, although under special Greek conditions—she belonged to the generation of Greeks who wrote in demotic Greek and quite literally invented modern Greek literature, like those Israelis who invented a language and a literature for their new nation. Penelope Benaki Delta, born in Alexandria, Egypt, in 1874, and buried in Kifissia, a green and wealthy suburb of Athens, in 1941, had virtually created the children's book in modern Greek, with the works she wrote and published between, roughly, the years 1909 and 1939. It is one of the paradoxes of modern Greek history that a nation so obsessed with its antiquity has a children's literature produced almost entirely in the twentieth century, and an adult literature not much older. Her children's books are fascinating, partly because of her particular charm as a narrator, partly because of the rare glimpses they give us into the social and domestic lives of the well-to-do Greeks of her period, and partly because of her utterly conscious effort, along with the other writers of her generation, to create a nation through literature. Penelope Delta writes not only to create Greek children's literature, but to create Greek children, to make models for them of Hellenism, and of what they should be as Greeks.

She was born into a wealthy and powerful cotton merchant's family in Alexandria, in one of the corners of the world whose cotton industry had become critically important to Europe during the interruption of cotton production in the United States during the American civil war. The Greek community of Alexandria had the reputation of being the richest and most exclusive foreign contingent in the city; the Baedeker guides of the day referred to the Greeks of Egypt as its "aristocrats," and Alexandrian Greeks like the Benakis, who arrived in the nineteenth century, felt less like colonials than like fundamental

Alexandrians, invoking Alexander the Great's foundation of the city, forgetting that Alexander the Great was himself a colonizer in Egypt. The Greek state was only sixty-odd years old when Penelope was growing up, poor, struggling, and bordered by Turkish-held territory. The Alexandrian expatriates helped sustain the Greek government and state enterprises with infusions of cash, and along with other expatriate communities, endowed charitable foundations and schools.

It was Penelope Delta's generation which succeeded in expanding Greece to its current boundaries, including her own native island of Chios, and tried and failed to reestablish a neo-Byzantine empire in the place of the disintegrating Ottoman Empire. When Penelope was a girl, her first glimpse of Turkish soldiers was on a visit to Chios, and she writes of how the sight of them in their red fezzes inspired a voluptuous hatred in her and the other children of the family. Chios, which claims to be the native island of Homer, was a steadily prosperous island under Byzantine and later Genoese rule. Its seamen were so skilled that Columbus is said to have learned the craft of navigation from Chiotes. When the Turks took the island, they followed their customary policy of leaving a profitable property largely to its own devices, governing with a light hand and enjoying the taxes generated by the Chiote production of silk, wine, and mastic, a natural gum produced by trees which grow exclusively on Chios, used throughout the Middle East as an ingredient in pastries and confections, and so popular in the mastic-chewing harems that various sultanas held the property rights to select Chiote mastic groves. The island is so close to the Turkish coast that one of Penelope's Chiote uncles, a strong swimmer, used to make a package of his business clothes, tie them to his head to stay above water, swim across to the busy Turkish ports of Chesme and Smyrna, dress there, go to work, and swim back home. Because of the laissez-faire Turkish jurisdiction on Chios, the island was lukewarm about joining the Greek uprising against the Turks in 1821. It was in fact Greek troops from the neighboring island of

Samos who first invaded the island, to pressure the Chiotes to join the rebellion.

The Turks, for their part, were stung by the betrayal of their leniently treated island, as if it were an unfaithful Greek wife who had been given every indulgence; a Turkish fleet descended on Chios in March of 1822, and the Turkish soldiers slaughtered at least twenty-five thousand citizens, by official execution and freelance murder. Appealing women and children were sold to harems and slavers. This was the massacre imagined in the Delacroix painting that created its image for the West. Penelope's maternal grandfather, a young man at the time, took his wife and children to sanctuary in a church, but when the Turks arrived, they took his family with them. He himself escaped and hid for weeks among the tombs, along with little children whose parents had been killed—they would emerge at night to scavenge for food, and then burrow into their hiding places again. He never saw his first family again, and presumed that they were burned to death when the Ottoman flagship was blown up in revenge by a famous Greek naval commander, Kanaris. But Penelope fantasized, in a turn of the imagination common to Greeks, that they might not have burned up, but that somewhere she had Turkish counterparts, a throng of little Turkish cousins. Her grandfather's second wife was completely illiterate because her school-age years were marked by political violence; she called her husband "Sir," and had sixteen children with him. Penelope remembers her in Alexandria, sitting in a velvet armchair, listening to the Benaki children recite mournful poems to her about starving children and freezing lambs.

Her Benaki grandparents fared differently during the massacres. The Benakis were originally from Mani, the region I visited for the Independence Day celebrations. They had scattered during an eighteenth-century attempt at revolution, and their Mani fortress was destroyed. Her grandfather, who was of the first generation to be born in Chios, could sing a song that began, "I am a son of the Benakis, who come from Kalamata." He was eighteen at the time of the slaughter, and his choice of refuge reflects his Mani heritage, perhaps, unlike her more urban Chiote grandfather, who chose a church to shelter his family. Antoni Benaki fled to the mountains with his brothers, sisters, nieces, and nephews. On the road, they realized the Turks were approaching fast, and found a cave to hide in. One of the babies cried, and in a phrase familiar in many Greek ballads, Antoni whispered to his sister, "Either quiet it or smother it." The Turks discovered them in the cave, and drew their scimitars to murder them. But a Turk who had been a former servant of Antoni's father recognized him and claimed him as a slave before the other Turks, warning them not to touch him, and gave him a place as a deckhand on his boat. He treated Benaki fairly, and soon Benaki was able to buy the caïque from his family's former servant with the money he had saved from his earnings. He then made trips to Alexandria, where he discovered and bought back all his sisters but two, who had been taken by the Turks into the depths of Asia Minor. One was lost without a trace, and the other, after a time, made her way back to Chios, leaving behind the two children she had had with her captor. After some years, when those boys were grown up, they set out to find her on Chios. They told her that they wanted her to return with them, that they were now independent and could give her a life of comfort. She answered that she loved them, "But you are Turkish children, and I am a Greek woman . . . so much blood divides us," and could not be persuaded to return with them, though they visited her often; and she had a poor and lonely life in Chios, "faithful in her faith and in her ethnicity to the end," as Penelope put it. Her Benaki grandmother was taken at age six by the Turks and sold to an Egyptian harem. She had a mole on her forehead, and her relatives found her again through the distinguishing mark. When, after her marriage, she wanted to have it removed, her husband forbade her, telling her, "That sign saved you from the harem. With that sign you will die." They are a forbidding-looking couple in their photographs. The wife wears a miniature of her son, not her husband, at her neck, as if it were a scapular, a charm of protection and power, a proof of her right to exist. Husband and wife both wear their faces like self-portraits, ruthless, bitter, humorless expressions, with indomitable stances and implacable gazes. What they permit their faces to reveal is threat, and they have hewn into their faces what they value—invincibility, pride, lethal honesty, contempt for others and for any tendernesses, absolutism, the sense of honor as a way of exacting a tribute from the world as much as giving something to it.

It was the slaughter in Chios which pushed Penelope's branch of the family to Egypt. By the time she was born, her father had a Liverpool factory and a commanding position in the Greek colony at Alexandria.

Penelope's Alexandria was a mansion in the Greek colony, beyond whose walls she could hear the chants of Arab beggars. Although her upbringing was luxurious, her world was one of jagged fragments which she could never fit together to make a whole. There was the odd circumstance of living a life of power and privilege in a country in which her only contacts with the indigenous population were as servants or beggars. She commented that beating Arabs was not only permitted, but obligatory, and the anecdotes she tells of her father beating their gardener for an imagined presumption, and of a British officer slashing an Arab's face with a whip, provoke the thought that the roots of Islamic fundamentalism may not lie in the Koran, but in Europe.

There were other splinterings in her affluent life. Although the Greek community had a grandiose sense of its power and importance, it also was tormented by a sense of inferiority in relation to the western Europeans in Alexandria. The Greeks felt self-conscious about their struggling, weak, and very new state, and both envied and mistrusted the French and English contingents in Alexandria. There was a glamour for them in the manners and lives of western Europeans, a sense of more secure and established traditions, and perhaps a half-acknowledged yearning for a less punitive family life than the tyrannical Greek family structure allowed. The

Benaki children grew up under the tutelage of various English and French governesses and teachers, and it was a source of shame later to Penelope that the Greek community of her day had a reputation as energetic capitalists whose passion for business left them indifferent to cultural affairs. She was embarrassed that the Greek community had no school of their own. Girls were not sent on to high school, but kept at home to learn housekeeping; boys were given higher education in Roman Catholic schools, where sometimes, as in her brother's case, they were proselytized. The Greek schoolteachers sent by the state were of such a poor standard, Penelope said, that none of the parents would entrust their children to them. Penelope grew up speaking English, French, and scraps of Arabic, like the brothers and sisters in one of her most famous novels for children, whose governess admonishes them perpetually to "Speik Ingliss," as the Greek children hear her command. The children's Greek lessons were all Katharevousa, which made them dislike the Greek books they read and distanced them from the spoken language of their own countrymen. It was as if American children's only instruction in English were in the language of the Tyndale Bible, all *doths* and *spakes;* and the result was that the Benaki children wolfed down their French and English books, but opened their Greek books only under orders. The stories Penelope describes herself as having a "mania" to write during her girlhood, with deaths and catastrophes on every page, were written in French. Penelope wrote her journals in French, too, until she was a grown-up married woman; and even as a prominent author, she anxiously pressed other Greek writers to assess her Greek, while many people say the Benaki children spoke Greek with foreign accents. This was not peculiar to Penelope's family—she records that all the Greek children of her acquaintance spoke English and French among themselves and with their parents. In fact, speaking Greek, among the very people who considered themselves, as Greeks, the "foam of the cream" in Alexandria, was the mark of someone who had had no cosmopolitan education—"Greek letters were for those who didn't know foreign languages," Penelope remarked, and domestic life reflected the doubleness of the Greeks' image of themselves. The children's clothes were marked with their initials in English, and when Penelope was asked as a bride how she wanted her silver wedding gifts monogrammed, she stunned her circle by asking that they be engraved with her initials in Greek.

There was an upstairs-downstairs atmosphere about being Greek. Above, the house was furnished with tables and chairs, linen, glassware, china, and silver imported from England, the library stocked with foreign literature. The cellar, Penelope remembers, seems to have belonged to Greece, with its great jars filled with olive oil, special earthenware urns filled with Chiote olives preserved in brine, flagons of *raki* from Chios, flower waters, rosewater, shelves full of Cretan soap (the olive oil–based soap that was once a staple of the Cretan economy), containers of figs and raisins from Smyrna, sweet wines, clay jars filled with Chiote mastic, and Penelope's favorite, confections made from almond and sesame, stored among dry bay leaves for fragrance. Despite this abundance drawn from both the Greek and the western European worlds, Penelope felt scorned for her ethnicity. The feeling of inferiority, she wrote, was inflicted on them by foreign nurses and teachers, who expressed scorn for the Greeks' general use of marriage as a purely financial transaction; it was compounded by teachers of "our own race," foreign-educated children they knew, the boys' Jesuit teachers. She was also wounded by a sense gleaned from the western European communities that Greece was not considered an influential, or even a politically mature, nation. She remembered with particular bitterness a cartoon of Greece she saw in an Italian paper, probably during the period in which Greece's ambitions to win back the territories of the former Byzantine Empire, to become "Greece of the two continents and five seas," had begun to be openly stated. The caricatures represented different countries in their military uniforms, and Greece was shown as a little foustanella-wearing child, crying with his mouth open and rubbing one eye with his fist. In front of him stood a bucket of water in which the moon was mirrored. The grown-ups surrounding the child asked him, "What do you want now?" and the boy called out, "I want, I want the moon!"

Penelope's novel *Trelantonis* (something like "Crazy Anthony," "Wild Anthony," or "Irrepressible Anthony") gives an idea of the scale of the Greece of her childhood. It is based on the summer of 1881, which the Benaki children spent with relatives in Piraeus, which then had a quarter that was valued as a summer refuge for its sea breezes and the access it gave to the sea for health-giving daily swims. There the children lived in the third of seven houses built by Ernst Ziller—a German architect who had also designed a house in central Athens known as the "Palace of Troy" for the philhellene archaeologist Schliemann, in 1878, where Schliemann and his wife Sofia brought up their two children, Agamemnon and Cassandra. In the largest of the row of Ziller houses in Piraeus, as Penelope's novel recorded, lived the king of Greece, who himself spoke Greek with a foreign accent. This was George I, a member of the Danish royal family, and founder of the Glucksberg dynasty, which never truly successfully rooted itself in Greece. No Glucksberg king ever had a hereditary connection to the Greek people. George had been a seventeen-year-old Danish naval cadet when the great powers of Europe selected him for the Greek throne. His accession to the throne had been revealed to him by a fish sandwich: he had left his house in Copenhagen carrying his lunch, consisting of sardine sandwiches which were carefully wrapped in newspaper so as not to leak oil. He happened to scan the paper as he unwrapped his lunch, and "read to my delighted amazement that I was King of the Hellenes." Just before the Greek delegation formally offered him the throne, he was promoted from naval cadet to captain.

In the Belle Epoque world of *Trelantonis,* the children's treats are *loukoumi,* what we call Turkish delight, prepared with mastic, and *vissinada,* a cherry syrup to flavor drinks beloved both in Turkey and in Greece, whose preparation by the daughters is described in one chapter. The boys' toy soldiers go to war divided into Greeks and

Turks, and when the children suffer at the hands of an English governess who tipples and scorns them as Greeks, it is the queen of
Greece who, sitting in her garden, sees that the governess is drunk
and informs the children's aunt, while in another adventure, the
hero, Antonis, is bitten by the Greek king's dog, Don.

To an outsider, though, this children's novel, with its conscious
domestic realism, reads like a fantasy of another world. The children
in the illustrations look like perfect specimens of European Edwardian childhood, with their sailor suits and straw hats; but at the same
time there is a strong undercurrent of hostility between Greece and
Europe, expressed by the struggles between the mischievous children and the malicious English governess, Miss Rice. When Miss
Rice unfairly brings down a punishment on the children from their
aunt, Antonis, the hero, says, "These are the kinds of things these foreigners do, the kinds of lies they tell . . . and they always do these
things!" These handsomely turned out children are also frequently
slapped, spanked, and beaten by nearly all the adults, foreign and
Greek, and there is something nauseating in the relentless contempt
expressed for girl characters by the boy-hero of a novel written by a
woman. The girls are drawn as weaklings, prudes, physical and moral
inferiors; the one who is most distinguishable from the others is the
one who praises Antonis in the end for his incorrigibility, calling him
a "little cockerel," with almost erotic undertones: "I like you," she
says, "because you are unruly and you are a *pallikari,* a brave, daring
boy. You are always making mischief, but you aren't afraid of any
punishment!" Antonis, for his part, orates with depressing frequency
about the inferiority of his sisters and of all women, and in a fight
with his sisters over which one will keep a beloved Greek servant
when they are grown up, says with doctrinal certainty that he will
have the privilege because he is a boy, and has first privileges in
everything. When Antonis for the first and only time admires a girl,
he says, "You are a daring boy yourself, you are a man!" The girl then
invokes the names of gallant fighting women of the Greek revolution, and asks Antonis if they too aren't *pallikaria.* She poses him a

surreal question about the heroines—the sentence reads literally: "And these women weren't gallant men?"

The world of *Trelantonis* is fascinating and disorienting, because of the strange encounter it records between Europe and the Orient; here a sailor-suited boy's idea of a prank is to smoke his uncle's narghile. The only narghile-smoking character I can conjure up in Western children's books is Lewis Carroll's caterpillar; *Trelantonis*, in Greek children's literature a work of realism, reads to us more like *Through the Looking Glass*.

The genre portrait of a Belle Epoque summer in Piraeus does not include another dissonance that disturbed Penelope in her childhood: the resentment of the indigenous Greeks for the *omoyeneis*, the expatriates of "the same race" who lived and made money outside Greece, who endowed the country with civic institutions, but always lived at a higher standard than the people they were benefitting could afford to do. In the Athens of Penelope's childhood, there were fields in the city's center, where the Hotel Grande-Bretagne now stands, and while the "outside" Greeks wore overcoats, the Athenians still wrapped themselves in oriental shawls. "Athenian" has been as malleable a word throughout its history as "Hellene"; in conversations overheard at the family dinner table, "Athenian" and "Plakiotis," man of Plaka (now the most romanticized, "old quarter" section of the city), conjured up covetous, jealous, hard-luck cases, ill-fated and cursed, whereas *omoyeneis*, expatriate, had nuances of cultured, patrician, polite. As a married woman living in an Athens utterly, unrecognizably different from the Athens of her occasional childhood visits, she remembered a bitter dialogue between an Athenian woman and a street flower seller, in which the woman coarsely drove the peddler away, seeming to almost hate the roses offered, for the pain their beauty and perfume gave her. At the Benaki dinner table, she winced hearing relatives saying they loved the Greek landscape but not the Greeks, and later, she recorded a remark of her grown brother's, "If I weren't a Greek, I would be a Greek-hater," a feeling she strove to repress in herself and in others. She puzzled over the

causes of the split Greek character, wondering why the same people
could be both heroes and deserters, as she put it.

But for all the ambiguity of the expatriate Greeks' relations with
their own countrymen, with other foreign colonials, and with the
local populations of the places where they did business, the most
unstable, ambiguous, and dangerous environment Penelope ever
knew was her parents' home, where public dignity, power, honor,
and lavish philanthropy coexisted with intimate cruelty and des-
potism. Penelope characterized child rearing in her day as strict,
merciless, without developmental education, caresses, love, an
upbringing based on terror and reverence, whose key phrase was
etsi prepei, this is how things must be. She described her household
not as a dual monarchy but a dual tyranny: her mother beautiful and
unapproachable, her father "straight as a column," with thick frowning brows, "two deities." It was a household in which disobedience,
complaint, and even terror itself were not tolerated.

Penelope was afraid of the grotesque shadows the lamplight
threw on the bedroom wall at night, but she never permitted herself
to call out, or even confessed the fear, because she was afraid her
father would hear about it, and find some way to express his contempt for her, or punish her. Her father seemed to her the archetype
of the *pallikari*: "Fearless, inflexible, implacable, untameable, big,
muscular, proud, handsome, he represented for us all the beauty of
virility. Whatever my father wanted, that was what happened. It
never entered the head of anyone to resist him or speak back to him."
Penelope remembered how once at the lunch table her father
berated her for biting her nails and called her to him, brandishing the
carving knife and threatening to cut her finger off. She was so terri-
fied that she couldn't move when he told her to sit down again. She
did not remember him whipping her with a horsewhip for the same
habit, but her mother described it to her when she was older. When
he entered the house, silence fell, and the main meal was served on
his arrival at any hour. The children had to wait, no matter how hungry they were, or leave their lessons, no matter how preoccupied

they were——her father himself suggested to her mother that the children eat dinner with her earlier, but she insisted that they eat with
the head of the house, the source of their food. When a European
governess, frustrated by the disruptions the moveable dinner hour
caused, criticized the arrangement, Penelope was partly grateful for
the sympathy she craved for her hunger headaches, but also disap-
proving of what she felt to be presumption, even a quality of blas-
phemy in the criticism. Her father, she wrote, was something like a
cult, a religion for her . . . "I cried horribly on his account. I cried
all my life. He dominated me always and tyrannized over me, know-
ingly and unknowingly . . . and nevertheless he remained," she said,
the great overarching love of her life.

Throughout her life, she continued to demonstrate this religious
devotion to charismatic leaders like General Nikolas Plastiras, and
above all, Eleftherios Venizelos, her father's own candidate and
political colleague and the most famous prime minister of modern
Greece. It was as if she found a way to assent to her father's treatment of her, and to submerge her own impermissible criticisms by
idealizing masculinity, in a sense participating in this charismatic
power as a sacrifice to it——if she was going to be crucified, at least
her torment would be at the hand of God the Father, in whose
divinity she would share. And above all, she resolutely idealized
Greece, and found a way through patriotism to craft a career in a
culture which barred women from any work not ultimately in the
service of a father or a husband——in Greece Penelope ingeniously
found a father to work for, and a way to justify her work. If her
books were created in the service of patriotism, then in a sense her
work was a sacrifice, and therefore not an act of independence.
Greece was a father that she could love and serve unreservedly and
uncritically——the problem of painful criticism was resolved, as in
her steely, heartfelt, charming, and oddly tragic political allegory
for children, *Fairy Tale Without a Name,* in which a young prince,
through leadership, and his sister, through service, set out to restore
the lost perfection of their kingdom, now corrupt and degraded.

The degraded condition of the kingdom is temporary, a momentary episode between a past perfection and a future restoration, and so cannot have its roots in the kingdom itself, since corruption would hardly have evolved from such perfection. The faint strain of tragedy comes through the evocation of the lost ideal, the nothingness of lost perfection which makes a nothingness of the future, a hopeless cycle in which an unattainable and unreal goodness is sought and never regained. Penelope is stymied in this book by the common problem of presenting goodness as ideal perfection, not as something living, complex, intricately, integrally, vitally connected to many qualities that are not good. And when good is seen only as an ideal quality, confused with the perfect, then evil is viewed only as a horrible flaw, a cyclical aberration, not a development that occurs in relation to other things. Critical thinking, vigilant revision, profound and lasting change, become impossible. If goodness is idealized, evil can only be repented.

Penelope's mother was as domineering as her father, a woman whose repressed fury at her own condition seems to have been vented on her household, her only realm of power, since she was utterly subject to her husband, who even read her letters as a matter of course, as later Penelope's husband read her correspondence—a practice Penelope wondered at only in retrospect. Poorly educated, almost pathologically without empathy, seethingly angry, but commandingly wealthy, emotionally and intellectually deprived, but materially spoiled, as a woman, abased, but as a wealthy wife, arrogant, vengeful, and self-important, Penelope's mother ruled her household with slaps, beatings, and constant vicious criticism. She was like a corrupt regional overlord, ruling her territory in the name of an absent but all-powerful sultan. She was gentle with her children only in one of her rare good moods, or when they were sick, and for the child Penelope, the "ne plus ultra of life's beauty" was a sentimental engraving she saw in an illustrated English magazine that showed a mother kneeling on a lawn and tenderly embracing a child, with the caption "My darling is better."

Early in her childhood, Penelope was possessed with the idea of suicide, the image of which was always mingled with the imagining of
her mother's tears, of feeling valued and loved. The thought of suicide, she reflected later, from early childhood, had never ceased to
live within her. As an adult, Penelope spent substantial time in German spas seeking cures for undiagnosable ailments, cramps, and
exhaustion.

Penelope imitated her mother in games with her toddler brother
in which she would alternately tease him and comfort him, baiting
him even as she caressed him, and becoming even more enraged as
he cried. Siblings often have distinctly, and even completely, different upbringings, depending on their parents' ambitions, fantasies,
and responses to them, and of the five surviving Benaki children
(one had died in infancy), Penelope seems to have been singled out
for the most brutal treatment—her father seemed to see her as a
competitor, and steadily undercut her intellectual gifts, telling her
that with her mind she ought to have been born a boy, conveying to
her that a woman's talents only emphasized her inferiority, while
her mother seemed to bitterly resent any possibility that Penelope
had capacities she did not, and might not share her own fate, jealous
of any interest of Penelope's that she herself did not understand. As
Penelope became more and more absorbed by reading and writing,
her mother increased her household duties, so that when she was
not having lessons she was nearly always occupied with sewing and
other housework. Her mother hated her reading and if she discovered Penelope with a book, she would invent an errand, saying,
"Stop your reading, I don't intend to make a philosopher of
you . . ."

Penelope had thoughts and emotions and capacities that, if not
destroyed or damaged, might enable her to escape from the loveless
web of the Benaki family, and it seemed they could not endure their
own lives if there was a richer hope in hers. If they could force her
life to resemble theirs, then the pain of their own disappointments
could be contained. Her misery would make their own seem justi-

fied, not a matter of choice, or of blind chance, but inevitable, the condition of life itself.

Her situation was, too, an example of the ironic social circularity that makes the lives of rich and poor abused children mirror each other, both classes of children equally vulnerable. The maltreated children of the poor are unprotected partly because of the difficulty of marshaling the human and financial resources to monitor and rescue them; the maltreated children of the rich are unprotected because their parents control those financial resources, surrounded by people they employ directly or indirectly, or colleagues with whom they are doing business, who are unlikely to risk their livelihoods and financial and social alliances by interfering.

One particular incident, with its atmosphere of almost luxurious brutality and voluptuous violence, marked Penelope throughout her life, and the memory of it brought tears to her eyes even as an adult. One day, Penelope, aged seven or so, simply couldn't stomach her French lesson, and declared a private holiday, drawing horses in her notebook. The next morning when the teacher asked for her homework, Penelope showed her the page with the cartoons, and told her that she didn't have the lesson prepared and didn't know who had drawn horses on the clean paper. She was sent into her mother's bedroom, where her mother, wearing a white peignoir with open sleeves that left her arms bare, asked her daughter who had ruined her notebook. Penelope said she didn't know, and her mother called her over to the bedside. Then, Penelope remembered, "The arms of my mother, white and powerful, fell on me like mallets . . . ," her mother striking her child's head, shoulders, back, chest, face with unappeasable rage. Penelope screamed and fell backward, and her mother continued to beat her, wherever the blows fell. A maid restrained the mother, holding back her "white, naked" arms, shouting that she would kill the child. The floor under Penelope was soaked with the little girl's urine; her mother noticed, stopped beating her, and ordered the maid, "Bring a mop." Penelope, hysterical with fear, rage, and shame, was taken from the room by the maid, and later that day was set again to her lessons, shut up in the schoolroom by herself. Her mother swept in, carrying Penelope's baby sister, and told Penelope that if her lessons weren't neatly written she would beat her again. Then she cuddled the baby, and said to the child in her arms, "Look out yourself that you don't grow up evil like that one." The incident was never mentioned again, although in Penelope it lived forever, intact, undiminished, inexhaustible, as love is supposed to be. Reading her English storybooks, Penelope wondered why it was only in books that mothers loved their children, and not in life.

When Penelope became a marriageable teenager, she began to participate in the highly chaperoned exhibitions at dances and opera evenings that were a prospective bride's work. Her older sister had been married to the son of an English partner of her father's, and under this system, a groom's potential as an administrator of the family business was perhaps his most important feature—his marriage to the bride was almost incidental, his marriage to her father was crucial. In addition, Penelope's maturity coincided with her father's developing political ambitions, so that a Greek groom would be important.

The Alexandrian community's courtships were conducted at family dinners, at the theater, at carnival and Easter dances. Young men from Greece and Constantinople as well as from Alexandria would be present, the boys' choices no freer than the girls', threatened with the loss of inheritances and career prospects if they differed from their parents' selection.

Negotiating the intricate social fissures of being Greek, the young couples courted each other in foreign languages, particularly English and French, and the fragments of such courtships recorded in diaries of the period like Penelope's give the impression that in this world of repressed sexuality, moving from language to language was itself an erotic experience, full of momentary revelations, glimpses of sudden unpredictable nakedness, charged secret vocabularies. They danced European dances, to fashionable new tunes like the "Carmen Sylva Waltz," named for the Queen of Rumania. There were no waltzes in their own country. The dances of Greece explore, most often in circular patterns, the expression of community, or of continuity between generations—they also, in men's solos, examine the nature of individuality, through improvisation and mesmerizing feats of movement, performed in relation to uniformly moving background dancers. But this dance-loving people's imagination of partnered dance, of the gestures a man and woman make in a conversation of motion together, face-to-face, of physical dialogue, is among the poorest in the world. In Greek discotheques, the couple dances are necessarily foreign ones, and when I left Greece briefly for the States and went with a friend to a Latin dance club, I was shocked to remember the wit, invention, erotic courage, reflection on the relation between passion and ethics, the burnished philosophical sensuality of those dances with partners. In Alexandria, in 1894, the year Penelope fell in love with a young man called Mavrocordatos, the girls wore dance cards which hung from their waists, along with lace fans, and the boys would approach, asking to sign for a particular number on the card. Neither partner could know each other well before marriage, so the courtship was managed through glances, waltzes, and code. Suitors proposed and were rejected in the interval between numbers; large questions about someone's ambitions and personal ethics were posed and answered on the way into the dining room for refreshments. Penelope described herself as proper to the point of priggishness, discouraging even lighthearted compliments, determined to behave correctly. She wanted both a husband she could care for and a son-in-law who would fulfill her father's desires. When a matchmaker approached her independently on behalf of a suitor, she answered that her father must be contacted instead, because she would only reply to such proposals through him. But for all her perfect decorum, what she longed for was a marriage of mutual love, a longing made more acute by a joyless childhood. When her mother discussed with her the possibility of living somewhere less appealing than Alexandria after her marriage, Penelope said she dreamed only of being devoted to someone, of making her husband happy. "Permit me to take a husband who I will like!" she begged. "I will be so miserable if I don't marry out of love." Her mother was so moved by Penelope's passionate sincerity that, in one of her caprices, she kissed her, and promised that Penelope would not be pressured when she came to make a choice.

The young man called Mavrocordatos Penelope met in 1894 was poor but socially distinguished, and had come out from Athens to work for her father. They fell in love in French and English, dancing at a carnival dance to a waltz they both thought "divine," called "The Dream of Love After the Dance." They explored each other's minds between dips and turns, both agreeing that they believed in fate. Mavrocordatos added that he had felt a magnet of fate drawing him from Athens to unknown joys in Alexandria. They described their feelings for each other in parables, telling each other stories about their attraction to each other so as not to violate propriety by direct declaration. Mavrocordatos, to let her know he couldn't forget her, told her he was puzzled by why there was no photograph of her in the office, mentioning significantly that he couldn't find one anywhere, telling a love story in which he himself was the male lead. He began to be a frequent visitor to the Benaki home, a guest at family dinners, received in an unspoken acceptance as a suitor, participating in conversations engineered by Penelope's mother to explore his philosophy of marriage. Mrs. Benaki spoke harshly of a nephew of hers who had declared he would only marry for money, testing Mavrocordatos, who replied that it was regrettable how common it was for gold to be more important than feelings in making a marriage. Penelope's mother declared before the company that feelings were more important, and when Penelope fervently thanked her later, she promised that this principle would govern the matter of Penelope's marriage. At Easter, the greatest of Greek seasonal feasts, Mavrocordatos was among the guests invited to the annual Benaki dinner. The company played whist, and at midnight a servant rang the bell to announce that Christ was risen. The guests stood up, kissing and offering Easter wishes for happiness to each other. When they went into the dining room, a family friend wished Penelope a happy Easter, and that he would see her a bride within the year.

When Mavrocordatos visited, staying within the correct boundaries of courtship by not attaching himself too obviously to Penelope, she would send him a coded message by playing "The Dream of Love After the Dance" on the piano. And when they finally shyly declared their love to each other, they used the polite plural "you."

For Penelope, loving and being loved was an unimaginable liberation and joy; for the first time, she understood other people's previously incomprehensible sense of life as a gift, not a painful ordeal, a waltz on burning coals, that had to be faced every day with hard-wrought bravery and incongruous public cheerfulness. But the innocent transparency of her happiness had unexpected effects. Families are not only personal but political entities; in fact, far from being exempt from politics, family relations in their political patterns are important seedbeds and training models for the conduct of a nation's political life, one reason that states and state churches struggle so arduously to shape them. What is considered just and acceptable in some versions of family life—as, for instance, ritual mutilation, wife or child beating, refusing women the right to drive or travel on their own authority, the abandonment of unwanted babies, or divorce only on the husband's initiative—will rarely be penalized by the state, particularly if the practice has been sacralized through theological sanction, and is presented as an expression of God's will. Penelope's family was a small-scale empire. Her mother, acting as go-between for her husband, reported that he was angry at Penelope's dancing whole waltzes with Mavrocordatos, and sitting near him at the dining table, eager for their conversations. Her father was fearfully jealous of Mavrocordatos; "he imagines that you love him." Penelope replied out of her exaltation that her father was right, that she loved Mavrocordatos with all her heart. Mrs. Benaki warned Penelope that she must disguise her feeling, telling her her father liked Mavrocordatos very much, "but only on the condition that his daughter will not love him . . . he wants your marriage, but he doesn't want you to love . . ." Penelope's love was, in terms of family politics, like an important territory declaring to an empire its intention to become an independent state.

Penelope's parents, having so publicly welcomed Mavrocordatos, began a ruthless campaign to destroy the attachment their tacit permission had helped secure. An exhausting round of fights began. At first Penelope's mother told her that the marriage was still possible, but that her father was infuriated by their appearing to be in love; but when her mother began to tell her that she had heard rumors that Mavrocordatos had had many adventures with wealthy prospective brides, Penelope realized that her father had turned against the marriage, and that her mother, however erratic her sympathies might be, was his envoy. Penelope asked her mother frankly if she thought Mavrocordatos only wanted her for her dowry. Why else would he want you, her mother replied; her new doctrine contradicted her old doctrine, but that made acceptance of it an even fiercer necessity. The family began to treat Mavrocordatos coldly on his visits, and to restrict even the couple's brief opportunities to speak. Penelope's father conveyed through her mother that he was angry she appeared to be suffering exaggeratedly, pale and losing weight, and Penelope prepared herself for a separation, girding herself for a heroic struggle, envisioning either a victory in which she would win her parents' consent to marry the man she loved, or not marry at all. She devised a way to correspond with Mavrocordatos through a trusted French governess, and prepared keepsakes to take with him to Athens, where he was being sent. She wanted to give him a charm from her bracelet as a talisman. It had been a gift from her parents, and like many parental gifts, it was a declaration of their own intentions, of the life they intended their daughter to have; it was an image of a sailing ship struggling through a tempest of high waves. The legend engraved on the charm read "Thus is life."

With Mavrocordatos removed from the scene, the Benakis waged a war of attrition against Penelope, with tortuous daily confrontations staged between her and her mother. Mrs. Benaki told Penelope that her idea of marrying for love was simply obsessive, and that her father would never consent to her marriage with a poor man. Her father called her in for private sessions as well, telling her that in her naiveté she could not recognize that Mavrocordatos was only a dowry hunter, and that he knew very well the techniques young men used to make young women believe in their fictitious love. Expertly, he worked to enclose her in the world he saw, the only real world, the world as he interpreted and willed it, from which he did not want her to escape. The tactics he and his wife employed to separate Penelope from her fiancé were models of political coercion, making full use of their material and emotional power over her. The intimate look Penelope's story gives at the logic of the arranged marriage shows us not only its social workings, but the opportunity it gave to play out emotional politics, unacknowledged family hostilities, favoritisms, fears, desires, revenges. It is not uncommon for family members to dislike each other, and the control over a child's future as an adult gave an enormous scope for expression of those feelings, particularly half-conscious ones, through the seemingly accidental choice of an incompatible marriage partner, human maneuvering wearing the costume and opulent maquillage of fate.

Even though Penelope considered that she and Mavrocordatos had pledged themselves to each other, that she was in fact engaged to him, her mother one morning peremptorily summoned her to her room, and read her a letter she had written in response to an uncle's embassy on behalf of a rich young Athenian. "My husband and I are agreed to accept the young man . . . as far as the dowry is concerned, the sum is 8,000 . . . We agree that our daughter will live in Athens with the parents of the young man whom she will respect . . ." She insisted on Penelope's consent to the wording of the letter, and when Penelope refused, she revised the letter to read, "My daughter has no objection, but wants to know the young man before we decide . . ." When Penelope, anguished in her disobedience, but true to her promise to Mavrocordatos, persisted in refusing, her mother told her that it would be her fault if she ruined the future of the man she loved, that her father would fire him from his job. When Penelope told her she preferred to stay unmarried if she could not marry Mavrocordatos, her mother declared that she would marry whomever they chose, and follow the examples set for her in the family. She was insulted, she said, that her daughter was treating her like a woman they knew who had used violence to obtain her daughter's consent to the marriage arranged for her. There was another conference, in which Penelope's father informed her that he was firing Mavrocordatos, that if he persisted in visiting them he would be ejected from the house with blows, and that he would break the teeth in her head if she attempted to meet with him. As for Penelope, if she was stubborn in her refusal to marry, she was welcome to remain in the Benaki household for all her life. Eat, drink, and rot, he told her.

Penelope drank her supply of medicinal arsenic, but there was not enough to kill her; she only vomited and convulsed throughout the night. She began to collect, drop by drop, arsenic from her brother's store, so that she would have enough to ensure her death next time. The impasse came to an end when Mavrocordatos wrote to Penelope releasing her from the engagement they had made between themselves, and asking her to release him. There had been a scene at his firing, and irrevocable insults had been exchanged on both sides, which now made any union between the families impossible. Perhaps he realized that not only would the Benakis not permit the marriage, but Penelope herself was so enmeshed with them that she could not marry without their involvement. Penelope herself seemed to expect him to remain loyal to her in unmarried devotion, while she lived out her days at home, unable either to marry or to leave the Benaki family. She wrote to him in a tone of imperious morality to return her letters and keepsakes, and never forgave him for what she considered his contemptible betrayal of their love. Her parents, she decided, had been proved right in their views of him and of marriage, and she resolved to marry according to their choice, to live her life as an obedient and honorable wife; as for love, she was so disillusioned that she felt she no longer had the capacity. She had thought during this worst of the struggles that having at first and last experienced love, to have it uprooted from her life meant uprooting her heart as well. As a mature married woman, she noted in her diary that her heart hadn't been uprooted; it had been killed. "I will no longer seek happiness in life . . . ," she wrote, ". . . the dream ended . . ." She never played "The Dream of Love After the Dance" again, and was almost nauseated if she heard it by chance.

Her father took the family on a trip to Europe partly to recover from the episode, and on the trip Penelope seems almost to have fallen in love with him, as prisoners sometimes do with their captors. ". . . I saw my father as he was," she wrote, "a golden heart . . . large-souled, proud . . ." If he had seemed merciless when she was suffering so much, it was because he knew nothing of her pain, she concluded. She felt he was superb, and she felt keenly her obligation as a caryatid of the Benaki name.

In the summer, in Lucerne, she encountered a palm reader who had established himself for a few days at the entrance of their hotel. He told her that she was proud above all, and that her arrogant pride would ruin her. When she asked him if a certain interpretation of the lines in her hand meant she would have no great joys, the fortune-teller told her that she herself had little luck in this area, but that her husband would have joys which she would share, although she herself would not often have what her heart desired. A little later, an uncle arrived in Lucerne to tell her family that he had found a fiancé for Penelope. His name was Delta, his family from Constantinople. He held a position with the railroad company of Thessaly, which would lead to a directorship; he was well-educated, *morfomenos* (a word which means, literally, shaped), speaking English, French, and German perfectly, the linguistic expertise which in Greece was the particular mark of an educated man or woman. He earned a great deal of money, she was told, although he had no personal property or expectation of a large inheritance. He was handsome, charming. Although she must leave Egypt and live with him in Athens—at the time, a less attractive prospect—he was alone in the world, without relatives, so that she would not face the universally dreaded struggles with a mother-in-law over her son's affections, domestic management, and child rearing. At first Penelope was shocked, unprepared for the reality that her family would actually marry her in the same way they would arrange a business trade, but she had resolved to follow her father's direction. She wrote her father, away on a business trip, that a marriage based on love no longer mattered to her, and that she promised to consent to any husband he chose. Having promised in advance to marry Delta, she was curious to learn what the man's first name was. No one knew. Nor did they have any idea what he looked like, and again Penelope was frightened and unnerved that they would so readily marry her to a man of whom they knew nothing except for rumors, most of those produced by associates who wanted to promote him as a marriage candidate. The elders of the family declared that they, in their greater experience, were better judges of marriage partners than their children; but they were prepared to commit her to a man they themselves didn't know, they were as ignorant of the future groom as she was. She wrote in her journal that what she was consenting to was her own ethical suicide, but that she could not escape it, and that in any case, she could no longer tolerate her mother's perpetual criticism and seeming malice toward her. The family and Penelope set out for Athens with the momentous knowledge that her fate was to be settled. Penelope, with a sense that Athens might be her future home, was so moved by the sight of the Parthenon that she wept.

Mr. Delta, on first meeting, turned out to be not handsome and charming and free of family ties, but corpulent, unattractive, and far from alone in the world—he had a brother whom he helped support, and also unexpectedly included in his marriage package a stepmother, the dreaded mother-in-law, the portent of domestic struggles for the Greek bride, the widow whose entire social status and emotional satisfaction depended now on her son. When Penelope married Delta, she was told, the mother-in-law would retire to Constantinople to live, the household would not be shared between them. Penelope, on the first encounter, found Stefanos Delta such an unappealing presence that she despaired, and again weighed the alternatives of continuing to live at home, which she found intolerable, or suicide, or a marriage to this candidate, an idea she found barely supportable. When her mother wished her good night, she told Penelope that her father had liked him so well that he would now refuse to consider another groom; it must be Delta or no one. The thought of engaging in another protracted struggle with her parents, the welcome prospect of freedom from at least her unhappy daily life with them, and the promise she had made to her father that she would abide by his decision resigned Penelope to accepting Delta. He also appeared more sympathetic in their next meetings—kindly, with a saving sense of humor unknown in Penelope's house, where the family's sense of the prestige due them ensured that there could be no hint of mocking or being mocked; and he turned out to be a man of scruples, a quality Penelope valued above all.

Before the engagement was officially finalized, Delta requested, as convention demanded, a private conversation with his future wife. The purpose of the interview revealed an unusual sensitivity, which moved Penelope and made her feel that if she could not love him, she at least might be able to trust him. He wanted to know if the marriage was taking place with her consent, if she was being offered against her will. It was a poignant—and futile—question, since the structure of their system of marriage meant that in truth she could only answer "both," that under this system, neither "yes" nor "no" was true. Ironically, in order to convey to her his honesty and good character, Delta could only reassure her that he didn't love her: he wouldn't pretend, he told her, that he had any feeling for her, but possibly it would come later. Penelope, combining grace and bitterness, excused him from any concern—"We are making a contractual marriage," she said, "nothing concerned with feelings!" At their engagement dinner, they were seated next to each other, to receive the toasts and good wishes of the families. Throughout the dinner, they correctly addressed each other as "Miss Benaki" and "Mr. Delta." The next morning, they were taken by Penelope's father to a photographer, where they posed separately for portraits to be sent to each other's relatives, so that each set could see for themselves what the future in-law looked like. The *arravonas* was official, that word in Greek which means both engagement and a sum of money deposited as security against the fulfillment of a contract. It is a word with a root so very old that it almost certainly predates Greek literacy; it comes from *arravon,* a word scholars identify as Phoenician, a term from the shipping business for a deposit against the delivery of a ship's cargo—an appropriate inheritance from that sailing people who probably brought Aphrodite and Adonis to Greece, developed from their own goddess Astarte and her Adonis-like consort; they certainly brought the Western world's first known alphabet, which was adapted to fit the sounds the Greeks made, as the divine figures were remolded to fit the native imagination of the sacred. As the Greek monks Cyril and Methodius were to the Slavs in the ninth century, bringing them the Greek alphabet, and the new divine personages of Christ and Mary, as well as trade and political alliances that last to this day, so the Phoenicians were to the Greeks. The debt Christianity owes to Semites is owed to Phoenicians equally as to Israelites, both for religious elements incorporated into the figures of Christ and Mary, and above all, for the Greek alphabet, which through Alexander's conquests became the lingua franca of the Mediterranean, later the language of the New Testament, and the medium of missionary Christianity. I hear the Phoenician word *arravon* often, as the base of the words for fiancée and fiancé, for the adjective "engaged"; when

I hear it, I am hearing the distant voice of Europa, who according to Homer was the daughter of Phoenix, the king of the Phoenicians.

For Penelope, another ordeal remained: she had grown up with an ideal of heroism, of facing danger for the sake of Hellenism, and as a woman, her equivalent of that heroism was to expose herself to the contempt of or even rejection by her future husband by a wrenching confession to him that she had loved another man, that she was not, in a sense, an emotional virgin, as she was expected to be. Perhaps, in part, too, she harbored a hope that the confession would free her from a marriage about which she had mixed feelings. After the initial confession, she brought up the subject so often that it also seems she might have made use of it as a way of expressing a rebellion against a marriage she didn't really want, even as a subtle and impersonal way of punishing the groom for not being the man she loved.

After Delta listened to her confession, he asked her if she had ever kissed the man she had been in love with, and she swore on God that she had not. Then it was possible for him to continue the engagement, he concluded, and asked her to kiss him. For Penelope, the first kiss was a wound, a repulsive obligation to a man to whom she was not attracted and did not love. It was a bizarre discovery for a sheltered and virginal young woman to make, that marriage itself could make prostitutes of women who would have consented to burn to death for the sake of morality.

Delta asked her for the details of her history with the other man, anxious to learn why her parents had forbidden the marriage. She said they had objected because of her emotional involvement with her suitor, and because he was poor. Delta told her frankly that he was poor, too, a shocking discovery for Penelope, since her parents had objected so strongly to Mavrocordatos on the ground that he had no money. Now it seemed that they were more than willing to accept her marriage to a poor man, as long as it was a poor man she didn't love. "The condition that they so feared several months before, today they accept because I don't love Mr. Delta," was the only conclusion she could draw.

Now that Stefanos and Penelope were committed, they were caught up in a strange charade, an engaged couple who had to impersonate an engaged couple. Now at their meetings, it would be almost impolite, ungenerous for Stefanos not to say he loved her, and she was obliged to reciprocate, to follow the dialogue written for her role as he recited his. As her future husband, he now had the right to read her diary, so she could not be sincere even in her private hours, until other matters preoccupied him and his interest in reading her journal waned. The engaged couple now sat next to each other at family meals, and went for lightly chaperoned walks along the quay at Phaleron, then a fashionable seaside resort near Athens, where there were theaters and opera, and respectable hotels, where the great Alexandrian Greek poet Cavafy stayed on his first visit to Greece. These meetings and walks were the foundation of the couple's personal knowledge of each other. On one stroll, Penelope wanted to know whether, if she offended Stefanos after they were married, he would be capable of beating her or killing her. "To kill you, yes, perhaps," he answered, "to beat you, never." This reply, she said, pleased her.

Penelope was determined to be impeccable in playing the devoted, affectionate fiancée as she was in any other matter of etiquette, resolved not to show any hint of hesitation, distaste, or ambivalence; she played the role of the bride-to-be charmed by her future husband so perfectly that her father again began to make jealous scenes, insisting that her absorption in Stefanos was coarse and rude, and their displays of affection for each other vulgar. It was a painful irony for Penelope to be attacked for efforts she was making partly to make her fiancé happy and partly to please her father, to demonstrate publicly that she embraced the future he had chosen for her. His displeasure with the couple's unseemly affection and her mother's fury with their selfish happiness continued even during Penelope's wedding day; as the bride dressed, she made a solemn vow to herself that if she ever had a daughter she would do all that was humanly possible to keep her from marrying as her mother was marrying.

The couple went to a hotel a bit outside of Alexandria for their honeymoon. Penelope faced her wedding night not only with the terror of an ignorant virgin, but with the despair of a young woman who knows that for all her life, she will never make love with a man she desires, or one she loves. When her husband left her alone to prepare herself, she undressed hurriedly, dove under the covers, and, hidden under the veils of the mosquito netting, put her face into her hands and began to pray.

Her married life was a lie, she recorded in her journal; her great success was in creating a kind of wax tableau of marriage, giving her husband the lifelike illusion of domestic content that was his preferred image and cherished hope. She worked to protect her parents too, from any public hint that she might be unhappy with the life they had chosen for her. Ironically, Penelope's public cheerfulness provoked her mother to say she was scandalized to see how quickly Penelope had fallen in love with her husband, while her father continued to lash out at her, saying public displays of affection between spouses disgusted him. When Penelope arrived in Athens, far from being mistress of her own household, she was subject to the mother-in-law, whose existence had been so unexpectedly revealed. They were to share the household for ten years, while she incessantly questioned the quality of Penelope's housekeeping, undermined her management of the house, and eventually, interfered with Penelope's rearing of her daughters. Delta, although Penelope described him as exceptionally kind, does not seem to have offered much in the way of companionship, coming home after work to read a newspaper, eat dinner, and fall asleep, determinedly oblivious to any household friction. For Penelope, it was a life of ashen joylessness, of struggling to accomplish meaningless work, of keeping her temper in the face of petty daily malice. Having children, although she had read about the great fulfillment of maternal love, the mother instinct, the miracle of maternal tenderness, was not the perfect consummation that the ideology of motherhood had led her to believe. Motherhood was work and caretaking—not

companionship, adult affection and conversation, intellectual and
moral dialogue, principled tenderness. For Penelope, who had
never experienced adult love, the always unequal love of parent and
child could never be adequate by itself. Only a profound adult companionship in work and in love could sustain her. She had never
been loved as a child, never experienced her own childhood, but
had been a symbol of her parents' parenthood, an architectural element of their dynasty, like the marble caryatids that sustain classical
buildings. As a parent, she was again a symbolic figure, this time for
her children, but inevitably not fully herself, not acknowledged and
thinking freely in a way that is possible in an adult companionship
but not between young children and parents. Motherhood was
rewarding in many ways, she reflected, but it could not alter her
emotional and intellectual starvation. She privately debated which
was more tortuous, to watch love die in a marriage of choice, or to
have one's capacity for love extinguished through a business marriage. She was painfully depressed, and dreamed of suicide, hating
herself for hating her life. True to her family's values, she felt a
ruthless contempt for herself. "My god," she wrote, "how repulsive
sick people are . . . myself among them . . . The world should be
cleansed of them . . . if all the sick people would have the courage
to plant a bullet in their heads, the world would get on much
better."

In 1905, almost miraculously, after the Deltas and their children
had moved to Alexandria so that Stefanos could take up a position in
the Benaki firm, Penelope met a man almost uncannily her match.
She had been told by the fortune-teller in Switzerland that her life
would hold little joy, but in retrospect, she annotated her record of
the prediction with a correction: she had known one great joy in her
life, she commented, referring to Ion Dragoumis. A diplomat,
ardent Hellenist, parliamentarian, the young Dragoumis, attached
to the Greek consulate at Alexandria, was to become one of the
most fascinating figures of modern Greece. His multivolumed journals, written from 1895 when he was a Cherubino living in Con-

stantinople through 1920 when, in his early forties, he was murdered, prove him to be one of the rare great diarists of the twentieth century. For his sensuous still-life descriptions of domestic
scenes and city vignettes, he might be compared to Virginia Woolf;
but as an urbane Greek, Constantinopolitan, and European, he
moves dizzyingly between worlds as the reclusive British writer did
not. The diaries also support his reputation as a fascinating personality and a desirable lover, even more than the photographs of his
finely planed, expressively ironic face, rich dark eyes, and elegant
body; they show him to have been a man with that most erotic of all
qualities, a capacity for sustained concentration, evident from his
earnest schoolboy annotated lists of favorite music and books, to a
detailed description of two little girls playing on the beach that he
watched one day during his final political exile on the island of
Skopelos.

Like Penelope, he loved the Parthenon, almost as if it were a
human presence, writing about how much he loved to sit on a rock
on its site, lose himself in thought, and look up to find it near him.
And like Penelope, he was an ardent cultural pioneer, in his efforts
to create a Greek nation. He was brother-in-law of a famous guerrilla leader in Macedonia, Pavlos Melas, who was killed the year
before Dragoumis met Penelope, and whose image is as famous in
Greece as Davy Crockett's is in the United States. Dragoumis's
influence on Penelope is palpable in her children's books, both in
their frequent preoccupation with Macedonia and in her choice to
write in demotic Greek. The year Dragoumis and Penelope met in
Alexandria, a controversial translation of the *Oresteia,* which they
must both have seen, was presented at a theater in Alexandria, with
Electra played by Marika Kotopouli, who was to become one of the
great figures of the modern Greek theater both as an artist and as a
master teacher. The struggle between the champions of demotic
Greek and Katharevousa was at one of its heights—the translation
of the Aeschylus plays performed in Alexandria was by a man named
Soteriades, and two years earlier its alleged vulgarization of the

Greek heritage had so enraged a professor at the University of
Athens that he led his students in a demonstration that turned violent, during which a spectator was killed. The Greek government in
response banned further performances of the translated plays,
agreeing with the professor and his party that demotic Greek was a
sacrilege against the Greek heritage, and that its use even violated
national interests. Still, there was a story reported in the newspapers that even this virulent champion of Katharevousa slipped into
demotic at the bedside of his sick daughter.

For Dragoumis and for Delta, and for their circle, the choice of
demotic was the choice of the Greek language as it had actually
developed, reflecting the history of the language and the people;
Katharevousa represented an idealized version of that history, like a
studio photograph instead of a candid shot, of Greek without Turkish, even without Latin, a dream of how fifth-century Greeks might
speak if they had also had the New Testament and were alive now—
the speech of statues wearing crosses. Katharevousa was itself a
fascinating creation. But for the demoticists, to commit to
Katharevousa would mean that the nation and its future literature
would be trapped forever in a dream of being Greek. Until she met
Dragoumis, Penelope had written her diaries in French, but after
her meeting with him she began to write wholly in Greek, becoming the only woman member of the circle of demoticists who
labored to bring modern Greek literature into being.

It is hard to chart the progress or much of the nature of Ion and
Penelope's affair. It seems the intensity of their feeling for each
other and their appetite for each other's companionship was open
enough for the Benakis to send the Delta family away from Alexandria to Frankfort, ostensibly to set up a new branch office there.
When Dragoumis eventually showed up in Frankfort, the Benakis
descended on Penelope in full force, with all the intimate psychological lacerations and threats with which they had managed her
before, and they succeeded in destroying any hope she had of making a life with Dragoumis. A curse runs through certain Greek fairy

tales: if the hero reveals certain secrets or exposes an evildoer, each time he makes the effort some part of his body will be turned to marble, his feet, then his knees, then his chest, until finally he becomes a statue. Penelope after the loss of Dragoumis, like one of those fairy-tale characters, seemed to be marble up to her neck. What was left her was speech, and she began to consider what she most wanted to write and publish. She wrote to the poet Palamas in 1909 about the nearly total absence of Greek children's books. Greek children read mostly books written for children in other countries, and there was little literature that reflected their own lives, their environment, the manners of the world they lived in. In a sense, then, even Greek children who could read were illiterate, without a literature that reflected their own experiences. Part of the enchantment of Penelope's work is exactly this invaluable glimpse of Greek manners and Greek domestic life—at their best her children's books have a miraculous freshness that reflects the delight and relief of speaking in your own tongue for the first time, the creativity of naming. Penelope was never at home in her parental family or in her marriage; her homecoming was to the house of Greek culture, helping to sustain and create it, and the best of her writing reflects the joyousness of that homecoming. She and her family eventually moved to Kifissia, then a leafy suburb of Athens filled with unpretentiously elegant villas, although it now looks like California, all shopping malls and "luxury" homes with elaborate security systems. The rest of Penelope's life was spent there, writing her books: historical novels for children, a life of Christ, *Trelantonis, Fairy Tale Without a Name,* and *Mangas,* a sort of *apologia pro vita sua* written by a dog. Her mother apparently never read any of Penelope's books, not even the life of Christ, which was dedicated to her.

Penelope's homecoming to Greekness, though, was also a homecoming to the doubled moral and social world that seems so much a part of being Greek. Her writings reflect her painfully divided feelings toward women and girls, and a gross idealization of boys and

men, almost jingoistic, which conflicts with their humane liberal-
ism, as does a strain of at times almost murderous nationalism. The
humaneness of Penelope's vision is movingly present in an episode of
Trelantonis, in which the children torment a little Jewish neighbor
with sanctimonious anti-Semitism, taunting her with the accusation
that Jews killed Christ, and showing her a cross to see if she will die,
since the devil in every Jew is supposed to burst at the sight of a
cross. After the incident their uncle calmly explains to them, in a
speech astonishing for its period—the book was first published in
1932—why Jews could not be held responsible for Christ's death
and should not be treated with theological fanaticism, but as people
who share Christian values; he wishes that all Christians might be
such good people as their Jewish neighbors, and defends the principle of religious freedom. In *Mangas,* on the other hand, the adventures of the dog narrator are interspersed with lessons in modern
Greek history. The children, who live in Alexandria, make a hero of
their Macedonian gardener, who delivers deadly sermons about the
Bulgarians, the chief opponents of the Greeks over Macedonia. The
gardener, a former guerrilla fighter with Dragoumis's brother-in-
law, Pavlos Melas, "straight like a cypress, eyes illuminated like the
sun, and the profile of an ancient Greek," declares that the Bulgarians are worse than the Turks, that they want Macedonia, which is
Greek, for themselves, as they wanted Eastern Rumelia, which is
Greek. "Macedonia is Greek," he declares. "We will take it for ourselves." When one of the boys tells him that his French governess
mocks his patriotism, the gardener replies, "Let her mock. They have
no business in our parts, the Europeans, nor do they know what our
dreams are," and tells them that the struggles of '21 are not finished,
that Greece remains a slave with Constantinople under Turkish jurisdiction. The gardener has a fight with a Bulgarian milkman in
revenge for Bulgarian terrorists having killed his family. The milkman is a symbol of Bulgarians; "All the Bulgarians are one," the gardener says, "wild beasts." The milkman is dismissed, although the
family's grandmother says he has served them well and never tried to

cheat them, but since he is Bulgarian, he must be expelled. Even the dog narrator comments, "Dogs hate cats, as the Greek hates the Bulgarian"; they are, he concludes, "ancestral enemies." In the end, the oldest boy of the family goes off to join the Macedonian struggle. By presenting the Bulgarians as hereditary enemies of the Greeks, Delta paints the whole people as a negative icon; she sacralizes political hatred in the way other people sacralize religious hatred. Deadly political dogma surprisingly crops up at moments in her books, offered to children along with her warmth and charm, and the delicious adventures of the protagonists.

Delta lived out her life writing her books, raising her children, and serving Greece on a grand scale, devoting her fortune to her country's service, even playing a role in creating Athens College, the famous Greek preparatory school. When the Germans invaded Greece in 1941, the suicide that had haunted Delta from childhood became possible. The German invasion was a violation of the one love left her, the love of her *patrida*, her fatherland. She took poison, succeeding in her calculation of a mortal dose. She was buried in her garden in Kifissia, requesting neither priest nor funeral. Her gravestone carries one word: Silence.

As for Dragoumis, after his affair with Penelope, he became the lifelong lover of the great actress Marika Kotopouli, who had starred as Electra in the presentation of the *Oresteia* during his year in Alexandria. He wrote and served in parliament as a member of the opposition to Venizelos. Sent into political exile under Venizelos's authority, he was murdered shortly after his return to Athens, in 1920, under the supervision of a former bodyguard of Venizelos's, the afternoon after an assassination attempt had been made on Venizelos in Paris. Penelope's father, Emmanuel Benaki, Venizelos's economic minister, told her he warned the leader of the band of renegade soldiers not to mishandle him, but the soldiers formed a firing squad and shot the great love of Penelope's life. Later on, the former bodyguard whose men had seized Dragoumis declared that the order for execution was given by Penelope's father. The

Benakis, including Penelope, were indignant over the accusation, which was never substantiated, although it does seem remarkable that a powerful Venizelist like Benaki apparently made no move to intervene or use his authority to order the party of soldiers, Venizelists all, to instantly set free a man whom they had no right to seize, much less execute.

Penelope died with her dreams unfulfilled. But Dragoumis, two years before his murder, had a dream that came true. He recorded that he had woken up drenched in sweat, having dreamed that some people in Kifissia surrounded him and tore at him from all sides, as if they meant to do him harm.

THE UNWRITTEN

Greece, with its some twenty-five hundred islands, is, like the human body, made up mostly of water, and like the body of someone you love, is finite, but inexhaustible. Now that my time here is getting short, I realize that the literal size of this country is deceptive, that I will leave here having never seen much that I dreamed of seeing. I cannot resist another brief but strenuous mountain trip to a region called Agrapha, partly because I am drawn by the meaning of its name, the unwritten, although it does not fit the intricate, if hidden, logic of my other routes. Agrapha borders Thessaly, and is famous guerrilla country, the site of savage medieval battles between the Byzantines and the Bulgarians, the boyhood training ground of one of the most famous strategists and soldiers of the War of Independence, Yiorgos Karaiskakis, the home of the national leader and soldier Nikolas Plastiras, whose role in the Asia Minor disaster saved many refugee lives after the war was lost, and a center for the Greek resistance during the Second World War. The region is called "the unwritten," according to most of the explanations I'm given, because the Turks never controlled the region, and so didn't include it in their tax books, as opposed to *grammena,* or "written," regions. It is, many say, still the least developed part of the country.

On the bus into the mountains, the radio station of the driver's choice repeatedly plays a soothing song for all the Greek students who are preparing to take their university entrance exams in June, an excruciating ordeal which, by all accounts I've heard, involves almost photographic memorization of the textbooks used to teach the subjects, and each year drives some children to suicide. The woman singing soothingly promises again and again in her refrain that everything will come out all right, a kind of national musical tranquilizer. I open my newspaper, which Paul says is the last I will see until I am back in Athens. A proverb forms one headline— "Beating comes from paradise." A teacher who beat a boy on the face with an unspecified blunt instrument was found innocent of wrong-doing by a court. The twelve-year-old boy had apparently refused to applaud a rival team when it won against his own, and the teacher had beaten the boy, with what I guess was a belt buckle, saying, "Such people are useless to society." The court found that the rights of teachers to correct children derive from society itself, and the special relation of submission to authority between student and teacher justified the teacher's actions.

Near the town of Karpenisi, where in 1823 one of the most dis-heartening moments of the Greek War for Independence occurred, when Markos Botsaris, one of the most respected of all the Greek revolutionaries, was killed in a skirmish with the Turks, the bus stops for a young woman with shining brown hair. She is about eighteen years old, carrying a baby and guiding a toddler; the ticket taker, who obviously knows her, approaches her in a familial way, and when she smiles at him, she shows a great-grandmother's mouth, with her front teeth missing. Paul tells me that this is common in these moun-tains, where people outside Karpenisi are cared for by a doctor who circulates in a Land Rover.

Local relationships are played out in miniature on the bus—the ticket taker is a hale, sociable man, who greets the boarding passengers, calling out bits of gossip and joking, teasing a woman who shouts to him when she wants the bus to stop, "It's not my job to let you off at your front gate." The bus lets us off some miles away from the village where our party will spend the night, at its last stop, a place that has an alpine feel, with its green meadows and dairy cows; we immediately acquire a small troop of children, who walk us to the local general store, where we wait to sort out our sleeping arrangements. Their warmth and curiosity make me think about what Greece must have been like before tourism reached its full intensity here, and make me wonder what its mixed blessings will bring to this region. Still, in a world that offers few unmixed blessings, it seems to me a civilized and hopeful way to make a living. As we walk through the village, a place that is all dust and watchful eyes, the bravest of the children asks me if I like Greece. I say yes, and ask her if she does. She hesitates and then says yes, with a hint that she might like to live in a larger town. Athens and Thessaloniki seem very far away here. Her parents' general store offers shelves of detergent, rice, and batteries; it is like a frontier store, except for the large color TV in one corner, tuned to a bodybuilding contest with bathing-suited men flexing their dramatic biceps and turning their finely muscled rears to the camera. Paul tells me that newspapers simply don't reach this countryside, so the approach to the outer world is virtually all through images. But when computers come here in full force, with their more literate technology, that may change. The twelve-year-old takes our orders for coffee with fierce concentration, skillfully matching us to our combinations of sugars and milks, showing her village proudly competent to meet the needs of *xenoi*. The littler children, in their shorts and plastic sandals, sit on benches near the door, whispering and giggling at us, entertained as if we were live toys. I ask the older girl if the village we are going to is pleasant, and she wrinkles her nose, saying, "It's smaller than this."

We set out for it in a truck, hanging on to slats on the side, a sight I associate with convoys of Greek soldiers, here where military service is obligatory and even boys of Greek descent who are citizens of other countries are encouraged to do service in the Greek army. When we thank the teenaged driver, I see that someone has lettered a plastic label for him to put over his glove compartment. It reads, "The hour always good and the holy Virgin always with Leonidas, the good and unforgettable guy." The village is a velvety refuge hidden in the rough mountains, looking uncannily Swiss, and we half expect to be greeted with a supply of chocolate and cheese, instead of fresh-killed chicken, the ubiquitous french fries, and beer. There is one shower in one of the houses in town, with only cold water, and we are distributed among the village houses; exactly as in a medieval inn, the sleeping arrangements put strangers of the same sex into a shared bed. The villagers are puzzled when some of the visitors hesitate, but I am well past the initial shock this medieval pattern of housekeeping used to provide—on overnight ferries, too, it is common for people to sleep in cabins with strangers. The village is gathered at the one taverna in town, drinking beer outdoors in the summer twilight, and the appealing, dignified proprietress chats to us every now and then between kitchen and customer. Her eight- and ten-year-old daughters board during the week with a family in the largest nearby town, so they can attend school, coming back on weekends. She says it is a hardship for all of them, but that she is determined for her girls to have the means to live independent lives—and to leave here if they want. She is a prodigy among the Greek mothers I have met, who often seem to be competing with each other in possessiveness, as if permanently dependent children were a glory of motherhood—in a world where women's personhood was determined only by the politics of motherhood, it is evident that surrendering children to adulthood meant a tremendous loss of social status, as well as being an emotional turning point. This village woman has more than one kind of courage.

Late that night, I wake up to the sound of someone shouting a catalogue of drunken curses. "He fucks the village," he says, "he fucks their mothers," and most loudly of all, "he fucks the Virgin Mary."

The mountains utterly change character from region to region of Greece. In Epirus, the region bordering on Albania, Lord Byron's haunt, where I spent a few days after Easter, the countryside is crystalline, the trees full of language in the form of murmuring bees, rock formations that look like the patterned seals stamped into the dough of the traditional Greek church bread, *prosfora.* There even the wooden interiors of the houses, designed and carved by the great itinerant craftsman of the region, who traveled the Balkans building houses for clients from Vienna to Constantinople, comment on the outer world, with their lacy carving, built-in beds, niches, and wooden grottoes, looking like versions of the pools and grottoes cut into these mountains by the clear rivers that run through them. The landscape there is startlingly erotic, and made sense for me of some modern popular paintings I had seen on wood of nymphs metamorphosing out of the mountain rivers, the waters streaming behind their heads like transparent veils. I watched a blue and white river coursing through a curved channel that seemed to have taken on the shape of a woman's body, the water spurting like a man's seed over the woman lying underneath. Here, in a neighboring region, in mountains that are part of the same chain, we are in another country. These mountains seem the creation of stress, with their battered rocky folds, and camouflaged villages, flocks of sheep crammed together on plateaus, guarded by sheep dogs who hate everyone but their owners.

After a day's hard walking, we approach the even tinier village where we will spend tonight. On an arched bridge with an old stone foundation, now covered coarsely with a thick slab of concrete like a piece of processed cheese on good bread, we are met by a grinning boy named Christos, who leads us into a village that consists mostly of the houses of his family, plus a sprinkling of others, a community office, and their family general store, the buildings arranged together on the buildable land like shelves in a cramped

closet. It is as if you opened a battered old cupboard and found
it inhabited by a tiny town. Christos's mother, Pareskevi, killed a
goat in the morning to make a special meal for us. We sit on what
approximates the traditional village *plateia* here, the concrete terrace of the general store, facing its green-painted door, a sign of
the family's affiliation with Andreas Papandreou's political party,
PASOK. Pareskevi tells us that because of the family's PASOK connections, they were forbidden to serve drinks and meals on this terrace by a district authority who was loyal to the opposition New
Democracy Party, and that they had had to serve their beers, coffees, and *mezedes* from a house until they negotiated permission to
reopen. Christos brings out a tray of beers, and heads off to feed the
things, *ta pragmata,* as domestic animals are called here. He carries
a bottle of milk for some motherless lambs. A neighbor, wearing a
long impressive beard and old army fatigues, arrives at the terrace
to drink his evening beer, and Pareskevi brings out for all of us new
feta cheese, as different from salty preserved feta as spring is from
winter. The village has a contingent of relatives who live in the
United States, in New Jersey, and at the insistence of the American
relatives who return each summer, the village acquired its one flush
toilet, and put in electricity a few years ago. Until 1991, the houses
were lit with kerosene lamps. There is still no washing machine, and
at Pareskevi's house no hot running water, and only an earth-
floored outhouse. She does have a television, though, where she and
her black-veiled mother can watch Greek detective shows and *I
Dream of Jeannie,* in one of the rooms of the house that are stacked
together like cardboard boxes, wherever there is a piece of earth
flat enough to support them. In the living room, there is an engagement photograph of her, taken on a special trip to Karpenisi,
with an elaborate upswept hairdo, kohl-rimmed eyes, and the Persian look many Greek faces have, with a distinctive lustrously dark
coloring.

It is still light when we finish dinner, ending with fresh sheep's
yogurt, like a plate of sour cream. We sit on the edge of the terrace

to watch the sunset. An old woman is coming down the neighboring hill from a house at the top. She is wearing an ankle-length black dress, a black kerchief over her thick white hair, carrying a woven shepherd's bag and two full sacks of *horta,* wild greens she has picked in the mountains to feed her rabbits. "My mother," Pareskevi says, and tells us that she climbs the impressively sharp peak we are looking at every day to look after the sheep. Her house is on the highest of the village hills, like a fortress, with the first view of visitors entering the village. She carried much of the building material up the hill herself, in sacks on her back, and it is her house that has the flush toilet. Pareskevi says she had all nine of her children by herself, in her old house, alone on the mountain, without a doctor. Pareskevi goes to meet her. From up close, she looks to be in her late seventies, and she greets us with hard eyes that never warm or trust. The greeting and wish and hospitality she offers is abstract, not personal; the convention is warm, the woman is not. She offers sweets to us in as prescribed a way as medicine. She is supposed to offer them and we are supposed to eat them, and none of us can continue until we have enacted the ritual, for her a domestic eucharist to be shared even and perhaps especially if she does not like us. She has the coldness of someone whose authority has been achieved because she has endured so much that some essential piece of caring has left her; you feel that she would be capable of murder, that somehow she has become a force, a fate, not a person, dissolved into clan and land, and that some detachment from this center would have to be possible for her to conceive of a world where people beyond her family had an equal claim on her sense of justice. She makes me wonder if the notion of loving your neighbor as yourself isn't flawed; turn over a sense of community conceived as an extension of yourself, and what is on the other side might be the blood feud, warfare against a group of people conceived only as extensions of your enemy. Maybe loving your neighbor not as yourself, but as profoundly other, might make a stronger commitment.

The old woman asks to see the American who is visiting, because she wants me to see an album of wedding pictures from a visit to

New Jersey. Even Christos went, and told me with an expression of rapturous remembrance that he had loved most of all the tunnel the cars took under the water from New Jersey to New York. I am taken through the album, from white limousine to banquet hall in a New Jersey wedding palace, all burlesque chandeliers and engraved matchbooks and weirdly sculpted pink napkins rising out of glasses. It was the wedding of twenty-three-year-old Elias, who had arrived last year for his summer visit and was told by *yiayia* that there would be no return ticket for him unless he married a local girl before he went back. Within two weeks, he was engaged to a girl from a neighboring village. "We didn't want him to marry an American girl," she said. "They leave men they don't like."

THE DREAM OF NARCISSUS

On my way to Ouranopolis, Heaven City, the last outpost on the Athos peninsula where women are permitted, I stop in Thessaloniki, the city I love best in Greece, for its civic sensuality, its hill neighborhoods, its views of the Thermaic Gulf, its hospitality to pedestrians, its small sweet parks where white-haired men and women sit on benches on summer nights singing old love songs, the rare old *rembetika* records you can hear being played in flea markets, its unabashed eccentrics and fine Ottoman cooking. I have a letter of introduction to a publisher based here, and on my way to meet him at his office, I stop in the church of Agios Dimitri, the patron saint of Thessaloniki, with its marvelous wavy patterns of bricks and some sort of healing moisture the saint causes to exude. On my way out, the clerk in charge of books and postcards hands me an English language booklet by the bishop of Konitsa, a town on the border of Albania, about northern Epirus, also known as southern Albania. I riffle through it on the way to my meeting—"History shows . . . ," it says, "that the Albanians never cared about their own freedom . . . Although they never admit it, they preferred to be slaves . . . The Albanians have no excuse to get nervous and angry whenever they hear the just demand of the northern Epirotes and of their Greek brothers for the union of northern Epirus with Greece. We are not asking anything more than what the Albanians are asking regarding the Kosovo area in Yugoslavia . . ."

The publisher turns out to be a small wiry man from Kefallonia, with a book-crammed office. I walk around the shelves to get an idea of what he has published, when suddenly there is a helping hand on my hair, then one on my shoulder, then one on my breast. I dodge away, having been trained in Anglo-Saxon–style martial arts, of which the basic underlying principle is to deny that anything has happened. So I crowd the room with remarks, telling him I am fascinated by children's literature, and trying to interest him in how little most of us really know about Scandinavian literature. I keep leaping out of his reach into intellectual frontiers, past a huge pictorial history of Salonika, and a solemn-looking Koran in Greek, as he bears down on me, his face sour with determination, only slightly unbalanced by clutching a camera, and shouting, to the consternation of a few people on a sofa in the waiting room, "Kiss me, kiss me on the mouth!" *Molon lave,* I think drily, "Come and get it," reverting to the legendary phrase of Leonidas to the Persians before the battle at Thermopylae, so beloved of all my Greek teachers. I am thinking, of course, of the practical problems the conference tables and desks and bookshelves present me in not getting kissed, but I am also thinking how this confirms an intuition about how kissing and not kissing are not only physical but metaphysical problems. This confrontation concerns something perhaps even more fundamental than the liturgy of sexual flight and pursuit. We are enacting an ancient argument, I realize, about the nature of reality, as the Kefallonian stumbles around his own obstacles of tables heaped with books, clutching his camera, his automatic flash making miniature explosions as he attempts to capture me in poses that could look convincingly welcoming. He is arguing that I am an image, as he chases me from corner to corner, and that his camera can prove it. I unfortunately, frustratedly, am sure that I am real—the proof that I am not an image is that I cannot disappear from this situation, however much I want to. In this crisis, my life does not pass before my eyes—his does. Because it is clear too that I am not even, in these circumstances, a feminine image. For this wiry old Kefallonian, I am an image of himself—he looks into the pool of me and sees his own face, thirty or forty years ago, sees his own trim torso, his own incontestable vigor—if he could touch me, he would have that lost young body of his back. By the magic which turns an image into a seer, I see that he is trying to turn me, at any price, into a young island boy—himself, once upon a time. But too many people are now sitting beyond the smoked glass doors of the reception room for him to continue his pursuit without public embarrassment, and I run down the stairs into the sunlit street, having witnessed again that historically cultivated Greek passion for the icon, one key to understanding not only Greek daily life, but Greek politics.

The bus's route to Heaven City runs through the cinnamon-colored Macedonian countryside, thick with sunflowers. I would have liked very much to be in this countryside for Anastenaria fire-walking, held every May, when women and men who have been possessed by the spirit of the emperor Constantine, who appears to them in dreams, often dressed as a policeman, army officer, or doctor, dance and walk across hot coals.

Domed beehives along the road look very much like the doll-house-sized Orthodox shrines scattered on small lanes and busy highways here, often commemorating traffic accidents—these look like small churches full of God's honey, and remind me of the story every Greek schoolchild knows about the bee and Agia Sofia. No architect brought the emperor Justinian a plan for the Church of Holy Wisdom that he liked. One day after mass, the patriarch handed the emperor the *antidoro,* a piece of blessed but not consecrated bread given after services in the Orthodox Church, which fell from the emperor's hand. He bent down to pick it up, but could not find it. Suddenly he saw a bee with the *antidoro* in its mouth fly out the window. He issued an order that whoever had a beehive was

to lure into it the bee with the holy bread. It happened that an architect had a beehive, and it was there the bee took refuge. But when
the architect looked inside, he saw not a hive, but a great domed
church, with a holy altar inside on which lay the *antidoro,* completely modeled by the bee through the grace of the *antidoro* it had
held in its mouth. It was the plan of the church of the beehive that
was submitted to Justinian and became the great church of Byzantium, Agia Sofia.

A number of the villages on the way to Heaven City have religious names, like Saint John the Baptist and Great Panagia. Heaven
City itself is a small town with a medieval tower, beautiful beaches,
and a large transient population of monks—we pass a pickup truck
full of produce driven by a pony-tailed, black-hatted monk. Other
monks board the men-only ferry for Athos itself, where no women
or female animals are allowed, with the exception of some female
cats that make kittens to control the children of the ungovernable
female mice. Athos is supposed to be the garden of the Virgin Mary,
who doesn't want to share her property with other women. The
story goes that the Virgin Mary made a sailing trip to Cyprus, accompanied by Saint John. She had been eager to see Lazarus, who
after his resurrection lived on the island. But a storm broke and the
tempest carried her to Athos. One monastery commemorates the
exact spot where her ship touched the shore, where there was at
the time a temple of Apollo. At the moment her ship anchored, the
statue of Apollo that stood in the temple called out ordering all men
down to the harbor to do homage to the mother of the great god
Christ. This kind of prohibition of women surely has pagan roots—
the Hellenistic poet Callimachus, in his hymn to Zeus, writes of a
temple on the spot where the goddess Rhea gave birth to Zeus,
where "no fourfooted creature that needs the help of the patron
goddess of childbirth," or any woman, approaches the holy place, a
hill called Rhea's childbearing bed. I would have liked to have been
able to see some of the monasteries, the one of which the Virgin
Mary is the abbot, her icon hanging on the back of the abbot's

throne, and the fresco showing the ship of the church battling the attacks of Muhammad, and the pope, who tries to use his pontifical cross as a grappling hook to draw the ship to him, and the final panel, in which Christ commands Saint Paul to cast anchor, and Orthodox priests draw the ship to shore. I have never seen it reproduced, and wonder if it is only a fable. I would have liked to have seen the icon of "the terrifying Protectress" that turned back an invasion of Turkish soldiers. But all that I can see on the little excursion boat that makes a semicircle around the holy mountain are occasional trucks, and paranoid-looking fortresslike monasteries. It reminds me of the gated and barbed-wire communities of South Africa.

I go to a tiny island later for a swim, what an island would be if it were a cottage. There I swim in a cove so calm you can swim laps, the waters clear as thought should be. An excited cry goes up from some children snorkeling farther out, "Octopus, octopus!" On the beach, there is a family group of a young couple and new baby, returning Greek-Americans from their accents, and some older Greek relatives, surely parents, and possibly some aunts and uncles. The baby is being given serial nurturing by all the female relatives, who fight gently over the changing of the diaper. But when it comes off, two of the women cry out in shock. The baby, apparently, is circumcised. The woman in a bathing suit relentlessly printed with purple flowers wrings her hands, and cannot stop herself from repeating, "Why did you ruin him? How could you ruin him?"

THE SLEEPING VIRGIN

Now that it is high summer, Athens has moved out of doors. Tavernas are full at two in the morning with family parties, including young children, eating in gardens and savoring the cool night breezes. Some of the smaller streets are looped from house to house with grapevines that shield the street from the summer sun, and the *laiki agora,* the farmers' markets on the streets, are filled with the magnificent Greek white peaches and melons, while competing vendors praise the perfumes and colors of their fruit with the chant "*Aromata kai khromata.*" Athens is above all a city of the personal, personal passions and tastes, loyalties and hatreds, and even straightforward information here has an atmosphere of personal declaration. An elegant dress shop in Kolonaki, whose windows I have often passed covetously, announces its summer closing with an exuberant handwritten message in the window— "We are not going for a coffee! We are not going to the square across the street! We are going to the sea! Goodbye for the month!" And I myself am saying goodbye to Stamatis, who is going to France for his summer holiday; I am leaving for the island of Mitilini tomorrow to spend the summer holidays honoring the

Panagia with Kostas, and when Stamatis returns from France, I will
have returned to the States.

We meet in Fokionos Negri, an endearing neighborhood with a
traffic-free area full of greenery and restaurants of unpretentious
charm. "What a zigzag route you are following," he says, "but it is
right for Greece, where my favorite of our proverbs is the question,
'Are we sailing straight, or is the shore crooked?' And now you have
sailed around the crooked shores of Athos, the most Islamic place in
Europe, where the Virgin Mary keeps her harem. And there, in my
theory, is where, in all probability, the murderer of Taktsis went to
ground." "Why on earth would you think that?" I ask. "Because the
civil courts have no jurisdiction there, for one thing. And for
another, the place has a reputation as a refuge for criminals—there
is a church canon which states that any male Christian, that is to say
Orthodox Christian, may choose to enter a monastery no matter
what crime he may have committed outside it, and that he may not
be obstructed in this choice. So that's my theory."

I tell him I will be spending the most important of the summer
holidays, which westerners call the Assumption of the Virgin, in
Mitilini. "Mitilini is a lovely island," he says approvingly, "and you
must try to see Chios too, while you are in the neighborhood. But
the key to the feast is in the icons which invariably show Mary dead
on her bier, and Christ behind her, with her soul in his arms in the
form of an infant. Because this holiday is about the death of woman
as goddess, and the appropriation of her divinity by Christ, who
becomes a greater mother than his mother, the male mother who
gives immortal life, the great gift men waited in vain for women to
give, holding his own infant mother in his arms. You can find this
appropriation of womanhood in the sacraments—in holy communion, for instance, when Christ's flesh and blood become food, previously the magic of the female mother. But her milk nourishes
children who will die, and his blood, replacing her milk, gives
immortal life to those who drink it. And baptism, in which the child
is reborn, with even the new amniotic fluid of holy water, through

a man. Christ, the divine transvestite, is the mother who makes the child live forever. This is why the Orthodox Church—and the Roman—are so vehemently opposed to women priests. It destroys the magic substitution they made to obtain immortal life, what you may call their *idées crucifixes.* If a creature who can become pregnant touches the flesh of Christ, she will render his body mortal, the old failure of her pagan divinity may corrupt his, and return him to manhood from deity, as she was returned to womanhood from deity."

I start to ask him how he will spend his time in France, but he breaks in. "I remember now you asked me how I read the image of the Jew Iefonia you saw in the Kimesis fresco at Mystras. I say it is not garden-variety anti-Semitism, which is basically a response to Jewish anti-Gentilism. After all, if a child comes to school and announces it is the chosen child and declares all the other children's lunches dirty food, it is likely to be bloodied by the end of the day. So I don't think Iefonia is this. I think his punishment at the hands of the angel for touching Mary is an expression of our resentment of the imposition of monotheism. Because the establishment of Christianity here can best be compared with the establishment of communism in Russia. Imagine the legislation against the pagan universities where the philosophers taught, imagine the jobs that were now given only to Christians, or people with solid Christian connections, not polytheists, just like the jobs that were given only to party members, imagine the arrival of soldiers to take the treasures from the polytheist temples, imagine the soldiers Constantine posted outside the caves all over the countryside to prevent polytheists from worshipping inside them. We needed Iefonia, and the accusation that he and his kind had killed a god, in order to distract ourselves from the truth that there is no more detailed record in religious history of the attempted murder of gods than our own. We tried to kill not one, but twelve. Not, I think, with great success." He looks at his watch, and calls for the bill, which I have only ever succeeded in paying here through the wildest subterfuge. "And I

wish you a good journey," he says, "but I warn you of what the novelist Vassilikos says about Greece—that it is the place where when
you are here you long to leave, and the minute you leave, you yearn
uncontrollably to come back. I know. When I am in Greece, I think
about my month in France. And in France, the whole month, of
Greece."

As with Easter, it had been difficult to decide where to spend the
holiday of the Kimesis, the Sleeping of the Virgin. I had been very
tempted by the island of Kefallonia, where in one village dozens of
snakes, called the "snakes of the Virgin," slither toward the church
dedicated to the Kimesis, climbing onto the faithful, the holy bread,
and the icons. When they don't appear, as in the two years of severe
earthquakes, it is considered a bad portent. And I would have liked
to have seen the ceremonies in some regions where the Virgin is
given an Easter, with funeral ceremonies and processions like
Christ's at Easter time, marking one season in Greece with man's
resurrection, and another with a woman's. But I had wanted to see
the paintings in the Theophilos Museum of one of the patron saints
of modern Greek painting, and Mitilini was a particularly favorite
island of Kostas's.

I buy some magazines for the ferry, which at this time of year feature special travel sections suggesting excursions to places where
there are miraculous icons of the Theotokos, one of which is on
Mitilini, along with letters from people who were saved by the Virgin's intervention. One woman living in Canada sends a photograph
of her son, resurrected by the Virgin when he was three years old
and three days dead. In the lounge someone is playing a radio, where
a suavely weary announcer celebrates the Virgin, in terms that
remind me of a charming hymn to Artemis by the Hellenistic
Alexandrian poet Callimachus, in which Artemis, sitting on her
father Zeus's knees, and clearly his pet, asks him to make her a goddess of many names. The announcer says, "She has been the fellow
warrior and benefactress of our race, the holy guide and the sweetly
kissing one during our struggles and suffering, the tender mother
and the fierce defender of whoever needs her. We call her the Guide,

the Sweetly Kissing One, the Life Giver, the Portrait, the Athenian Woman, the Woman of the Sea, the Panegyriotissa, the Virgin of the Festivals, the Peponiotissa, the Virgin of the Melons, when her church is near melon patches, the Virgin of the Cold Waters, when her church is near a spring. But whatever name we call her, she is the mother of Greece and of the Greek people." The announcer pauses to take an audible drag of his cigarette. Always when I am reminded of the great gift of the Greek language for epithet, I think that the language is something like an iconostasis, picture related to picture, stories concealed in the twining imagery. "She is the invincible commander, the highest general in battles, the doctor for the sick, the protectress of all who are suffering unjustly, the food and drink of those who hunger and thirst, the co-ruler of Heaven and first of all the Saints . . ." August is particularly the Virgin's month, the August 15, 23, and 31 holidays known collectively as the Virgin's. The official name of August, like July's, respectively Augustus and Julius here, reminds me powerfully of the new ordering of time that came with the Roman emperors these months were renamed for, but in the popular view, the days of August are given to the Virgin Mary like bars of gold. In old print shops, you can see prints of fruit or sheaves of wheat, with the traditional verse "August, my lovely month, come twice a year." This is the month that gives the greatest feeling of security, overflowing abundance, of ease and earned pleasure, when the farmers have stored in their cellars grains and corn, hay and feed for their animals, wood for their fires. August is the month of the richest eating, with its seemingly endless fruits and vegetables, "so many you need shawls to gather them," one verse says. In Greece it is a month in which you might imagine life would never end. But it is also a duplicitous month, a month also commemorated in foreboding verses about getting winter clothes ready, about the short days beginning, the summer *meltemia* gales prefiguring the sharp winter winds.

The walls of the ferry lounge are decorated with posters of the Greek museums, a glowing Theophilos magical realist view of Mitilini town, and a poster for a wax museum in the northern town of Ioannina, where I have been on a trip with Leda. The memory of the animated wax death of Socrates still sends us into paroxysms of giggles: at intervals the wax Socrates would point to the cup of hemlock, and with the same regularity, the friend holding the cup would roll his mechanical eyes. We strike up a conversation with a young soldier who is on the way home for the holiday. He sees that Kostas is reading a book about Chinese art, and he produces some of his own work, drawings of men dancing the *zembekiko* with rapt self-absorption, and some studies of a soldier sitting on an iron cot, masturbating. His face glows when he talks of Matisse, and darkens when he talks about what has gone wrong in the world. "The fault is with humanism," he says, "the humanism of the Renaissance, which places man at the center of the Universe where God should be, man in all his arrogance, egoism, and materialism. This is why we are in a world where we destroy the environment and value money above life, this idea of the greatness of humanity." It is hard to imagine a more arrogant and uncomprehending dismissal of humanism, whatever its flaws, I think as we drink coffee with the round-cheeked soldier.

We dock a little after dawn in Mitilini town with its delightful neoclassical houses, ornate tiles covering their doorsteps, probably from the period of the Balkan Wars, when tiles like these were made in Piraeus. The day is still waiting for the full seal of sunrise, a sunrise that comes like the fulfillment of a great promise, like Prince Hal becoming King Henry the Fifth. We pass one tiled entrance which reads *Khairete,* the old but still used greeting, which literally means "rejoice," written in an oceanic script of waves and swags and flourishes, and bordered by pleasant cherubs, who anchor themselves by holding on to the ends of the word. In a niche carved over one formerly impressive door is a bunch of carved and painted wooden grapes. On another door hangs a bunch of garlic, stabbed through with a fork, to pierce the evil eye. It gives me a new question about the nature of the evil eye, reminding me of Polyphemus the Cyclops in the *Odyssey,* who was stabbed through the eye by Odysseus. I have always wondered whether the *Odyssey* wasn't full of hidden sexual jokes, remembering a Greek epigram which refers to female genitals as the eye of the Cyclops, and this particular *gouri* against the evil eye, of a kind I haven't seen before, makes me wonder if there isn't also some sexual undercurrent in the metaphysic of the evil eye.

We have a coffee, and find a taxi driver to take us to the other end of the island to the fishing village where we will stay, with a stop at Panagia Petra, painted by Theophilos, with its church, like our Lady of Vertigo, madly placed on a jagged cliff, as dictated by the Virgin Mary in a dream. A long time ago, the story goes, a sea captain of Mitilini had an icon of the Virgin. He didn't realize that his icon was miraculous. The village of Petra that you see today was covered with the sea, and only a jagged piece of the cliff on which the church is built today was visible. One night the sea captain dreamed of the Virgin, who told him she wanted to live on this very cliff. The captain took his boat out, and sailed along the coast, trying to find the cliff she had meant. Suddenly the boat stopped moving, although there was a good breeze. The captain called out, "Come help us travel, Panagia!" And when he looked to his left, he saw a radiant light glowing on the cliff, and in the center of the light, his own icon, miraculously suspended in the air. The captain sailed closer, wanting to recover his icon, and as he approached, the sea itself lowered and the cliff got higher, as if the earth were sculpted into a new shape. Still, the captain was determined to have his family icon back, and he clambered onto the cliff and managed to secure it. The next day when he was fishing, the boat again stopped dead in the waters, and the icon disappeared again. Again, he sailed toward the cliff, and saw it on the peak. This time, after he brought the picture down, he nailed it to his mast. That night he dreamed of the Virgin again. She said, "Nail me to your mast if you want, but I will always run away, back to the rock where I want to build my house." And in the morning, when he went down to his boat, the icon had disappeared from the mast.

Meanwhile, the Virgin had appeared to another person, a young village girl, and told her to go the mayor and tell him to build a church on the rocky cliff of Petra where every day the waters receded even more. The girl went bravely to the mayor, but he paid no attention. Again the Virgin appeared to her, and again, she tried her luck with the mayor. He didn't lift a finger to help. Then the Virgin beat the girl, and warned the mayor in a dream that she would harm him too, if he didn't build her church. His baby sleeping in its cradle was seized with racking spasms. When he saw this, the mayor begged the Virgin for mercy and promised that she would have her church. The baby immediately recovered. When the craftsmen went to look over the site to plan the church, they had no idea how to handle the problem of making a stairway up the rock to make the church accessible. Suddenly the icon of the Virgin began to move around the cliff top as if it had invisible legs, and it made an architectural design using twigs that it collected. So the craftsmen built according to its plan. Finally the church was done, and the day of the first liturgy arrived. The priest sprinkled all the corners of the church outside and in with holy water, and after the service, a young apprentice to the church builder ascended the stairway up the cliff, carrying a tray of *raki* and glasses for the craftsmen to celebrate their good work. But the boy slipped off the steep stone steps, and fell screaming. *Panagia mou,* everyone shouted at once, and ran to the edge of the cliff to look. As they got to the edge, they saw the boy rising through the air with the tray of *raki,* and the white towel draped neatly over his right arm, just fluttering a little in the breeze. When his feet touched the solid cliff, he walked toward the craftsmen, holding out his tray. None of the *raki* had spilled from the glasses.

As we drive, Pericles's radio plays a song of unrequited love, the Greek no, *okhi,* with its round absolute *o* sound making a world in which what has been proposed will never come to pass, the *okhi* punctuated by the *aaaakh vaaakh* sounds that transcribe Greek sighs, very different from the quality of our gentle resigned sighs, that leave us like the perfume of dying flowers. Greek *aaaakhs* bleed and flood and empty the body, and I am reminded that Greek sounds of laughter, refusal, and desire are very different from ours. A song of the great Greek singer of the sixties who calls herself Katie Grey comes on. Her style is something between a torch singer and a Patsy Cline, with a voice of passionate flexibility, and her life, by all accounts, has been a drama to match. She is singing one of her classics, "Whoever is brought up in strangers' hands knows what pain is . . . strangers' hands are like knives." We turn onto a narrow dirt road to reach our fishing village, the distance between us and the coast of Turkey narrowing to what looks like swimming distance. The radio of its own accord now emits songs that sound like the *mikrasiatika,* Asia Minor Greek songs I know, but these songs are in Turkish. "From here," says Pericles, "the reception is better for the Turkish station than for the Greek one." We nearly collide with a speeding car, and then with a truck full of farm produce speeding on the pebbly road, and Pericles says, "You know why our accident rate is so high?" Greece is one of the European leaders in automobile accidents, and the newspapers and magazines steadily report the accident statistics. "Because of drinking and driving. Family problems, business problems, they drink and drive. Just here a friend of mine, a farmer, drove a tractor off the road last winter and lay under it until dawn, bleeding to death." We pass his friend's farm, and Pericles points out the memorial, and further on, the tractor that killed him, isolated like an animal so savage it needs a pen to itself. "God pardon him," Kostas says to Pericles, in a traditional phrase of blessing for the dead. "God pardon him," Pericles echoes.

"As for me," he says, as if wanting his stories not to end with death, "I got married this summer." We congratulate him, and he says, "But don't tell anyone, it's a secret. You see, my wife is fifty, and I am forty, and my boss doesn't like me to go out with her. So I tell him that she is just my girlfriend, that I sleep with her maybe once or twice a month, to do her a favor," he says, miming a look of sexual condescension. "You see, he knows," he says, pointing to Kostas, "but you don't, that here it is all *zilia,* jealousy, and *koutsombolia,* gossip, maybe I don't get the good jobs and the big fares if they don't like how I live. In America, it's very free, isn't it, the life there, you can do just what you like. I watch *The Bold and the Beautiful* every day in winter when we live in Athens, and I see how free it is." Again, I marvel at the utter faith in the image I have met so often here. "But you know, I love this nice woman so much that it surprised me, I wanted to marry her. When I met her in Athens, she was so shy she couldn't say a word. I asked my friends, 'Why does this nice woman have nothing to say?' And they told me her story, how she came from a famous military family, and her house was like a soldiers' camp. They didn't let her wear short skirts, they would slap her if her blouse wasn't fastened all the way up to her neck. They arranged for her to work in the Middle East, and for all her youth her life was being picked up to go to work, and picked up by car to go back to her apartment. She typed during the day and watched television alone at night. Her brother became a general, with medals on his chest, and he would taunt her when she came home for Easter, telling her, 'You cannot marry until I marry, the younger doesn't marry before the elder, and I will never marry.' He is sixty-one, and he never married. Can you imagine such a story? But when I met her I liked her so much, and her style is good, she doesn't look fifty, she keeps a good figure. And in our house, you don't mind my telling you this, she often wears only a slip all day, or walks around naked, from having been kept in her clothes like a prison all her life. At first, she didn't believe I could want her, and then she said, But you must have children, and I am too old now for children. And I said, Don't worry, I have a boy, I had him with a Swedish girl, they come once a year to see me. So I don't need children. And an older woman is what I want, you know they know how to do things in the house that the younger women don't any more. At five, she gets up, brings me my coffee, makes my bed, always the clean house, the clean clothes, and she knows how to do this beautifully. Every day she cooks a special meal. Today she is making me *imam baildi* with four cheeses. Then at night, we drink Bacardi and Coke, we dance, we start the love machine, sometimes we stay up all night, like she is making up for so many years. And she is always so warm with me, I come home, and cuddle next to her, and she says, How is my sweet boy, it's like having a mother. And she told me, I understand if sometimes you want a younger woman, you can sleep with your Swedish girl when she comes, can you imagine a wife so unselfish as she is? Our only trouble is her family, we have tried to make peace with them, but they hate this good woman, they call her names you wouldn't believe, her brother calls and screams how she is a whore, who wants nothing more than to eat penis, that she is a whore who takes a young boy for her lust, and now marries without permission. Once we had her mother to visit, and I swear, this woman spent the night looking through the keyhole to our room. My wife makes a little noise during *erotas,* and the mother says in the morning, 'All night I hear you, whore, like a bitch in heat.' And then we had friends to dinner, and the mother says in front of them, 'I suppose tonight you all four fuck each other.' So I told my wife, 'It is over with your family, I am your family now.' I hope you don't mind my telling you about all this, but I am so happy with her, and I need to tell someone about my secret, and it looked to me like you would understand."

Pericles crosses himself as we pass a simple white chapel overlooking the sea and enter the village. We want to look in the chapel where a famous novelist named Myrivilis wrote a book called *The Mermaid Madonna,* for an icon of the Panagia as a mermaid that inspired him. But it is not in the church. I ask the proprietress of the local souvenir shop, who is reading a novel by Marguerite Duras, where we can find the icon. She smiles and says, "You can't. It's a dream. Only Myrivilis's dream. There was never such an icon."

After a lunch of white wine and stuffed sautéed zucchini blossoms filled with feta cheese, egg, and fresh mint, we go up to the nearby town of Molivos, romantically beautiful topped by a castle that sits on a great, dynamic rock, the cluster of stone houses below it looking like infant castles it is giving birth to. A mule carrying panniers of zucchini looking like torches with their flame-colored flowers passes us on the cobbled street. We pass some fine marble public fountains, with marble plaques over them expressing wishes and identifying the donors in Turkish, in the Arabic alphabet used before Atatürk's reforms. Mitilini was occupied by the Turks until 1912, and until the Asia Minor catastrophe maintained a constant social interchange with the port of Aïvali across the water, one of the towns on the coast of Turkey where large numbers of Greeks lived. Over the fortress in Molivos is another inscription in Turkish, and a Greek family panting outside after their climb look up at it. "What is it, this writing?" asks the thirtyish wife, holding the hands of her two children and catching her breath. "What language is this?" She is free not to know. Across the blue waters the coast of Turkey faces us, looking at Turkey in Greece. And I wonder if tomorrow, when we go to Aïvali, we will feel Greece staring back, looking at Greece in Turkey.

Early next morning, we take a bus to Mitilini town to catch the daily ferry to Aïvali. There are only six passengers on the bus after we board, and a woman climbs on after us, wishing the bus driver and the passengers a general *kalimera*. Hanging over the windshield dangles a gold evil-eye charm, a madonna, a pomegranate, and a decal of the Playboy bunny. The bus driver is wearing the gold bracelets and neck chains favored by Greeks and Turks and Arabs and Israelis, more of the golden chains which link Greece to the East. The graffiti along the road have changed topics from the spring graffiti, and now written everywhere in PASOK green ink is the sentence "The selling of Greece will not be tolerated," a reference to the opposition party's plans to sell off the national telephone company to private investors. Two elderly gentlemen take front seats, diagnosing each other through information like a pair of social doctors. "You have grandchildren?" one asks the other, who replies, "My daughter is making my first grandchild now." They discuss the care and feeding of pigs, which leads almost inevitably to political discussion. "Andreas will make souvlaki of us all, if he is prime minister again," the one on the right predicts. At a village two stops later, he descends, calling to his new acquaintance, although he is probably going no more than ten minutes further, "Have a good journey, and a good week," using the polite plural you. An army tank has broken down, so the road is filled with soldiers—Mitilini is so close to Turkey that it is one of the prime sites for military duty. We arrive in town in time to wander a bit in the market district, where I see something I can't stop looking at, a turn-of-the-century needlepoint sampler: worked in red and green threads, the color of fruits, there are two ornamental alphabets, Greek and Roman, row by row, as if they were sown seeds germinating, waiting to find their way into the fruit of speech. The letters of both alphabets are decorated with leaves and petals, and at the bottom of the sampler, the young girl has signed her work in threads with her name, Eleni in Greek, Helen in the Roman alphabet. She has made a work of art of her double heritage. Kostas goes inside to see if he can buy it for me, and arrange to pick it up later from the shop. The shop owner pours us out two coffees, quotes a justifiably unaffordable price, and says in any case that the shop is closing for several days. He smiles a restrained smile with his mouth, but an overjoyed one with his eyes, and asks if I have seen what is in the corner of the shop. It is a gleaming baby carriage with an awning. "It is for my first grandchild, who was born yesterday," he says. "My daughter and son-in-law have waited ten years, and had given up hope. Can you imagine our joy? After ten years, there is a child at last. So the baby will come home tomorrow, and my wife and I will be there to welcome our grandchild." We congratulate him, and he inclines his head. There is a stateliness, a dignity in the face of joy that I think is as wonderful as dignity before sorrow. It communicates the more subtle bravery joy demands, the willingness to give oneself fully to joy without the illusion that you are no longer at risk. It demands a greater steeliness, since there is nothing more terrible than the destruction of what is most precious to you, than the loss of your greatest joy. In loving so fully you expose yourself to hell itself; the courage of heroism is not courage so ultimate as this grandfather's, or this young couple's, who must now love in a way that leaves them completely vulnerable.

Aïvali, the Turkish coastal town, was the home of the important Greek novelist Venezis, and of the neo-Byzantine painter Kondoglou, whose bitterness toward the West must surely have been colored by the loss of his childhood home in 1922. Like many others, Kondoglou found refuge in Mitilini, where many families have Aïvaliote roots. On the ferry, I study a postcard of the popular painter Tsironis's image of Aïvali, framed in painted flowers and laurel leaves, with a superimposed image of the painter Kondoglou hovering above it, also wreathed, both like the kind of photograph of the dead you see on the walls of houses all over Greece, where keeping their images before the family's eyes functions as a proof of the survival of the living as much as a remembrance of the dead. In their daily seeing of the image is the proof and reminder of their own consciousness, their eyes light the candle of life as only the living can. The dead can only be looked at by the living, they cannot look back.

We sail into Aïvali, which is held between two outstretched arms of land like an infant. As you sail in, you see an island with a ruined Orthodox church, one of those maritime churches so often overlaid on sites dedicated to Poseidon, shrines for sailors to acknowledge as they embarked and as they returned home safely. Some of the Greeks on the day excursion are going with the special purpose of photographing grandparents' houses to which they can never return.

As we put into port, a sailboat passes us on its way out, flying the bright red Turkish flag with its crescent moon, its thin curve the sign of a fault line that opened into an abyss, so that between Aïvali and Mitilini, where there was once a short span of sea, there is now a gulf. We are processed through the customs house under the obligatory picture of Atatürk, who wears a fur coat, with a mocking expression in his eyes, the color developed in the photograph designed to make them a supernaturally piercing blue. As we assemble to meet the bus for Pergamon, we are surrounded by Turkish boys and men, no women entrepreneurs among them. One of them whispers to me, "Fruit of Dalloum, fruit of Dalloum," and I wonder if this conceals some voluptuous suggestion, until I see his partner holding a stack of men's T-shirts and underwear sealed in factory packages marked "Fruit of the Loom."

Pergamon was a spa sacred to Asclepius, like the ones on Kos and at Epidaurus, and it has the usual elements of Asclepiad spas: statues, therapeutic baths, and theater. These spas must have been very like Baden-Baden in the nineteenth century, and Canyon Ranch or the Golden Door today, with their mixture of entertainment, physical and mental therapy, designed to improve the health of the patient by refreshing him mentally as well. There is a soldiers' encampment directly in front of the site: as Greece keeps concentrations of soldiers at its nearest points to Turkey, so Turkey keeps soldiers at its points nearest Greece, it seems. We walk to the theater, where there is a small cultural skirmish between a Greek tourist and the Turkish guide, a pleasant young woman whom I imagine as having a taste for historical novels, who is telling us about the theater's fine acoustics, saying that they resemble the acoustics of the theater at Epidaurus. The Greek lady in shorts says rather severely, "Yes, possibly they do, but Epidaurus is known to have the best acoustics in the world." Another lady echoes her, "We have learned this in school." Vans filled with camera equipment overlook the site, and a handsome group of men and women in bright clothes with strong makeup are ordering the same drinks again and again as they are filmed for a soft drink commercial. Along the road as we drive to the restaurant where we will have lunch, we pass women wearing Turkish trousers bent over in the fields, hanging laundry, bringing dishes of food to groups of men seated under trees. It is clear that the women's trousers are garments designed for work—they allow the woman to work bent over, in strong winds, and in any position her labor requires without exposing any flesh. They are practical, not romantic garments, and

I am reminded of a Turkish proverb I read once, "A woman for
work, a boy for love, and a melon for ecstasy." Along the road there
are also many coffee houses, where men are drinking at tables set
under trees. As in Greece, the women do not sit in coffee houses,
and I am struck that so many of them are wearing, in this heat,
ground-length housecoat-like overgarments, and by how many of
them are fully veiled. The men in the coffee houses look up at the
women in our bus, unveiled and unswaddled, with angry speculative stares. Cars pass us on the road, but none are driven by women;
they sit in the back, swaddled in the housecoat garments, with their
heads covered, the winds thick with dust circulating through the
open windows of the cars. The Eastern negative mysticism about
women driving cars, being free to come and go, seems to be operating here. Along with cars and passing trucks, I see men driving
horsedrawn wooden carts on the precisely laned asphalt, as Mercedes and Toyotas speed by them.

We spend the rest of the afternoon in Aïvali, in the central market of the town, a place of chaotic commerce. Kostas and I look in
some of the secondhand storefronts to see if we can find any pages
from late-nineteenth- and early-twentieth-century calendars; I have
been told that the calendars of the period in use here, and in cities
like Smyrna and Constantinople, would often have the date and year
printed according to the Muslim, Jewish, Eastern Christian, Julian,
and Western Christian Gregorian calendars, a tribute to all these
imperial religions' ambition to control time itself. It feels strange
and painful to amble past the corpses of the elegant neoclassical
Greek houses, recognizable for the marble reliefs over their doors
which carry Greek imagery, a baby Dionysus holding a cluster of
grapes, a ship sailing confidently over marble waves, that give a
glimpse of the voluptuous domesticity prosperous Ionia seems to
have meant to so many Greeks. The market itself is a maze of abundance—a wagon full of olives, tableware, brightly colored fruit and
vegetables, encyclopedic collections of spices, some to make you
sleep, some to make your hair gleam, or to make you potent. Along

the crowded cobbled streets are motorcycles, donkeys, dwarfs, cripples, sellers of cherry syrup blended with water to quench your thirst, birds to slaughter at home or here. A horse drawing a wooden cart whose sides are painted with brilliant poppies and vines stops to piss on the street, its urine swirling through the interstices of the cobblestones, past the feet of a seated bread seller.

As there were no women entrepreneurs this morning, there are no male shoppers this afternoon. The women shopping wear their long overcoats and scarves; some are fully veiled in black, some in Turkish trousers in electric color combinations, topped with blouses in flaming colors covered with sequins, these last unveiled. Although most of the women in the market are lumpen with coverings, in many of the shop windows you see posters of belly dancers, marking a hopeless sexual polarity. On the one hand, there are the women in sequins and flames, jeweled bras and pubic coverings, the stuff of sexual fairy tale; on the other, women covered like people guilty of a great crime, or hideously disfigured, objects as much of fear and loathing as of desire. These women can have no reality on either side of the veil. And the veil posits in an ugly way that men's sexual relations with women are fundamentally rapes, enactments of uncontrollable lust and violence; but the veil is itself a violation, a woman who wears it has already been raped. It occurs to me, too, as I watch the great amethyst eggplants and brilliant green beans changing hands, to be made into dishes like the ones I will eat tonight in Greece, that one indication of a country's capacity for diplomacy, for compromise, negotiation, promise making and keeping, may be found in the relations of its men and women, which are the models and training grounds for making alliances, for the negotiation, discussion, and maintenance of common interests without the use of physical force, for the cultivation and sustaining of trust.

It also strikes me that this market could be Mitilini's: the manners of the people, their gestures, with the same raised head and closed eyes to signify a "no," the radio music which sounds familiar except for its Turkish lyrics, the exclusively male *kafeneia,* the combination of mistrust and appetite for contact with the foreigners, the civic entertainment of the *corso,* the love of bright colors, all mirror the world across the water. When we walk through the streets, with their handsome dilapidated mansions like the ones in Mitilini town, to take the return ferry, I stop for a moment to look at the ornament on one door, hung with a bunch of garlic, a fork stabbed through one clove to pierce the evil eye. All the way back through the pine-forested hills of the island to the tiny village on the coast, Mitilini glows in the evening sun, caramel-colored, like the skin of the beautiful interracial child it is.

If you go to the Theophilos Museum, you will see—along with the strange, beautiful Theophilos paintings, which transmute everything they touch, heroes from history, battles, airplanes, prosperous Greek-Americans visiting for Easter, into fairy tale—a Tsarouchis portrait made from a photograph of about 1910 or so, of the itinerant painter himself, dressed as Alexander the Great, in an outfit drawn from the shadow puppet Alexanders who appear in some of the Karaghiozis plays. The squat little painter stands holding a tiny shield, his plump belly causing his cheap masquerader's cuirass with its flaking gilt to hang unevenly over his dirty trousers, his hair and beard unkempt, his fat-cheeked, tired face utterly unlike the chiseled coinage of Alexander's. His eyes have an expression that is both tragic and visionary, since he knows that he is not Alexander, and at the same time dreams he is, both Karaghiozis and Alexander, a man and a dream of himself. It is something Alexander himself must have felt at times, and I think it is one of the great portraits of the twentieth century. Kostas hums a fragment of one of his favorite Savopoulos songs: "The thing that destroys me and that saves me/ is that I dream like Karaghiozis . . ."

THE MARBLE KING

A Greek friend of mine who is taking Turkish lessons lent me a book he had bought recently called *Turkish Culture for Americans* the week before I went for my brief visit to Istanbul. Put together by a Turkish team of authors, it consisted of scenarios illustrating Turkish manners and customs, and explanations of them for Americans. In one, an American couple having dinner with a Turkish couple become too engaged in a discussion of education with the Turkish schoolteacher wife. Her husband falls silent, indicating displeasure. The explanation follows: "Ayse had behaved like a submissive Turkish wife until the conversation turned to her profession. Her husband's withdrawal from the conversation signaled Ayse that she had overstepped her role." In another scenario, an American Fulbright scholar visiting Atatürk's mausoleum is accosted by a screaming guard for keeping his hands in his pockets and continuing to approach the tomb during the playing of a martial tune—the book explains that he was perceived as not displaying adequate reverence to the memory of Atatürk, or the national anthem. There is a tale of a man who is insulted by receiving a gift from his Western employee of a framed picture of two village women in traditional dress. The breach here is that the gift is thought to denigrate by showing Turkey represented by peasant women rather than modern achievements—"Turks are sensitive to how their country is perceived. They want to be seen as European . . . ," write the authors. It is a glimpse of a *filotimo,* a readiness to be insulted, a preoccupation with public image, that mirrors Greek *filotimo.* Finally, there is the visiting professor who leaves the room during a calculus quiz and is upset by being handed exams in which answers have been copied from paper to paper. The writers explain, "Turkish students may often . . . help each other with their homework. This may extend to the test situation as well. It is not seen as cheating, but rather as helping a friend. This is an important cultural point . . ." It is little more than a utilitarian book, but I have to admire its authors' rigorous and public candor, facing a culture which, like Greece's, turns on a gyre of humiliation and pride, and can seem more preoccupied with public perception than with private behavior, a culture which takes everything personally and, like Greece's, is a culture of doppelgangers, whose capital, once Constantinople, the chief city of the eastern Roman Empire, became after years of decaying relations between two of the most diplomatically inept empires in history, the great city Istanbul, the queen city of the Muslim world. It seems now to be, above all, Atatürkopolis, judging from the relentless presence of his image, which appears, it seems to me, on every denomination of Turkish currency, not to mention walls, sculptures, books, schools. And Atatürk was another man in whom East and West strained against each other, the bisexual from Thessaloniki who longed for Turkey to become a Western nation, and imposed the reforms to make that goal possible in the style of an Eastern potentate, in a means that may have made some of those reforms only a veneer, an exhibition to please a feared and beloved father, Kemal Atatürk, the perfect father of the Turks, which was the meaning of the name that Mustafa assembled during his career.

In modern Greek folklore, Constantinople is the city of the marble king, the last Byzantine emperor, who will one day become incarnate again, and drive the Turks back to the "Red Apple Tree," their mythical birthplace. It is another irony of the shadow play of history here that the conquering Turkish Mehmet II may very well have had as much if not more Greek blood than Constantine Paleologus, whose mother was Serbian and father half-Italian. Mehmet also had Serbian kin through his father, but the identity of his mother is intriguingly unknown. What is known is that she was not born a Muslim, and she may very well have been Greek.

The last emperor of Byzantium, according to legend, was supposed to be named Constantine like the first one, and if the popular songs of 1922 are any indication, there was a mystical excitement about the King Constantine under whose rule the Asia Minor campaign was undertaken, the campaign which definitively ended Greek and Turkish coexistence on the same soil. In these songs, the Glucksberg Constantine is often identified with the marble king. But as is often the case with oracle and prophecy, the marble king did not take the form he was expected to, and 1922 remains a bitter influence on Greek and Turkish relations—in Greece, the prime minister Venizelos, who mercilessly badgered the European allies for cooperation in his plan to occupy Smyrna, with an eye on the rest of the Asia Minor coast, and on Istanbul, is called the *ethnarkhis,* the national leader. In Turkey, you hear him called Venizelos the murderer. Venizelos's mother had had a dream, I was told when I visited his memorial outside of Khania in Crete. She had dreamed that he would be a great liberator of the Greek people, and because of this dream, she had chosen the name Eleftherios, from the Greek word for freedom, for her son. But the Turks dream too, and those dreams flow too, as dreams do, in the veins of their lives. Atatürk's mother had also had a dream, I was told in Istanbul, a dream that had changed the future of the Turkish people. She had wanted him first to become a teacher of the Koran, and when he proved recalcitrant, she changed her ambition, wanting him to become the rich merchant his father should have been. But Atatürk fought with her, wanting a military career above all. He had passed the entrance to military school, but needed her permission for acceptance, which she refused to give. One night, she had a dream in which she saw her son hovering in a golden tray on top of a minaret. A bodiless voice spoke to her, saying that a military career would give her son this height, but another choice would cast him down. So she agreed, a decision in which the military victories that won nationhood for modern Turkey now seem implicit. And I was told of another dream that ominously helped lead to the viciously unresolved and dangerous situation on Cyprus now, a dream of Atatürk which Denktas, the leader of Turkish Cyprus, had in 1974, a dream in which Atatürk's response to his pleas for help seemed to him to prophesy the coming Turkish invasion of the island. Like a dysfunctional family, the Turks and Greeks have lived the same events, but have no common memories of them, few common interpretations of those events.

But Turkey is veined with Greece as Greece is veined with Turkey. The keenness and beauty that is also a part of the dialogue between the Greeks and the Turks makes their mutual hatreds tragic not only for themselves, but for the world. I have never seen a city more dazzlingly situated than Istanbul, nor one with a keener sense of what domestic pleasure might be. The wooden villas along the Bosphorus construct a relation between sea and garden that makes Venice seem myopic; their combination of the ingenious, the playful, and the comfortable is a vision of domestic beauty. They often have the *krokalia* pebble mosaic decoration that Greek villas do, and the beautifully detailed woodwork that I have seen in the houses in Greece in Epirus; I learn from my hostess that the finest carpenter in Istanbul at the end of the nineteenth century was a Greek named Antonis Politis. And these waterfront houses are themselves called *yialis,* from the Greek word for waterfront. The Turks had their own version of the Katharevousa and demoticist quarrel—in 1932, it was estimated that thirty-five percent of Turkish vocabulary was of Turkish origin, a percentage which changed drastically after the linguistic reforms decreed by Atatürk. I wonder sadly how much of the repressed vocabulary was Greek, feeling how much the Greek incorporation of Turkish vocabulary adds to the Greek language and sensibility, and thinking that the presence of its Greek vocabulary must be as valuable for Turkish.

On the way back to my hotel, I see several boys of five or six, dressed in satin and sequin costumes with plumed gendarmes' hats on their heads, carrying sequined and plumed sceptres. The costumes have an odd look of theatrical and class pastiche, like the disguised counts' costumes in Viennese operettas. "Is it a children's party?" I ask. The driver—as in the countryside, I never saw a woman driving in Istanbul—answers, "Today they go to cut the peepee." My hostess explains to me, "The costumes show that they celebrate their circumcision, which takes place today. They used to have marvelous carved wooden beds on which the operation took place, very prized today. I know antique dealers who hoard them."

At my hotel, which is more luxurious than the finest hotel I have stayed in in Greece, with impeccable room service, sheets such as I have never slept on, like flower petals, there is a fridge stocked with Turkish *raki,* wines, and champagne. A prayer mat has been set down for use during the taped calls to prayer audible from the minarets of the neighborhood. I drink a glass of white wine before dinner, and open the memoirs of Halide Edib, the only woman member of Atatürk's circle, whose Greek-infused memories of her childhood in Istanbul fascinate me. Her first lessons were from a Greek kindergarten teacher, and she remembers visiting her in her house, with its typical Turkish furnishings of divans, and its typical Greek corner for icons, before which an oil flame burned. The child would mimic the Greek funerals she saw passing in the neighborhood, in a favorite game, in which she would march up and down her room carrying a pet, and solemnly chant "Kyrie Eleison." Even the proverbs she quotes as childhood touchstones seem interchangeable with Greek ones. Her older sister scolds her one day, telling her "No child can learn without being beaten. Beating has come out of heaven." And the legendary tales she tells of the Paul

Bunyan-esque Turkish warrior Battal Gazi remind me of the Greek
Byzantine legends of Diyenis Akritas; but for Akritas defending the
borders of Byzantium, and Battal Gazi attacking them, happy endings have different meanings. Battal's magical war whoop dispatches
twenty Christian infidels to hell when he sounds it; the Byzantine
Caesar builds a tower in the middle of the Bosphorus to hide the
most beautiful Greek princess. But Battal Gazi outwits him, kidnaps
the princess, and marries her. It is like the Zeus and Europa story;
but this princess is not Phoenician, she is Greek.

The pilgrimage I am most anxious to make, given that I have
such a short time, and must give it to Greek sites, is the monastery
church at Khora, in what is now a suburb of Istanbul, the creation of
the brilliant Byzantine politician and scholar Metochites, who died
in 1332, not long before the empire fell. I have to make my way
there by myself, since my hostess's child unexpectedly needs
stitches. I have noticed, to my surprise, how many women here
wear scarves and veils, and I dress carefully for the expedition,
knowing from Greece that sexual etiquette toward foreign women
differs in unpredictable ways. I put on a long dress, wear a scarf and
no makeup. I look at myself in the mirror. I look like something out
of *Little Women*. I look like hell. The taxi driver, nevertheless, goes
wild, and when I arrive at the monastery after many unwelcome
suggestions, he flails his arms, gesticulating toward the women in
the houses around the monastery, who are all scarfed, and wearing
those hideous overcoats that look like the overcoats clients of
pornographic films wear into the movie houses. He shrieks, "Turkish madams no good, not sexy like you!" I catch a glimpse of myself
in the rearview mirror, bewildered by this response to the little
puritan I see there. I pay, and hasten to church.

Theodore Metochites, under whose supervision this church
was restored, was one of the most vital figures of the fourteenth
century. He was born in Constantinople in 1270 to a father who
supported the reunion of the Roman Catholic and Orthodox
Churches, and was, at one point in his career, the Byzantine em-

peror's ambassador to the pope. The family was banished to Asia Minor when an anti-union emperor came to power. It was his training in classical rhetoric that won Metochites a place in the service of the emperor Andronicus II, who heard a speech he had written in praise of the city of Nicaea and was impressed. Metochites acted as an ambassador of the emperor, and eventually became the most powerful minister in the empire, managing to marry a daughter into the imperial family. He also acquired enormous wealth by selling positions and titles and access to the emperor, and an ugly reputation as a man who was a parasite on the poor, and a brilliant reputation as a mathematician and astronomer. He seemed to struggle with his admiration of ancient philosophy, praising secular philosophy, but cautious so as not to be accused of heresy. Christians, he said, having received the Revelation, only needed to follow the scriptures, having escaped the theological problems of the ancient philosophers, although his training in classical rhetoric made for an odd mixture of images in moments of his work. He praised an abbot friend for his performance of the liturgy's Bloodless Sacrifice with "holy Bacchic frenzy." And he also seemed to struggle with a foreboding that the empire was doomed. "We are all caught in an enormous net," he wrote, "and tossed about in it without hope of escape." From about 1316 to 1321, he supervised the decoration of this church. A little after Easter of 1321, civil war broke out between the emperor and his grandson. Metochites dreamed of a thief stealing the key to his treasure room, and when Constantinople fell to the emperor's grandson, Andronicus II, Metochites was exiled to a provincial town called Didimotikho in Thrace, whose bad wine he complained of bitterly. He was permitted to return to Constantinople after a period, and died at the monastery he had restored, as a monk who had taken the name Theoleptos.

The church is famous for the freshness and beauty of its mosaics, and also for some extraordinary frescoes, an almost sensual Jesus as Pantokrator, and an angel holding the scroll of the Last Judgment in the air, a celestial athlete lifting a weight as great as the world. What also strikes me is an intenser concentration on the girlhood of the Virgin Mary than I have seen in a Byzantine church, not only images of the Virgin in relation to Christ, but a separate cycle of the events of her own childhood, the annunciation of her birth, her birth, the first seven steps she took as a toddler, being tenderly caressed by both her parents, as always in Byzantine art, deliberately sacrificing the rendering of space so that time too will disappear into eternity.

It is when I see the mosaics of the Virgin entrusted to Joseph, and of Joseph leading the little girl to his house, an image I have never seen, that I sense the pressure of autobiography, Metochites's autobiography. Mary is presented in the mosaics as a child, a little girl. The bearded Joseph who leads her away is old enough to be her grandfather. "And the priest said unto Joseph: Unto thee it hath fallen to take the Virgin of the Lord and keep her thyself. And Joseph refused saying: I have sons, and I am an old man, she is but a girl . . ." runs the account in an apocryphal gospel. In the mosaic, Mary's protector, the priest Zacharias, mediates between Joseph and the Virgin, holding and controlling the flowering rod that signals Joseph's election, while his hand is placed tenderly and protectively on the doll-like little girl's head. The image stirs the memory that it was Metochites who arranged the complicated marriage negotiations for his emperor Andronicus II's daughter Simonis and the Serbian king Stephen Milutin. In those days in the Balkans, marriages were one of the primary means of negotiating national boundaries, and settling other political disputes. The work of crafting the marriage contract took Metochites to Serbia five times. The Serbian king Stephen Milutin had been already been married twice, and repudiated a third wife to marry Simonis. The engagement was celebrated and Simonis was sent to Serbia, to be trained and educated to be what Milutin wanted as a wife. Milutin was forty years old. Simonis was six. He raped his six-year-old bride, rendering her sterile. When Simonis later fled to a cloister to escape him, she was forced to put off her habit and return.

I look again at the images of the little girl Virgin, looking up trustingly at Joseph, who looks down at her, utterly safe in the divinely ordained procession of these mosaics, not to be raped by this bearded man, not to be sterile, but to be the mother of a divine child. And I think there is a lesson here in Balkan politics, in the utter separation of this sacred dream of the world from the real events Metochites presided over, in this divorce of history and art, of the imagination and time. For when legend extinguishes history, when the imagination is not allowed to play over the world in time, the events on earth that might have no consequences in legend destroy and entrap generations of human life. In legend, when time does not pass, the marriage of a child is a miracle, and death is not death. In history, when time does not pass, there is blood vendetta, the feud that never ends, that begins again in the next generation the feud that never ends. As Mary can never be truly harmed, Simonis can never stop being raped. If we value the great poem of Christianity, we cannot reject one meaning of Christ's incarnation, that while God's relationship to humans may not change, humans' relationship to God must, as Christ's did, even on the cross, ranging from the certainty with which he promises the thieves on their crosses that they will see paradise together, to the mournful cry to God in the question "Why have you forsaken me?", experiencing in death both despair and hope.

THE STATUES DANCING

On my last night in Athens, I go to roughly five parties and two nightclubs. All week too, there have been last meals, and visits from neighbors carrying sweets, while at each visit, I promise myself I won't cry, but do. Tonight I am saying goodbye the way Athenians do, that is, by staying up all night and trying to stop time. At the third party, the host and hostess declare that I am not allowed to leave Greece without ever having seen a Greek pornographic film, so all during the wine and the chatter, films with names like *Hot Nights* and *Sensual Days in the Aegean* unwind on their VCR. People have sex in village costumes, with much visual joking about foustanellas; people have sex in fishing boats; one woman has sex with a coffin that has an erection, while she moans that this is what the angels do in paradise, that this is resurrection. I make my way on to the next party and the next, and then to a nightclub. The Greeks have made going to nightclubs a national art, a form of collective lovemaking, and one of the signals of enjoyment in their movies is the nightclub scene, with singing and dancing, and a table littered with bottles, glasses, fruit, and dancers. You go in search of *kefi,* of joyous abandonment. Tonight, a woman is moved by the first act to leap from table to table to join the opening singer on the stage. Women circulate with baskets of carnations to buy to throw at the singers you appreciate—passionate enjoyment is demonstrated by buying the whole basket, and having it overturned on the singer, who continues the song through a rain of flowers. People in parties at tables leap up onto the tables and dance the *tsifteteli,* the belly dance that is both Turkish and Greek. Tonight, teenagers in Versace jeans climb onto the tables and sway to one of the hits of the season, "You remind me of my mother/That's why I love you . . ." The show goes on for hours, but we leave as three baskets of carnations are poured over another singer, whose last line I catch as we are getting our coats, "Because it doesn't exist, immortality . . ." At the *rembetika* club where we wind up, there is a sort of raised wooden platform for people who are inspired to dance to get on, the tables are too small. So, like people who in church get the spirit and come forward to testify, dancers come forward to the platform when a song moves them. An old man dances a *zembekiko* like a dying eagle's flight, a middle-aged husband kneels at the feet of his wife and claps as she dances around him in an intricate circle. I see the most beautiful *tsifteteli* I will probably ever see, performed by two girls of completely different physical types, one heavy and voluptuous, the other reedy, both wearing ordinary jeans and T-shirts, but moving so liquidly that you would swear they could cross the borders between the great river of dreams and the earth of reality. Like a great river whose changing course alters the boundaries of the earth that contains it, the changing boundaries of dream and reality can never be permanently fixed, as they destroy and create and recreate each other. Like those fertile rivers that sustain settlements and cities, dreams make life possible, bring it into reality; we ourselves are bred in dreams. And like great rivers, dreams can destroy us if we do not patiently, delicately observe their barely perceptible changes in breadth and depth, the new tributaries and branches they sculpt. Watching the dance makes me think of this, and of the traditional phrase that ends a Greek fairy tale: "And they lived happily, but we live better." But like dreams, "they" are in our lives, and "we" are in their story. They lived happily, but we live better. Who are they, then, and who are we?

I get home a little after dawn. The streets are already full of the sound of people going to early morning jobs on motorcycles. I spend the little of the morning I have left doing last-minute packing, and waiting for my farewell call from Kostas. "I knew you wouldn't stay," he says sadly. "Why is that?" I ask. "Because your favorite of all the Shakespeare plays is *A Winter's Tale.*" "Kostaki," I say, "I have been up all night being very happy and very very sad. Don't torment me with your tarot of Shakespeare. How did you know I wouldn't stay?" "All right," he says. "In *A Winter's Tale,* a girl whose past has been severed from her is restored to her own history when she sees a statue move. When the statue moves, the play ends. You saw the statue move."

I made myself look out the window as the plane took off, leaping over the cliffs and the Aegean Sea like a champion horse clearing a jump, as we moved away from the adamantine glitter of the sun on the white buildings and the Saronic Gulf to skies of a more diaphanous blue, the plane ascending delicately, securely, as if on a current of breath, a breath calibrated with precisely enough force to blow a candle out.

THE ROAD FROM COORAIN
by Jill Ker Conway

A remarkable woman's clear-sighted memoir of growing up Australian; from the vastness of a sheep station in the outback to the stifling propriety of postwar Sydney; from an untutored childhood to a life in academia; and from the shelter of a protective family to the lessons of independence.

Autobiography/0-679-72436-2

SHOOTING THE BOH
A Woman's Voyage Down the Wildest River in Borneo
by Tracy Johnston

When Tracy Johnston signed up for a rafting expedition down Borneo's Boh River, she had no idea that it had never been fully navigated, nor did she know about the local wildlife, which included swimming cobras and swarms of sweat-eating bees. But perhaps the most revealing discovery was what she learned about herself: about what it means to be an adventurer—a woman adventurer—in a world that seems to be made exclusively for the young.

Travel/Adventure/0-679-74010-4

MAIDEN VOYAGES
Writings of Women Travelers
edited and with an Introduction by Mary Morris

Whether it is Edith Wharton, marveling at the magical beauty of a Marrakech palace garden, or Mildred Cable, wondering at dust demons and phantom voices in the Gobi Desert, the women gathered in this generous and delightful anthology show as much of themselves as they show of the strange and wonderful places they visit.

Travel/Women's Studies/0-679-74030-9